Studies in Soviet History and Society

edited by Joseph S. Berliner, Seweryn Bialer, *and* Sheila Fitzpatrick

---

Revolution on the Volga: 1917 in Saratov
by Donald J. Raleigh

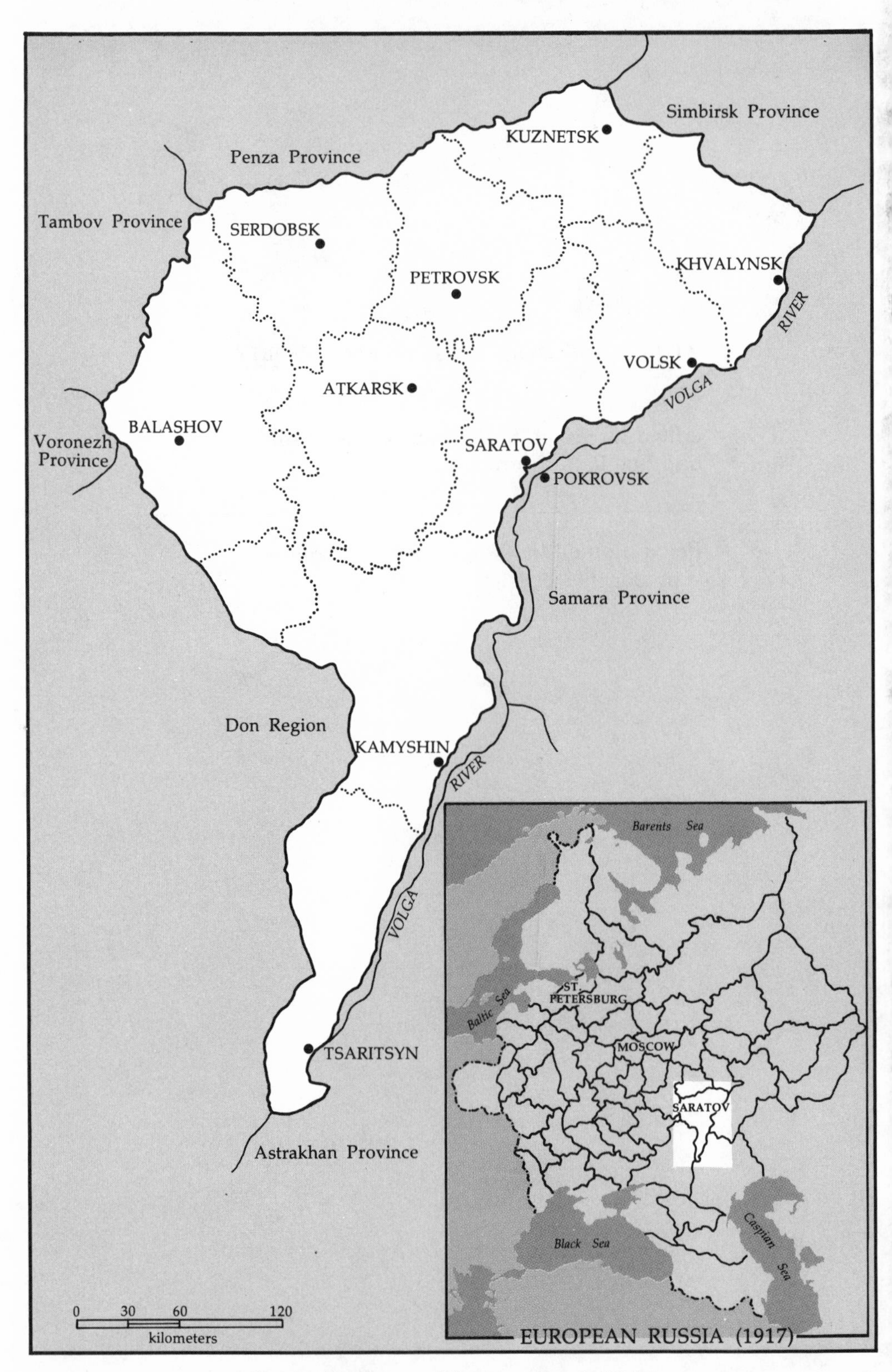

Saratov Province and European Russia (1917)

REVOLUTION ON THE VOLGA

1917 in Saratov

DONALD J. RALEIGH

CORNELL UNIVERSITY PRESS

Ithaca and London

First published 1986 by Cornell University Press.

International Standard Book Number 0-8014-1790-2
Library of Congress Catalog Number 85-12792
Printed in the United States of America
Librarians: Library of Congress cataloging information appears on the last page of the book.

The paper in this book is acid-free and meets the guidelines for permanence and durability of the Committee on Production Guidelines for Book Longevity of the Council on Library Resources.

To Karen

Contents

Maps

Preface

My aim in this book is to trace the course of the Russian Revolution in the provincial city of Saratov and thereby to shed light on the kaleidoscopic events that tore apart the social and political fabric of the old regime in 1917. This book is the first non-Soviet consideration of the revolution in a provincial town of European Russia. Presuming that a study of the revolution in a provincial capital within the Central Industrial Region or black-earth zone would illuminate the events on which our understanding of the revolution is based, I specifically sought out an administrative, trade, and cultural center that had some, but limited, industrial development. Such a city was more representative of provincial Russia than a major factory town with a sizable working class. Saratov struck me as an ideal choice on several counts. In its economic relationships, it had the general characteristics I was seeking. For a variety of objective and fortuitous reasons, sources on Saratov were more plentiful and diverse than those available for other towns.[1] Furthermore, the peasant problem loomed so large in Saratov province that its capital city became one of the most important centers of Russian populism and

1. Available sources include newspapers representing most political factions, memoirs, published documents, and a growing corpus of Soviet secondary literature. Further, the protocols of the Saratov Soviet have been published. According to E. N. Burdzhalov, the protocols of only two provincial soviets have survived. See "Istochniki i literatura po istorii vtoroi russkoi revoliutsii," in *Sverzhenie samoderzhaviia: Sbornik statei*, ed. I. I. Mints et al. (Moscow, 1970), p. 252.

of the Socialist Revolutionary party. In dealing with Saratov, I directly address the problem of the political fate of provincial populism. Finally, because Saratov housed a large army garrison, the town's social geography allowed for an examination of those concerns that affected soldiers as well as workers, peasants, and members of the middle class.

Still, the reader rightfully may ask, "How representative is Saratov?" This question cannot be answered confidently until more regional studies are completed. Reginald E. Zelnik, author of a pioneering social history of St. Petersburg factory workers, observed more than a decade ago that "the general state of the field of Russian history in the United States requires more concentration on regional studies, confined within fairly narrow chronological limits."[2] It still does. Indeed, probably because of our early tendency to view Bolshevism as an alien force in Russian history and also because of the scarcity of primary source materials outside the Soviet Union, the revolution in provincial Russia has received comparatively little scholarly attention in the West.[3] Moreover, since the few available book-length regional studies deal with Russia's borderlands, where nationality conflicts gave a peculiarly local flavor to social tensions and politics, we really have no historiography to speak of concerning the spread of the revolution in the Russian heartland. This state of affairs is reflected in the pages of standard textbook accounts of the revolution: it's not a matter of knowing which interpretation seems most plausible, but a matter of even finding a decent account of what happened.

My purpose, then, is to explain what happened in Saratov. By showing

2. Reginald E. Zelnik, *Labor and Society in Tsarist Russia: The Factory Workers of St. Petersburg, 1855–1870* (Stanford, 1971), p. 3.

3. With the exception of Ronald G. Suny's examination of class and nationality in Baku, Andrew Ezergailis's narrow investigation of Latvian Social Democracy, Russell Snow's preliminary findings on Bolshevism in Siberia, Rex A. Wade's work on the Red Guard, and a few scholarly articles, the stormy events of 1917 in provincial Russia have been neglected. See Ronald G. Suny, *The Baku Commune, 1917–1918: Class and Nationality in the Russian Revolution* (Princeton, 1972); Andrew Ezergailis, *The 1917 Revolution in Latvia* (Boulder, 1974); Russell E. Snow, *The Bolsheviks in Siberia, 1917–1918* (Rutherford, O., 1977); and Rex. A. Wade, *Red Guards and Workers' Militias in the Russian Revolution* (Stanford, 1983). Although it concentrates on Petrograd, Wade's study includes chapters on the Red Guard in Kharkov and Saratov. See also W. E. Mosse, "Revolution in Saratov (October–November 1917)," *Slavonic and East European Review,* 49 (1971), 586–602; Richard A. Pierce, "Toward Soviet Power in Tashkent, February–October 1917," *Canadian Slavonic Papers,* 17 (1975), 261–70; and Donald J. Raleigh, "Revolutionary Politics in Provincial Russia: The Tsaritsyn 'Republic' in 1917," *Slavic Review,* 40 (1981), 194–209. Several broad accounts of popular institutions and government policies also have dealt with provincial events. See Marc Ferro, *La Révolution de 1917,* vol. 1, *La Chute du tsarisme et les origines d'Octobre;* vol. 2, *Octobre: Naissance d'une société* (Paris, 1967, 1976); Roger Pethybridge, *The Spread of the Revolution: Essays on 1917* (London, 1972); and John L. H. Keep, *The Russian Revolution: A Study in Mass Mobilization* (New York, 1976).

what was distinctive about Saratov, I hope to bring into sharper focus the features it shared with European Russia as a whole. In a sense, Saratov was Russia. For generations of educated Russians, Saratov was the stereotype of a provincial town. The city probably will never shed the undeserved image evoked by the playwright A. S. Griboedov, who in *Wit Works Woes* has Famusov, a corrupt government official, punish his crafty daughter by ordering her out of Moscow to the provinces: "To the country, to your aunt, to the backwoods, to Saratov!"[4]

This book wrestles with several major problems. As a sociopolitical history, it analyzes the nature of political power in a revolutionary setting and the changing social support various political factions enjoyed within the intricate, ambiguous institutional framework that surfaced willy-nilly after the collapse of the Romanov autocracy. Focusing on the role of popular organs that flourished after February, this book evaluates Saratov Bolshevism and seeks to explain its ultimate success among workers and soldiers in this populist stronghold. Throughout the narrative I describe relations between local organs and central organs in Petrograd, between authoritative institutions in Saratov and the various and overlapping executive committees and class-oriented committees that cropped up in district centers and villages in the province. The district center of Tsaritsyn (later Stalingrad, now Volgograd) receives special consideration because of the town's sheer size, economic importance, and early move to the left. I likewise assess the unfolding of the revolution in the Saratov countryside and the forces that worked to shatter the delicate nexus between town and country. I weigh the impact of national events on local affairs and consider how the course of the revolution in the localities affected national issues in turn. By concentrating my attention on the backwater of Saratov I hope to demonstrate that the conflicts and conditions that brought about the revolution were by no means confined to the urban capitals. The infrequency with which this fact has been acknowledged contributes to the erroneous view that 1917 was somehow a historical metropolitan accident.

In writing this book, I have made a conscious effort to keep my thinking within the context of 1917 and to avoid what I consider a far too common pitfall in Western scholarship on so admittedly emotional a topic: a tendency to permit our knowledge of or reaction to subsequent Soviet history to intrude upon and color our understanding of the revolution itself. Such detachment is not always easy, particularly when one's request to consult archival holdings is met with the bland assurance that no such documents exist. Since Saratov is a closed city, my familiarity with it thus remains confined to academic literature, made human by the personal accounts of my Saratov friends. Uncertain access

4. A. S. Griboedov, *Gore ot uma* (Moscow, 1967), p. 119.

to Bolshevik and non-Bolshevik primary materials, the tendentious quality of some sources, and the glaring lacunae in others have forced me to countenance imbalances and omissions in my narrative and analysis or to rely on Soviet writing. Whenever I have leaned on Soviet scholarship, I have tried to establish the integrity and professionalism of individual historians before accepting their conclusions or reconstruction of events. On a more positive note, I must emphasize that I could not have completed this book had I not been able to carry out research in the Soviet Union. The richness of the many local newspapers and of published documents and memoirs available nowhere else provided me with ample, if incomplete, material for this investigation. Despite the occasional antithetical perspectives reflected in the sources, a certain general agreement nonetheless emerges, which makes me strongly suspect that access to archives would not have altered in any major way the conclusions I have reached.

All dates in this book are given according to the Julian calendar. In use in Russia until 1918, it was thirteen days behind the Gregorian calendar of the West. Transliteration from Russian is based on the Library of Congress system. For stylistic considerations I have taken the liberty of deleting the soft sign from place names and proper nouns (e.g., Kazan rather than Kazan'; Zhest metalworks instead of Zhest'). In some surnames "ii" is rendered "y" to conform with common usage: Kerensky, Chernyshevsky, Trotsky.

I owe a deep personal debt to Alexander Rabinowitch, who has been a constant source of inspiration, encouragement, and support. John M. Thompson has also guided my thinking and has offered perceptive criticisms of various versions of this book, for which I am grateful. Ronald G. Suny, Richard Stites, William G. Rosenberg, Rex A. Wade, and Daniel T. Orlovsky have given me invaluable advice. I am particularly grateful to Michael S. Melancon for his unflagging enthusiasm and critical eye, and for forcing me to think differently about the Socialist Revolutionaries. Louise McReynolds read my manuscript as I revised it, and with good humor persuaded me not to toss it into the wastebasket. I subjected my colleagues Jerry H. Bentley, Richard H. Immerman, and Herbert F. Ziegler to my draft conclusion and benefited from their thoughtful criticisms. Reginald E. Zelnik caught some errors and confusion in my background chapter. Thank you all.

I record my indebtedness as well to the many people who facilitated my research along the way. My thanks go to the staffs of the Indiana University Library, University of Illinois Library, University of Chicago Library, Columbia University Library, New York Public Library, Library of Congress, University of California at Berkeley Library, University of Helsinki Library, and the Hoover Institution. I am also grateful to the staffs at the State Historical Library, Lenin Library, and Fundamental Library of the Social Sciences (now INION) in Moscow, and to the Saltykov-Shchedrin Library and Library of the Academy of Sciences in Leningrad. I express special appreciation to Patricia A. Polansky, Russian bibliographer at the University of Hawaii's Hamilton Library. Her unstinting assistance, resourcefulness, and boundless energy often made me forget that I was living in the middle of the Pacific Ocean. Sincere thanks also to John M. Bushnell, Thomas S. Fallows, and John J. Stephan, who shared materials with me, and to G. A. Gerasimenko, who so liberally gave of his time, personal library, and encyclopedic knowledge of Saratov's revolutionary past. N. G. Kozin of Saratov University took time from his busy schedule to obtain the photographs published in this volume. In the process we became friends. Elizabeth K. Taitano typed the tables and spent many hours providing meticulous clerical support. Everett A. Wingert of the University of Hawaii supervised Patricia A. Pennywell's preparation of the maps. Gayle Yoshida of the University of Hawaii Press prepared the index. John G. Ackerman, editor at Cornell University Press, has shown confidence in this book from the start. Senior Manuscript Editor Barbara H. Salazar improved the manuscript. It has been a real pleasure to work with them.

I benefited from the generous financial support of the International Research and Exchanges Board, which made it possible for me to conduct research in the Soviet Union during 1974–75. Thanks to a grant from the University of Hawaii's Research Council, I was able to return to the Soviet Union in June 1980. A grant-in-aid from the American Council of Learned Societies enabled me to carry out research on the U.S. mainland during the summer of 1981.

I am grateful to the *Slavic Review* for permission to include here, in altered form, material from my article "Revolutionary Politics in Provincial Russia: The Tsaritsyn 'Republic' in 1917," published in volume 40 of that journal (Summer 1981).

Over the years my Soviet friends O. A. Kling, E. I. Orlova, L. S. Obraztsova, P. A. Obraztsov, A. V. Matveev, A. N. Petrova, T. A. Shpak, N. V. Liubina, O. E. Kudriavtseva, and V. I. Zavorotnyi have shared their families, friends, and homes with me. Finally, I must acknowledge the enormous contribution of my wife, Karen, who allowed my unsatiable interest in Russian history to become a major part of her life, too. And, in grateful fulfillment of a promise made back in 1967, I thank Michael Pagliaro for introducing me to Russian history and to critical historical thinking.

DONALD J. RALEIGH

Honolulu, Hawaii

REVOLUTION ON THE VOLGA

CHAPTER 1

Saratov on the Eve of Revolution

They call it the river of rivers, the Main Street of Russia. For hundreds of years the Volga both witnessed and shaped the development of the Muscovite state. In folklore and song the murky waters took on near-mystical powers of nourishment, comfort, sorrow—and resurrection. During the consolidation and spread of the empire in the sixteenth century, the Volga River, which linked European Russia with trade routes in Persia, already played a prominent role in the state's economy. Each summer fishermen and merchants from central Russia trekked to the Volga and from there to the exotic markets of Kazan and Astrakhan, searching for salt and coveted luxury items brought by southern caravans. Threatened by Turkish expansion in the Don River region, Cossack horsemen drifted eastward toward the unfortified Volga and assaulted Russian merchants, jeopardizing their lucrative trade. The Muscovite government, responding to these Cossack raids and those of various nomadic tribes, built a chain of fortresses in the late sixteenth century—Samara (Kuibyshev), Tsaritsyn (Volgograd), and Saratov—to protect its commercial interests.[1]

Historians know little about Saratov's settlement by a group of state servitors in 1590.[2] Because of inadequate and contradictory evidence,

1. A. A. Geraklitov, *Saratov: Kratkii istoricheskii ocherk* (Saratov, 1919), p. 10; P. A. Kavunov, *Goroda Saratovskoi oblasti* (Saratov, 1963), p. 23.

2. According to an early account, a Prince Grigorii Osipovich Zasekin "of the Kazan regiment," a nobleman named Fedor Mikhailovich Turov, and a group of state servitors

writers even disagree about the location of the first Saratov fortress.[3] Wherever the original site, the general area served as a natural bridge between Moscow and Central Asia and the Caspian Sea. Nomadic peoples may have founded a settlement near present-day Saratov as early as 500 B.C. Later the region hosted the Khazar and Mongol empires. The Khazars, who developed a prosperous, cosmopolitan society noted for its extensive trade connections with the Arab and Byzantine worlds, occupied the territory in the seventh century. Toward the end of the thirteenth century the Mongols seized the lower river basin. As their control disintegrated some two hundred years later, the region fell to the successor states of the Golden Horde, the Tatar khanates of Kazan and Astrakhan. When the expanding Muscovite state reached the Volga, it confronted the Tatars, Kalmyks, Kirghiz, and Mordvinians. The very name Saratov may well be a compound of two Turkic-Mongol words, *sary* or *sara* and *tai* or *tau* or *tar*, meaning yellow (beautiful) mountain.[4]

Located in the eastern tip of the fertile black-earth zone some 50 degrees north latitude and 49 degrees east longitude, where forest and steppe meet in a hilly area some 200 to 300 meters above sea level, Saratov has a continental climate. Tall hills—"mountains," as the locals call them—nestle up against the city on three sides, making it warmer, dustier, and more arid than the rest of the oblast, or province. Valleys honeycomb the northern, richly wooded hilly part of the province, while the southern half shows little variety in altitude. The province's boundaries today differ from those of 1917. Before the revolution, the territory that makes up contemporary Saratov oblast belonged to two provinces: the right-bank lands fell in Saratov province and the left-bank territory in Samara. At the time of the revolution Saratov province was divided into ten districts *(uezds)*. Now, however, the two northernmost districts (Ser-

---

founded Saratov in 1590. Recurring fires destroyed most local records that otherwise would shed light on Saratov's formative years. The oldest existing official documents date from the early 18th century. Apart from them, travelers' accounts remain the main source of information on 17th-century Saratov. The peripatetic Dutch emissary Olearius, for instance, journeyed down the Volga in 1636, and took back a fragmented description and drawing of the fortress and region. See Geraklitov, *Saratov*, pp. 2–3; N. A. Bondar' and I. N. Steshin, *Saratov* (Moscow, 1951), p. 7; N. Il'in, *Saratov: Istoricheskii ocherk* (Saratov, 1952), p. 6.

3. The most popular and probably correct account holds that the town's founders erected the stronghold on the right bank of the Volga River near the Soviet city of Engels (formerly Pokrovsk), that it moved to the left bank during the Time of Troubles (1598–1613), and that it was relocated on the right bank once again (its present locale) in 1674 (M. I. Skliar, "Gorod Saratov [Ekonomiko-geograficheskaia kharakteristika]," candidate dissertation, Moscow State University, 1958, pp. 16, 38).

4. A. Ia. Maizel', *Putevoditel' po gorodu Saratovu s 2-ia planami v kraskakh i svedeniiami o gubernii* (Saratov, 1917), pp. 1–3; *Sputnik po gorodu Saratovu s illiustratsiiami i planom goroda* (Saratov, 1898), p. 4.

dobsk and Kuznetsk) lie within Penza and Ulianov oblasts, while the southernmost districts (Tsaritsyn and Kamyshin) lie in Volgograd oblast.[5]

Early Russian towns existed primarily for reasons of state. As a typical military settlement, Saratov was headed by an official *(voevoda)* subordinate to authorities in Kazan. Throughout the seventeenth century, 300 to 500 professional musketeers *(strel'tsy)* made up most of the fortress's inhabitants. The nonservitors or townspeople *(posadskie liudi)* involved in trade, commerce, and manufacturing constituted but a small fraction of the population. Old drawings show wooden houses and churches pressed together within a log stockade and a Tatar bazaar flourishing outside the fortress walls. Guarding Muscovy's shaky eastern frontier, Saratov repeatedly fell under siege at this time. Kalmyk forces sacked Saratov in 1643; in 1671 the peasant rebel Stenka Razin torched the town; and as late as 1693 Tatar tribesmen laid waste to the settlement.

By the eighteenth century, when the expansion of Russia's frontiers beyond the Volga had reduced Saratov's military importance, the fortress had acquired a new, commercial significance. In the beginning of the seventeenth century fishing communities, usually founded by monasteries, arose along the riverbank; appropriately, Saratov's official coat of arms depicts three small sturgeon against a bluish background that symbolizes the life-giving waters of the Volga. After 1700, Saratov rapidly evolved into a commercial center. To promote the salt industry, Empress Elizabeth (1741–1762) moved peasants from other provinces to Saratov to labor in local salt mines. By this time a major trade route stretched from Astrakhan to Saratov and on to Simbirsk, while another one meandered from Saratov to Penza, Tambov, and eventually Moscow and the central regions of the country. In July and October Saratov hosted markets and fairs that drew craftsmen and peasants from the neighboring countryside. In the course of the administrative reforms of Catherine the Great (1762–1796), the town, which had been part of Astrakhan province, was designated the administrative, commercial, and cultural center of newly created Saratov province.[6]

By the beginning of the nineteenth century the city's future had become vitally linked to the rich black earth of the northern part of the province and to the processing and shipping of grain and agricultural products. A hundred years later Saratov province occupied first place in Russia in volume of flour production.[7] In fact, Saratov's reputation as a

5. Skliar, "Gorod Saratov," pp. 29–30; N. S. Frolova, ed., *Saratovskaia oblast'* (Saratov, 1947), p. 37.

6. N. F. Khovanskii, *O proshlom goroda Saratova* (Saratov, 1891), pp. 6–7.

7. A. M. Starkmet, *Saratov: Putevoditel'* (Saratov, 1963), p. 9; G. A. Malinin, "Saratovskie zheleznodorozhniki v revoliutsii 1905–1907 gg.," *Uchenye zapiski Saratovskogo gosudarstvennogo universiteta,* 55 (1956), 124.

grain producer and supplier made the region especially prominent during the revolution and civil war. The introduction of steamships and railroads in the nineteenth century and the completion of the Volga–Baltic Sea canals contributed to Saratov's commercial significance by enabling it to ship grain southward to the Rostov market as well as to the interior of the country. The Moscow–Saratov railroad line was opened in 1871, and its extension to Uralsk and Astrakhan formed the important Riazan–Uralsk trade artery.

Unfortunately for Saratov, unfavorable reputations are hard to shake. At the end of the eighteenth century Gabriel Derzhavin, tsarist administrator and poet, had described Saratov as "a city in name only."[8] A hundred years later many visitors still considered it a dull, dirty provincial capital even though it had been transformed into an urban center with 17,000 buildings, of which 3,000 were brick, and almost 3,000 stores and shops. Saratov, the reading public surmised, was the woefully provincial town of Chekhov's "Lady with a Dog." At least those who had been there probably thought so. Fin-de-siècle Saratov made this none-too-flattering first impression on Maria Stolypin, the governor's daughter: "Saratov, itself, my God, how I hated it . . . everything there only spelled despondency and anguish for me. The streets were laid out as if with a ruler, with small, sad little houses along each side. . . . There were so many drunks."[9]

But to the illiterate Saratov muzhik living on the edge of pauperism or to the inhabitant of one of the province's scrubby district towns, Saratov evoked an altogether different image. Like many other Russian urban centers, Saratov had registered dramatic population growth and progress in connection with the boom years of Russian industrial expansion in the 1890s and once again after 1910. By 1914 the city had become the eleventh largest in the Russian empire. In official area Saratov occupied 2,000 square *desiatinas* of land (about nine square miles). Expansion within the city limits was carried out according to an architectural plan drawn up in 1870, but slums shot up helter-skelter on the outskirts of town and in two large ravines that divided Saratov into three separate districts. Old town Saratov, the center of the city, extended from the Volga River on the east to the mountains and steppe on the west. Glebuchev and Beloglinskii ravines bordered old town on the north and south, respectively. The "mountain" region commenced on the other side of Glebuchev ravine and continued northward to Sokolov Mountain. The southern region stretching from the Volga to the slopes of

8. Cited in Khovanskii, *O proshlom*, p. 21.

9. M. S. Bock, *Reminiscences of My Father, Peter A. Stolypin* (Metuchen, N.J., 1970), p. 98. Also see the description of Saratov found in *Spravochnik-putevoditel' po gorodu Saratovu* (Saratov, 1902), pp. 176–77.

Saratov, c. 1900

Lysaia (Bald) Mountain was the industrial settlement, where many of Saratov's largest factories were concentrated.[10]

The disparity between Saratov's rich and poor neighborhoods was glaring. The rectangle formed by Moscow, Ilin, Konstantinov, and Nicholas streets, in the west-central part of the city, enclosed the "downtown" area. Residents of this neighborhood enjoyed such modern technological advances as telephones, electricity, and a Belgian-built tram system. The downtown district featured a university founded in 1909 and named after Nicholas II, a music conservatory and drama theater, technical schools, and the headquarters of educational, cultural, and social clubs. Well-to-do Saratovites might join the local chapter of the Esperanto Society or the Vegetarian Club. Theaters, museums, libraries, and cinemas added to the cultural attractiveness of the neighborhood. Moscow Street, the major commercial thoroughfare, cut through the city to Moscow Square, where peasants, artisans, and local merchants hawked their produce and wares. The strolling public could stop in one of the several pavillions here to buy ice cream or sip a cool yoghurt or Tatar kumiss. On Sundays the regimental band, ensconced in a makeshift wooden bandshell, performed for the public. During World War I an impressive covered market, designed in the modernist style by the architect V. A. Liukshin, opened. The City Duma building, the scene of much political activity in 1917, loomed over the square. Most of the buildings lining the street dated from the early nineteenth century and were squat and heavy-looking, with thick walls and narrow windows. "Just like the Arbat section in Moscow," a modern Saratovite observed. Nemetskaia (German) Street, the other major boulevard in the district, called the Nevskii Prospekt of Saratov, lured shoppers, pleasure seekers, and tourists, and on holidays was the site of parades and festivals. The shops catered to the affluent; expensive food items, gold and silver jewelry and artifacts, cosmetics, musical instruments, and rich pastries were displayed, as one 1911 guidebook put it, "just like in the capital."[11] A city of lilac bushes, elms, lindens, and poplars, Saratov had a certain provincial rusticity and quaintness despite its modern pretensions. The writer Konstantin Fedin described it as a city "of gingham, retired generals, and flour kings."[12]

The poorer sections of Saratov stretched along the riverfront, the city's ravines, and the town's outer perimeter. Lacking multistory buildings, these areas were less densely populated than the downtown area. Few of the streets were paved, and indoor plumbing and electricity were rare.

10. I. N. Kokshaiskii, *Gorod Saratov v zhilishchnom otnoshenii* (Saratov, 1922), pp. 1–11.

11. *Saratov: Sputnik-ukazatel' 1911 god* (Saratov, 1911), p. 28.

12. Konstantin Fedin, *Early Joys*, trans. G. Kazanina (New York, 1960), p. 232.

Housing varied from log or brick structures to run-down hovels. The outskirts of town differed little from the surrounding countryside. What Moscow Street was to middle-class Saratovites the Upper Bazaar was to the poor: "harsh, grasping, ferociously desperate, and violent."[13]

Medical reports, guidebooks, and travelers' accounts stressed the unsanitary and unaesthetic condition of lower-class Saratov. In 1910 Saratov's death rate equaled that of Petrograd and Moscow thirty years earlier. Poor sanitation was the major, if indirect, cause of death and sickness. Pointing to the terrible conditions in the densely populated ravines, a 1910 medical report observed that "epidemics never cease in Saratov; one infectious disease merely replaces another." Workers and petty artisans constituted 78 percent of the inhabitants of the largest ravine, Glebuchev. The primitively constructed dwellings there, often coated with clay or mud, lacked garbage removal and toilet facilities. As early as 1891 City Duma reports had expressed concern over the potential dangers in these areas, but no effective law regulating living conditions was ever enacted.[14]

Well before the Revolution of 1917, Saratov had acquired a reputation as one of the most radical Volga provinces. Nineteenth-century writers often argued that the territory's unusual mixture of independent-minded people encouraged a local spirit of defiance. Casual observation suggests that there may have been something to this assessment. Throughout the seventeenth century, freebooters, fugitives, religious dissenters, and disgruntled peasants fled to the undergoverned Volga area from central Russia. Slavic peasants soon composed the bulk of the population, diversified by pockets of indigenous Mordvinians, Tatars, Chuvash, and Kalmyks. Subsequent administrative assimilation of the frontier during the eighteenth century resulted in state-sponsored colonization and economic development of the Saratov region. In addition to the government's recruitment of Ukrainian peasants to work the local salt mines, Catherine the Great subsidized the resettlement along the Volga of German colonists and Old Believers who had been living abroad. Later, Saratov province became a refuge for evacuees from regions threatened by Napoleon and a new home to prisoners of war from the multinational French army. Gypsy bands and Jews also settled in the area.[15] More im-

13. Ibid., p. 358.

14. "Gorod Saratov: Sanitarno-topograficheskii ocherk," *Vestnik obshchestvennoi gigieny, sudebnoi i prakticheskoi meditsiny,* no. 11–13 (1910), pp. 201, 205, 211.

15. Migration to Saratov is discussed in *Statisticheskii sbornik po Saratovskoi gubernii* (Saratov, 1923), p. 58. For an analysis of the settlement of German colonists and Old Believers, see Roger P. Bartlett, *Human Capital: The Settlement of Foreigners in Russia, 1762–1804* (Cambridge, Eng., 1979), p. 155. Information on the arrival of various groups during the 19th century comes from Khovanskii, *O proshlom,* p. 11.

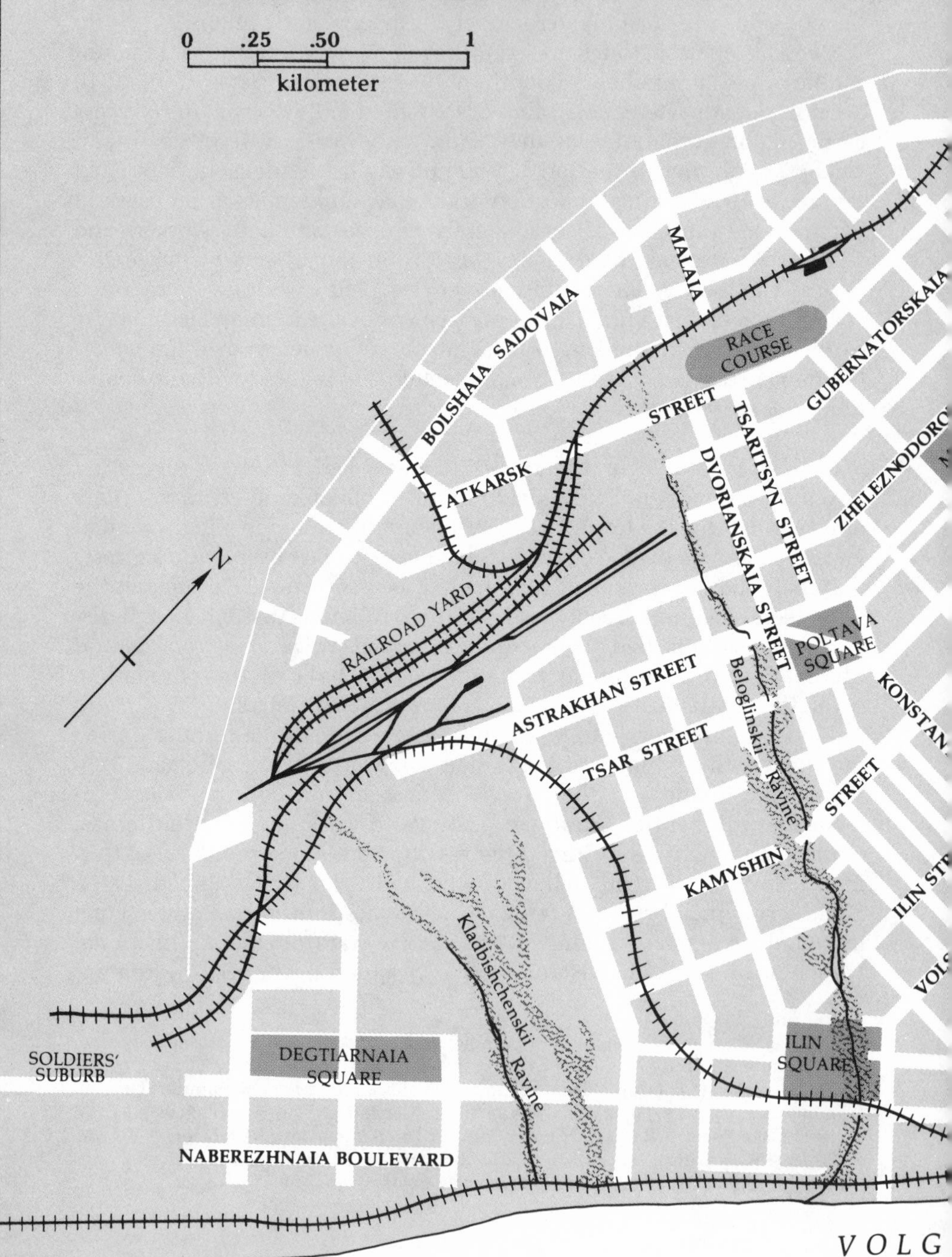
SARATOV
0
.25
.50
1
kilometer
N
MALAIA
BOLSHAIA SADOVAIA
RACE COURSE
GUBERNATORSKAIA
STREET
TSARITSYN STREET
DVORIANSKAIA STREET
ATKARSK
RAILROAD YARD
POLTAVA SQUARE
ASTRAKHAN STREET
Beloglinskii Ravine
TSAR STREET
STREET
KAMYSHIN
Kladbishchenskii Ravine
ILIN SQUARE
SOLDIERS' SUBURB
DEGTIARNAIA SQUARE
NABEREZHNAIA BOULEVARD

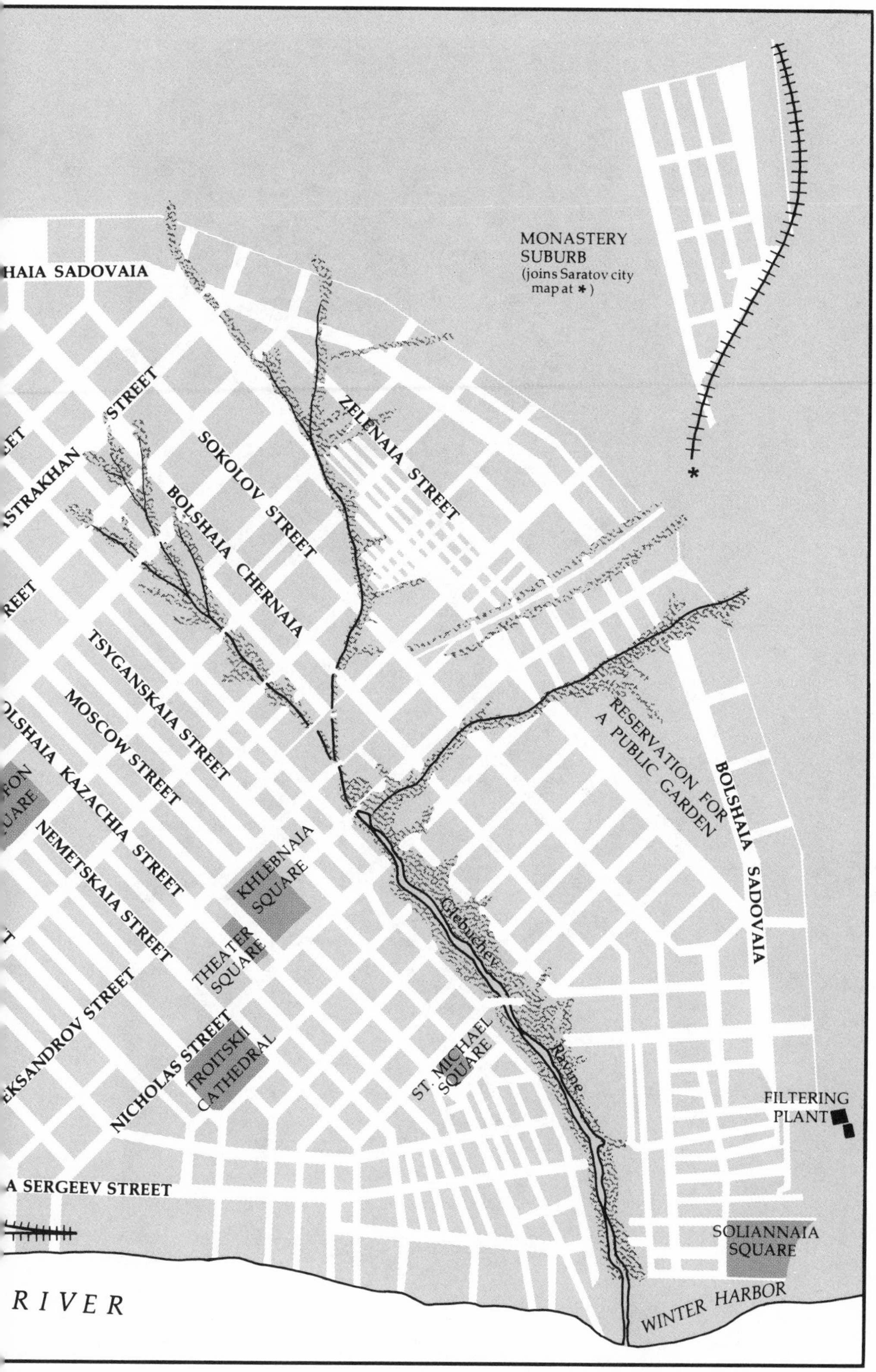

HAIA SADOVAIA

MONASTERY
SUBURB
(joins Saratov city
map at *)

STREET
EET
ASTRAKHAN
SOKOLOV STREET
ZELENAIA STREET
BOLSHAIA CHERNAIA
REET
TSYGANSKAIA STREET
MOSCOW STREET
OLSHAIA KAZACHIA STREET
FON
UARE
NEMETSKAIA STREET
KHLEBNAIA
SQUARE
THEATER
SQUARE
EKSANDROV STREET
NICHOLAS STREET
TROITSKII
CATHEDRAL
ST. MICHAEL
SQUARE
Glebuchev
Ravine
RESERVATION FOR
A PUBLIC GARDEN
BOLSHAIA SADOVAIA
FILTERING
PLANT
A SERGEEV STREET
SOLIANNAIA
SQUARE
WINTER HARBOR
RIVER

Saratov town center

Saratov at the turn of the century

TABLE 1
Percentage of Slavs and major minorities in Saratov province, 1897, by district

		Major minorities	
District	*Slavs*	*Ethnic group*	*Percent*
Serdobsk	99.77%	—	—
Balashov	99.73	—	—
Tsaritsyn	95.50	Germans, Kalmyks	—
Atkarsk	94.66	Germans	—
Volsk	94.61	Tatars, Chuvash, Germans	—
Saratov	89.73	Germans, Mordvinians	—
Petrovsk	72.00	Mordvinians	20.0%
		Tatars	5.5
Kuznetsk	61.86	Tatars	20.0
		Mordvinians	16.0
Kamyshin	59.47[a]	Germans	40.0
Khvalynsk	56.00	Mordvinians	20.0
		Tatars	20.0
		Chuvash	—

Data based on 1897 census.
[a]Russians, 44.46%; Ukrainians, 15.01%.

portant, Saratov was an attractive destination for peasant migrants from central Russia until the second half of the nineteenth century, when out-migration—reflecting the stagnant nature of local agriculture—overpopulation, and unemployment reversed earlier trends.[16]

As Saratov province entered the twentieth century its population was predominantly rural and Slavic. According to the 1897 census, the province's population was 2,405,829, 76.75 percent of whom were Russians; all Slavs combined made up 83.1 percent of the total. Important minority nationalities included the Germans (6.92 percent), Mordvinians (5.15 percent), and Tatars (3.94 percent). In the province's ten districts the percentage of Russians varied from Serdobsk uezd, where they composed 99.7 percent of the total population, to Kamyshin uezd, where they made up only 44.46 percent of the inhabitants. (See Table 1.) Few non-Slavs had been assimilated into the Russian population with the exception of those residing in the cities of Saratov and Tsaritsyn. In Kamyshin, for example, the Volga Germans, who constituted 40 percent

16. V. M. Kabuzan, *Izmeneniia v razmeshchenii naseleniia Rossii v XVIII-pervoi polovine XIX v.* (Moscow, 1971), pp. 28, 31–32; V. K. Iatsunskii, "Izmeneniia v razmeshchenii naseleniia Rossii v 1724–1916 gg.," *Istoriia SSSR*, no. 1 (1957), p. 211; A. A. Mal'kov, *Estestvennoe dvizhenie naseleniia Saratovskoi gubernii* (Saratov, 1926), pp. 3, 5.

of the uezd's population, lived in distinct ethnic communities.[17] So did the Mordvinians, Tatars, Chuvash, and Kalmyks. Census data show that few of the rural minorities could pass a literacy test in Russian, and that most practiced religions other than Orthodoxy. These demographic data take on meaning when they are put into a sociopolitical context: districts with the strongest and most violent peasant movements in 1905 and 1917 tended to be those with the greatest concentration of Russians and other Slavs. These districts also had the densest populations and the largest urban centers. Without diminishing the importance of the ethnic minorities, whose history remains to be written, we may say that because of their relative isolation from the Slavs they did not to any discernible extent shape the course of events in Saratov in 1917.

Before Saratov became a provincial capital in the eighteenth century, its population grew slowly. From an estimated population of 3,000 in 1720, the number of inhabitants had increased to a mere 7,000 in 1774. Nineteenth-century sources cite the number of inhabitants as 15,000 in 1815, 27,000 in 1825, and 49,600 in 1838. In the second half of the nineteenth century the city's growth paralleled the tremendous increase in the population of the country at large. By 1897 the city's population had reached 137,147 (92 percent were Russian); by 1904, industrialization had pushed it to 202,848. Afterward Saratov's expansion tapered off a bit; nonetheless, by 1910 the city's population had expanded to 235,300 (see Table 2), and it reached 242,425 in 1913.[18]

The extraordinary population dislocation caused by World War I had a profound impact on Saratov's population and the course of the local revolution. Emigration from Saratov to Siberia and other areas, which had relieved local overpopulation in the countryside since the end of the 1890s, stopped altogether.[19] Military conscription changed the population profile in both city and village. The government drafted roughly one-third of the city's working class. In rural areas military mobilization vastly altered the ratio between men and women. Before the war there had been 102.5 women per 100 men in the countryside; in 1916 there were 121.8 women per 100 men. By 1917, 47.3 percent of the province's "able-bodied" men had been put into uniform.[20] As a center of noncom-

17. N. A. Troinitskii et al., eds., *Pervaia vseobshchaia perepis' naseleniia Rossiiskoi Imperii, 1897 god,* vol. 38, *Saratovskaia guberniia* (St. Petersburg, 1904), passim. See also James W. Long, "Agricultural Conditions in the German Colonies of Novouzensk District, Samara Province," *Slavonic and East European Review,* 57, no. 4 (1979), 531–51.

18. Geraklitov, *Saratov,* pp. 24–25; Il'in, *Saratov,* p. 27; Kavunov, *Goroda Saratovskoi oblasti,* p. 32.

19. See *Statisticheskii ezhegodnik Rossii za 1916,* no. 1 (Petrograd, 1918), pp. 98–99.

20. Stanislas Kohn and Alexander F. Meyendorff, *The Cost of the War to Russia* (New Haven, 1932), pp. 24, 27.

Table 2
Populations and annual growth rates of six Volga cities, 1897–1910

City	*Population* 1897	1910	*Average yearly growth rate*
Tsaritsyn	55,200	100,800	6.4%
Saratov	137,100	235,300	5.4
Samara	90,000	143,800	4.6
Kazan	130,000	194,200	3.8
Astrakhan	112,800	162,400	3.3
Simbirsk	41,700	55,200	2.5

Source: I. N. Kokshaiskii, *Predvaritel'nye dannye perepisi naseleniia goroda Saratova i ego prigorodov* (Saratov, 1916), p. 21.

bat military activity, Saratov belonged to the Kazan Military District, which was one of the largest war machines in the country. All of the district centers within Saratov province housed garrisons except Khvalynsk.[21]

The Great War altered Saratov's ethnic makeup. When the Central Powers threatened Russia's western border, the government evacuated entire defense-related factories, including their Latvian and Polish workers, to safer locales, such as the Volga region. By the fall of 1917 more than 20,000 Poles, an additional 6,000 Polish Jews, and thousands of Latvians had been evacuated to Saratov province. Arriving from areas with histories of greater labor unrest than Saratov, the evacuated Latvian and Polish workers proved more militant than their local counterparts in 1917, especially those employed at the Russian-Baltic plant, the Zhest metalworks, and the Titanik factory, relocated from Riga and Revel. Thousands of students from the western provinces and Jews from the Pale also ended up along the Volga. The Transactions of the Saratov City Duma reported that in 1916, 50,000 to 75,000 displaced people were living in Saratov town. Crammed together in inferior housing, the refugees had an unsettling impact on the city. Epidemics broke out frequently among them. Town authorities had to cope not only with housing and health problems but also with increasingly erratic food supplies, sanitation problems, and crime. Finally, as in the rest of the empire, war conditions separated families and brought about a decline in the birth rate. The number of illegitimate births shot up, accompanied by widespread public concern over the growing incidence of venereal disease.[22]

21. S. E. Topaz, *Nekotorye voprosy zakhvata vlasti sovetami i podavleniia imi soprotivleniia ekspluatatorov v pervyi god Sovetskoi vlasti* (Ashkhabad, 1960), p. 20.

22. Walentyna Najdus, *Polacy w Rewolucji 1917 roku* (Warsaw, 1967), pp. 6, 8, 17, 50,

Because of the fluidity of the population during the war, statistics on Saratov's population in 1917 must be used cautiously. Estimates range from 204,000 to roughly 250,000 inhabitants. Refugees, transferred workers, students, and soldiers in the garrison, however, tended to be excluded from these figures. Their inclusion would put the population of the greater metropolitan area in 1917 closer to 300,000. If one takes into account that this figure included 25,000 to 75,000 refugees, 60,000 to 70,000 soldiers, thousands of evacuated Latvian and Polish workers, Jews, and students, and then recalls that one-third of the indigenous industrial proletariat and at least as many unskilled workers had been drafted, one can conclude that, at a very conservative estimate, one-third of the city's 1917 population had not been there before the war.

The city's social makeup in 1917 is as difficult to assess as its fluctuating population. The Saratov City Duma decided in December 1915 to conduct a local census in early 1916 in order to ensure better handling of food supplies. Census takers divided the town's population into five defined social categories that are much more revealing than the old-fashioned government classification by legal estates *(soslovie)*. The 1916 classifications were: (1) workers—factory workers, artisans, unskilled workers, domestic and industrial servants, and others; (2) *sluzhashchie* and officials—salaried employees, white-collar workers in commercial and industrial enterprises, government officials, people of free professions (military officers, clergy, teachers, lawyers, doctors, etc.); (3) merchants and factory owners, including people who owned businesses and those who lived on income from rented dwellings—capitalists; (4) students in secondary or higher educational institutions, living independently in the city without their parents (a transient group); and (5) those who belonged to no category, mainly refugees without specified employment.

According to the 1916 census, Saratov's population was 232,015. The compiler of the published proceedings informed readers, however, that the city's real size was greater because the figures excluded the troops who lived in barracks (most of them did) and those recuperating in military hospitals. Slightly more than half of the population belonged to the working class, as Table 3 shows. The compilers of the census suggested that this group, too, was actually larger, because the statistics

---

52; L. I. Lubny-Gertsyk, *Dvizhenie naseleniia na territorii SSSR za vremia mirovoi voiny i revoliutsii* (Moscow, 1926), p. 23; V. G. Khodakov, "Bor'ba rabochikh Saratovskoi gubernii pod rukovodstvom Kommunisticheskoi organizatsii za rabochii kontrol' nad proizvodstvom v 1917–18 gg.," candidate dissertation, Saratov Pedagogical Institute, 1953, p. 4; "Professional'nye soiuzy Saratovskoi gubernii za 10 let," *Nizhnee Povolzh'e*, no. 10 (1927), p. 152; V. Ts. Urlanik, "Dinamika naseleniia Rossii," *Uchenye zapiski Vsesoiuznogo zaochno-ekonomicheskogo instituta*, no. 2 (1957), p. 124; A. G. Kovalevskii, *Ocherki po demografii Saratova (rozhdaemost' i smertnost' za 1914–1927 gg.)* (Saratov, 1928), p. 11.

TABLE 3

Population of Saratov, 1916, by sex and social class

Class	*Males*		*Females*		*Both sexes*	
	Number	*Percent*	*Number*	*Percent*	*Number*	*Percent*
Working class	56,533	53.6%	66,509	52.5%	123,042	53.0%
Professional middle class	17,136	16.2	18,883	15.0	36,019	15.5
Commercial middle class	9,688	9.1	13,191	10.5	22,879	9.8
Students boarding in Saratov	5,190	4.9	3,718	3.0	8,908	3.8
Refugees and others	17,128	16.2	24,039	19.0	41,167	17.9
All classes	105,675	100.0%	126,340	100.0%	232,015	100.0%

Source: I. N. Kokshaiskii, *Predvaritel'nye dannye perepisi naseleniia goroda Saratova i ego prigorodov* (Saratov, 1916), p. 15.

neglected some workers who rented dwellings and small shops, tailors who took in work at home, and others who lived in special housing facilities. Since one-third of the population had not yet reached the age of 15, it may be assumed that of the 123,042 members of the working class, about 80,000 were adults and thus part of the labor force.[23] Yet other sources note that only a portion of these workers—about 25,000—could be classified as "industrial proletariat," employed in approximately 150 factories in town. The city housed 23 metal-processing and machine-building plants employing about 4,000 workers; 17 wood-processing enterprises, 11 butter creameries and vegetable oil presses, 8 flour mills, and numerous brick, leather, chemical, textile, and tobacco factories. The flour mills employed about 1,500 workers; the butter creameries about 560; the Zhest factory from Riga about 2,000; the Gantke metalworks, approximately 650; and the Bering factory, 450. There also were an estimated 2,000 railroad workers in Saratov, 400 transportation workers hired by the Belgian-owned tram company, 1,100 workers employed in print works, and about 1,000 tobacco workers. The ten brick factories employed approximately 1,000; the three leather plants, 260; the sawmills, 440; and the shipyard, 400. The remaining part of the population classified as working class by the 1916 census included large numbers of artisan workers, domestics, dock hands, and other unskilled types. Once again, the true impact of the war can be seen in the fact that refugees made up the second largest social group in town. What can be called Saratov's middle class—merchants, factory owners, "flour kings," professionals, and the large number of office workers—constituted one-fourth of Saratov's population in 1917.

Much of the analysis in subsequent chapters will focus on Saratov's workers, who became one of the most reliable sources of support for the Bolshevik movement. It therefore is appropriate to trace in some detail the evolution of the local working class. As one of the last regions of European Russia to industrialize, the Lower Volga in general and Saratov in particular through 1917 and afterward remained more vital as an entrepôt than as an industrial center. Both Saratov and Tsaritsyn had become transfer points for Donets coal, Baku oil, Volga lumber and grains, Ural ores and metals, Astrakhan fish, and machines and tools manufactured in Moscow and St. Petersburg. Grain processing and the manufacturing of food and consumer items prepared from agricultural or animal products accounted for the bulk of the province's output in the

23. I. N. Kokshaiskii, *Predvaritel'nye dannye perepisi naseleniia goroda Saratova i ego prigorodov* (Saratov, 1916), pp. 9, 13.

early twentieth century.[24] A modest consumer goods industry catering to local needs had also developed in Saratov from the eighteenth century. Paralleling economic changes in the country as a whole, Saratov's commercial and industrial development after the 1860s sped up dramatically. Steam-run flour mills and vegetable oil presses appeared simultaneously with the opening of local banks, extension of a railroad network, and establishment of the Saratov Stock Exchange. Metal-processing factories founded toward the end of the century employed more skilled elements of the proletariat. The machine-building Bering plant began production in 1888, the Gantke metalworks (nail and wire manufacturing) in 1897, the Volga iron foundry and the Kolesnikov boiler factory in 1899.

Few Saratov workers, however, were classified as industrial laborers in 1900. Manufacturing in the province remained concentrated in villages and industrial suburbs in four districts (Saratov, Tsaritsyn, Kuznetsk, and Volsk), and included a large percentage of handicraft and artisan production. The increase in the number of workers in small enterprises actually outpaced that of factory wage earners. The location of factories in the countryside, characteristic of Russian industrialization before World War I, meant that workers were employed in the vicinity of their home village. Within the city of Saratov a growing number of unskilled and often transient workers flocked to the fetid working-class slums sprawling around the city limits. In the 1890s the butter creameries, flour mills, and tobacco and brick factories employed seasonal workers among the poorer strata of the local peasantry.[25] Many others found work as dock hands and barge haulers. The peculiarities of the country's economic transformation confused revolutionary activists, many of whom doubted whether one really could speak of a "Russian industrialization." Even the government took a long time to shake its view of factory workers as nothing more than peasants.

A steady rise of large, urban-centered industrial enterprises staffed by a more or less permanent, city-dwelling work force accompanied the growth of small-scale, rural-based manufacturing. Although little is known about them, a cadre of urban workers toiling in the tobacco factories and various other enterprises manufacturing consumer items evolved in Saratov throughout the nineteenth century. But it was the government-sponsored industrialization program of Minister of Finance Sergei Witte, which resulted in the opening of metalworks in Saratov

24. See P. Topilin et al., *Saratovskaia oblast' za 40 let* (Saratov, 1957), p. 9; and A. Kh. Kliachko, "Krizis pereproizvodstva 1900–1903 godov v Saratovskoi gubernii," *Trudy Saratovskogo ekonomicheskogo instituta*, no. 3 (1951), pp. 123–24.

25. G. P. Saar, *Saratovskaia promyshlennost' v 90-kh godakh i v nachale 900-kh godov* (Saratov, 1928), pp. 3–5, 10, 27.

Saratov Stock Exchange

and an extension of railway facilities in the 1890s, that led to the formation of a skilled work force: the new factories recruited workers from more industrialized towns. By 1903 the total number of enterprises in Saratov had grown to 186, with 9,201 workers. (Since small enterprises were not included in the factory inspectorate's statistics, the number of workers was actually higher. Further, the artisan population shot up during the same period, from 4,894 in 1891 to 16,080 in 1903.)[26] By 1903–4, however, a nationwide economic crisis temporarily interrupted industrial expansion and local metalworkers and railroad workers lost their jobs.[27] Strikes over bread-and-butter issues broke out in Saratov in the first years of the century. These workers not only were the most politicized at the time but also dominated labor politics in 1905 and again in 1917.

Saratov recovered slowly from the depression. In the decade before World War I, Tsaritsyn eclipsed Saratov in its rate of industrial growth, and with the completion of the Orenburg–Tashkent rail line in 1906, the volume of rail activity shifted southward to Tsaritsyn. Moreover, Saratov still had few large factories, while in neighboring Tsaritsyn several factories employed more than 2,500 workers.[28] Most Saratov workers continued to labor in small enterprises processing agricultural and animal products. By 1914 a cadre of skilled workers existed only in the town's metal-processing and machine-building factories, large mechanized food-processing establishments, and railroad yards.

The economic situation of the Saratov working class differed little from that of workers elsewhere in provincial Russian towns. Because the local economy was tied to agriculture, the bulk of the working class remained an unstable urban element that maintained ties with the countryside. The legacy of social subordination and of a low cultural level in the villages carried over into the cities. During most of the nineteenth century the government denied workers the right to strike or organize, thus all but guaranteeing that economic protests would turn political. Ignoring the existence of a labor problem, the tsarist regime favored a patriarchal relationship between employer and worker.[29]

Long hours, low wages, neglect of basic sanitation, and an accident rate higher than the national norm characterized working conditions in

26. See G. F. Khodakov, "Bor'ba Saratovskikh rabochikh pod rukovodstvom bol'shevikov v period revoliutsii 1905–1907 gg.," *Uchenye zapiski Saratovskogo gosudarstvennogo universiteta*, 55 (1956), 86–87.

27. G. Minkin, "Rabochee dvizhenie 1905 goda na Volge," *Kommunisticheskii put'*, no. 21–22 (1930), p. 66.

28. Khodakov, "Bor'ba rabochikh Saratovskoi gubernii," p. 5.

29. Gaston V. Rimlinger, "The Management of Labor Protest in Tsarist Russia, 1870–1905," *International Review of Social History*, 5 (1961), 230.

Saratov at the turn of the century. Skilled metalworkers, whose earnings topped national averages, received the best wages locally and enjoyed the highest standard of living. Unskilled workers, including women and adolescents, engaged in food-processing industries and the like, usually earned less than workers elsewhere. The whistle blast marking the end of the workday sent most unskilled workers home to a shack or factory barrack in the town's ravines or on the slopes surrounding the city, which also housed an estimated 4,000 tramps and beggars. Smallpox, scarlet fever, diphtheria, dysentery, cholera, plague, and venereal disease were an inevitable part of the lives of workers who lived in these slums. So was alcohol.[30]

A 1911 factory inspector's report shows a crude dichotomy in living and working conditions between skilled and unskilled laborers, which was in no way unusual in Russia at the time. Admitting that factory owners had a clear advantage over workers in prescribing terms of employment, the inspector adopted an almost relentlessly critical tone in his report. He censured all food-processing industries for widespread filth and lack of sanitation measures, and found fault with the poor diet, medical care, and factory housing available to workers. Admonishing the city administration to do more to look after workers' health, the report recommended that factories be placed under constant sanitary inspection and proposed the implementation of a program through which the workers themselves, after proper training in sanitation and hygiene, would participate in future inspections.[31]

If any improvements in work conditions came about after 1911, the impact of the war soon negated them. During the first months of hostilities overall output in Saratov fell off. At one point production at the Bering factory had plunged 80 percent. After the organization of the Saratov War Industries Committee in 1915, set up to assume responsibility for military supplies, this negative trend temporarily reversed itself. Measures that initially revived food and light industries were adopted during the war, and they resulted in the diversification of local industry and an upsurge in war-related production, especially after the evacuation of factories from the Baltic provinces to Saratov. This wartime expansion, however, did not alter the predominantly agricultural character of the Volga region.[32] According to the report of the Saratov Labor Ex-

30. N. L. Klein, "Ob osobennostiakh polozheniia i urovne ekspluatatsii promyshlennykh rabochikh Srednego Povolzh'ia v period kapitalizma," *Nash krai* (Kuibyshev), no. 1 (1974), pp. 22–23; A. Kh. Kliachko, "Materialy o polozhenii promyshlennykh rabochikh Saratovskoi gubernii," *Trudy Saratovskogo ekonomicheskogo instituta*, 2 (1949), 63–67.

31. Inspectors examined 98 Saratov factories representing 27 industries. See *Fabriki i zavody g. Saratova v sanitarnom otnoshenii* (Saratov, 1911).

32. E. N. Burdzhalov, *Vtoraia russkaia revoliutsiia: Moskva, front, periferiia* (Moscow, 1971), p. 202.

change, an institution concerned with the problems of unemployment and job placement, the war at first increased unemployment among certain categories of unskilled workers because many light industries curtailed or even shut down production, whereas it increased demand for skilled labor to staff the defense industries.[33] Skilled workers and unskilled female laborers employed as domestics had the easiest time getting placed, while some salaried workers, such as office workers, bookkeepers, and sales clerks, had the greatest difficulty. The flood of refugees into Saratov after August 1915 complicated the tasks of the Labor Exchange, which now sought to broaden its activities to aid the more than 3,000 refugees who had registered with it during the five-month period before January 1916. As the war progressed, lack of fuel, raw materials, and inefficient transport caused many enterprises to reduce their output or close. Unemployment became still more of a problem.

Data on living conditions reported in the 1916 census corroborate the unenviable situation of Saratov's working people and the burden the war placed upon them. Other social groups—even the refugees—ate better than local workers, whose diet was high in starchy products and contained little meat, fish, eggs, and sugar. Workers also made do with less kerosene, soap, and other necessities. The compiler of the census cautioned that the working class had misunderstood the purpose of the questioning and the proposed ration-card system. Believing that the size of subsequent rations would reflect earlier consumption levels, workers had tended to exaggerate their access to desirable food items.[34]

During 1905 and again in 1917 peasant disorders, punctuated by occasional paroxyms of violence, swept across the Saratov countryside, securing for the province a reputation for rural unrest. More than anything else, local economic conditions had transformed the plain folk in the villages into peasant rebels and potential revolutionaries. The two state-directed attempts to reshape the social structure of the countryside, the emancipation of the serfs in 1861 and the Stolypin reforms in the decade before 1917, failed to transform the countryside rapidly enough or in the manner envisaged by the government. Climatic considerations also contributed to the precarious economic situation in the village. Between 1871 and 1925 Saratov province suffered nineteen famine years, two-thirds of them caused by drought.[35] Despite the fact that the Volga area had become a breadbasket for the country, many in the overpopulated villages lived on the edge of poverty.

33. E. E. Diakevich, *Ocherk o deiatel'nosti Saratovskoi 'Birzhi truda' za god sushchestvovaniia (27 noiabria 1914 g. po 1 ianvaria 1916 g.)* (Saratov, 1916), p. 7.

34. Kokshaiskii, *Predvaritel'nye dannye perepisi*, pp. 30–32.

35. Long, "Agricultural Conditions," p. 540.

Agricultural and economic relations varied considerably within this province, to which serfdom had come late. From the reign of Catherine the Great on the government had awarded large parcels of land to its favorites, creating gentry latifundia and extending serfdom. The large estates with serf populations were found in the northern and western districts and to a somewhat lesser degree in the central section. The northwestern and central districts of Serdobsk, Balashov, Atkarsk, and Petrovsk lay in the rich black-earth, or *chernozem*, region, which grew rye, barley, and oats. Running along the Volga on the east, Saratov and Volsk districts also enjoyed favorable soil, although only parts could be classified as chernozem. The northeastern forested uezds of Kuznetsk and Khvalynsk, populated by a sizable number of Tatars and Mordvinians, had a diverse peasant economy that relied heavily on trade and handicraft production. The southern strip of the province fell into an altogether different agricultural zone. The loamy steppe soil here, known as *suglinok*, was less fertile than the black earth to the north, and made fruit orchards and livestock breeding more profitable than grain growing. Because the region was populated by state serfs, the peasant holdings tended to be larger and landlord holdings smaller. Saratov province, then, could be divided roughly into two diverse economic zones with a transition belt in the middle.[36]

Local conditions confirm our worst suspicions about the terms and effects of emancipation, from which few Saratov peasants benefited. The proportion of land retained by landowners was higher in Saratov than in any other province in European Russia; emancipation actually resulted in a 37.9 percent reduction in peasant holdings in the province.[37] Fully one-third of the former landlord peasants opted for the so-called beggar's portion, which granted them one-fourth of the local maximum allotment without payment of redemption fees, thus guaranteeing that they would become entrapped in an exploitive system of rent and labor relationships (*otrabotka*) with local landowners (*pomeshchiki*).[38] As elsewhere, crown and state serfs fared better under the legislation. By 1900 those who had received the smallest allotments rented a far greater amount of land than

36. Before emancipation, *barshchina* (labor and services to the gentry) prevailed in the northern districts of Kuznetsk, Khvalynsk, Volsk, and Serdobsk, settled by peasants from central Russia. More complicated and varied agricultural techniques existed in the southern half of the province, where peasants from the Don and Ukraine acquired holdings by *obrok* or cash payments. Statistics on serfdom before 1861 are found in L. N. Iurovskii, *Saratovskie votchiny* (Saratov, 1923), pp. 232–33.

37. Harry T. Willetts, "The Agrarian Problem," in *Russia Enters the Twentieth Century, 1894–1917*, ed. George Katkov et al. (London, 1971), p. 117.

38. S. E. Topaz, "Pobeda Velikoi Oktiabr'skoi sotsialisticheskoi revoliutsii v Povolzh'e," *Uchenye zapiski Turkmenskogo universiteta*, no. 12 (1957), p. 139; *Materialy k voprosu o nuzhdakh sel'sko-khoziaistvennoi promyshlennosti v Saratovskoi gubernii* (Saratov, 1903), pp. 52–53.

the former state serfs, who had been given more generous holdings.[39] Concentrated in several uezds in Saratov province, the peasant movement was most truculent in those fertile, black-earth districts of the northwest and central areas in which the terms of emancipation had been the least favorable.

Low productivity, the discouragement of modern farming methods inherent in the communal structure, and the burden of taxation to provide capital for Minister of Finance Sergei Witte's industrialization drive further limited modernization. Throughout the 1861–1914 period acquisition of additional land became the peasant's answer to poverty. But the population burgeoned far more rapidly than the availability of land, especially in the black-earth districts with the highest population density.[40] The problem in much of the Russian countryside at the turn of the century had become one of too many peasants rather than too little land. A study carried out in 1903 of changes in the Saratov village since 1861 reported that 64.1 percent of the total rural male population had suffered a reduction in their allotments, whereas only 7.4 percent experienced an increase in the size of their holdings.[41] The contraction in landholding turned out to be greater in densely populated Serdobsk uezd, which stood in the vanguard of the peasant movement in 1917. Volsk and Saratov districts followed closely behind Serdobsk. Given the economic significance of agriculture in Saratov province, the 1903 report concluded that peasant holdings remained dangerously inadequate.

Available land and the establishment of banks to help peasants buy plots simply could not satisfy the peasants' craving for land. Landowners' holdings declined 61.5 percent between 1861 and 1905, but city dwellers who frequently rented land to peasants purchased more than half of what had slipped from the hands of pomeshchiki. On the eve of the Revolution of 1905 the state, church, and other institutions still owned 14 percent of the land in Saratov province and private owners 31 percent. Most peasants had become inescapably involved in complicated rent and labor arrangements with local landlords, especially in black-earth Balashov, Serdobsk, and Atkarsk districts, where by 1900 one-third of the land they cultivated was rented.[42] Others migrated to

39. M. Ia. Kosenko, "Agrarnaia reforma Stolypina v Saratovskoi gubernii," candidate dissertation, Moscow State Historical-Archival Institute, 1951, p. 32.

40. In Balashov uezd, for example, the population shot up 52% between 1858 and 1901, whereas land under peasant cultivation increased by only 17%. See Timothy Mixter, "Of Grandfather-Beaters and Fat-Heeled Pacifists: Perceptions of Agricultural Labor and Hiring Market Disturbances in Saratov, 1872–1905," *Russian History*, 7 (1980), 141.

41. *Materialy k voprosu*, p. 14.

42. The 1903 report, however, criticized peasant renting of land because of the arbitrariness of rents and terms (ibid., p. 62). See also *Materialy dlia otsenki zemel' Saratovskoi gubernii*, vol. 1, *Zemlevladenie* (Saratov, 1906), p. 41; I. I. Babikov, "Krest'ianskoe

urban areas or Siberia to escape the grip of poverty, or turned to trade and handicraft production to survive.

Constant change challenged the traditional way of life and the intricate economic nexus of rent relationships trapped the peasant and created social tensions that "lay just below the surface of Russian society in the late nineteenth and twentieth centuries." There was a growing movement back and forth between town and country. Collective actions against perceived social injustice now combined traditional forms of protest with more organized behavior reflecting "the spasmodic effects of slowly developing capitalism at the turn of the century."[43] The economic depression of the early 1900s struck local agricultural production, too. Low prices for grain on the world market hurt all of the Eastern European countries that exported cereals. A poor harvest hit Russia in 1901 and Saratov province in particular, increasing food prices there. During a resulting famine, peasants in Balashov, Serdobsk, and Petrovsk uezds rose up against landowners. In isolated cases peasants vented their rage against Cossack troops sent to pacify the villages.[44] A commission set up in the wake of the disorders to analyze the problems of local agriculture concluded that the weighty burdens of the landowners' property rights and the anachronistic village commune had caused a sharp decline in agricultural profitability and increased peasant unrest.[45] Zemstvo statistics on peasant landholding provided compelling objective data to support the commission's findings.

P. A. Stolypin, who became Russia's prime minister in 1906, was appointed governor of Saratov province in 1903. His experience governing a rebellious region during the Revolution of 1905 undoubtedly strengthened his resolve to drive through the land reforms drafted earlier under Witte's influence, which bore Stolypin's name. Providing a legal and administrative framework for social transformation, the Stolypin reforms consisted of two 1906 laws facilitating the release of peasants from the confines of the commune and an edict of June 14, 1910, decreeing that members of communes who had not carried out a repartitioning of land recently became outright proprietors of their holdings. The comparative strength of the commune, overpopulation and poverty, and the manifest vestiges of subordination to the landlords shaped the response to the reforms in Saratov. In roughly 30 percent of the counties *(volosts)*

---

dvizhenie v Saratovskoi gubernii nakanune pervoi russkoi revoliutsii," *Uchenye zapiski Saratovskogo gosudarstvennogo universiteta,* 55 (1956), 175–79.

43. Mixter, "Of Grandfather-Beaters," pp. 166–67.

44. R. I. Klimov, *Revoliutsionnaia deiatel'nost' rabochikh v derevne v 1905–1907 gg.* (Moscow, 1960), p. 20. See M. A. Morokhovets, *Krest'ianskoe dvizhenie i sotsial-demokratiia v epokhu pervoi russkoi revoliutsii* (Moscow, 1926), p. 8; S. M. Dubrovskii, ed., *Krest'ianskoe dvizhenie v revoliutsii 1905–1907 gg.* (Moscow, 1956), p. 31.

45. Kosenko, "Agrarnaia reforma Stolypina," pp. 48–49.

Governor's house

peasants refused to elect representatives to local commissions that carried out the laws. Before the war only 7 percent of the 140,661 peasant households that applied to leave the commune received permission from their fellow villagers; force had to be used to implement the laws elsewhere. Peasants who remained in the commune often showed hostility toward those who left the collective fold. The reforms met with the greatest success in uezds with the most differentiated and advanced forms of agricultural production (Balashov, Serdobsk, Petrovsk, Atkarsk, Saratov, and Kamyshin), and appealed primarily to the richer peasants and to the very poor, who often immediately sold their land.[46]

Designed to shatter the peasant commune and create a class of conservative, loyal peasant farmers, the Stolypin reforms left a mixed record of success and failure in Saratov. Applications for withdrawal peaked in 1909 and afterward fell sharply; few among the ethnic minorities showed any enthusiasm for special legislation earmarked for them. Between 1907 and 1915, 97,229 households (27.9 percent of the total, higher than the national average) left the commune (went on *otrub*). Slightly more than one-third (34 percent) sold their allotments.[47] About 6 percent of the Saratov peasants who left the commune, roughly twice the national average, established the ideal *khutor*-like farms, which were independent, self-contained units that included the owners' homestead.[48] A small class of comparatively well-off peasants had emerged locally. Peasants who already owned 15 to 25 desiatinas of land or more purchased 94 percent of all land sold in the province in 1912. At approximately the same time some 6,411 landowners plus the government and church held half of all land in the province.[49] Moreover, the reforms did not alleviate the unhealthy system of rent and hired labor relationships.[50] On the eve of revolution the population of Saratov province consisted of

46. Ibid., pp. 104, 110, 125, and passim. See also G. F. Khodakov, *Ocherki istorii Saratovskoi organizatsii* KPSS: *Chast' pervaia, 1898–1918*, 2d ed. (Saratov, 1968), p. 165. For evidence of hostility toward the Stolypin peasants see A. V. Shapkarin, ed., *Krest'ianskoe dvizhenie v Rossii, iiun' 1907 g.–iiul' 1914 g.: Sbornik dokumentov* (Moscow, 1966), pp. 289–90; and A. M. Anfimov, ed., *Krest'ianskoe dvizhenie v Rossii v gody pervoi mirovoi voiny, iiul' 1914 g.–fevral' 1917: Sbornik dokumentov* (Moscow, 1965), p. 120.

47. Khodakov, *Ocherki istorii*, pp. 166–67; V. V. Kondrat'ev, *Bor'ba bol'shevikov v gody Stolypinskoi reaktsii za sokhranenie i ukreplenie nelegal'noi partii i ispol'zovanie legal'nykh vozmozhnostei* (Saratov, 1960), p. 8. Peasant farmers who set up such farms were called *khutoriane*. Peasants who left the commune but still lived in the villages were *otrub* farmers or *otrubshchiki*.

48. S. M. Dubrovskii, *Stolypinskaia zemel'naia reforma: Iz istorii sel'skogo khoziaistva i krest'ianstva Rossii v nachale XX veka* (Moscow, 1963), p. 585.

49. *Saratovskoe oblastnoe sel'skokhoziaistvennoe soveshchanie: Materialy*, 2 vols. (St. Petersburg, 1911), 1:1, 20; 2:108–9.

50. P. S. Kabytov, "Vliianie Stolypinskoi agrarnoi reformy na sel'skoe khoziaistvo Povolzh'ia (1907–1914 gg.)," *Ocherki istorii i kul'tury Povolzh'ia*, no. 1 (Kuibyshev, 1976), p. 55.

2,702,000 rural and 673,371 urban dwellers. Roughly 5 percent of the 405,495 peasant households lacked land altogether and another 15 percent, classified as *besposevnye* (without sowing area), had but a marginal amount of land.[51] Some of these families did not farm at all because of shortages of seed or labor. Some grew crops for themselves only and earned cash in other ways. In the preceding twenty-year period, the number of households in the landless and near-landless category had increased from 13 percent to 21.2 percent.[52]

War and revolution interrupted the rhythm of change in rural Russia, making historical analysis of the government's efforts to improve conditions in the countryside difficult. The war disrupted grain exports and transport, and it disturbed the equilibrium of trade and money turnover. Requisitioning and conscription reduced the number of available draft animals in the villages and sent the rural labor force into the army, thus undermining cultivation and production. After one year of war the total area under cultivation diminished. The poorer peasants, despite aid from zemstvos and cooperatives, and large landowners suffered most. (Relying heavily on cheap farm labor, the large estate owners found that the colossal outpouring of peasants into the war effort had led the cost of hired hands to rise by as much as 100 percent and more.)[53] Small peasant households often had to reduce the area sowed because of labor shortages within the family. By the summer of 1917, 30.7 percent of all households lacked male laborers.[54]

Each year of war brought greater strain to the countryside, complicating relations with the towns and foreshadowing the food-supply problems that were to become so acute in 1917–22. The amount of cultivated land decreased steadily, as did the availability of manufactured items for rural consumption. By 1917, after a good harvest and at a time when virtually no grain was exported, prices for Russian wheat skyrocketed 50 percent. War also abruptly halted the flow of applications for withdrawal from the commune and actually brought about its revival. By the summer of 1917, many local peasant committees voted to force all consolidated property back into the communal fold.

Saratov was not only a city of "gingham, retired generals, and flour kings"; it was also a city of revolutionaries. Current scholarship underes-

51. M. O. Sagrad'ian, *Osushchestvlenie Leninskogo dekreta o zemle v Saratovskoi gubernii* (Saratov, 1966), pp. 10–11.

52. Ibid., p. 9. The rise was most dramatic in Tsaritsyn (14.2 to 30.0%), Kamyshin, Balashov, and Atkarsk uezds.

53. A. F. Milovzorov, *Krest'ianskoe chastnovladel'cheskoe khoziaistvo Saratovskoi gubernii posle goda voiny* (Saratov, 1916), p. 9.

54. A. M. Anfimov, *Rossiiskaia derevnia v gody pervoi mirovoi voiny (1914–fevral' 1917 g.)* (Moscow, 1962), p. 189.

timates the strength of an indigenous socialist political culture in provincial Russia that helped doom conventional liberal solutions to political crisis in 1917. To understand what happened in Saratov during the revolution it is necessary to take into account the full sweep of antigovernment activities since the 1890s, which paralleled the evolution of a revolutionary movement in European Russia as a whole.

Soviet historiography links Saratov in the seventeenth and eighteenth centuries with peasant rebels Stenka Razin and Emilian Pugachev, whose leveling appeals struck fear into the hearts of Russia's landowning class and elicited a sympathetic response from local peasants. Aleksandr Radishchev, author of the famous *Journey from St. Petersburg to Moscow*, published in 1790, was born in Saratov province at a time when the autocracy extended serfdom by parceling out large tracts of land along the Volga to its favorites. N. G. Chernyshevsky, whose *What Is to Be Done?*, published in 1863, long appealed to the country's alienated youth, left engaging memoirs describing his coming of age in mid-nineteenth-century Saratov. Today an arrogant, defiant statue of Chernyshevsky stands guard over a town square and the local university carries his name. Dmitrii Karakazov, member of a clandestine revolutionary circle and would-be assassin of Tsar Alexander II, claims a Saratov lineage, too. Such prominent populists as Vera Figner, M. A. Natanson, A. A. Argunov, Viktor Chernov, and Stepka Balmashev, whose well-placed bullet struck down Minister of the Interior D. S. Sipiagin in 1902, all spent time in the Saratov underground.

An impressive array of Bolsheviks also conducted illicit activities in Saratov during their peripatetic days in the underground. Born in Saratov in 1881, A. I. Rykov, Lenin's successor as chairman of the fledgling Soviet government in the early 1920s, had turned Marxist in Saratov at the turn of the century. Local police arrested Lenin's sisters Maria and Anna for antigovernment work there in 1910–11, a period captured by Saratov-born Konstantin Fedin in his novel *Early Joys*, the first volume of a trilogy set along the banks of the Volga. L. M. Kaganovich served as a young Bolshevik soldier in the Saratov garrison in 1917. M. S. Ol'minskii (Aleksandrov) and V. P. Nogin, who directed the Moscow Bolsheviks in 1917, carried on party work in Saratov during the early days of World War I. Even more important, P. A. Lebedev, M. I. (Misha) Vasil'ev-Iuzhin, V. P. Antonov (Saratovskii), and V. P. Miliutin not only spent part of their formative years in the Saratov underground but stood at the helm of the local Bolshevik movement throughout 1917. After serving as the first chairman of the Saratov Soviet in 1917, Miliutin left Saratov for Petrograd upon his election to the Central Committee of the Bolshevik party in April.

The lives of other prominent political leaders, such as Prime Minister

Stolypin, are likewise linked to Saratov. The potent Saratov zemstvo movement elevated the well-known liberals N. N. L'vov, S. A. Kotliarevskii, and A. D. Iumatov to the national political scene. In 1912 the province elected A. F. Kerensky, head of the provisional government that fell to the Bolsheviks in October 1917, to the Fourth State Duma.

Local conditions reflecting the overall political health of the country created favorable soil for the nourishment of radical ideas in Saratov. The plight of the rural masses brought about by acute land shortage and overpopulation had exalted the peasant in the eyes of the local intelligentsia, many of whom pined for pastoral utopias. Saratov province emerged as a center of Russian populism and remained so throughout the revolutionary period. A constant influx of political exiles into the city contributed further to the development and diversification of the local radical movement. By the turn of the century, Russian populists began to call the town the "Athens of the Volga" because of its heavy concentration of revolutionary-minded members of the intelligentsia *(intelligenty)*.

According to one account, Chernyshevsky's legacy had created a more progressive and liberal public in Saratov than in other Volga cities. As early as the 1860s, members of the local intelligentsia had tried unsuccessfully to acquaint Saratov workers with European socialist ideas.[55] In the following decade self-education circles *(kruzhki)* dominated the local radical movement, producing activists who joined the Saratov populist or *narodnik* movement and went into the unreceptive villages to politicize the peasantry. Iu. N. Bogdanovich, Vera Figner, G. V. Plekhanov (who later became the "father of Russian Marxism"), and other populist luminaries conducted illegal activity along the Volga, where virtually all strains of populist thought then prevalent in Russia found at least a handful of adherents.[56] The central committee of the People's Will moved to Saratov and issued inflammatory proclamations calling upon the oppressed to rise up and smash the autocracy and propertied elements.[57]

The conservative crackdown in the aftermath of the assassination of Alexander II in 1881 made illicit activity more difficult but by no means impossible. During the 1880s the political police *(okhranka)* monitored the numerous self-education circles in Saratov, including the first ones conducted by Saratov workers. By the end of the decade, Marxist litera-

55. F. D'dova et al., *Revoliutsionnye kruzhki v Saratove* (St. Petersburg, 1906), pp. 5–7.

56. See F. Venturi, *Roots of Revolution: A History of the Populist and Socialist Movements in Nineteenth-Century Russia* (New York, 1966), pp. 592–93; D'dova, *Revoliutsionnye kruzhki*, pp. 7–9.

57. G. P. Saar, "Pervye popytki sotsial-demokraticheskoi raboty sredi Saratovskikh rabochikh," *Proletarskaia revoliutsiia*, no. 4/75 (1928), pp. 133–40, 151–53.

ture circulated among local students, radicals, and workers. The great famine of 1891–92 heightened political awareness. Mark Natanson, a respected populist leader from the past, returned from exile to Saratov, where he founded the Party of the People's Right *(Partiia Narodnogo prava)*. Seeking to meld the social activism sparked by the 1891 famine with traditional populist sentiments, Natanson evaded police infiltration and crackdowns until 1894. Across much of Russia, the public initiative permitted by the government to extend famine relief boiled over into heated debates between populists and those who embraced the more "scientific" laws of Marxism. Although local conditions and experiences initially limited Saratov society's receptiveness to Marxism, by the turn of the century the intense debate between populism and Marxism common to larger industrial centers had flared up in Saratov as well, under the influence of the expansion and modernization of local industry and the abundance of political exiles. The formation of the Moscow Workers' Union and the St. Petersburg textile strikes of 1896 appeared to vindicate those who had claimed that capitalism had come to Russia. Branches of labor organizations modeled on the Moscow Workers' Union opened elsewhere. Many involved in these organizations were exiled to Saratov, and by the second half of the 1890s Marxist circles had taken root in town.[58]

In the 1890s, Social Democrats (SDs) banished from the large industrial towns organized workers' self-education circles in Saratov lumber mills, wood-processing plants, railway shops, and metal-processing factories. The Kharkovite E. O. Zelenskii, who arrived in Saratov in 1898, and an activist named A. Panfilov linked together several of the circles in the metalworks into a "Saratov Democratic Workers' Group," and pushed it to adopt the Manifesto of the Russian Social Democratic Labor Party (RSDRP), drawn up at the founding congress the same year. Until this point the Marxist-minded intelligentsia had largely ignored workers, and workers, not surprisingly, hesitated to cooperate with the intelligentsia for fear of attracting police attention. As elsewhere, relations between the intelligentsia and workers were not always amiable. When the okhranka arrested the leaders of the Workers' Group in 1899, many of them blamed Zelenskii for inciting them to action. Afterward ties between workers' circles and those of the intelligentsia temporarily collapsed.[59]

58. Ibid., pp. 128–33; G. P. Saar, "Saratovskaia organizatsiia RSDRP v nachale 900-kh godov," *Proletarskaia revoliutsiia*, no. 11/12 (82/83) (1928), p. 122.

59. According to police files, the first SD circles had appeared in Saratov in the 1880s. See G. P. Saar, "Saratovskaia organizatsiia RSDRP do 1907 g.," *Vestnik Saratovskogo Gubkoma RKP*, no. 3/28 (1923), pp. 37–39; Z. S. Petrov, "Stranichki iz istorii Saratovskoi organizatsii VKP(b) (1898–1899 gg.)," *Kommunisticheskii put'*, no. 5 (1928), p. 41.

Soviet scholarship has praised these first Social Democratic stirrings in Saratov, but in fact they paled in comparison with the activities of local populists. Widespread peasant disturbances and an economic crisis that struck Russian industry at the start of the new century had revitalized populism, challenging any inroads Marxism may have made. Rival Social Democratic and populist-oriented salons competed for the hearts of the Saratov intelligentsia. But the competition remained friendly. As one participant admitted, "there was no precise line between these two groups at this time." The liberal public *(periferiia)* sympathized with all the revolutionaries, usually without making distinctions among them.[60] This was a significant feature of Saratov's prerevolutionary legacy.

It took the Marxist intelligentsia considerable effort, in the meanwhile, to bridge the tremendous cultural gap and mistrust between them and workers. For one thing, the SDs expended their energy on theoretical discussions, particularly on the debate over economism, a new current within Marxism that neglected the political struggle in favor of waging battle to gain economic improvement for the proletariat. Economism also advocated collaboration with liberals in a joint struggle to win a constitution. The debate over economism in Saratov complicated the reestablishment of contact with workers, who for the most part disliked the theoretical squabbles among the intelligentsia and failed to understand what they were all about. Workers began to go their separate way. In 1901 some Saratov workers—most of whom had come from other cities, where they had been "contaminated by economism"—issued several numbers of an underground newspaper, *Rabochaia gazeta* (The Workers' Newspaper), and organized the first labor strikes in Saratov without the guidance of the radical intelligentsia. Exposed to what they considered to be

---

Information on the SD circles of the 1890s can be found in T. K. Chugunov, "Iz istorii Saratovskoi organizatsii 1902–1907," *Vestnik Saratovskogo Gubkoma RKP,* no. 5/30 (1923), p. 44; S. Koblents, "Iz istorii Saratovskoi organizatsii (1902–1907) (Iz besedy so starym podpol'nikom T. K. Chugunovym)," *Vestnik Saratovskogo Gubkoma RKP,* no. 3/28 (1923), p. 44; E. N. Bogdanova, "Iz lichnykh vospominanii," *Vestnik Saratovskogo Gubkoma RKP,* no. 3/28 (1923), p. 46. Zelenskii's activities are illuminated in G. Lushnikov, "Vospominaniia o vozniknovenii v Saratove sots-demokraticheskoi rabochei gruppy, 1896–1899 gg.," *Kommunisticheskii put',* no. 10/35 (1923), pp. 174–85 passim. On relations between workers and the intelligentsia see A. Stanchinskii, "S. D. podpol'e v Saratove i zhurnal 'Saratovskii Rabochii' v 1899 g.," *Proletarskaia revoliutsiia,* no. 2/14 (1923), p. 89; G. P. Saar, "Saratovskaia Sotsial-demokraticheskaia gruppa 1898–1899 gg.," *Vestnik Saratovskogo Gubkoma RKP,* no. 5/30 (1923), pp. 75–77; L. K., "Pervo-maiskie proklamatsii Saratovskogo komiteta (Po materialam Saratovskoi okhranki)," in *Pervoe maia: Sbornik vospominanii* (Saratov, 1922), pp. 16–17.

60. P. A. Lebedev, "K istorii Saratovskoi organizatsii RSDRP (1901–1902 g.)," *Proletarskaia revoliutsiia,* no. 15 (1923), pp. 233–34. See also S. Kanatchikov, *Iz istorii moego byt'ia,* bk. 1 (Moscow and Leningrad, 1929), pp. 19–21.

an arbitrary fine system and other economic injustices, railway shop workers and linemen and metalworkers from the Bering plant went out on strike, hoping to improve work conditions. Workers' groups and the Marxist intelligentsia even commemorated May Day separately that year.[61]

The appearance of the newspaper *Iskra* (The Spark) in 1900, founded by Lenin, Iu. O. Martov, and others, helped bring the SD intelligentsia and workers together. *Iskra* was available in Saratov because neighboring Samara served as a center for the dissemination of the newspaper along the Volga. Encouraging the intelligentsia to forge links with the workers' movement and form Social Democratic organizations, the newspaper urged activists to move beyond propaganda to political agitation. By the end of 1902, local *Iskra* supporters declared a victory over economism and announced the formation of an SD organization that formally subscribed to the *Iskra* line.[62] Soviet accounts, however, cloud the fact that many local SDs viewed *Iskra*'s tone as a mixed blessing. M. N. Liadov (Mandel'shtam), one of the delegates elected by Saratov workers' circles to the Second Congress of the Russian Social Democratic Labor party in 1903, reported that it would have been better for the Saratov committee if *Iskra* had not attacked economism and the populists so harshly. Two seasoned worker activists, S. Kanatchikov and G. M. Fisher (A. Fisher), shared Liadov's misgivings. Kanatchikov recalled that *Iskra*'s "first issues were met rather coldly by the workers' groups," while Fisher noted that "we considered it a militant revolutionary Social Democratic newspaper, but simply too intellectual and unfit for broad dissemination." Workers also resented the intelligentsia's disdainful attitude toward workers' concern over economic issues and therefore "had rather strong anti-intelligentsia feelings."[63]

As a center of Russian populism in the 1870s, Saratov naturally enough stood in the vanguard of the movement when it was revived in the 1890s. Throughout the second half of the 1890s local cells concentrated their efforts on establishing ties with other centers and forming a political party. For a time the Saratov Society of Fine Arts served as a

61. F. Ivanov, "Pod rukovodstvom rabochikh bol'shevikov," *Vestnik Saratovskogo Gubkoma RKP*, no. 3/28 (1923), pp. 43–44; and S. Koblents, "Zabastovochnoe dvizhenie 1901 goda: Iz besed s rabochimi zh. d. masterskikh," *Vestnik Saratovskogo Gubkoma RKP*, no. 3/28 (1923), pp. 72–73.

62. The dissemination of *Iskra* in Saratov is discussed in G. A. Malinin, *Sviazhite nas s "Vavilonom": Iz istorii rastprostraneniia proizvedeniia V. I. Lenina v Saratovskoi gubernii* (Saratov, 1973), pp. 39–66; and D. M. Konovalov, *Saratovskii agent "Iskry"* (Saratov, 1969).

63. M. N. Liadov, "Moi vstrechi," in *Vospominaniia o II s"ezde RSDRP* (Moscow, 1959), p. 54; Kanatchikov, *Iz istorii moego byt'ia*, pp. 36–37; and G. M. Fisher, *V Rossii i v Anglii: Nabliudeniia i vospominaniia Peterburgskogo rabochego (1890–1921)* (Moscow, 1922), pp. 46–47, 49.

meeting ground for populist-minded intelligenty. In 1896, A. A. Argunov founded in Saratov the Union of Socialist Revolutionaries, better known as the Union of the North, which contributed to the formation of the Socialist Revolutionary party in the summer of 1900. Until the party elected a central committee in 1901, the Saratov organization fulfilled this function. Saratov cultural activists *(kul'turniki)* maintained close bonds with liberal zemstvo officials, professional groups, students, merchants, and workers' circles. The party mustered a particularly strong following among city and zemstvo employees, in the offices of the Riazan-Uralsk railroad line, and among the staff of the city zemstvo publication, *Saratovskaia zemskaia nedelia* (Saratov Zemstvo Weekly).[64]

By 1900 such Saratov populist leaders as I. I. and N. I. Rakitnikov, Ekaterina Breshko-Breshkovskaia (the "grandmother of the Russian Revolution"), and Viktor Chernov concluded that the peasant masses were now far more favorably disposed toward revolutionary propaganda than in the past. By the end of 1900 Saratov SRs had begun to conduct agitational work in local villages. The Mariinskii Agricultural School in Nikolaev and the village of Turki in Balashov uezd gained fame for their success in winning over the peasants' sympathies. The distribution of old populist tracts, Tolstoyan literature, and hectographed leaflets flourished, contributing to the particularly volatile nature of peasant disorders in Saratov province in 1902. Following a bad harvest, peasant disturbances, during which peasants clashed with landlords and conducted wage strikes and rent boycotts, ripped through Poltava, Kharkov, and Saratov provinces. Reevaluating its priorities, the SR Central Committee now decided to redirect the party's main efforts from the urban peasant worker to the villages. In the aftermath of the turmoil, Breshkovskaia and N. I. Rakitnikov founded the national Peasant Union to direct party activities in the countryside. Before long the union boasted a broad following among the peasantry along the Volga and in the Ukraine, while the Agrarian Socialist League, founded by Chernov, formally joined the SR party. Saratov SRs, however, like SRs elsewhere, continued to agitate among local workers; some party members joined a United Group of SRs and SDs, which advocated the use of terror and purportedly published a joint newspaper.[65]

64. A. A. Argunov, "Iz proshlogo partii sotsialistov-revoliutsionerov," *Byloe,* no. 10 (1907), pp. 103–5.

65. Saar, "Saratovskaia organizatsiia do 1907," p. 39; L. Martov et al., eds., *Obshchestvennoe dvizhenie v Rossii v nachale XX-go veka* (St. Petersburg, 1909), 1:40. Lebedev recalled that relations with the SRs were so friendly that talks of unification remained widespread. See "K istorii Saratovskoi organizatsii," p. 239. Another SD participant noted that the newcomer to the revolutionary movement had trouble differentiating between SDs and SRs. See M. Samsonov, "Saratovskaia organizatsiia RSDRP v 1901–1905 gg.," in *1905 god v Saratovskoi gubernii (Po materialam zhandarmskogo upravleniia): Sbornik statei* (Saratov, 1925), pp. 106–7, 111.

Saratov revolutionaries likewise maintained cordial relations with local liberal circles. Thomas S. Fallows has demonstrated that what made the local zemstvo movement particularly significant "was the liberal-radical alliance" characteristic of the province and "a tradition of cooperation between moderates and extremists which became manifest in the personal and political bonds uniting the gentry liberals of the zemstvo with the radical doctors, statisticians, teachers and other 'democratic intelligenty' employed by that democratic institution."[66] Some liberals even funded radical publications and ventures. The Saratov liberal N. N. L'vov supported the Social Democrats' *Iskra* financially. A. A. Tokarskii, a future leader of the Saratov Kadets, frequently sponsored evening gatherings to which he invited political activists of all persuasions and also sympathetic individuals from the periferiia. Such cooperation had long-term repercussions: N. I. Rakitnikov, A. A. Tokarskii, Pavel Lebedev (one of the most active local SDs), and others emerged as leaders of rival political parties in Saratov during the revolution. This early work together created a degree of toleration that later shaped the alignment of political forces in Saratov immediately following the collapse of the autocracy in February 1917.

The assassination of Minister of the Interior Sipiagin in April 1902 by the Saratov populist Stepka Balmashev resulted in a major police crackdown on all illicit activities, which especially hurt local SDs.[67] The arrest and exile of SD leaders at this time occurred against a background of factional strife that split the party into Bolshevik and Menshevik factions at the Second Congress in 1903. The resulting battles that so fiercely rocked émigré circles, however, were much less important inside Russia. In theory, and to a greater extent in practice than often is believed, Social Democracy remained a single party until 1912 and even afterward. Bolshevik and Menshevik factions existed in Saratov after the Second Congress, but workers failed to understand the differences, and the local committee remained united.[68] Having accepted the rulings of the Second Congress, the Saratov committee maintained closer ties with the party center, operated a printing machine, supported a lecture series, and established an agrarian league in the countryside (which, interestingly

66. Thomas S. Fallows "Forging the Zemstvo Movement: Liberalism and Radicalism on the Volga, 1890–1905," Ph.D. dissertation, Harvard University, 1981, p. 8.

67. Rykov was so badly pummelled by the police during this demonstration that he "attributed his noticeable stammer to the beating he had taken that May Day in 1902" (Samuel A. Oppenheim, "The Making of a Right Communist—A. I. Rykov to 1917," *Slavic Review*, 36 [1977], 423).

68. I. P. Gol'denberg (Meshkovskii), who became a member of the Bolshevik Central Committee in 1905, represented the Bolshevik point of view, while D. A. Topuridze, leader of the local Menshevik committee in 1917, took the Menshevik side (Chugunov, "Iz istorii Saratovskoi organizatsii," p. 45; M. N. Liadov, *Iz zhizni partii v 1903–1907 godakh* [*Vospominaniia*] [Moscow, 1956], p. 78).

Building that housed the underground SD press in 1905

enough, often distributed SR publications and popular legal brochures). By 1905, SD worker circles existed on the railroad lines, at the foundries, the Bering factory, the nail plant, the oil press, and the butter creameries, and among tailors, joiners, and students at the artisan school. After the outbreak of the Russo-Japanese War, the Saratov SD committee even agitated among soldiers in the Saratov garrison and published a *Soldier's Leaflet.*[69]

On the eve of the Revolution of 1905 liberal Saratov society also had become outspokenly critical of the autocracy. Local liberals initiated a series of public banquets in the spirit of the 1848 banquet movement in France, hoping to promote their political demands, which had taken on new urgency in view of the Russo-Japanese War and a renewal of government censorship. The local campaign, which began in mid-November 1904, was one of the most successful in the nation.[70] Working side by side with revolutionaries, who enthusiastically took part in the banquets, the Saratov zemstvo liberals distributed inflammatory leaflets and

69. G. P. Saar, "Iz proshlogo Saratovskoi organizatsii (1904–1906)," *Vestnik Saratovskogo Gubkoma RKP,* no. 24 (1922), p. 71; M. Morshanskaia, "Pervaia konferentsiia voennykh i boevykh organizatsii RSDRP v noiabre 1906 g.," *Proletarskaia revoliutsiia,* no. 5/28 (1942), pp. 96–97.

70. Terence Emmons, "Russia's Banquet Campaign," *California Slavic Studies,* 10 (1977), 45–86.

in general helped heighten antigovernment sentiment in Saratov to an alarming degree. Such was the political climate on the banks of the Volga when news arrived from St. Petersburg that government troops had fired on unarmed workers and their families at the Winter Palace.

For good reason Lenin called the Revolution of 1905 a "dress rehearsal" for 1917: 1917 was not an isolated phenomenon. News of "Bloody Sunday," as the slaying of the Petersburg workers came to be known, resulted in one of the most formidable labor strikes in the country, which broke out in Saratov on January 12. Beginning at the Bering metalworks, the strike quickly spread to the railroad lines. Soon workers from the lumberyards, flour mills, tobacco plants, and printing offices, as well as barbers, students, and shop assistants, joined the ranks of an estimated 10,000 strikers. During the course of the strike massive street demonstrations, the likes of which Saratov had not seen before, ended in clashes with Cossack troops.[71]

Bloodshed was probably inevitable in Saratov because Governor Stolypin remained determined to suppress all disturbances. Fearing that he would be unable to make good his threats, he requested additional battalions of soldiers from Penza. Arriving in Saratov in mid-January, these troops emboldened Stolypin, and he arrested leading revolutionaries. Their imprisonment coincided with the decision of factory owners to grant the striking workers pay increases and reduced hours; consequently the strike died out on January 20–22.[72] But a second strike wave hit Saratov on February 7–8, when it became clear that some factory owners had no intention of implementing all of the economic concessions promised earlier. Demanding the eight-hour workday and a 25 percent pay hike, the mill workers triggered this second strike, which

71. See G. P. Saar, "Ianvarskaia zabastovka v Saratove," in *1905 god v Saratovskoi gubernii*, p. 10; G. M. Derenkovskii et al., "1905 god v Saratove," *Istoricheskie zapiski*, 54 (1955), 74; V. Nevskii, "Ianvarskie dni 1905 g. v provintsii," *Krasnaia letopis'*, no. 4 (1922), pp. 122–29; Akademiia nauk SSSR, *Revoliutsiia 1905–1907 gg. v Rossii: Dokumenty i materialy. Nachalo pervoi russkoi revoliutsii, ianvar'–mart 1905* (Moscow, 1955), p. 386; V. P. Antonov-Saratovskii, *Krasnyi god* (Moscow and Leningrad, 1927), p. 54. A Saratov delegate to the Third Congress stressed that the response of Saratov workers to Bloody Sunday would not have been so spirited had it not been for the constant political activity the SD committee had conducted during the preceding month. See Institut marksizma-leninizma pri TsK KPSS, *Tret'ii s"ezd RSDRP aprel'mai 1905 goda: Protokoly* (Moscow, 1959), pp. 136, 169.

72. Revolutionaries prepared lists of demands for workers to present to their bosses. The first three items on the lists were political—convocation of a constituent assembly, an end to the war, and the cessation of legal action against political prisoners. According to Stolypin's agents, "workers often tore them off" and told their bosses to "begin reading from the fourth point." See *Nachalo pervoi russkoi revoliutsii, ianvar'–mart 1905*, p. 390, and I. S. Sokolov, *1905 god na Riazano-Ural'skoi zheleznoi doroge: Po vospominaniiam uchastnikov i materialam Saratovskogo gubernskogo arkhiva* (Saratov, 1925), p. 9.

immediately involved the metalworkers from the Gantke plant. Within days the strike spread to the province's district centers. In industrialized Tsaritsyn more than 10,000 workers quit their jobs, paralyzing economic life in the city. The Saratov strike ended on February 22, when factory owners bowed to workers' demands.[73]

Soviet historians writing after the 1920s attribute the success of the 1905 strikes to local Bolsheviks. But the sources present a far more complex picture. The differences between Bolshevism and Menshevism continued to mean little in Saratov. I. P. Gol'denberg, who chaired the Saratov SD committee throughout most of 1905, advocated an end to factionalism within Russian Social Democracy. A 1905 okhranka report on the activities of the local SD committee did not even mention the terms Bolshevism and Menshevism.[74] The Leninist M. N. Liadov, who arrived in Saratov in early 1905 to drum up support for a party congress, observed that the "Saratov organization strongly wavered between Bolshevism and Menshevism." Further, the Saratov committee, made up almost exclusively of the intelligentsia until fall, cooperated closely with SRs in organizing strikes and disseminating and publishing illegal literature.[75] In fact, Saratov SDs and SRs formed a joint strike committee to direct the local movement. The Saratov representative was chastised at the Third Congress, convened in London in April, for his committee's open cooperation with SRs and liberals and its failure to recruit working-class members. Justifying the committee's behavior in view of the strong

73. B. S. Kirillov, *Bol'sheviki vo glave massovykh politicheskikh stachek v period pod"ema revoliutsii 1905–1907* gg. (Moscow, 1961), pp. 115–16, 123–24.

74. G. P. Saar, "Okhrannoe otdelenie o deiatel'nosti Saratovskoi organizatsii RSDRP," *Kommunisticheskii put'*, no. 9/34 (1923), pp. 199–201.

75. It is interesting to note what became of the most prominent Saratov SDs after 1905. Gol'denberg, who had been committed to coalition with the Mensheviks, maintained his moderate outlook when he became a Bolshevik Central Committee member and party newspaper editor. During World War I he sided with the defensists, who were not ready to advocate the defeat of their country, even in the name of revolution. In the spring of 1917 he rejected Lenin's April Theses. N. M. Druzhinin joined the Bolsheviks as a young student, served as a party agitator and propagandist in Saratov during 1905, and later matured into a leading Soviet historian of the Russian peasantry. In 1905 the Menshevik D. A. Topuridze edited the SD committee's newspaper *Privolzhskii krai*. Afterward he continued to represent local Social Democrats who sought to end factionalism. Another Menshevik, I. M. Liakhovetskii, better known as Maiskii, a hero during the armed clashes with the police in the fall of 1905 in Saratov, converted to Bolshevism during the Civil War of 1918–21, and was fated to become a famous Soviet diplomat, academician, and memoirist. A young Bolshevik agitator named G. P. Fedotov, who enjoyed widespread popularity in working-class circles, emigrated after 1917 and became an eminent specialist on Orthodox church history. Another young Bolshevik activist named A. I. Alekseev (Lobov) turned into a police informant after 1911. In 1918 he was exposed by a revolutionary tribunal and executed. See N. M. Druzhinin, "V Saratove v 1905 g. (Vospominaniia)," *Voprosy istorii KPSS*, no. 10 (1979), pp. 100–102; Derenkovskii, "1905 god v Saratove," pp. 83–84; Saar, "Okhrannoe otdelenie," p. 202.

grip populism had over the local intelligentsia, the Saratov delegate V. M. Obukhov (Kamskii) responded that Saratov SDs favored a united leftist organization from which polemics would be barred. Local needs and factors, he emphasized, accounted for and exonerated the behavior of Saratov SDs.[76] Local considerations also shaped the Saratov committee's response to changes called for by the congress. The Saratov organization challenged the very validity of the "Bolshevik"-stacked Third Congress and later rejected its decision on agrarian matters, as well as the stance taken by a rival Menshevik conference.[77]

As the year progressed, Saratov society became further politicized. Trade unions affiliated with a national coordinating board (the Union of Unions) were founded in town and contributed to a growing sense of class consciousness among workers. Social Democratic and Socialist Revolutionary committees and cells emerged in most of the district centers and in virtually every railroad depot.[78] The Revolution of 1905 in Saratov reached its most critical stage in the fall, when an unusually high degree of violence, reflecting the vitality of the revolutionary-liberal alliance as well as that of extremely conservative elements, colored local developments. In early October Saratov railroad workers, metalworkers, and flour mill workers went out on strike. When the mayor convened the City Duma to assess its relationship to the labor movement, the Duma elected a central strike committee made up of Kadets, SDs, and SRs, including the mayor and a known terrorist.[79] Between October 12 and 14 a general strike froze economic life and transportation in Saratov. Local factory inspectors noted the political character of the movement. Saratov workers, who earlier in the year eschewed "political demands," now petitioned for a constituent assembly and political freedoms along with their familiar economic claims. On October 12 open battle broke out between the demonstrating public and mounted Cossacks and police, leaving behind several dead and wounded.[80]

Instead of quieting things, the October Manifesto, calling for election of a duma and the establishment of a democratic republic, only served to push the street movement to new levels of violence. Fed up with the

76. *Tret'ii s"ezd RSDRP,* p. 383.

77. Derenkovskii, "1905 god v Saratove," pp. 84–85; Iu. K. Milonov, "Partiia i professional'nye soiuzy v 1905 godu," *Proletarskaia revoliutsiia,* no. 1/48 (1925), pp. 94–95.

78. See, for example, radical activities in Volsk in P. G. Kutyrev and A. G. Chulkov, "Sobytiia pervoi rossiiskoi revoliutsii v Vol'ske," *Voprosy istorii,* no. 6 (1981), pp. 184–87.

79. Saar, "Okhrannoe otdelenie," pp. 202–6.

80. E. E. Gershtein, "Oktiabr'skaia politicheskaia stachka 1905 goda v Saratove," *Uchenye zapiski Saratovskogo gosudarstvennogo universiteta,* 55 (1956), 324; A. Gerasimov, "God pervoi revoliutsii v Saratove," *Molodaia gvardiia,* no. 12 (1925), p. 125; G. G. Sushkin, "Oktiabr', noiabr' i dekabr' 1905 g. na Riazano-Ural'skoi zheleznoi doroge," *Katorga i ssylka,* no. 12/73 (1930), p. 148.

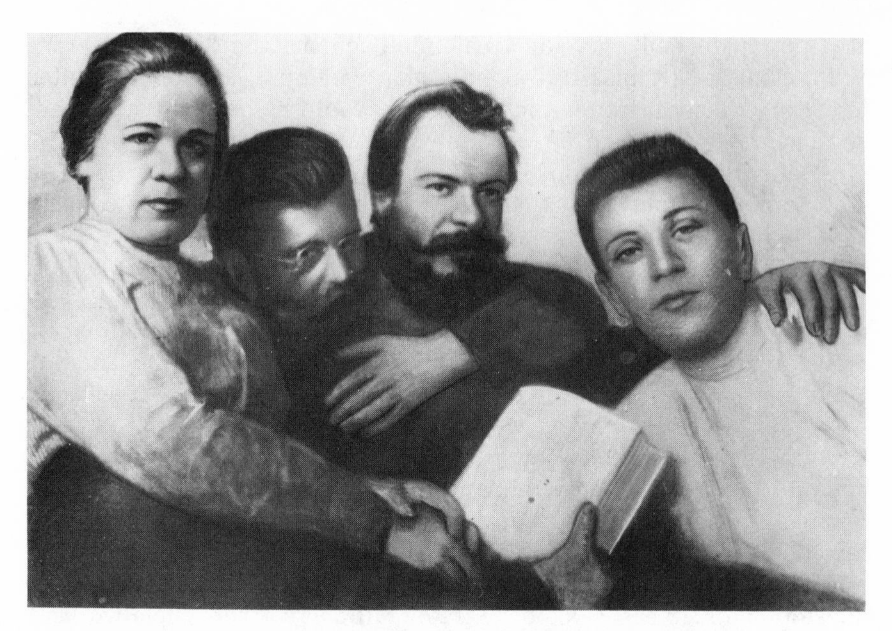

Saratov SD Railway Committee, 1905

permissive street movement of the past year, the ultraconservatives now organized a local branch of the Union of the Russian People, one of several right-wing organizations formed in Russia at this time and commonly known as Black Hundreds. After publication of the October Manifesto, Bishop Germogen (an acquaintance of Rasputin's and a popular figure among the conservative-minded citizenry) marched at the head of a demonstration in support of the tsarist regime. The assemblage of Black Hundreds set off for Theater Square, where the Saratov SD and SR committees had sponsored a rally that attracted an estimated 10,000 workers, students, professionals, and revolutionaries. Although a workers' armed guard rose to defend the proletariat, the guard was forced to retreat. Many were severely beaten and one member of the armed guard was killed.[81]

That evening rightist elements launched a pogrom against Jews, the intelligentsia, and radical workers. Under the approving glance of Cossack guards, who often joined the looting, Black Hundreds sacked the small shops and businesses owned by Saratov Jews and raided the office of the legal SD newspaper. The pogrom ended only after Stolypin, who had left the city before its outbreak, returned to Saratov with a large

81. See K. V. Avgustovskii, "'Soiuz russkogo naroda' (Iz zhizni Saratovskogo otdeleniia)," *Sovremennyi mir*, no. 9 (1907), pp. 61–73.

contingent of troops. Within leftist circles many believed that Stolypin's timely disappearance and reappearance suggested that he tacitly approved of the rightist offensive. Although estimates of the damage and of the number injured vary, they all indicate that destruction was extensive.[82] When the February Revolution reached Saratov twelve years later, workers and soldiers moved first of all to arrest Black Hundred leaders, police officials, and prominent monarchists.

Throughout Russia workers' councils, or soviets, had been elected in late 1905 to direct the strike movement. These first soviets were nonparty organizations that usually formed fighting detachments of armed workers. The success of the St. Petersburg Soviet encouraged the growth of soviets elsewhere, and both the St. Petersburg and Moscow soviets sent delegates to the provinces to promote the election of local councils.[83] Saratov revolutionaries elected a workers' soviet as part of preparations for the December general strike planned by the soviets in the two capitals.[84] Local workers chose twenty-eight deputies (twenty-two SDs and six SRs) to their soviet. Railroad workers, metalworkers from Gantke and Bering, printers, workers from the Levkovich tobacco factory, and students from the feldsher school composed the bulk of the Soviet's membership. A Bolshevik railroad worker named A. A. Petrov was elected chairman. Because of shifting political allegiances at the local level at this time, the insignificance of the Bolshevik–Menshevik rivalry, and the united front between Saratov SDs and SRs, Soviet historians find it difficult to deal objectively with the first local soviet. After rejecting the program of the Bolshevik Third Congress, the Soviet passed an SR

82. According to the police, during the pogrom 10 people were murdered, 124 were injured (66 seriously), and 168 apartments and shops were looted (Saar, "Okhrannoe otdelenie," pp. 207–8). See also P. Argunov, "Iz vospominanii o pervoi russkoi revoliutsii," *Katorga i ssylka*, no. 1/74 (1931), pp. 156–60; M. N. Pokrovskii, *1905 god: Istoriia revoliutsionnogo dvizheniia v otdel'nykh ocherkakh* (Moscow, 1925), 1:346; M. Semenov, "1905 god v Saratovskoi gubernii," *Proletarskaia revoliutsiia*, no. 3/50 (1926), p. 207.

83. On November 26, after heated debate, the Saratov SD committee, which had enrolled more than 1,000 members, passed a resolution calling for "the election of a soviet of workers' deputies" (G. A. Malinin, "Saratovskii Sovet rabochikh deputatov v 1905 god," *Uchenye zapiski Saratovskogo gosudarstvennogo universiteta*, 55 [1956], 156–57).

84. As background to the strike, local revolutionaries founded a united fighting detachment of 300 workers in November. The SRs intensified their campaign in the countryside, and also operated an illicit hideout for the preparation of bombs and planning of terrorist activities (V. I. Nevskii, comp., *1905: Sovetskaia pechat' i literatura o sovetakh* [Moscow, 1925], p. 494). Local authorities were also prepared for battle and were indignant over a bold act of political violence: an SR female terrorist named A. A. Bitsenko, who one day would be a member of the Soviet peace delegation sent to Brest-Litovsk, assassinated Adjutant General Sakharov in Stolypin's home on November 22. (A prominent lawyer and Saratov liberal, A. M. Maslennikov, sent flowers to Bitsenko in an act of solidarity with the revolutionaries.) See Mary E. Schaeffer, "The Political Policies of P. A. Stolypin," Ph.D. dissertation, Indiana University, 1964, p. 120.

resolution that it "must be the single leader of the revolutionary parties of the proletariat in its struggle with the government and must not adopt the program of any one party."[85] Although weakened by the arrest of many of its leaders, the Saratov Soviet made plans to participate in a general strike promoted by the St. Petersburg Soviet, scheduled to begin on the railway lines. The Soviet organized an armed guard and raised money for arms. More than 2,000 townspeople responded to its call to demonstrate on December 16. This time its armed guard answered the Cossacks' volleys and whips with a staccato of revolver shots, which left eight dead and others wounded. The street clash in Saratov, echoed in Tsaritsyn, Atkarsk, Volsk, Kamyshin, and Balashov, marked both the high point and the demise of the labor movement in 1905.

Saratov province registered more peasant disturbances during the Revolution of 1905 than any other European province except parts of the Ukraine.[86] The agrarian turmoil that erupted in late summer can be ascribed to both immediate and long-term causes, to both local and outside influences and pressures. Two consecutive bad harvests provided the initial impulse to revolt.[87] Long-term rural poverty brought on by post-emancipation rent and labor relationships also shaped events. By 1905, belief that the land should belong to those who tilled it had found universal acceptance in the villages. Moreover, a tradition of peasant violence, whose legacy was kept alive by revolutionaries, guaranteed that tension in the Saratov area would remain high.

The most volatile outbreak began in Atkarsk uezd in mid-October. From there looting and arson spread throughout most of the province, particularly to those uezds with the most intense economic inequalities—Petrovsk, Atkarsk, Balashov, Serdobsk, and Saratov districts.[88] Often the first and most sustained flare-ups took place in the same villages that had risen up in 1901–2. Conversely, the least unrest occurred in districts where a large percentage of peasants had been former state peasants and where pomeshchik landholding had been underdeveloped. Faced with reduced food supplies for their families and livestock, Saratov peasants seized the meadows and pasturelands of large landowners, failing to discriminate in favor of liberal landowners who took pride in their progressive attitudes toward local peasants. Peasants dev-

85. N. N. Demochkin, "Partiia i Sovety v 1905 g.," *Voprosy istorii KPSS,* no. 2 (1965), p. 89.

86. E. A. Morokhovets, "Krest'ianskoe dvizhenie 1905–1907 gg. i sotsial-demokratiia," *Proletarskaia revoliutsiia,* no. 2/37 (1925), p. 15.

87. V. Frantsev, "Agrarnye volneniia v 1905 godu po Saratovskoi gubernii," *Kommunisticheskii put',* no. 37 (1925), pp. 37–38.

88. See N. Karpov, *Krest'ianskoe dvizhenie v revoliutsii 1905 goda v dokumentakh* (Leningrad, 1926), pp. 258–59.

astated and burned estates and carted off seed, sheaves of grain, and livestock, occasionally keeping detailed records of what was taken and how it was distributed. In some instances outside agitators assumed leadership of the disturbances. Peasants vented their rage at the symbols of landlord Russia. As Stolypin's daughter recalled, "peasants set fire to estates of landowners, destroying everything they could lay hands on, libraries, pictures, porcelain, antique furniture, even cattle and crops. Although the peasants never stole anything, they burned the landowners' homes with blazing torches, also their cattle pens, sheds, storehouses. Everything the proprietors tried to rescue from the burning houses, the peasants cut to chips, trampled with their feet, demolished, and tore to pieces."[89]

Vindicating predictions made by SRs, official reports stress the militancy of the "middle peasants," and complement findings on comparative peasant rebellions in other countries.[90] Richer peasants tended to show restraint, while the impoverished and middle strata tended to exhibit hostility toward the better off.[91] Virtually everywhere young peasants were the driving force behind the disturbances, just as young workers seemed the most prone to rebel in the cities. With some dramatic exceptions, women appear to have played a passive role in the agrarian movement. Government officials noted now and then that outside revolutionaries instigated uprisings, but more often the external encouragement came from the SR-oriented rural intelligentsia entrenched in SR brotherhoods *(zemliachestva)*, the SR Peasant Union, and the All-Russian Peasant Union, organized in May by zemstvo activists. (More than 10,000 Saratov peasants had joined the All-Russian Peasant Union in 1905.) Peasant soldiers demobilized after the war with Japan also figured prominently in the movement, just as demobilized soldiers would in 1917.[92]

Officials investigating the causes of the unrest heard such justifications and explanations from the peasants as "The land is a gift of God and must belong to the population that works on it" and "We consider it unjust that capitalists have taken in their hands this gift of God, forcing us to work for them." Popular sentiments to the effect that "the land once was ours" at times took the form of rumors of golden charters, suppressed by the landlords, which declared that the land belonged to

89. Quoted in Bock, *Reminiscences*, p. 122.

90. Eric R. Wolf, *Peasant Wars of the Twentieth Century* (New York, 1969); Hamza Alavi, "Peasants and Revolution," in *The Socialist Register*, ed. Ralph Miliband and John Saville (London, 1965), pp. 241–77.

91. Maureen Perrie, "The Russian Peasant Movement of 1905–1907: Its Social Composition and Revolutionary Significance," *Past and Present*, no. 57 (1972), p. 141.

92. Ibid., p. 147.

those who toiled upon it. Government reports cited lack of land, high rent prices, and related problems of low pay for hired hands and bad harvests as the major causes of unrest. In the language of the documents, "peasant need in all areas," an "eternal life of semistarvation," and an unusual "class hatred" accounted for the rebellion. These same factors explained the receptivity to radical doctrines in the villages as well.[93]

Viewed by progressive society as a vicious martinet, Stolypin called in troops to pacify peasants and abort the organizational efforts of political groups. He shut down a congress of the Saratov Peasant Union in December and unleashed a contingent of Cossacks against a congress of zemstvo doctors in Balashov.[94] Nevertheless, radical activity threatened the regime's stability through mid-1907.[95] By the end of 1907 a deceptive calm had returned to rural Saratov. Visiting villages in the province at this time, a correspondent observed a widespread feeling of despondency and hopelessness among the peasants, who spoke apocalyptically of coming famines and of how tough it was going to be to eke out a living. Many of the landlords had hired armed guards to protect their property; others put their land up for sale. But the more politically "conscious" peasants, the young, refused to buy the land that they believed rightfully belonged to them, even though prices of land for sale or rent had fallen. A report of the Free Economic Society commented that as a result of the rural unrest, tensions among the various strata of the peasantry had risen. In some areas conflicts broke out between villages competing to rent pomeshchik land. Another observer saw strong opposition among the peasantry to early measures of the Stolypin legislation and the idea of migrating to Siberia. "Let the pomeshchiki go [there]," peasants told him.[96]

The government's quelling of the December 1905 strike marked the beginning of the autocracy's assault on the revolution. In June 1907 Prime Minister Stolypin drastically changed the Duma electoral laws,

93. I. V. Chernyshev, "Otchet komiteta po okazaniiu pomoshchi golodaiushchim, sostoiavshego pri I. V. E. Obshchestve za 1906–1907 prodovol'stvennyi god," *Trudy imperatorskogo Vol'nogo Ekonomicheskogo Obshchestva*, no. 1–2 (1908), p. 131.

94. For a description of the Balashov pogrom see Gerasimov, "God pervoi revoliutsii," pp. 122–23.

95. Semenov, "1905 god v Saratovskoi gubernii," p. 214; V. M. Gokhlerner, "Iz istorii krest'ianskogo dvizheniia v Saratovskoi gubernii v gody pervoi russkoi revoliutsii (1905–1907 gg.)," *Uchenye zapiski Saratovskogo gosudarstvennogo universiteta*, 55 (1956), 239, 245.

96. Chernyshev, "Otchet komiteta," pp. 149–51; P. Maslov, *Kak krest'iane borolis' za zemliu v 1905–1906 godu, dvadtsat' let tomu nazad* (Moscow and Leningrad, 1925), p. 93; I. Konovalov, "V derevne (Iz Saratovskoi gubernii)," *Sovremennyi mir*, no. 2 (1909), pp. 14–33.

effectively disenfranchising masses of people to create a docile legislature. Across the country the "system of the third of June" abruptly curbed revolutionary activity and drove antigovernment groups underground once again. In Saratov successive waves of arrests and police infiltration had already begun to check revolutionary activities by midsummer 1906, when authorities shut down the SD newspaper edited by the Bolshevik P. A. Lebedev. Saratov Social Democrats held fewer meetings as ties with workers' circles were severed. Permeated with police provocateurs, the local party organization curtailed its work. The provincial organization registered 795 members at the beginning of the year, but had lost 265 members by June.[97] Individuals who carried on party work during 1908–9 often did so in isolation, without regular ties with the party center or even with the skeleton Saratov SD committee.

Police repression, fear, loss of leaders, and widespread demoralization slowed the growth of trade unions and dampened workers' willingness and ability to strike. Employer opposition and government repression also circumscribed the union movement, a circumstance that in the long run may have weakened workers' inclinations to trust reformist strategies and led them to turn instead to militant revolutionary ones.[98] The government's basically hostile attitude toward workers' organizations is reflected in the fate of trade unionism in Saratov. Thirty-two trade unions had been registered in the province in 1906; by 1909 there were only seven.[99] Strike activity dropped off precipitously as well.[100]

Determined police crackdowns turned the revolutionary leadership's attention once again to heated debates over appropriate strategies. Despite the formal reunification of Russia's Social Democrats in the spring

97. Khodakov, *Ocherki istorii*, pp. 172–73.

98. Victoria E. Bonnell, "Trade Unions, Parties, and the State in Tsarist Russia: A Study of Labor Politics in St. Petersburg and Moscow," *Politics and Society*, 9 (1980), 299–322.

99. "Professional'nye soiuzy," p. 150; V. Sviatlovskii, "Professional'noe dvizhenie rabochikh v 1905 g.," *Krasnaia letopis'*, no. 2–3 (1922), pp. 181–82. Tailors and clerical workers appear to have retained the strongest union organizations. See A. Ezhov, "V Saratove (1907–1917 gg.)," *Kommunisticheskii put'*, no. 10 (1923), p. 189. A collection of police documents on the Saratov metalworkers' union offers some interesting insights into this politically active stratum of Saratov workers, and reveals how influential SRs were among Volga-area metalworkers at this time. See F. Bulkin, "Soiuz metallistov i departament politsii," *Krasnaia letopis'*, no. 5 (1923), pp. 252–67.

100. In 1906, 61.2% of the workers in Saratov were on strike; by 1908 the proportion had dropped to 6.5%. See V. R. Varzar, *Statistika stachek rabochikh na fabrikakh i zavodakh za trekhletie za 1906–1908* (St. Petersburg, 1910), pp. 4, 17, 62, 80, 134, 140, 179, 186. Some Soviet historians have criticized Varzar's statistics for excluding certain categories of workers, but until more evidence is produced, Varzar's statistics, whatever their inadequacies, remain the best available. See A. S. Amal'rik, "K voprosu o chislennosti i geograficheskom razmeshchenii stachechnikov v Evropeiskoi Rossii v 1905 godu," *Istoricheskie zapiski*, 52 (1955), 142; Kliachko, "Materialy o polozhenii rabochikh," p. 74.

of 1906, the leaders of both factions continued to maneuver for hegemony. As before 1905, factionalism and personality clashes consumed émigré energies, with the result that there again rose rival centers, rival newspapers, and rival conferences, few of which could claim to be representative of Russian Social Democracy. Even the main factions were now riven by subfactions.[101]

Local conditions, as well as the personal inclinations of prominent revolutionaries, continued to shape the behavior of Saratov Social Democracy. Factionalism continued to be unpopular within working-class circles, while the renewed factionalism abroad merely complicated relations between local groups and émigré centers. In 1906 the Saratov SD committee, ignoring the party's call for a boycott of all electoral activities, responded to working-class pressure from the Bering and Gantke plants and railroad workers by actively participating in the campaign for election to the First Duma.[102] Ironically, after the dismissal of the Second Duma and the change in the electoral law in 1907, the SD party leaders, including Lenin, supported participation in elections to the Third Duma. But sentiment at the local level now favored a boycott, and local Social Democrats carried resolutions denouncing the Duma elections. In 1908 the Saratov committee demanded the recall of the Social Democratic deputies from the Third Duma; apparently Bolshevik sentiments—albeit "recallist" ones—ran high locally. Saratov-born G. I. Lomov (Oppokov), who had directed the workers' armed guard in Saratov in 1905, may have

101. After the Fifth Party Conference in 1908, Lenin denounced such "new revisionists" as the right-wing Menshevik "liquidators" *(likvidatory)*, who shunned illegal conspiratorial work on the grounds that it would compromise possible gains through legal activities in trade unions, cooperatives, and the dumas. Arguing that party work at the local level should develop organically, the liquidators believed that the SD Central Committee should function as a coordinating organ, not as a policy-making body for all party groups. G. V. Plekhanov and the so-called Party Mensheviks now sided with Lenin against the liquidators while a third group of Mensheviks fought to preserve party unity. Lenin likewise battled against left-wing and conciliationist elements within his own faction. The Bolshevik "boycotters" and "recallists" *(otzovisti)* and ultimatists—"upside-down" liquidators, as Lenin called them—insisted that all legal activities were illusory, especially after the change in the electoral law in June 1907. As a consequence they demanded the recall of SD delegates elected to the Duma. In addition, such left-wing Bolshevik intellectuals as A. A. Bogdanov, A. V. Lunacharsky, the writer Maksim Gorky, and Saratov's Liadov not only rejected Duma activities but also espoused a variety of quasi-religious philosophical ideas referred to as "God-building" *(bogostroitel'stvo)*. By 1909 the left Bolsheviks launched their own paper, *Vpered!* (Forward!), with the goal of challenging Lenin's hold on the party paper, *Proletarii*, and opened their own party school in Italy. Moreover, a group of "Party Bolsheviks," led by Saratov-born A. I. Rykov, tried to reconcile the various factions. Trotsky headed yet another "nonfactional" SD center.

102. Saratov province sent ten leftist deputies to the Second Duma, including four SDs, among whom was the Bolshevik V. M. Serov. No conservative candidates or even Kadets were elected. See Khodakov, "Bor'ba saratovskikh rabochikh," p. 116.

been partially responsible for the Saratov SDs' position. A Bolshevik recallist active in the Moscow and St. Petersburg committees, Lomov often traveled to his hometown to lobby on behalf of recallism.[103]

Disappointed by the poor results of their political involvement and demoralized by ubiquitous police spies, many workers abandoned revolution. In describing a strike at the cotton-padding factory, a revolutionary named Ezhov, who arrived in Saratov in 1907, noted that among the Riazan peasants who worked there, strike sentiments appealed only to young workers, who made economic demands. The older, married workers with children protested against the strike, fearing reprisals and loss of their jobs.[104] As Ralph C. Elwood has demonstrated in regard to the Ukraine, both the arrest or emigration of much of the revolutionary leadership and the tendency of the radical intelligentsia to abandon the cause at this time led to an increase in proletarian influence in the underground Saratov SD organization. By mid-1907 workers ran the local skeletal organization and those in the province's district centers.[105] Another wave of arrests in 1909 destroyed all coordinated committee work. Cells *(iacheiki)* and small study circles now predominated, as before 1905. One participant recalled that by 1909 party work consisted merely of discussing SD Duma activity, and that this situation continued until 1912.[106]

Despite the autocracy's efforts to contain the radical movement, several indicators suggest that the revolutionary camp had already begun to recover in 1910. A second industrialization spurt in 1909–10 contributed to a rise in working-class activism. Members of the local underground distributed émigré newspapers that managed to make their way to the banks of the Volga, and occasionally hectographed nonfactional

103. V. N. Pozoiskaia, "Saratovskaia partiinaia organizatsiia v gody tsarskoi reaktsii (1907–1910 gg.)," *Povolzhskii krai*, no. 4 (1975), pp. 46–56 passim.

104. Ezhov, "V Saratove," pp. 186–87. Ezhov finally linked up with a group of like-minded students he had met at a public cafeteria subsidized by local liberals. The students were from the technical high school and could well have been prototypes for Fedin's Kirill Izvekov in *Early Joys*.

105. Pozoiskaia, "Saratovskaia partiinaia organizatsiia," p. 43, and "Bor'ba bol'shevikov pod rukovodstvom V. I. Lenina protiv otzovistov i ul'timatistov po voprosu dumskoi taktiki (1907–1910 gg.)," *Uchenye zapiski Saratovskogo gosudarstvennogo universiteta*, 59 (1958), 161; V. I. Tomarev, "Tsaritsynskaia gruppa RSDRP mezhdu dvumia revoliutsiiami (1907–1917 gg.)," *Istoriko-kraevedcheskie zapiski*, no. 5 (1977), p. 45. For elsewhere in Russia, see R. C. Elwood, *Russian Social Democracy in the Underground: A Study of the RSDRP in the Ukraine, 1907–1914* (Assen, Netherlands, 1974), pp. 64–65.

106. Ch., "Saratovskaia organizatsiia s 1909 po 1917," *Vestnik Saratovskogo Gubkoma RKP*, no. 3/28 (1923), p. 50. A handful of workers led by a young tobacco worker, I. A. Galaktionov, managed to issue a leaflet criticizing the Duma and calling for the unification of the proletariat in a single workers' party. See Pozoiskaia, "Saratovskaia partiinaia organizatsiia," pp. 59–60.

leaflets and proclamations. At the same time, the SD intelligentsia involved themselves in legal literary activities.[107] Lenin's sisters Anna and Maria moved to Saratov in late 1910, with Anna's husband, M. T. Elizarov. The local police soon arrested Anna for her role in publishing the *Privolzhskaia gazeta* (Volga Region Newspaper). Maria, the Saratov police purportedly observed, was the "central figure among local Bolsheviks."[108] The popular Menshevik D. A. Topuridze collaborated with Lenin's sisters on the newspaper, which in Aesopian but popular language sought to spread news on conditions among Saratov workers. At this time the Saratov governor reported to the capital that local Social Democrats had resurrected their committee. In fact, Saratov had one of twenty local party organizations represented at the Prague Conference in 1912, where, according to most writers, Bolsheviks and Mensheviks became two distinct parties. Although émigré leaders who returned to Russia after the split at Prague introduced a new wave of factionalism at the local level, Saratov SDs petitioned the Bolsheviks' *Pravda* (Truth) and the Menshevik liquidators' *Luch* (Ray [of light]) to end their bickering.[109]

A renewed strike movement also suggests that political activity was recovering. During 1911 Saratov railroad workers, lumberyard workers, dock hands, and tailors went out on strike and tried to organize an illegal May Day celebration. The next April government troops gunned down more than 150 unarmed striking workers in the Lena goldfields, an event that prompted sympathy strikes throughout the country, including Saratov, where the Bering workers and others struck. Weeks later Saratov SDs sponsored a May Day strike in which an estimated 2,000 workers from 24 factories participated.[110] Moreover, Lenin now encouraged Bolsheviks to infiltrate such legal channels as trade unions, consumer

107. I. V. Mgeladze (Vardin), who in 1917 became a prominent Saratov Bolshevik leader and proponent of merger with the Mensheviks, arrived in Volsk in 1910, where he published a newspaper for two years, together with two SRs. S. K. Minin, leader of the Tsaritsyn Bolsheviks in 1917, returned to Tsaritsyn at this time to help the local SD committee put out a legal party journal. See G. Rubashkina, "Vol'skaia organizatsiia SDRP (bol'shevikov)," *Vestnik Saratovskogo Gubkoma RKP,* no. 5/30 (1923), p. 80; Tomarev, "Tsaritsynskaia gruppa," p. 46.

108. P. Kudelli, "Svetloi pamiati Anny Il'inichny Elizarovoi-Ul'ianovoi," *Krasnaia letopis',* no. 1 (1936), pp. 200–204; A. I. Ul'ianova-Elizarova," Iz aftobiografii Anny Il'inichny Ul'ianovoi Elizarovoi," *Proletarskaia revoliutsiia,* no. 6 (1935), p. 134. The police report is found in V. I. Tomarev, "Pod"em rabochego dvizheniia v Povolzh'e v 1910–1914 gg.," *Povolzhskii krai,* no. 1 (1972), p. 88.

109. Khodakov, *Ocherki istorii,* p. 215. In neighboring Samara united SD groups agitated in factories and workshops and published a nonfactional newspaper that printed articles written by all of the émigré leaders. See O. Piatnitsky, *Memoirs of a Bolshevik* (New York, n.d.), pp. 191–95.

110. Malinin, *Sviazhite nas,* p. 155; Tomarev, "Pod"em," p. 92.

societies, and medical funds *(bol'nichnye kassy)*. Laws issued in June 1912, permitting the creation of workers' funds to aid victims of illness and accident, led to a proliferation of mutual aid societies. By the summer of 1914, workers had set up fifteen medical funds in Saratov.[111] Saratov SDs also joined cultural and educational clubs, where, as in other endeavors, they collaborated with SRs and local liberals.

For the most part, the fortunes of the other revolutionary parties in this era paralleled those of Saratov Social Democracy. Perhaps because of the local SR committee's advocacy of terrorism, police repression against SRs had been especially fierce after 1907. But by 1912 local SR activists could boast broad involvement in legal operations, particularly in the cooperative movement, and support among workers. Further, legal liberal parties became increasingly critical of the government at roughly the same time that revolutionaries were expanding their activities. Nationally, a surge of interest in municipal affairs and local politics had taken hold by 1909. In Saratov middle-class "progressives," "the party of the third element and the free professions," had triumphed in local politics.[112]

A few other incidents likewise indicate that antigovernment feelings had mounted. In the winter of 1910–11, university students and faculty and professional groups in Saratov took part in illegal ceremonies marking the death of the great writer Lev Tolstoy, who had fallen out of favor with the government and church during his later years. The government rightly interpreted the flood of emotion unleashed by Tolstoy's death as a rebuke to its policies. Demanding that a portrait of him be hung in the university library, student demonstrators faced strong reprisals from the authorities, and soon found themselves drafted.[113] Saratov society also denounced the government's shooting of workers in 1912. In a report to the Ministry of the Interior, the Saratov governor noted a move to the left by zemstvo organs and a revitalization of the third element.[114] Together with the revolutionaries, Saratov liberals intensified their activities within various clubs and educational societies as well as in the people's university movement. On the eve of the Great War, society's dissatisfaction was once again serving as the basis for a rising tide of political activism. As Elwood so aptly put it, the war neither postponed revolu-

111. M. Korbut, "Strakhovaia kampaniia 1912–1914 gg.," *Proletarskaia revoliutsiia*, no. 2/73 (1928), p. 107; A. Ezhov, "Moi vospominaniia o Maiake," *Vestnik Saratovskogo Gubkoma RKP*, no. 6/31 (1923), p. 69.

112. Cited in Michael F. Hamm, "Kharkov's Progressive Duma, 1910–1914: A Study in Russian Municipal Reform," *Slavic Review*, 40 (1981), 20, 26, 33, 36.

113. P. A. Bugaenko et al., *Saratovskii universitet, 1909–1959* (Saratov, 1959), pp. 12–13.

114. E. D. Chermenskii, "Vybory v IV gosudarstvennuiu dumu," *Voprosy istorii*, no. 4 (1947), p. 23.

tion nor caused it; it "merely served to define and to intensify grievances felt since the beginning of the century."[115]

The World War destroyed the unity of world socialism; most socialists reacted to the outbreak of hostilities along national lines. Confusion was exacerbated in Russia by Lenin's astounding advocacy of his own country's defeat. In Saratov and other Volga cities, arrests on the eve of the war once again had debilitated party groups. During the first months of war Saratov Bolsheviks had no ties whatever with the party center, a situation not uncommon in the country as a whole.[116] Deep uncertainty over how to relate to the war held sway within local Bolshevik ranks. V. P. Antonov (Antonov-Saratovskii), who became one of Saratov's most influential Bolsheviks in 1917, is a case in point. Despite claims that he adopted an internationalist, Leninist position from the start, other, more convincing evidence shows that he supported Plekhanov's defensist position until mid-1915.[117]

Information trickling into Saratov from elsewhere eventually broke down defensist attitudes among local Bolsheviks. The arrival in town at this time of an impressive contingent of activists who had closer contact with the émigré center also influenced local attitudes. By the spring of 1915, Nogin, Ol'minskii, S. I. Mitskevich, Miliutin, V. A. Radus-Zenkovich, Iu. K. Milonov, and Vasil'ev-Iuzhin had linked up with such local SDs as Antonov and Lebedev. Ol'minskii, who brought to Saratov

115. Elwood, *Russian Social Democracy in the Underground*, p. 273.

116. Lenin's theses on the war first became known in Petrograd in September 1914, and no. 33 of the Bolshevik newspaper *Sotsial-Demokrat* published with the antiwar manifesto of the Central Committee in November 1914. S. V. Tiutiukin admits that the tactical stance of the Bolshevik Central Committee remained unknown in some localities until early 1915 and that "in these conditions many complex questions had to be resolved independently in the provinces, without ruling directives from the party center." See his *Voina, mir, revoliutsiia: Ideinaia bor'ba v rabochem dvizhenii Rossii, 1914–1917* gg. (Moscow, 1972), p. 13. For a description of the situation in Saratov when war broke out see V. I. Tomarev, *Bol'sheviki Povolzh'ia vo glave bor'by proletariev protiv tsarizma* (Volgograd, 1977), pp. 244–45; and V. Podsumkov, "Bol'shevistskaia gazeta v Saratove 25 let tomu nazad," in the newspaper *Kommunist* (Saratov), June 7, 1941, p. 2.

117. Antonov's claims can be found in V. P. Antonov-Saratovskii, *Pod stiagom proletarskoi bor'by: Otryvki iz vospominanii o rabote v Saratove* (Moscow and Leningrad, 1925), p. 8. Also see M. G. "Iz istorii Saratovskoi bol'shevistskoi organizatsii (1916–1918)," *Kommunisticheskii put'*, no. 17/80 (1927), p. 34. G. I. Lomov endorsed Antonov's statement years later. See. G. I. Lomov et al., eds., *Nasha gazeta, no. 1–9, 1915* (Saratov, 1935), p. vii. The year after Antonov's memoir was serialized in *Proletarskaia revoliutsiia* (1926), however, several prominent Bolsheviks—including Lomov—wrote letters to the editors insisting that even Antonov had supported the Menshevik position until mid-1915. See G. Lomov et al., "Pis'ma v redaktsiiu zh. 'Proletarskaia revoliutsiia,'" *Proletarskaia revoliutsiia*, no. 2/49 (1926), p. 276. Even earlier, in 1922, Ol'minskii wrote that during his exile in 1916, Lomov was the first advocate of the inevitability of October and Antonov was his main opponent. See "Tri pis'ma," *Proletarskaia revoliutsiia*, no. 4 (1922), p. 276.

copies of Lenin's *War and Social Democracy* published in *Sotsial-Demokrat* (Social Democrat), recreated ties with the center through Moscow contacts. Some eight months passed after the outbreak of war before Saratov Bolsheviks became acquainted with the position of their central committee.[118]

It took strong conviction to advocate Lenin's position on the war because the Russian public, like that of other countries, had backed its country's entry into the hostilities. After the Russian victory at Przemysl in March 1915, a massive demonstration, supported even by some of Saratov's more "conscious" workers, celebrated Russia's military triumph. The Union of Michael the Archangel, led by local landlords, mobilized support for the war, and although its successes were negligible among skilled workers, it made inroads among the "ignorant lower middle classes on the outskirts of the city." The Black Hundreds opened a cafeteria-club for workers and "spread slander" against Saratov Germans, Jews, and revolutionaries. Rumors of an anti-German pogrom spread throughout the province and the Black Hundreds purportedly threatened local radicals.[119]

Not everyone, to be sure, had met the declaration of war with enthusiasm. Antiwar disturbances had broken out at induction centers in Volsk and Tsaritsyn; peasant disturbances had flared up in some districts in the countryside.[120] In Saratov itself workers at the Gantke plant had responded to the declaration of war by going out on strike. The head of the Saratov police reported to his superiors that the tranquillity of local workers should not be taken for granted. "The novelty of the attitudes evoked by the war, interpreted as a growth in patriotic feeling, will pass," he predicted, "and an old mood capable of turning into open rebellion will replace it at the first appropriate moment."[121]

Working-class attitudes toward the war are admittedly difficult to assess, but evidence shows that sympathetic feelings in Saratov gradually cooled. For one thing, the government relocated more radically disposed Latvian and Polish workers to Saratov. For another, bread-and-butter issues shaped the attitudes of the indigenous work force toward the war. Only those establishments that filled war orders now operated at full capacity. The number of workers at cement and lumber-processing plants, at flour mills, print shops, and even metalworks decreased. By

118. *Kommunist*, January 7, 1941, p. 2. (These personal bonds forged in the underground may well have weighed heavily on later factional developments within the party. In November 1917 Nogin and Miliutin resigned from the Soviet government because they opposed single-party rule. Ol'minskii and Nogin worked together within the Moscow Bolshevik organization in 1917.)

119. Antonov-Saratovskii, *Pod stiagom*, p. 35.

120. Tomarev, *Bol'sheviki Povolzh'ia*, pp. 247–48.

121. Tiutiukin, *Voina, mir, revoliutsiia*, p. 82.

1915, despite some pay increases, wages already failed to match the rising costs of consumer and food items. In August and November 1914 workers struck for higher wages in Tsaritsyn. The strike movement broadened in 1915, when workers from the Bering plant (Sotrudnik), Gantke plant, Iakovlev print works, and Medvedev lumberyards went out on strike. While the economic vicissitudes of war were driving workers to strike, the government continued to send political exiles, mainly revolutionaries, to Saratov. The governor complained in 1915 that more than 100 exiles had already registered in Saratov and about 500 in Tsaritsyn.[122]

Growing economic unrest among the Saratov proletariat helped to revive activities among the revolutionary intelligentsia. Government-created guardianships or trusteeships *(popechitel'stva),* cooperatives, various educational organizations, and clubs continued to be the main legal institutions open to socialists. The war necessitated an increase in the scope of these institutions, especially after refugees and evacuees flooded Saratov. Antonov, moreover, promoted the opening of a labor exchange to deal with growing unemployment. Socialists similarly infiltrated cooperatives, clubs, and institutions set up to assist displaced persons.[123] The most important center for SD activity at this time was the club Maiak (Lighthouse), which had opened in 1912. Such adult education organizations in Russia resembled the Verdandi, Chautauqua, and Sillon movements in Sweden, the United States, and France. Initially Maiak had served as a meetingplace for the liberal intelligentsia, but once war had broken out more revolutionary types, including Bolshevik exiles who arrived in 1915, began to congregate there. During the war Kerensky, now a deputy to the Fourth Duma elected from Saratov, frequently visited town and addressed gatherings at Maiak. In May 1915 Saratov Bolsheviks decided to concentrate their efforts there to attract working-class support, rather than continue agitational work within student circles. It was at this time that Ol'minskii and Nogin showed up in Saratov with copies of *Sotsial-Demokrat.* Antonov claimed that by late spring 1915, Maiak and the Saratov committee of the RSDRP had become synonymous and that working-class membership had swelled.[124]

Growing working-class unrest, a replenished Social Democratic group, and the establishment of ties with party circles in Petrograd, Moscow, Baku, and Astrakhan encouraged Saratov SDs to publish a newspaper in

122. Tomarev, *Bol'sheviki Povolzh'ia,* pp. 257–62.

123. Khodakov, *Ocherki istorii,* pp. 227–28.

124. Antonov-Saratovskii, *Pod stiagom,* pp. 129–33; S. Poltavskii, "O Saratovskom Maiake," *Otkliki,* no. 12 (1913), p. 13. See V. V. Babushkin, "Maiak," in *Fevral': Sbornik vospominanii o 1917 g. Kniga pervaia* (Saratov, 1922), pp. 13–15; and Ezhov, "Moi vospominaniia o Maiake," p. 69.

Maiak headquarters, 1912–1917

the summer of 1915. Despite claims of Soviet writers, the circumstances surrounding publication of a paper revealed the multiplicity of opinions within local Social Democracy and the extent to which differing attitudes on the war began to break down the traditional camaraderie of local socialists. Ol'minskii, Mitskevich, and Antonov, who was making rapid progress in his intellectual journey to Bolshevism, had to contend with a large group of SD intelligenty, both local and from the outside, who insisted on an editorial board free from party control. What was at stake was their desire to avoid a formal split within the mixed Bolshevik-Menshevik group, and to keep factionalism to a minimum so as not to alienate workers. Such prominent figures as Nogin and Lebedev remained critical of their party's stance on the war and did not wish to drive away several Menshevik comrades from Samara, who participated in the preliminary discussions on starting up a publication. But in the process of reaching a consensus on critical issues it became clear that the Bolsheviks held the upper hand, for it was decided to opt for a "party" paper. Articles in the first issues of *Nasha gazeta* (Our Paper)[125] criticized

125. A Soviet treatment of *Nasha gazeta* can be found in I. Bas, *Bol'shevistskaia pechat' v gody imperialisticheskoi voiny* (Moscow, 1939), pp. 121–53. See also Antonov-Saratovskii, *Pod stiagom*, pp. 19–43. At first the editorial board was made up of Lebedev, Lomov, and Antonov. "But almost immediately," wrote Lomov, "our party men of letters considered Antonov and me too undiplomatic, people who under the repressive condi-

election of workers' groups to war industries committees (the Bolshevik position). Outvoted on this issue, the Mensheviks withdrew from the newspaper's editorial board and eventually left for Samara, where they put out a defensist paper.

In all, ten issues of *Nasha gazeta* went to press between August 8 and October 20, 1915. By the time the police shut it down, the number of copies printed had increased from 2,000 to 10,000 (the leading Saratov dailies had circulations of 6,000 copies).[126] The paper provides valuable insights into labor conditions in Saratov, as it devoted extensive coverage to medical funds and management's purported threats to take advantage of wartime conditions to counter workers' demands for improved wages. Workers complained of arbitrary fine systems, niggardly pay, the hiring of prisoners of war for low wages, and constant threats from their bosses to hire refugees, prisoners of war, or women if workers dared to voice their discontent.[127] Monitoring *Nasha gazeta*'s contents and impact on the labor movement, the okhranka maintained that the paper "from the very first issue obviously aimed at inciting the workers not only against the government but in general against the propertied classes as well."[128] Police confiscated two of the ten issues and censors purged others of provocative writing. Local industrialists, who complained that the paper encouraged strikes, pressured the police to increase surveillance. On October 15 local courts closed down *Nasha gazeta* and ordered the arrest of several of its editors.[129]

The publication of *Nasha gazeta* had paralleled a resurgence in strike activity; yet the paper's role in influencing this revival of the workers' movement is difficult to evaluate. The growth of a strike movement in Saratov seems to have been part of a national phenomenon brought about by unpopular governmental policies and a worsening economic situation. In the summer of 1915, for instance, troops shot at striking workers in Ivanovo-Voznesensk and on September 3 the government

---

tions of tsarism would be unable to hold out even for a few issues . . . the editorial board now co-opted Ol'minskii into its makeup." See Lomov, *Nasha gazeta*, pp. vii–viii.

126. Sh. Levin, "Sotsialisticheskaia pechat' vo vremia imperialisticheskoi voiny," *Krasnyi arkhiv*, no. 2 (1922), p. 220; Antonov-Saratovskii, *Pod stiagom*, p. 24. See *Nasha gazeta*, no. 6, September 18, 1915.

127. For additional evidence see A. Martsinovskii, *Zapiski rabochego-bol'shevika* (Saratov, 1923), p. 70.

128. Quoted in Levin, "Sotsialisticheskaia pechat'," pp. 222–23; see also *Kommunist*, no. 49, February 27, 1959, p. 2.

129. S. I. Mitskevich, "Vospominaniia o revoliutsii v Saratove," *Rabotnik prosveshcheniia*, no. 8 (1922), p. 26. The editors themselves expressed surprise that they were able to publish ten issues before being shut down. Antonov mentioned that rumors had circulated that the paper lasted as long as it had because a newly appointed police chief had not yet arrived from Astrakhan. See *Pod stiagom*, p. 25.

dismissed the State Duma. The local workers' movement had already revived on its own initiative by 1915, just as it had in Petrograd, and may have actually encouraged the SD intelligentsia to organize a party committee and publish a paper. More strikes had broken out in 1915 in Saratov than during any other year between 1912 and 1916. The May Day strike of 1915 shut down almost all large plants and factories.[130]

Nevertheless, the local strike movement intensified during the period *Nasha gazeta* was being published. Tailors, bakers, printers, and workers at the Kostemolnyi plant went out first, and the movement soon spread to oil press, lumberyard, and other workers.[131] Increasing strike activity reflected the growing financial burden the war had placed on the Saratov working class—a point *Nasha gazeta* repeatedly emphasized. Each month of hostilities brought greater economic difficulties to Saratov workers. The government scrapped decrees regulating work hours and limiting female, adolescent, and child labor. Prices of food and manufactured items shot up 40 percent by 1916, making many products unattainable for the wage earner. The cost of such commodities as sugar and kerosene skyrocketed 100 to 200 percent. Long queues became commonplace in the city. Victimized by the priorities of war and threatened by the possibility of being sent to the front, workers turned more and more to the revolutionary underground for direction. By September 1915, concomitant with the publication of *Nasha gazeta*, the strike movement had acquired new intensity, and by November inspectors reported a political strike.[132] Moreover, Saratov workers boycotted the War Industries Committee, as *Nasha gazeta* and the Bolsheviks had been urging them to do.[133]

The revival in revolutionary activities in the second half of 1915 must also be viewed as part of a broader concern within Saratov society over the government's bungling of the war cause. Shortly after the publication of *Nasha gazeta*, Kerensky visited Saratov and organized a meeting of local representatives of all the major liberal and radical groups. If Antonov's account of this gathering is to be trusted, the various individuals exhibited enormous camaraderie and shared the sentiment that revolution would shortly break out.[134] An additional factor in the intensifi-

130. "Professional'nye soiuzy," p. 15. For events in Petrograd see Tsuyoshi Hasegawa, *The February Revolution: Petrograd, 1917* (Seattle, 1981), pp. 73–103; and S. A. Smith, *Red Petrograd: Revolution in the Factories, 1917–18* (Cambridge, Eng., 1983), pp. 48–53.

131. Antonov-Saratovskii, *Pod stiagom*, p. 34; Bas, *Bol'shevistskaia pechat'*, pp. 139–40.

132. M. G. Fleer, ed., *Rabochee dvizhenie v gody voiny (Materialy po istorii rabochego dvizheniia v Rossii)* (Moscow, 1925), pp. 98, 101.

133. Ch., "Saratovskaia organizatsiia," p. 51.

134. Antonov-Saratovskii, *Pod stiagom*, p. 41.

cation of antigovernment feelings at this time was the arrival in Saratov of evacuated students from Kiev University and the city's commercial institute and higher educational programs for women. Local revolutionaries noted that the evacuated students helped fill the need for political instructors and propagandists, and that the Kievan students were more radical than local ones. The police concurred.[135]

About the same time that Kerensky convened the meeting of the opposition parties, a demonstration took place in Saratov to commemorate the death of V. B. Lomtatidze, a Menshevik member of the Second Duma. Later that week, the police questioned Antonov, Lebedev, and several others responsible for it. A sharp rise in the price of flour a few weeks later prompted railroad workers and others to strike. Local SDs issued appeals and printed leaflets articulating the workers' demands. Within days the authorities arrested Antonov, Lebedev, and Lomov.[136]

More arrests in early 1916 all but destroyed the SD underground. Plans to conduct a May Day demonstration under the slogans "Down with the War," "The Eight-Hour Workday," and "A 100 Percent Pay Increase" were foiled by the police, who arrested all the revolutionaries they could find, dealing a crippling blow to Maiak and the SD movement in general.[137] When the Bolshevik T. V. Sapronov arrived in Saratov in June 1916, he found the party organization in shambles. Another recent newcomer to Saratov, A. M. Martsinovskii, reported dishearteningly that many workers still expressed patriotic sentiments and were unaware of the existence of trade unions.[138] Party cells at most factories had broken down. As before, however, party members still free met at Maiak, and there Sapronov and Martsinovskii made their first contacts in Saratov, despite the fact that the okhranka was methodically observing all activity on the premises.[139]

As was often the case in the history of Saratov Social Democracy, the arrival of such outside activists as Sapronov and Martsinovskii strengthened the underground. But the greatest initiative came from the Bolshevik workers K. I. Plaksin, Ignat, V. F. Bukin, R. Iu. Gul'bis, Vorob'ev, and others, who formed the "Initiative Group," which for the next seven months tried to restore ties via medical funds with metal-

135. Iu. K. Milonov, "Nakanune velikikh sobytii," in *Za vlast' sovetov (Sbornik vospominanii starykh bol'shevikov)*, ed. A. V. Babushkin et al. (Saratov, 1968), p. 12.

136. Ibid., pp. 10–11; Institut marksizma-leninizma pri TsK KPSS, *Bol'sheviki v gody imperialisticheskoi voiny, 1914–fevral' 1917 gg.: Sbornik dokumentov mestnykh bol'shevistskikh organizatsii* (Moscow, 1939), p. 97; Antonov-Saratovskii, *Pod stiagom*, p. 58.

137. V. V. Babushkin, "Razgrom organizatsii," in *Pervoe maia*, pp. 53–57.

138. Martsinovskii, *Zapiski*, p. 71.

139. T. V. Sapronov, "Tri mesiatsa na Volge (1916)," *Proletarskaia revoliutsiia*, no. 8/43 (1925), pp. 216–17.

workers, carpenters, lumberyard workers, Latvian workers, and local tailors. The Initiative Group also attempted with little success to revive ties with SD committees in other Volga cities.[140] Lacking theoreticians—people able to deliver lectures, write proclamations, and the like—the Initiative Group failed to organize an actual SD committee. Members of the local Bolshevik intelligentsia still in town now shied away from contact with workers, while some workers viewed the underground with suspicion or hostility. Not surprisingly, the Initiative Group cooperated with other elements of the opposition. It joined the illegal political Red Cross, an organization of intellectuals, mainly Mensheviks and Kadets, to aid political prisoners, and linked up with the Bund (the General Union of Jewish Workers, an organization allied with the Mensheviks).[141] But attempts to interest such Bolshevik intellectuals as Miliutin, Mitskevich, and Vasil'ev-Iuzhin in practical work failed.

January 1917. The economic and social strains of two and a half years of war had created broad anxieties among the townspeople. Saratov newspapers documented these concerns, both the minor ones and those of a graver nature. Even the minor complaints and apprehensions were directly tied to the war. City officials discussed the construction of a much-needed bridge across the Volga, but the project had to be scrapped under the pressure of wartime needs. Irate citizens complained of rampant hooliganism, while local medical funds at factories campaigned for a new clinic. Even more seriously, the growing incidence of draft evasion and desertion caused city officials to crack down on men who tried to elude military service. Health inspectors, meanwhile, had to cope with mange and typhus epidemics. After reporting that half of the city's public baths should be closed because of unsanitary conditions, the sanitation commission nevertheless grudgingly kept them open. Saratov simply lacked other facilities. Supply problems, ironically, also bred discontent in this food-producing province. Real and anticipated shortages of food items had locked the city administration and food-supply committee in heated debate over the introduction of a rationing system for bread and other products. City officials expressed hope that rationing would end speculation and make it easier to handle decreases in available grain supplies projected for February and March. Authorities reluctantly agreed to a system that was scheduled to begin in April. Yet rumors concerning the upcoming rationing increased speculation and

140. V. P. Antonov-Saratovskii, "Saratov s fevralia po oktiabr' 1917," *Proletarskaia revoliutsiia*, no. 2/25 (1924), pp. 154–55; K. I. Plaksin, "Nakanune," in *Fevral': Sbornik vospominanii*, p. 9; Martsinovskii, *Zapiski*, pp. 73–74.

141. Plaksin, "Nakanune," pp. 9–11.

higher bread prices heightened discontent. Long lines at bread shops now were common. Meat became a luxury. The city exhausted its tea reserves.[142]

Food deficits coincided with an energy and transport crisis that caused factories to close. Those industries forced to convert to electrical energy overburdened the city's few power stations. To compensate, the public and private sectors reduced their lighting of public buildings and shop windows. Lack of coal gravely threatened the Riazan-Uralsk railroad line, which reduced its services, thereby further complicating the food-supply issue. The city's labor exchange reported that unemployment in 1916 was twice as high as during 1915. The closing of more factories in early 1917 made matters worse. In addition, the 8,060 refugees in Saratov sorely needed clothing and food at a time when the city expected the imminent arrival of a group of Rumanian evacuees.[143]

Although the pressing problems and discontent linked with the war contributed immensely to a rising critical sentiment within Saratov society, the broad legacy of the past quarter century determined political relationships that emerged in Saratov after the autocratic regime had been swept away. Since 1905, if not before, the mixed record of reform and reaction had engendered much hostility in Saratov toward the government. The resulting vitality of progressive and leftist forces more than anything else shaped the post-February political alignment. Patterns of behavior and relationships among and within political groups that had formed back in the early days of political activism at the turn of the century and later survived in the underground after 1907 were to cast a heavy shadow over 1917.

142. See the reports in *Pochta*, no. 1, January 1, 1917, p. 3; no. 13, January 17, p. 3; and no. 19, January 25, p. 3; in *Saratovskii golos*, no. 63, January 12, 1917, p. 3; no. 64, January 13, p. 3; no. 69, January 19, p. 4; no. 92, February 18, p. 4; and no. 94, February 21, p. 4; *Saratovskii vestnik*, no. 24, January 29, 1917, p. 6.

143. *Saratovskii golos*, no. 63, January 12, 1917, p. 4; no. 64, January 13, p. 3; *Pochta*, no. 4, January 4, 1917, p. 3; no. 15, January 19, p. 3; no. 35, February 17, p. 3; *Saratovskii vestnik*, no. 24, January 29, 1917, p. 2.

CHAPTER 2

"May the Lord God Help Russia": The February Revolution in Saratov

"May the Lord God help Russia." The text of his abdication ready, Nicholas left for headquarters at Mogilev. "All around me," he recorded in his notebook, "is nothing but treason, cowardice, and deceit!" The next day reports of the formation of a provisional government flashed by telegraph across the empire, into the depths of Siberia. Almost everywhere the news stunned local populations. In Petrograd the collapse of the dynasty had taken place quickly and with few excesses. Equally striking was the rapid spread of the revolution in the provinces, where spontaneous public initiative and widespread euphoria resulted in the formation of new administrative institutions.

But the most important result of the February Revolution was not so much new institutions as an entirely different approach to politics, for the revolution inaugurated direct participation in politics by the heretofore disenfranchised, unlettered Russian masses. Public executive committees, soviets, legalized party committees, and social and political organizations representing a myriad of interest groups sprouted throughout the country. In Saratov as elsewhere the revolution unfolded without detailed directives from the center; in a few days a new political apparatus emerged locally. At first glance the change seems to have taken place calmly and with considerable cooperation among various interest groups. But beneath the smooth veneer discord threatened to undermine the frail political structure almost from the start.

The initial reaction of local political leaders on February 28 to the astounding news from the capital that the autocracy had collapsed matched the understandable apprehensions of the State Duma and Soviet leaders in Petrograd. Irregular receipt of official telegrams created confusion and uncertainty in Saratov. Belated communiqués and bulletins on the dissolution of the State Duma, followed by the inexplicable interruption of these dispatches, gave rise to all sorts of rumors. Unable to satiate their readers' curiosity, local newspapers fed them details of the British seizure of Baghdad and other war episodes. Not until early morning on March 1 did any authoritative message from the new government reach Saratov; then M. V. Rodzianko, president of the State Duma, cabled provincial governors of the Duma's need to form a new government. Intending to keep the important news secret, Governor S. D. Tverskoi of Saratov province held back the telegram's contents from the public.

As people set off to work at daybreak and Saratov resumed its ordinary functions, nothing outwardly distinguished March 1 from the day before. As yet only a chosen few were aware of the gravity of the moment. In the early morning the governor had summoned a small group of leading public figures—the marshal of the nobility, leaders of the City Duma and zemstvo—to a clandestine meeting. Informing them that the State Duma had declared the government deposed and that it had appointed a provisional government made up of Duma members led by Rodzianko, Tverskoi admonished the city fathers to proceed cautiously to prevent public disorders in Saratov. The governor reminded those assembled that he was compelled by oath to support the old regime and suppress any illegal public excesses. "Petrograd, Moscow, and the army," he concluded, "determine events . . . [here] it is necessary only to wait."[1]

But many public officials feared that Tverskoi's withholding of news would lead to those very excesses he was determined to prevent. By late morning, the people of Saratov had an inkling that something of consequence had come about in the capital. The newspaper *Pochta* (The Post) reported that "toward noon a sensational rumor arose that a provisional government had been formed, composed of members of the State Duma." Eagerly awaiting any information, crowds formed near the city's newspaper offices. In the afternoon more official telegrams reached Saratov. Before the police seized them, the texts of several somehow reached people in the streets, where they were "literally snatched from hand to hand" and "read aloud."[2] The morning's rumors seemed to be confirmed. Now everyone's attention focused on Tverskoi's plans.

1. *Saratovskii vestnik*, no. 51, March 5, 1917, p. 4; F. Morozov, "Fevral'skaia revoliutsiia v Saratove," in *Fevral': Sbornik vospominanii*, p. 24; *Saratovskii listok*, no. 49, March 2, 1917, p. 2. Deputy Mayor A. A. Iakovlev's account of this meeting can be found in *Izvestiia Saratovskoi gorodskoi dumy* (Saratov, 1917), p. 65.

2. *Pochta*, no. 58, March 3, 1917, p. 3.

Before the governor had a chance to take preemptive measures, the Saratov City Duma convened at five o'clock, insisting Tverskoi report to it. His morose tone contrasted sharply with the brighter but understandably anxious mood of most Duma members. Tverskoi again expressed his fear of a mass movement. "I know by experience that even the very best feelings, when thrown into the street, become soiled and trampled upon." After encouraging the Duma to work to prevent any demonstrations, he closed by stating his intention to retain his post until he was removed by imperial decree. "I recognize no other authority," he said, "and will use all of my efforts to preserve order." After Tverskoi's withdrawal the delegates reassembled in the mayor's office, where Deputy Mayor A. A. Iakovlev opened the meeting, from which the public was barred. Iakovlev recounted what had taken place at the governor's that morning and read the telegram issued in Petrograd by Rodzianko: "Under the difficult conditions of internal chaos brought on by the measures of the old regime, the Provisional Committee of the State Duma has found itself compelled to assume responsibility for restoring national and public order." During the ensuing discussion of how the city administration should respond to the events in the capital, the Duma implored newspaper editors to publish all cables and censured Tverskoi for ordering the police to stand guard over the printing presses. A representative from *Saratovskii vestnik* (Saratov Herald) then divulged the contents of the two latest telegrams: the old government had been arrested and the Petrograd garrison had placed itself at the disposal of the Committee of the State Duma. Upon hearing this news, some delegates suggested sending messages of support to the new government; Tverskoi, however, had posted police to prevent such messages from being sent. Steering the meeting away from further discussion, Iakovlev stressed the need for a general plan of action and for soothing the population by publishing all communiqués from the capital. Agreeing with his suggestions, the Duma members decided to send a delegation to the governor to persuade him to allow the dispatch of telegrams to Petrograd. They also agreed to reconvene that evening to talk over what steps to take. By now many were recommending the creation of a committee to direct the local transfer of power. Representatives of the War Industries Committee, university administration, Society of Shop Assistants and Merchants, City Cooperative Board, garrison command, and administration of the Riazan-Uralsk railroad line were invited to the evening session.[3]

3. This discussion is based on *Izvestiia Saratovskoi gorodskoi dumy*, pp. 64–68; *Saratovskii listok*, no. 49, March 2, 1917, p. 2; P. Kul'manov, "Pered grozoi," in *Fevral': Sbornik vospominanii*, p. 21; and M. I. Vasil'ev-Iuzhin, "Nakanune Fevral'skoi revoliutsii," in *Za vlast' sovetov: Vospominaniia uchastnikov revoliutsionnykh sobytii 1917 goda v Saratovskoi gubernii*, ed. G. Sukharev et al. (Saratov, 1957), p. 10.

City officials were unaware that a group of revolutionaries gathered at Maiak the same day decided to send their own delegation to the Duma that evening. Vasil'ev-Iuzhin, Miliutin, and a tailor named Stepanov were chosen to attend the important meeting.[4] Although details of what happened at Maiak that afternoon are blurred, those assembled apparently agreed to organize a soviet of workers' deputies. Local revolutionary activists, who formed a "workers' group" at Maiak, took it upon themselves to conduct elections to the soviet at Saratov's industrial enterprises and issue proclamations to the garrison. Yet despite the conclusion of a plan of action, the revolutionaries naturally remained apprehensive. Vasil'ev-Iuzhin worried about the weak ties the SDs had both among the 60,000 to 70,000 men of the garrison and among workers.[5] Nevertheless, the news of the downfall of the Romanovs relieved many fears. Any doubts that lingered probably melted away when a youth smashed his fist through the portrait of Nicholas II, which until this point had witnessed the goings on at Maiak.[6]

Shortly after nine o'clock Iakovlev opened the evening Duma session. Throngs of curious citizens disrupted the order that generally prevailed in the building. Wearing heavy fur and cloth coats and clumsy galoshes, townspeople packed themselves along the stairways leading to the meeting hall. Inside, interrupted by thunderous applause, the deputy mayor read the most recent telegrams from Rodzianko, listing the members of the new government. The assembled deputies unanimously agreed to ignore the governor and send a telegram of support to the newly established national government. Speaking on behalf of, in his words, the "organized workers of Saratov," the Bolshevik M. I. Vasil'ev (Vasil'ev-Iuzhin) suggested that a greeting likewise be sent to the "heroic Petrograd proletariat," a proposal received with enthusiastic applause. But the general goodwill was destroyed by the polemical remarks of the tailor Stepanov, whose emotional blast against the old regime was interrupted by cries of dissent. The chairman of the local zemstvo board and several others left city hall in protest.[7]

In the ensuing debate over an appropriate course of action, fanned by the reading of four new telegrams from the capital, including a greeting from the Petrograd Soviet, two factions emerged. One, represented by such leading Kadets as S. P. Krasnikov and A. A. Nikonov, opposed the formation of an executive committee in Saratov until the situation in

4. Antonov-Saratovskii, "Saratov s fevralia," p. 157.

5. Vasil'ev-Iuzhin, "Nakanune Fevral'skoi revoliutsii," p. 16.

6. Ts. A. Kogan, "V te istoricheskie dni," in *Za vlast' sovetov* (Saratov, 1957), p. 164.

7. *Izvestiia Saratovskoi gorodskoi dumy*, pp. 71–73; Kul'manov, "Pered grozoi," p. 21; Antonov-Saratovskii, "Saratov s fevralia," p. 180; *Saratovskii listok*, no. 50, March 3, 1917, p. 3; Antonov-Saratovskii, *Pod stiagom*, p. 103.

Petrograd had been clarified further. The other faction, led by Bolsheviks Vasil'ev and Miliutin and by N. I. Semenov from the War Industries Committee, clamored for the immediate organization of a new local authority. Arguing that "the task of the present moment is organization, organization of all of Russia," Vasil'ev maintained that the Provisional Government should keep in mind that it was just that—provisional—and that a prompt convening of a constituent assembly was expected. Workers' and students' vocal support of Vasil'ev's remarks prompted disapproving outcries from the more cautious delegates of industry and commerce. After further emotional exchanges, those present agreed to cable their support to the new government and to publish an appeal to the city's populace to remain calm. The city's political forces were already aligning themselves differently from those in the capital. The head of the War Industries Committee, Semenov, the old People's Will activist N. N. Miasoedov, and the Bolshevik Vasil'ev drafted the statement to the townspeople on behalf of the Duma. General apprehension and a hesitancy to act without orders from the new government prevented more concrete measures. Postponing the creation of a new executive body, the meeting adjourned until the next evening.[8]

On March 2 the governor continued to withhold information from all but his closest confidants and threatened to use armed force against the population if necessary. Beginning in early morning, regular news dispatches from Petrograd arrived in Saratov, but police kept them from being printed. Many people in the streets remained ignorant of the rapidly unfolding events in the capital. When M. A. Golubov struck up a conversation with a cabman, the cabman advised against going to the bazaar. "It's not worth it. It's probably not open today. There's trouble. They say a levorution [*livoriutsiia*] is going on in town. They took Batiushka Tsar away from his throne. Some sort of duma took over. God's punished us." Another observer related that the crowds he mingled with feared the soldiers billeted in the city's garrison. "Whose side are they on? Will they shoot us?" Aware of the apprehensions of the townspeople and annoyed by what they considered the pernicious interference of the governor, the editors of the two major newspapers, *Saratovskii listok* (Saratov Sheet) and *Saratovskii vestnik*, managed to send a telegram to Petrograd, addressed to Rodzianko, Kerensky, and A. M. Maslennikov: "Governor Tverskoi is putting obstacles in the way of printing telegrams of the [wire service] agencies, is demanding changes in the texts, and is confiscating newspapers. . . ." Tverskoi also banned meetings and dem-

8. For a description of the Duma meeting that evening see *Izvestiia Saratovskogo Soveta rabochikh i soldatskikh deputatov* (hereafter cited as *Izvestiia Saratovskogo Soveta*), no. 6, March 14, 1917, p. 2. See also *Saratovskii vestnik*, no. 49, March 2, 1917, p. 3; Morozov, "Fevral'skaia revoliutsiia," p. 26.

onstrations, but crowds continued to gather near newspaper offices and in the city's largest squares. Rumors abounded. Tverskoi's veiled activities gave rise to widespread talk that he was secretly deliberating with members of the Black Hundreds and military authorities. While concerned Saratovites took to the streets, hoping to catch the latest news, representatives of various public organizations and institutions ignored Tverskoi's decrees and met privately.[9]

March 2, when the Provisional Government took office in Petrograd, was also a day of organization in Saratov. A joint meeting of the administrations of the Stock Exchange and War Industries Committee issued a congratulatory telegram to the new government. Students from higher educational institutions elected delegates to an all-city student committee. The district zemstvo selected a special committee to promote law and order and supervise food distribution. At the same time, workers in Saratov's plants and factories elected representatives to the workers' soviet. In a few cases the proletariat greeted the revolutionary leaders organizing the elections with indifference, if not hostility. Sent to the Egorov factory, the Bolshevik K. I. Plaksin discovered that the workers refused to cooperate: "For us it's all the same whether there are soviets or not; our situation won't be improved by it."[10] But apparently most of the city's working class responded more enthusiastically, because that evening fifty-eight delegates representing twenty-nine enterprises attended the first meeting of the Saratov Soviet of Workers' Deputies.[11]

An uncanny similarity existed between the atmosphere of the first meeting of the Saratov Soviet and that of the Petrograd Soviet in the Tauride Palace on February 27. In Saratov, the gathering took place in the basement of the city hall, while the enlarged Duma session convened in the upper auditorium. Eyewitnesses refer to the "continual movement from the lower hall to the upper and back."[12] As in the capital, the existence of the Soviet pressured Duma leaders to be more decisive than they had been the previous evening. The Duma members became dead-

9. M. A. Golubov, "Saratov v 1917 g.: Vospominaniia pomoshchika Kursovogo ofitsera Saratovskoi shkoly praporshchikov," manuscript dated Innsbruck, Austria, 1955, Columbia University, Butler Library, p. 15; *Saratovskii listok,* no. 51, March 5, 1917, p. 5; *Izvestiia Saratovskogo Soveta,* no. 6, March 14, 1917, p. 2; *Pochta,* no. 58, March 3, 1917, p. 3; for a description of Tverskoi's actions see B. A. Osipov, ed., *1917 god v Saratovskoi gubernii: Sbornik dokumentov, fevral' 1917–dekabr' 1918* gg. (Saratov, 1957), p. 44; Morozov, "Fevral'skaia revoliutsiia," pp. 26–27.

10. K. I. Plaksin, "Nakanune," in *Fevral': Sbornik vospominanii,* p. 11.

11. V. P. Antonov-Saratovskii, ed., *Saratovskii Sovet rabochikh deputatov, 1917–1918: Sbornik dokumentov* (Moscow, 1931), p. 3 (hereafter cited as *Saratovskii Sovet*); Vasil'ev-Iuzhin, "Nakanune Fevral'skoi revoliutsii," p. 16; Z. Petrov, "Saratovskii proletariat v bor'be za vlast'," in *1917 god v Saratove* (Saratov, 1927), p. 6. Burdzhalov gives larger figures: 88 deputies from 49 organizations (*Vtoraia russkaia revoliutsiia,* p. 206).

12. Morozov, "Fevral'skaia revoliutsiia," p. 28.

locked again in a debate over a suitable course of action, while the Soviet addressed itself to important organizational questions. Under the chairmanship of I. A. Skvortsov, a Menshevik worker from the Bering factory, the Soviet elected an executive committee, a chairman, and representatives to the public executive committee being formed by the Duma. Included in the Soviet's Executive Committee were the Bolshevik intelligenty Vasil'ev and Miliutin, the Bolshevik workers I. A. Galaktionov from the Levkovich tobacco factory and K. I. Plaksin from Zhest; the Mensheviks P. Ia. Kolesnikov (a typesetter), Skvortsov, and K. A. Tkachev from the Sotrudnik plant, and the SR flour mill worker M. I. Sadaev.[13] Milituin was elected chairman and Vasil'ev and Skvortsov vice-chairmen. It bears pointing out that the workers who played key roles in the formation of the Soviet came from those enterprises where SD and SR activities had been most active even before 1905. Moreover, in contrast with the Petrograd and Moscow soviets, Bolsheviks not only were included in the Executive Committee of the Saratov Soviet but occupied two of its three top leadership positions. Having settled organizational matters, the Soviet called for a one-day strike and demonstration on March 3, which would complement a parade of garrison soldiers. On the morning of the demonstration, workers were to report to their factories to elect factory committees. At two o'clock the proletariat were to converge on Moscow Square "in order to greet our revolutionary army, which has joined the people and defends their rights."[14]

In any revolutionary situation armed force usually serves as a determining factor. Despite the high command's efforts to keep the garrison isolated, members of the workers' committee formed by revolutionary activists had managed to inform some military units of the revolution in Petrograd. The Third Machine-Gun Regiment, no ordinary unit, mutinied first, although it is impossible to say just how or when it did so. The entire imperial army had only four such units: the First and Second regiments in Petrograd, the Third and Fourth in Saratov. These regiments trained machine-gun instructors, who typically were metalworkers or other skilled workers. As in Petrograd, this particular category of soldier figured prominently in local affairs during the spring of 1917. On the evening of March 2, soldiers from the Third Machine-Gun Regiment and

13. Ibid.; *Saratovskii Sovet*, p. 3.

14. The text of the resolution can be found in *Saratovskii listok*, no. 50, March 3, 1917, p. 3, and in *Izvestiia Saratovskogo Soveta*, no. 16, March 29, 1917, p. 2. Also see G. A. Gerasimenko, *Sovety Nizhnego Povolzh'ia v Oktiabr'skoi revoliutsii* (Saratov, 1972), p. 21. Requesting help, three workers from Samara attended this first meeting of the Saratov Soviet. Two hundred workers in Samara had been arrested for participating in an economic strike, some of whom were being shipped to the front for their activism. See *Saratovskii listok*, no. 51, March 5, 1917, p. 4.

Executive Committee of the Saratov Soviet, March 1917

others headed for the Duma building. As several officers and soldiers made their way to the upper hall, throngs of soldiers, demanding to see Duma leaders, milled about outside the building.[15]

Back in the hall, an officer reported to the Duma on the creation of a provisional military committee. "On-the-spot meetings of soldiers from all units of the garrison just took place," he declared. "It was decided to send a telegram to the Provisional Government that the garrison of the city of Saratov is at the disposal of the [State Duma] Committee." Adding that each unit elected one officer and one soldier to take part in the military committee, the officer yielded the floor to a soldier, who informed the gathering that the military units would assemble the next day in one of the city's main squares to demonstrate their solidarity with the new regime. "Commanders were found in several barracks who hindered some from coming here," he said in parting. "But we're not afraid of them."[16]

The formation of a soviet and a military committee had added an element of urgency to what the Duma members would decide that evening. The factions that had developed the night before, however, promptly resurfaced. Arguing that the proposed executive committee should limit itself strictly to informational matters, Kadet leaders strongly opposed the formation of a body with executive authority. But as the well-respected Popular Socialist P. A. Medvedev argued, "events are developing so quickly that now no one doubts the need for such a committee. The question is only about its functions—informational or executive. Maybe we're on the verge of pogroms. And if we wait for the center, that'll be a big mistake. The center won't save us from anarchy. We're not saying that the committee should arrest the administration. But we must be ready for that." The old narodnik N. N. Miasoedov then suggested that the governor might close the Duma; Vasil'ev cautioned that if an executive organ were not created, "the democracy would take that task upon itself," and that the military might take extreme measures, since one officer had already complained about the vacillations of the Duma leaders ("rats," as he called them). This comment precipitated an uproar of excitement and confusion. Vasil'ev was shouted down; only with persistence could the chairman restore order.[17]

The majority now recognized the need to create a local organ of the Provisional Government. The resulting deliberations, continuing until the early morning of March 3, produced the Obshchestvennyi ispolnitel'nyi komitet, or Public Executive Committee (hereafter referred to as the PEC), composed initially of sixteen representatives. As the

15. *Saratovskii listok*, no. 50, March 3, 1917, p. 3.
16. *Izvestiia Saratovskoi gorodskoi dumy*, p. 78.
17. Ibid., pp. 78–80; *Izvestiia Saratovskogo Soveta*, no. 6, March 14, 1917, pp. 2–3.

Duma had stipulated, the PEC was to include six representatives from the City Duma, three from the city's organization of lawyers, one from the zemstvo, one from the cooperatives, and five from the Soviet. The PEC's main purposes were to preserve order, to function as an impartial government, and to work with the army "for a decisive victory over the enemy."[18] On March 5 the committee declared itself to be the legal organ of power in Saratov province. A. A. Tokarskii, a respected lawyer and member of the First State Duma, served as chairman, and Semenov, the Popular Socialist from the War Industries Committee, assumed the responsibilities of provincial commissar, as governors now were called.

No sooner had the committee been formed, however, than it faced its first serious crisis. While the delegates had argued over the judiciousness of arresting the governor and other members of the old administration, the street had taken matters into its own hands. The Provisional Military Committee, made up of SRs and Bolsheviks, had ordered the arrest of the governor and other prominent officials of the old regime. Crowds of soldiers, mainly from the Third Machine-Gun Regiment, and some townspeople, led by the zealous officer V. N. Sokolov, made numerous arrests throughout the morning. Included among the immured were the police chief, gendarmes, leading Black Hundred activists, Tverskoi, the deputy governor, and about 300 others whom the crowds associated with the old regime, some of whom later were sent to Petrograd. The soldiers next turned their wrath on the barracks at the outskirts of the city, where they locked up officers against whom they had special grievances—Commander Sos'e of the Ninetieth Regiment, an army doctor, military censors, and others.[19]

The Provisional Military Committee's independent actions alarmed both the commanding officers in the garrison and the PEC, for the arrests reflected considerable hostility toward men of the old regime. Newspapers on the morning of March 3 called for complete order in the garrison, and members of the PEC and high-ranking officers visited the barracks, appealing to rank-and-file soldiers to remain calm. Several officers tried all morning to have the demonstration planned for that day canceled. One officer proposed turning loyal artillery cadets ("junkers" or officer trainees) from the local military school on the marchers.[20] Under pressure from the high command, the PEC urged troops to obey

18. Petrov, "Saratovskii proletariat," p. 6.

19. Morozov, "Fevral'skaia revoliutsiia," p. 29; *Izvestiia Saratovskogo Soveta*, no. 8, March 17, 1917, p. 1; Martsinovskii, *Zapiski rabochego-bol'shevika*, p. 84; V. V. Vas'kin, "Iz istorii bor'by za bol'shevizatsiiu Saratovskogo garnizona v 1917 g.," in *Materialy k nauchnoi konferentsii aspirantov i molodykh nauchnykh sotrudnikov*, no. 1 (Saratov, 1965), pp. 100–101. Born in 1896, the young Sokolov had participated in SD circles since 1915. In 1917 he joined the Bolshevik party and in 1918 served as provincial commissar of war.

20. M. Blinov, "Iz fevral'skikh vospominanii," in *Fevral': Sbornik vospominanii*, p. 35.

their officers and, with the exception of the five representatives from the Soviet, voted to abolish the Provisional Military Committee. But once again the PEC realized the limits of its power. The call to the committee to disband during the demonstration that afternoon evoked disorders among the marching soldiers. Returning to their barracks, they ignored the PEC's ruling altogether and elected a "permanent" military committee. Colonel Milovanov and other officers who tried to block this move found themselves under arrest.[21]

All in all, the demonstration on the afternoon of March 3 represented mass acceptance of the revolution on the part of most Saratovites. Converging on Moscow Square about 2:00 P.M., an enormous parade of troops and officers "joined the people" in the "name of the homeland and victory." Accompanied by workers, students, and members of various national minorities dressed in colorful native costumes, the parade filed through the city and past a centrally located podium where the participants were greeted by members of the PEC, members of the Riazan-Uralsk railroad administration, and other prominent citizens. During the parade a telegram from Kerensky, granting full amnesty to political prisoners, was read to the marchers, who proceeded to the city's prison and freed an estimated sixty political prisoners. *Saratovskii vestnik* reported that "at four o'clock a grandiose demonstration with red flags took place on German Square. A brass band played the Marseillaise. News about the abdication of Nicholas II was met with incredible ecstasy."[22] Another paper commented that "on the streets there are demonstrators, meetings. In the crowd of demonstrators—red flags. People are singing the Marseillaise. . . . From one end of the city to the other there is the booming of popular rejoicing."[23] Such activity continued until late evening. To be sure, not everyone celebrated that day, but those who lamented the demise of the old regime remained prudently silent. As the Bolshevik V. P. Antonov later commented, "The 'bloodlessness' of the February Revolution in Piter [Petrograd] is to a considerable extent a liberal legend. But in Saratov, it indeed was bloodless."[24]

The most significant observation that can be made about the spread of the revolution to the district towns is how quickly it took place. Despite efforts by officials in many centers to suppress news, the town populations everywhere knew of the formation of the Provisional Government by March 4. Between March 4 and March 8 new executive committees or

21. *Izvestiia Saratovskogo Soveta*, no. 16, March 29, 1917, p. 2; also in *Saratovskii listok*, no. 51, March 5, 1917, p. 4.
22. *Saratovskii vestnik*, no. 51, March 5, 1917, p. 4.
23. *Saratovskii listok*, no. 51, March 5, 1917, p. 4.
24. Antonov-Saratovskii, *Pod stiagom*, p. 105.

soviets had replaced the old administrations in *all* of the province's district centers. Broadly speaking, the social geography of these towns affected the response to the revolution. For the most part the populations were involved in trade and handicraft activities and there were few industrial workers. Populism and liberalism represented the most significant political currents among the intelligentsia. Occasionally one comes across an isolated Social Democrat, but such activists exhibited few partisan sentiments at this time. Such factors as the record of progressive elements locally before 1917 and proximity to Saratov or Tsaritsyn also shaped the way the revolution unfolded at the district level. Yet in virtually every instance the army emerged as the truly decisive element in shifting the balance of forces against the old administrations. All of the district centers except remote Khvalynsk housed garrisons, which often were more populous than the towns themselves, as Table 4 shows. Without exception garrison troops, often joined by workers, arrested the old tsarist police and gendarmes and unpopular garrison commanders and officers.[25]

In Tsaritsyn, representatives of the city duma, political parties, consumer cooperatives, and newspaper offices formed a provisional execu-

Table 4

Populations and strength of garrisons in district towns, Saratov province, 1917

Town	*Population*	*Size of garrison or regiment number**
Atkarsk	12,500	9,000
Balashov	17,400	135th and 145th
Kamyshin	24,800	?
Khvalynsk	19,300	None
Kuznetsk	29,500	147th and 148th
Petrovsk	19,800	134th and 145th
Serdobsk	10,100	161st
Tsaritsyn	134,683	93rd, 143rd, and 155th
Volsk	36,000	150th and 245th

*Regiments normally ranged from 5,000 to 13,000 soldiers.

Sources: A. F. Milovzorov, *Sel'skokhoziaistvennye raiony Saratovskoi gubernii* (Saratov, 1924), p. 18; I. Romanov and N. Sokolov, *Ocherk istorii revoliutsii 1917 goda v Tsaritsyne (Stalingrade)* (Saratov, 1930), p. 6; A. I. Razgon, "O sostave sovetov Nizhnego Povolzh'ia v marte–aprele 1917 g.," in *Sovety i soiuz rabochego klassa i krest'ianstva v Oktiabr'skoi revoliutsii* (Moscow, 1964), p. 93; M. Frenkin, *Zakhvat vlasti bol'shevikami v Rossii i rol' tylovykh garnizonov armii: Podgotovka i provedenie Oktiabr'skogo miatezha, 1917–1918 gg.* (Jerusalem, 1982), p. 16.

25. Khvalynsk is the only town about which I was unable to find information on the local transfer of power. The absence of troops there may explain why. For the role of the garrisons in the uezd towns see V. V. Vas'kin, "Soldaty Nizhnego Povolzh'ia v Fevral'sko-martovskie dni 1917 goda," *Iz istorii Saratovskogo Povolzh'ia* (Saratov, 1968), pp. 92–110.

tive committee on March 1, even before the population of Saratov had established a similar organ. The next day soldiers, prodded by the so-called *frontoviki*—soldiers who had been wounded at the front and sent to recuperate in military hospitals at the rear—surged forth from their barracks into the city and joined workers from the large armament and metal-processing plants. The crowd of soldiers and workers freed political prisoners, set fire to the jail, and arrested tsarist police officials. That same day the Workers' Group of the War Industries Committee elected a soviet; on March 3, under strong Menshevik influence, a workers' council held its first meeting. In contrast with events in Saratov, soldiers formed a separate soviet.[26]

In the settlement of Nikolaevsk, on the left bank of the Volga directly across the river from Kamyshin, and in Kamyshin and Balashov, new political organs replaced the old order the day after the news of the formation of a provisional government in Petrograd arrived. In Nikolaevsk soldiers elected a soviet, disarmed the tsarist police, and helped organize a workers' soviet.[27] Soldiers also set up a soviet on March 3 in Kamyshin and apprehended the police. In Balashov the existence of SD cells in the railroad yards and butter creameries as well as an element of pure chance colored the February days. On the evening of March 2, armed soldiers en route from Moscow to Kamyshin stopped at the Balashov station. Disarming the local railroad police and town gendarmes, the soldiers soon had the local garrison out in the streets too, despite the duma's efforts to keep the troops in their barracks. In response, the duma and zemstvo formed a committee of public safety while a local Bolshevik activist, A. L. Bankvitser, appealed to Balashov workers to elect representatives to a soviet. Late that evening armed workers and soldiers rounded up tsarist police officials, some of whom resisted. Shooting broke out between the police and forces of the soviet before the former were subdued.[28] A separate soldiers' soviet appeared in late March.

Proximity to Saratov helps explain the prompt establishment of a new revolutionary order in Pokrovsk. Several prominent local citizens who had witnessed the formation of the PEC in Saratov returned home to

26. For a description of the February Revolution in Tsaritsyn see M. A. Vodolagin, *Krasnyi Tsaritsyn* (Volgograd, 1967), pp. 37–40; V. V. Vas'kin and G. A. Gerasimenko, *Fevral'skaia revoliutsiia v Nizhnem Povolzh'e* (Saratov, 1976), pp. 29–31, 14–15; G. A. Gerasimenko, *Vozniknovenie sovetov rabochikh, soldatskikh i krest'ianskikh deputatov v Nizhnem Povolzh'e (1917–pervaia polovina 1918 gg.)* (Saratov, 1966), p. 5; and I. Presniakov, "Iz podpol'ia na prostor," *Partiinyi sputnik*, no. 9–10 (1923), pp. 68–72.

27. The Bolshevik V. I. Ermoshchenko, a drafted mine worker, chaired the local soviet (Vas'kin and Gerasimenko, *Fevral'skaia revoliutsiia*, pp. 37–38).

28. Ibid., pp. 40–41. For a description of the events in Kamyshin see S. Manturov, *Iz revoliutsionnogo proshlogo Kamyshina (1905–1920)* (Volgograd, 1963), passim.

direct the transfer of power there. Workers and soldiers took to the streets upon hearing of demonstrations in Saratov, and local liberals and populists formed a committee of public safety and immured gendarmes and the garrison commander. A week later workers elected a soviet, which soon enrolled 2,000 members.[29]

In Atkarsk, Volsk, Kuznetsk, and Petrovsk the town dumas and district zemstvo boards established executive committees before local workers and soldiers organized soviets. *Saratovskii listok* reported that in Atkarsk the initiative for forming an executive committee "fell to the city and zemstvo workers, who organized a committee of twenty townspeople, workers, and railroad employees."[30] A local Bolshevik remembered that "early in the morning I ran to the [railroad] station, where soldiers traveling from Moscow had confined the gendarmes. That evening we decided to arrest the local police. All of this was so hard to fathom—that people were arresting the police!"[31] A few weeks later soldiers locked up the garrison commanders because of their refusal to recognize the new government.[32] In Volsk, the largest of the district centers after Tsaritsyn, local soldiers arrested unpopular officers while the revolutionary intelligentsia set up a public executive committee made up of Mensheviks, SRs, Popular Socialists, and Kadets. No prominent Bolsheviks were on hand here. In fact, when a Bolshevik named G. Rubashkina brought copies of the Saratov Bolshevik paper to town later in the month, street vendors refused to sell them and she had to find children to distribute the papers free. Soon the united committee of intelligenty began to publish its own newspaper. A Bolshevik named S. K. Kukushkin, who had stalked the Volga underground for years, participated in this joint publication. "In the beginning I didn't know that he was a Bolshevik," admitted Rubashkina. Despite the relatively large concentration of factories, "there was not a single Bolshevik, and not a single person who sympathized with the Bolsheviks."[33] Railroad workers and soldiers in Kuznetsk formed voluntary squads on March 3 and arrested the tsarist police. The squads later created a new people's militia, shut down the zemstvo court, and imprisoned the unpopular Colonel Uspenskii. Duma and zemstvo officials had announced on March 4 the birth of a provisional executive committee, which, intimidated by public demonstra-

29. Vas'kin and Gerasimenko, *Fevral'skaia revoliutsiia*, pp. 41–43; *Izvestiia Saratovskogo Soveta*, no. 4, March 10, 1917, p. 4.

30. *Saratovskii listok*, no. 68, March 28, 1917, p. 4.

31. Ezhov, "V Saratove (1907–1917 gg.)," p. 189. Also see a report in *Saratovskii listok*, no. 51, March 5, 1917, p. 4.

32. *Protokoly zasedanii Saratovskogo Voennogo Komiteta: Protokoly zasedanii Presidiuma Saratovskogo Voennogo Komiteta*, no. 4, March 16, 1917, pp. 32–33.

33. Rubashkina, "Vol'skaia organizatsiia SDRP," p. 80.

tions, agreed to include soldier and worker deputies.[34] In Petrovsk the regiment commander withheld news for several days and kept his troops impounded in their barracks. But on March 5 soldiers and townspeople demonstrated, and the troops locked up their commander. A new administrative organ, however, was not formed until later.[35]

In Serdobsk uezd the location of a heavily trafficked railroad junction in Rtishchevo and a sizable number of railroad workers in Serdobsk town shaped the local response to the revolution. Revolutionary tradition was important here, too. Back in 1902 and in 1905 railroad workers had supported the strike movement initiated by their Saratov coworkers, while violent peasant disturbances had given the district a reputation for radicalism. Now in 1917, during the first few days of March, soldiers and workers participated in public meetings and disarmed local police after authorities tried unsuccessfully to suppress news. The arrival of a contingent of Saratov railroad workers and soldiers further encouraged the revolutionary forces. On March 4 a public executive committee assumed power; on March 9 the Saratov Soviet resolved to send agitators to Serdobsk to form a soviet. In Rtishchevo railroad workers disarmed police and set up a people's militia. On March 23 a workers' soviet convened for the first time.[36]

Soviets or workers' groups in the district towns turned to the Saratov Soviet for guidance. Even before any formal, hierarchical structure of soviets emerged, workers' and soldiers' soviets seem to have looked instinctively to the Saratov Soviet for direction. In early March the flow of appeals from district soviets and villages for agitators, literature, and advisers inundated the Saratov Soviet. On March 10 it sent delegates into the province to promote the organization of local soviets wherever they did not yet exist. Agitators from Saratov helped set up soviets in Khvalynsk, Atkarsk, Rtishchevo, and Volsk. But lack of funds and trained cadres kept the Soviet from honoring the large number of requests from the villages. The Executive Committee lamented that its representatives penetrated only the countryside near Saratov.[37]

Nevertheless, news of the formation of a provisional government spread from the district centers into villages in the countryside. Virtually

34. I. I. Ponomarchuk, *Kuznetskii uezd posle Fevral'skoi revoliutsii* (Kuznetsk, 1958), p. 7; Vas'kin and Gerasimenko, *Fevral'skaia revoliutsiia*, pp. 46–47. See the memoir of the uezd commissar, F. Bobylev, "Kuznetskaia respublika," in *Fevral': Sbornik vospominanii*, pp. 37–40.

35. Vas'kin and Gerasimenko, *Fevral'skaia revoliutsiia*, pp. 46–48. See a Petrovsk soldier's report at a regional military conference in *Izvestiia Kazanskogo Voenno-okruzhnogo Komiteta*, no. 14, June 6, 1917, p. 3.

36. N. P. Bul'in et al., *Stranitsy zhizni (Iz istorii Serdobskoi organizatsii KPSS)* (Penza, 1961), pp. 6–11; and Vas'kin and Gerasimenko, *Fevral'skaia revoliutsiia*, *pp. 52–55*.

37. *Saratovskii vestnik*, no. 64, March 22, 1917, p. 3.

everywhere in the rural areas peasants accepted the news of the formation of the new government calmly. Not one known village meeting or resolution or cable expressed opposition to the new order. In Saratov district as in much of the rest of the province, peasants arrested or removed from office local administrators, zemstvo officials, and village and district police. Without any directives from the center or from Saratov, they then set about electing new executive organs that differed widely in name, size, and method of selection.

On the eve of 1917 each of the ten districts in Saratov province was divided administratively into a number—ranging from eight to forty—of smaller units called volosts or counties. Each volost was managed by a volost assembly *(skhod),* elected by the local village communes, usually for a three-year period. According to local custom, every ten households had one voice in the volost assembly. At the top stood an executive board of foremen, clerks, and village elders. During March and April the peasants replaced this authority structure with a myriad of peasant committees, often called volost executive committees, committees of public safety, or something similar. As *Saratovskii listok* informed readers, "in the villages of Saratov uezd one can observe the universal removal of volost foremen. The populations are arresting village elders."[38] As was true in other cases of popular spontaneity in the spring of 1917, the Provisional Government had no choice but to legalize the new self-proclaimed committees. On March 19 the government recognized the legitimacy of volost executive committees, transferring to them the responsibilities of the old volost administrations until the zemstvos were reelected along democratic lines.

The peasant committees, which varied in size from three or five up to as many as a hundred members, differed greatly from one another. In many localities peasants elected their committees according to the traditional ten-household system. But in contrast with old practices, about half of the elections now were secret, and the age requirement was lowered. Perhaps the most unusual practice was that common to Khvalynsk and Serdobsk districts, where all eligible males assembled and tried to shout each other down. Those who survived this ordeal best—and sometimes it dragged on for days—found themselves chosen for influential roles in their villages.[39] The countryside had its own understanding of freedom.

38. Cited in Vas'kin and Gerasimenko, *Fevral'skaia revoliutsiia,* p. 163. See also G. A. Gerasimenko, "Local Peasant Organizations in 1917 and the First Half of 1918," ed. Donald J. Raleigh, *Soviet Studies in History,* 16, no. 3 (Winter 1977–78), 12–18.

39. G. A. Gerasimenko, "Vozniknovenie volostnykh obshchestvennykh ispolnitel'nykh komitetov v Nizhnem Povolzh'e (mart–mai 1917 goda)," *Povolzhskii krai,* no. 2 (1973), p. 55.

Although far removed from the urban centers where the revolution was being made, Saratov peasants displayed keen interest in what the revolution meant. After the first news trickled in via telegram, telephone, or newspaper, peasants sought to find out for themselves what was going on. Some villages dispatched representatives to neighboring towns for information. Others greeted delegations of workers and soldiers or speakers sent from some town or soviet. Once news about a new government had been confirmed, peasants summarily dealt with tsarist police officials. To the peasants there was little difference between the police and the governmental administrative apparatus in the village. Hand in hand with the formation of peasant committees went the establishment of a militia elected at village meetings. In the majority of cases peasants disarmed and arrested the old police. Typical was the situation in Balashov, where local peasants seized officials and turned them over to the town authorities.[40] As was customary in rural Russia, village bathhouses served as detention centers until those arrested were transferred to volost centers.

Evidence suggests that to the peasantry the revolution signified the end of an unfair property system and the beginning of a new era in which those who backed the peasants' timeless claim to the land would now govern. In March 1917 peasant villages sent numerous resolutions and congratulatory messages to the Saratov Soviet, the PEC, the Provisional Government, and the Petrograd Soviet. Peasants patriotically made contributions in money and kind to the army and war cause. But when the government admonished peasants to wait for the promised constituent assembly to resolve the land problem, they began to take independent actions. In Saratov province patterns of rural unrest seen in 1902–3 and 1905–7 now repeated themselves. In March local peasants already expressed dissatisfaction with existing economic relationships. Clashes between large property owners or rich peasants and renters were the most widespread manifestation of peasant unrest at this time. In one village peasants appealed to the Petrograd Soviet to help them work out favorable terms for renting land.[41] But the minor disorders that broke out in March 1917 were only a prelude to what would become a widespread and at times violent peasant movement that aggravated the food situation in the cities and played a major role in bringing down the Provisional Government.

40. A. Zhagar, "Put' k oktiabriu: g. Balashov, Saratovskoi gubernii," *Kommunisticheskii put'*, no. 58 (1926), p. 45. See also the Balashov representative's report at the oblast congress of soviets on March 23 in *Izvestiia Saratovskogo Soveta*, no. 15, March 28, 1917, p. 2.

41. Akademiia nauk SSSR, Institut istorii et al., *Revoliutsionnoe dvizhenie v Rossii posle sverzheniia samoderzhaviia*, ed. L. S. Gaponenko et al. (Moscow, 1957), p. 681.

The nearly simultaneous appearance of the Provisional Government and Petrograd Soviet had fashioned an ambivalent power structure at the national level, which contemporaries called dual power or *dvoevlastie*. Although it acknowledged the legitimacy of the Provisional Government, the Petrograd Soviet commanded real power within Petrograd's working-class districts and garrison; the Provisional Government could not enact any significant legislation or make any important policy announcement without the Soviet's endorsement. With the exception of Kerensky, who accepted the portfolio of minister of justice, the socialist parties within the Soviet abstained from participating in the government. Most socialists interpreted February as a bourgeois revolution and therefore did not wish to be associated with the policies of the new regime until the revolution entered the socialist stage. Meanwhile, the Soviet offered conditional support to the government headed by Prince G. E. L'vov, a government later described by Lenin as "ten capitalist ministers and Kerensky as hostage of the democracy."

In Saratov and elsewhere in the provinces the alignment of political forces differed from that at the national level. True, as in Petrograd both a soviet and a local organ of the Provisional Government were formed. A fairly broad examination of the February Revolution in other provincial towns reveals that there, too, besides soviets, variously titled public executive committees were set up by city dumas, zemstvos, representatives of such public organizations as war industries committees, cooperatives, and industrial enterprises, and by revolutionary activists, soldiers, officers, and workers. What is striking about these new executive committees in such cities as Saratov, Simbirsk, Kazan, Iakutsk, Vladivostok, Baku, Odessa, Minsk, Petrozavodsk, Tashkent, Tomsk, Astrakhan, Rostov-on-the-Don, Tver, Arkhangelsk, Voronezh, Kiev, Samara, and Novgorod—to name a few—is that the majority of soviets not only cooperated closely with them *but took part in them* (and sometimes even formed them), creating broadly representative coalition organs. Local conditions and experiences in each case determined the specific strength of *tsenzovoe obshchestvo* or "census society," the privileged classes of the old regime, vis-à-vis the "democratic" elements. In a few unusual cases, such as Khabarovsk and Nikolaevsk, Bolsheviks headed the local public executive committees. But again, the significance lay in the coalition itself, in the willingness of all political groups to cooperate, perhaps because no one in Russia in March expected a socialist revolution. In fact, the flood of cables and appeals to Kerensky from throughout Russia suggests that the provincial populations took a favorable view of his participation in the otherwise bourgeois government. This particular turn of events has been largely ignored in Western historical literature, while most Soviet historians criticize Bolshevik participation in public executive committees.[42] A striking exception is V. I. Startsev, who recently acknowledged that "perhaps only in Petrograd, the capital of the government, no coalition organ of local power such as a committee of public safety or a committee of public organizations was created."[43]

Before the February Revolution power in provincial Russia had been concentrated in the hands of local governors. Reporting to the Ministry of the Interior, they bore responsibility for the activities of city mayors, police chiefs, town dumas, and zemstvos. The new provisional government circulated a telegram on March 5, replacing tsarist governors with provincial commissars and calling for the removal of the old police. On March 19 the government announced the liquidation of the office of *zemskii nachal'nik* or land captain. The land captains' political functions were to be transferred to newly appointed district commissars and their juridical functions to provisional judges named by the provincial commissars. Furthermore, the government sanctioned the formation of volost executive committees until the zemstvos were reelected. The Provisional Government admonished local authorities to rely on those groups who mustered the most trust among local populations. Yet in Saratov and elsewhere the enormous amount of independent initiative in the very first days of March resulted in local power transfers *before* the government had enacted its decrees. The government merely institutionalized what already had taken place, for the February Revolution had dealt a death blow to centralized government.

The active participation of Saratov socialists in the coalition Public Executive Committee, the emergence of a powerful military committee commanding nearly universal support in the garrison, the soon to be recognized weakness of the City Duma, and the Soviet's growing popularity suggest that dual power inappropriately describes the political situation in Saratov in March 1917. Power was in the streets, waiting to be wielded by those who acted decisively. By the end of March, as the Soviet and Military Committee discussed their merger and the Soviet established control over the Duma, political power in Saratov appeared to be moving toward dual power shared between the Soviet and the PEC. But at this point the impact of the coalition within the PEC and the overriding strength of the socialist parties in Saratov gave an interesting twist to local events. As we shall see in Chapter 3, the PEC quietly faded away, its leadership undermined from the very beginning by the inclusion in it of socialists and representatives of the Saratov Soviet. Political

42. Representative examples can be found in V. I. Tomarev, "Fevral' 1917 goda v Povolzh'e," *Povolzhskii krai*, no. 3 (1975), p. 149, and more recently in A. M. Andreev, *Mestnye Sovety i organy burzhuaznoi vlasti (1917 g.)* (Moscow, 1983), p. 43.

43. V. I. Startsev, *Vnutrenniaia politika Vremennogo Pravitel'stva pervogo sostava* (Leningrad, 1980), p. 198.

developments in Saratov evidently had a logic of their own. It bears repeating that most socialists considered the February Revolution a bourgeois one and hence they did not look upon the Soviet as the focus of political power in the city. Moreover, at the end of March the Petrograd Soviet instructed local soviets to work in conjunction with other organizations and under no circumstances to assume governmental functions. Be that as it may, in Saratov a small number of socialist activists dominated the Soviet, provided leadership for the nonbourgeois political parties, edited their respective party newspapers, participated in the PEC, and gained control over the City Duma. When these same few individuals began to ignore the Public Executive Committee, it simply stopped meeting. In effect a situation bordering on the single power, or *edinovlastie,* of the local soviet was taking shape regardless of any theoretical notions about the nature of the revolution. By the summer of 1917 the real question of political power in Saratov concerned not so much the transfer of power to the Soviet as the outcome of the intrasoviet party fighting barely felt in March, but felt quite noticeably by April.

Nonetheless, for the first month or so after the February Revolution the PEC remained the leading authority in Saratov. Prominent, well-known individuals who led the city's political parties served on the Public Executive Committee. Its membership, initially limited to sixteen, expanded as previously unrepresented interest groups lobbied to be included. The Soviet delegated almost all of its presidium to the PEC: Miliutin, Vasil'ev, Miasoedov, Skvortsov, and Kolesnikov. Among important new members co-opted into the committee were the local Menshevik D. A. Topuridze and officers from the Military Committee. Soon Saratov's lower middle class *(meshchantsvo)* demanded a voice in the PEC and elected four representatives.[44]

In March the Public Executive Committee had to delineate its authority in the presence of competing loci of power—both real and potential—and establish a working relationship with the Provisional Government. In Saratov, as in many towns, the consolidation of a new administration demanded a reorganization of the police force, alleviation of food-supply problems, and liquidation of vestiges of the tsarist regime. Since soldiers and workers had arrested members of the tsarist political police and gendarmes during the evening of March 1–2, the establishment of a new police force had particular urgency. The setting up of a new militia, as the police were to be called, revealed all the ambiguities of the post-February political settlement.

44. *Saratovskii vestnik,* no. 55, March 9, 1917, p. 3.

In the first days of March the Saratov Soviet worked out a plan for the creation of a people's militia to keep order in the city and protect Saratov's factories and plants. After having drafted the proposal for the people's militia, the Soviet turned the project over to the Public Executive Committee, which officially replaced the former police with the new militia on March 9. A. A. Minkh, who took charge of the security forces, announced that students, workers, and soldiers had responded enthusiastically to the call to enlist in the militia, and that by March 5, 400 students and 400 workers had already expressed their willingness to serve.[45] Although the PEC had chosen Minkh as well as neighborhood police chiefs, the regulations drawn up by the Soviet gave it the right to supervise the militia's activities. The Soviet also had a direct hand in selecting the factory militia, or *druzhina.* Factory committees submitted lists of eligible workers to the Soviet's Executive Committee, which in turn selected the militiamen *(druzhiniki).* Despite the uncertainty of what Soviet supervision over the activities of the militia actually meant, the creation of a new security force proceeded smoothly except for a debate over what should be done with the tsarist gendarmes arrested during the February days. Declaring their allegiance to the new order from their prison cells, the tsarist police petitioned that the healthy among them be given the opportunity to serve at the front, and that the sick and old be taken back into service. It is impossible to say with any assurance what became of this proposal.[46]

In the immediate aftermath of the February Revolution, the PEC, Soviet, and people's militia sought to preserve order and gain the population's trust. The new administration faced serious problems inherited from the old regime, as well as a host of new ones created by the revolution itself. As in the past, newspaper editors fretted over the large number of haunts in and near Saratov where thieves and other criminals hid.[47] Another matter attracting broad concern was public drunkenness. In March the Public Executive Committee issued proclamations calling for the curtailment of alcohol consumption, and announced stringent measures against anyone who sold illegal spirits or who was arrested for

45. *Revoliutsionnoe dvizhenie posle sverzheniia samoderzhaviia,* pp. 32–34; *Saratovskii vestnik,* no. 51, March 5, 1917, p. 4. (A Provisional Government decree calling for the formation of temporary militias to replace the old police first circulated on March 22.)

46. V. S. Gol'dman claims that many tsarist gendarmes kept their posts in the new power structure, but it is difficult to say with any assurance how widespread this practice may have been ("Istoriia sozdaniia i uprocheniia Saratovskogo Soveta rabochikh, krest'ianskikh, krasnoarmeiskikh i kazach'ikh deputatov v 1917–1918 gg.," candidate dissertation, Leningrad Law Institute, 1954, p. 65).

47. See, for example, *Pochta,* no. 61, March 8, 1917, p. 3.

intoxication.[48] Rumors abounded, though newspaper articles repeatedly attempted to dispel them. Yet another problem involved both criminal elements and zealous revolutionaries who conducted illegal searches, confiscations, and arrests. The PEC had to assure the citizenry that confiscation of weapons and searches were invalid unless they were carried out under orders signed by the PEC and Soviet.[49] The PEC, in its desire to dissipate rumors, instituted censorship of all pamphlets and brochures. It also established an information commission to coordinate lectures and discussions on political problems.

Recent studies on Petrograd, Moscow, Latvia, Baku, and Siberia document the destabilizing impact of food shortages on the course of the revolution at the local level. As a food-producing region, Saratov at this time was spared the nagging food shortages that aggravated social tensions elsewhere. But fear of reduced rations heightened tensions, while inflated prices and transportation problems made it hard to obtain commodities that were not produced locally. As a supply center for other areas, Saratov faced constant pressure to guarantee that the flow of raw grain from the villages and processed grain from Saratov mills did not taper off. Naturally, the matter of food supplies had top priority for the new administration in Saratov. The Soviet formed a food-supply committee at one of its very first meetings and the PEC created a food-supply department for the whole city, made up of representatives of all prominent public organizations. According to newspaper accounts, food speculation was rife in March and rumors abounded that mill owners had hoarded caches of grain. Forming a commission to investigate these matters, the PEC set up a food-supply organ for the entire province. At a provincial conference of food-supply committees, delegates elected a presidium to coordinate intraprovincial matters. Before long supply committees functioned at the uezd, volost, and in some cases factory level. Meanwhile the Saratov Soviet outlined a detailed plan for electing a food-supply assembly for the city. The plan called for the election of one delegate for every 600 inhabitants, about 400 in all. These elections, the first general, secret ones ever held in town, may have strengthened the politically unsophisticated masses' trust in the new order, especially in the Soviet, which announced that any necessary reductions in food items would be the same for all social groups. *Saratovskii listok* reported that public participation in the regulation of food supplies helped curb grain speculation considerably.[50]

Another sensitive problem facing the new order in Saratov in the

48. *Saratovskii listok*, no. 53, March 8, 1917, p. 4.

49. Ibid., no. 52, March 7, 1917, p. 3; *Pochta*, no. 60, March 7, 1917, p. 2.

50. *Pochta*, no. 72, March 22, 1917, p. 1; *Saratovskii vestnik*, no. 64, March 22, 1917, p. 1; *Saratovskii listok*, no. 64, March 22, 1917, pp. 1, 3.

spring of 1917 involved democratization of the city and town dumas and zemstvos, elected by "census society." After the Duma rejected a proposal to add delegates from the Soviet, the Military Committee, and the sizable Jewish population, the Soviet took the lead in trying to democratize the City Duma by means of general elections. Succumbing to such pressure from the Soviet, the Duma agreed to double its membership to eighty while excusing present members from submitting to reelection. But only eight of the forty new members were to be chosen by the Soviet and the remainder by the propertied, commercial, and professional classes.[51] By a vote of 9 to 8 the Public Executive Committee barely approved the Duma's recommendation, which strained the relationship between socialists and liberals within the PEC. Despite the support of the PEC, the Duma realized that it was marked for change. A meeting in mid-March was "boring and listless, like a funeral feast after the burial of the old order."[52] The Duma failed to meet again until April 19, further revealing its weakness and growing obsolescence. During this time the Soviet and Military Committee criticized the Duma's proposal, "since representatives of the genuine democracy would be included in the Duma in an altogether trifling proportion."[53] On March 30 the Soviet issued an alternative plan drawn up by the Bolshevik Lebedev. Each political party would present its municipal program and slate of candidates. The population would vote for parties and programs; candidates would be picked proportionately, according to the percentage of the total vote a given party had received. The plan also demanded that present Duma members submit to reelection. The PEC had no choice but to adopt the Soviet's project in full.

Change came more smoothly to the provincial zemstvo, which succumbed to pressures to broaden its constituency more willingly than the Duma. Yet even here friction colored the transformation that took place. Declaring its allegiance to the Provisional Government, the Saratov uezd zemstvo organized a temporary committee charged with the task of keeping abreast of political developments. On March 5 the zemstvo met with representatives of various political groups to discuss broadening its membership. At this meeting a rumor spread that delegates from the Soviet had not been allowed to participate. A large crowd of angry workers soon assembled to protest the alleged exclusion of representatives

51. *Izvestiia Saratovskoi gorodskoi dumy*, 1917, pp. 84–86, 91; also in *Saratovskii listok*, no. 61, March 18, 1917, p. 3.

52. *Saratovskii listok*, no. 66, March 24, 1917, p. 3.

53. Ibid., no. 64, March 22, 1917, p. 3; *Izvestiia Saratovskogo Soveta*, no. 11, March 21, 1917, p. 1; A. I. Lepeshkin, *Mestnye organy vlasti Sovetskogo gosudarstva (1917–1920 gg.)* (Moscow, 1957), p. 102.

from the Soviet and even threatened the zemstvo leaders. Only after a student convinced the workers that its delegates were taking part in the proceedings did the people disperse. The zemstvo, having already received a reorganization proposal from the All-Russian Zemstvo Union, accepted a plan drawn up by the Soviet to revamp volost zemstvos on the basis of universal suffrage.[54]

Existing historical literature does not illuminate the relationship between the Provisional Government and its local organs; therefore, attempts to work out a hierarchical institutional relationship in Saratov merit attention. Two congresses of executive committees from Saratov province took place in Saratov in March. Called prematurely before all of the districts' representatives assembled, the first congress dealt only with the issue of prisoners of war, resolving that they should work for the families of drafted peasants and banning their cheap hire by prosperous farmers and landowners.[55] Opening on March 26, the more important second congress discussed the role and functions of the executive committees at all levels and their relationship to the national government. The congress did not always proceed smoothly, in part because it consisted of delegates representing a variety of political leanings.[56] The major resolution passed by the congress stated that the official organs of the Provisional Government at the local level were the executive committees of the province, uezds, and volosts, and where warranted of the cities, villages, and settlements. These temporary bodies would be replaced by permanent institutions through universal direct election. Recognized as the provincial executive committee, the Saratov PEC would be enlarged to include representatives from the districts.[57] At the same time the Saratov PEC announced that apart from its administrative functions, it would strengthen the new order by exhibiting "law-governed controls" over the activities of all local governmental and public institutions, organize elections to democratize elective bodies, promote the formation of trade unions, and support the army and all institutions working for defense.[58] The Saratov PEC certainly saw itself as the legitimate successor to the old order.

Public executive committees in March 1917 were compelled to take

54. *Pochta*, no. 60, March 7, 1917, p. 3; *Saratovskii Sovet*, p. 56; V. K. Medvedev, "Saratovskii Sovet ot fevralia k oktiabriu 1917 g.," *Uchenye zapiski Saratovskoi oblastnoi partiinoi shkoly*, no. 1 (1948), p. 60.

55. G. A. Gerasimenko et al., eds., *Khronika revoliutsionnykh sobytii v Saratovskom Povolzh'e, 1917–1918 gg.* (Saratov, 1968), p. 18 (hereafter cited as *Khronika*).

56. See *Saratovskii listok*, no. 70, March 30, 1917, p. 5.

57. *Saratovskii vestnik*, no. 72, April 2, 1917, p. 5.

58. Ibid. The Provisional Government's circular called upon the chairmen of the local zemstvo boards to replace governors. See *Sbornik tsirkuliarov Ministerstva Vnutrennykh del za period mart–iiun' 1917 goda* (Petrograd, 1917), p. 5.

local conditions into account when they considered directives from the Provisional Government. Crucial issues were decided on the spot. At the local level the new administrative organs had to bow to public sentiment and rely on their own resources to keep order. In the provinces, as opposed to Petrograd, the state structure almost immediately began to yield to pressures from progressive forces. The Saratov PEC, for example, had elected Semenov provincial commissar before the L'vov government had appointed K. N. Grimm to the same post. Upon receiving the government's announcement of Grimm's appointment, the Saratov PEC wired Petrograd that if the government wanted support in the provinces it was imperative that it "appoint representatives of the new order only in exceptional cases and only when elected public committees were not yet formed in a given locality." Grimm, incidentally, declined the post, whereupon the government accepted Semenov's appointment. The Kamyshin Public Executive Committee also rejected the Provisional Government's appointee and instead elected its own district commissar. Responding to local pressure, committees elsewhere in the province removed individuals who did not enjoy the local population's trust.[59]

The Saratov Public Executive Committee and uezd committees as well had to contend with continual pressure from the ubiquitous garrisons and soviets. As part of the Kazan Military District, the Volga provinces served as the most important center for the formation of reserve troops. The 150,000 soldiers and officers stationed in Saratov province alone made it a major training center in the rear. After Kazan, Saratov housed the largest garrison in the region, and another sizable garrison of about 20,000 soldiers was located in Tsaritsyn. In March 1917 the 60,000-man Saratov garrison consisted of three reserve regiments, two artillery brigades, two machine-gun regiments, two artillery units, and the 692nd infantry troop guard or druzhina.[60] The local revolution would have unfolded altogether differently had it not been for the presence of so many troops.

The unusual history of the Saratov Military Committee serves as a striking example of the breakdown of the state structure and atomization of power at the local level after February. It also demonstrates the popularity of socialist tendencies within the army. Until the Military Committee merged with the Soviet on June 1, the MC represented a potent political force in the city. Despite opposition from the garrison command and the PEC, rank-and-file soldiers and junior officers had elected a permanent military committee on March 5, made up of forty officers and eighty soldiers. The committee named General Major Gaase, commander

59. Vas'kin and Gerasimenko, *Fevral'skaia revoliutsiia*, pp. 88–90.
60. Vas'kin, "Soldaty Nizhnego Povolzh'ia," pp. 91–93.

of the 108th Army Brigade, as head of the garrison. Second Lieutenant Pontriagin assumed the chairmanship of the MC and directed the nine-member Presidium, which included only one Bolshevik, the soldier Vasilii Kulikov, who also sat on the Presidium of the Soviet's Military Section. Other important members of the Presidium were the SR soldier and former teacher M. T. Didenko; the SR Captain Stankevich; the well-known Popular Socialist ophthalmologist N. I. Maksimovich, who was elected to his party's city committee as well; and the SR N. Megaritskii. The Ukrainian SR Second Lieutenant N. S. Neimichenko became the MC's first representative to the PEC. Pontriagin, Didenko, and Neimichenko, who later emerged as leaders within the Soviet, were among the most determined opponents of the Bolsheviks' bid for an all-socialist government in October. The relatively junior rank of most of these officers and their adherence to populist parties bore heavily on local politics. During the war junior line officers had advanced rapidly from lower to middle ranks; with the collapse of the old command structure, they surfaced as leaders of the new revolutionary army. Not surprisingly, the MC's published protocols reveal that conflicts arose between the younger junior officers and older cadre soldiers sitting on the committee.[61]

The manner in which the Saratov Military Committee emerged says a great deal about local initiative during the revolution. On March 6 the commander of the Kazan Military District issued Order 412, announcing the formation of the Kazan Military Committee and calling for the establishment of similar committees within the district. The order reached the garrison commands of Saratov province on March 10–11. But the Saratov Military Committee had already been elected on March 5; similar committees had arisen in Rtishchevo, Pokrovsk, Petrovsk, Kuznetsk, and Novouzensk between March 4 and 7, days before the arrival of Order 412. Moreover, on March 9 the Saratov MC had sent delegates to neighboring towns to promote the election of military committees where they had not yet been formed. Like the Saratov MC, those in the district towns elected deputies according to a 2-to-1 ratio of soldiers to officers, thus departing from Order 412's recommendation of an equal number of soldiers and officers.[62] Independent initiative ruled in this matter.

As it turned out, the activities of the Saratov Military Committee soon went far beyond the intentions of Order 412, which called for the creation of military committees "to regulate questions of internal affairs of a

61. *Protokoly zasedaniia Saratovskogo Voennogo Komiteta* (Saratov, 1917), no. 12, March 24, p. 5; no. 16, March 31, p. 12.

62. Vas'kin and Gerasimenko, *Fevral'skaia revoliutsiia*, pp. 113–15; I. M. Ionenko, *Soldaty tylovykh garnizonov v bor'be za vlast' sovetov (Po materialam Povolzh'ia i Urala)* (Kazan, 1976), p. 113.

unit and to consider needs of an everyday nature." Ignoring the restrictions established by Order 412, the Saratov MC successfully limited the power of the command, forced the garrison and unit commanders to subordinate themselves to it, and interfered in the activities of other military committees. Born of controversy, the MC faced opposition from staff officers throughout March. When they demanded the dismissal of the Military Committee in mid-March, however, they found themselves under arrest. The MC then elevated its own candidate to the post of commander of the Fourteenth Infantry Brigade, thereby infringing on the prerogative of the commander of the Kazan District. The MC also bypassed several colonels who would normally have been elevated to the command post before its candidate. Back on March 6, the MC had established a special personnel commission of officers and soldiers to replace officers who had been arrested during the February Revolution. Afterward this commission continued to function, involving itself in the investigation of soldiers' complaints against officers and replacing them when such action seemed necessary.[63] Toward the end of March, officers, military officials, and medical personnel who had formed a republican officers' club that excluded enlisted men tested the MC's authority by declaring that any resolution passed by the club would be binding on the Military Committee. But the MC held its ground, ruling that any potential measures taken by the officers had to be cleared by the MC first.[64]

The existence of the MC did not weaken military discipline. The revolution had done that. Even though soldiers constituted two-thirds of the committee's membership and few cadre officers were elected to it, the MC took a strong stand against insubordination. To be sure, the Military Committee occasionally found itself at odds with its constituency, especially when it tried to release some officers arrested on March 2.[65] Thereafter the MC acted more carefully, maintaining order by availing itself of the general enthusiasm unleashed by the revolution and by appealing to the soldiers' patriotism. When deserters began to return to their units after the revolution had triumphed, the Military Committee in most cases granted pardons.[66] An estimated 600 soldiers imprisoned locally for desertion were sent back to their regiments.[67] The MC also issued a mandate to the entire garrison delimiting the responsibilities of both soldiers and officers. Calling for the strengthening of the new system and

63. The extraordinary power of the Saratov Military Committee was an exception in the Lower Volga region. See Vas'kin and Gerasimenko, *Fevral'skaia revoliutsiia*, pp. 120–22.

64. *Protokoly zasedaniia Saratovskogo Voennogo Komiteta*, no. 13, March 26, pp. 5–6.

65. Vas'kin, "Iz istorii bor'by," p. 104.

66. *Saratovskii vestnik*, no. 58, March 14, 1917, p. 5; *Pochta*, no. 62, March 9, 1917, p. 3.

67. *Saratovskii listok*, no. 52, March 7, 1917, p. 3.

supporting order and discipline in the army, the mandate served as a guide for the garrison until a regional conference of military organizations substituted another.[68] Yet officers remained uneasy about, if not mistrustful of, their troops, who pushed to initiate their own version of Order Number 1. Published by the Petrograd Soviet during the first week of March, the document authorized the election of soldier and sailor committees with broad administrative authority, and made local military units responsible to the Petrograd Soviet. Although intended for the Petrograd garrison, the order spread throughout the armed forces as military units everywhere emulated it. Paradoxically, as Allan K. Wildman has argued, Order Number 1 helped curb excessive revolutionary ardor and had a stabilizing effect on the army at this time.[69]

The Saratov Soviet printed the text of Order Number 1—without any accompanying editorial—a few days after the order was written. Within days the spirit of Order Number 1 had inspired the creation of democratically elected soldier committees at the company, battery, detachment, and regimental level, which gave soldiers a direct, lower-level vehicle for expressing their aspirations. By March 15, company committees had been formed in the majority of units in the Saratov garrison and other garrisons in the province. Most committees seem to have been elected by the soldiers themselves, though officers subsequently tended to play a prominent role in them. Occasionally these committees excluded officers. Apart from company committees, the Saratov Soviet also organized regimental soldier committees, made up exclusively of soldiers who were Soviet deputies. Elsewhere in the region officers participated in regimental committees along with soldiers.[70]

The Saratov Soviet's call for the election of regimental military committees guaranteed the army's further politicization and required the Military Committee to compete with the Soviet for the soldiers' support. During March the Soviet laid the foundation for later popularity in the garrison. On March 3 workers went to the barracks to urge soldiers to elect delegates to the Soviet. By March 6, fifty garrison representatives had joined the Soviet, which assumed the title Saratov Soviet of Workers' and Soldiers' Deputies.[71] Electing two delegates from each company—with no special preference given to officers—common soldiers were actually more broadly represented in the Soviet than in the MC, which contained a fixed number of officers. Not until the end of March,

68. *Izvestiia Saratovskogo Soveta*, no. 8, March 17, 1917, p. 3; Antonov-Saratovskii, *Pod stiagom*, pp. 286–88.

69. Allan K. Wildman, *The End of the Imperial Army: The Old Army and the Soldiers' Revolt (March–April 1917)* (Princeton, 1980), pp. 191–98.

70. Vas'kin and Gerasimenko, *Fevral'skaia revoliutsiia*, pp. 128–33.

71. Gol'dman, "Istoriia sozdaniia i uprocheniia Saratovskogo Soveta," p. 61.

when the Soviet created a military section, would its influence over garrison units grow.

The Bolshevik P. A. Lebedev has argued that the Military Committee functioned more as an administrative than as a political organ, thus liberating the Executive Committee of the Soviet from mundane worries. Yet Lebedev insists that the Soviet was not able to trust the Military Committee, that competing interests led to conflict at this time.[72] The Military Committee strove to delineate the rights and responsibilities of each organ. It sought to preserve the loyalties of the revolutionary army to the Provisional Government and consequently viewed certain actions taken by the Soviet with alarm. The MC wanted the Soviet to deal only with "activities of a general civilian nature," such as political issues. At a meeting of the presidiums of both bodies the MC voiced its opposition to discussion of the end of the war with the masses. It demanded that political slogans be discouraged and the proposed eight-hour workday be postponed, that questions of internal order not be discussed in the military units, and that all leaflets prepared by the Soviet for the troops submit to military censorship.[73] The MC proved equally hostile to any debate on the seizure of land. In line with pronouncements of the Petrograd Soviet, the Saratov MC passed a resolution calling for a continuation of the war "to a victorious end" and summoning the government "to publish conditions upon which Russia and her allies could conclude peace."[74]

During March the Saratov Military Committee coordinated the first regional (oblast) conference of military committees held in Russia after the February Revolution. Representing thirty-nine military organizations in the area, the district meeting convened in Saratov on March 27, under the chairmanship of Korvin-Krukovskii, head of the Saratov officer training school.[75] After debating the character of the war, delegates passed a resolution based on the peace program put forth by the Provisional Government and Petrograd Soviet, which supported the carrying out of the war to a victorious end, but without annexations and indemnities. The delegates likewise accepted in principle self-determination for ethnic minorities, neutralization of the Straits, and the formula "peace but no armistice." When the delegates discussed the Provisional Government, some representatives from the rank and file spoke out strongly against it.

72. P. A. Lebedev, "Fevral'–oktiabr' v Saratove," *Proletarskaia revoliutsiia*, no. 10 (1922), p. 250.

73. Vas'kin, "Iz istorii bor'by," pp. 105–6.

74. *Saratovskii vestnik*, no. 58, March 14, 1917, p. 5.

75. *Saratovskii listok*, no. 68, March 28, 1917, p. 3. There is no consensus on the number of military organizations represented. *Saratovskii vestnik* cites 40 organizations (no. 69, March 29, 1917, p. 5), while *Khronika* claims there were 54 (p. 30).

But the majority voted to support the government, provided it worked closely with the Petrograd Soviet, which, the resolution added, should be enlarged to include representatives of military organizations, soviets of workers' deputies, and peasant congresses from all of Russia. The statement admonished the Petrograd Soviet, however, not to undermine the Provisional Government by issuing orders of national significance.[76]

Opinions differed most over the issue of the eight-hour workday. Fearing the curtailment of production of military equipment, many speakers argued that introduction of a shortened workday should be postponed until after the war. Following lively debate, the delegates agreed to the introduction of the eight-hour day, but only by governmental decree; they demanded that the Provisional Government and All-Russian Soviet jointly examine the industrial crisis, particularly in defense-related industries. If it were to do so, their declarations declared, "We believe that we can boldly tell our comrades in the trenches 'don't spare shells.'" Finally, the conference adopted a series of mandates delineating the functions and responsibilities of the various military organs. The powers of the lower-level regimental and company committees were now curtailed, except for disciplinary functions. These last measures marked an attempt to instill order and discipline into the fluid situation that emerged after February. But it already may have been too late.

The Saratov Soviet even more than the Military Committee came to rival the political authority of the Public Executive Committee. Within a week of the Soviet's creation approximately 60 percent of the industrial enterprises in town had elected deputies to it. Resembling the joint workers' and soldiers' councils in Petrograd, Krasnoiarsk, Kronstadt, and other towns rather than the separate soldiers' and workers' soviets that had emerged in Moscow, Kharkov, Odessa, Kiev, and elsewhere, the Saratov Soviet was divided into a workers' and soldiers' section, each with its own presidium, directed by a joint "Presidium of the Executive Committee." SR officers controlled the Soldiers' Section, formed at the end of March, while intelligenty and professionals dominated the Workers' Section. By April the Soldiers' Section and the SR officers in particular began to attract much of the support previously enjoyed by the Military Committee.[77]

Organizational matters consumed most of the Soviet's energies in March. Initially it met daily, but later it convened regularly three times a week. The Executive Committee continued to hold disorderly, nonagenda sessions each day; when faced with usually pressing problems, it

76. *Saratovskii vestnik*, no. 70, March 30, 1917, pp. 3–4; no. 72, April 2, p. 5.
77. Lebedev, "Fevral'–oktiabr' v Saratove," p. 2.

called extemporaneous meetings. It formed committees to handle specific needs and set up additional committees as the functions of the Soviet diversified further. Bombarded by requests from across the province for agitators and literature, the Soviet also established a department for provincial matters, which supervised a collective of agitators. The size and importance of these committees changed frequently during the following months as different needs arose and as representation in the Soviet expanded. The Executive Committee increased its membership for the same reason. Often prominent activists returning from exile, such as Antonov and Lebedev, both of whom were widely respected in labor circles, were promptly co-opted into it.

By the end of March the Executive Committee had expanded to twenty-four members, considerably strengthening the representation of the heretofore underrepresented SRs. The Soviet plenum elected at large fifteen delegates and the political parties chose the remaining nine. (The Trudoviks, SRs, SDs, and Military Committee had two representatives on the committee, and the Bund one.)[78] Varying in size from five to nine during its first month, the Presidium contained only one SR delegate until after the formation of the Soldiers' Section, when SR strength significantly increased. Bolsheviks played a leading role in the Presidium; in early April three of five members belonged to the party and somewhat later six of nine members were Bolsheviks.[79] Miliutin, Khrynin, and Vasil'ev helped launch the Soviet's newspaper, *Izvestiia Saratovskogo Soveta* (News of the Saratov Soviet), which first went to press on March 5. Antonov accounted for Bolshevik strength within the Executive Committee, unusual for this time, by underscoring the existence of a sizable group of old underground activists in town on the eve of the February Revolution, and "the group, perhaps rare for the provinces, of theoretically versed old-guard intellectuals."[80] Some of these intelligenty, such as Miliutin, who belonged to the moderate wing of the party, enjoyed popularity among non-Bolshevik revolutionaries. Considerable goodwill prevailed in the spring of 1917, and in this atmosphere of camaraderie one's overall stature and length of service in the revolutionary underground counted more than party affiliation. Finally,

78. *Izvestiia Saratovskogo Soveta*, no. 18, April 2, 1917, p. 2. Razgon gives more complete statistics. According to him, 37 members eventually sat on the Executive Committee, of whom 16 were Bolsheviks, 10 were Mensheviks, 3 were SRs, 1 was a PS, and 7 did not belong to any party. See "Sovety Srednego i Nizhnego Povolzh'ia v bor'be za demokraticheskie perevybory gorodskogo samoupravleniia (mart–avgust 1917 g.)," in *Oktiabr' i grazhdanskaia voina v* SSSR (Moscow, 1966), p. 121.

79. A. I. Razgon, "O sostave sovetov Nizhnego Povolzh'ia v marte-aprele 1917 g.," in *Sovety i soiuz rabochego klassa i krest'ianstva v Oktiabr'skoi revoliutsii* (Moscow, 1964), p. 115.

80. Antonov-Saratovskii, "Saratov s fevralia," p. 178.

the Bolshevik Initiative Group, formed in 1916 by worker activists, contributed to the party's influence after February. Infiltrating all possible legal channels, the group had revived party cells in the largest factories on the eve of 1917.

In the first weeks of March the Saratov Soviet tried to keep in line with the Petrograd Soviet and Provisional Government on all national issues, but otherwise bowed to local pressures. On such matters as the eight-hour day and the war the Executive Committee hesitated to take a stand until it ascertained "what Kerensky and Chkheidze think." Some deputies criticized such caution. The Polish Bolshevik Ia. G. Fenigshtein complained that the Soviet "has no program, and is only an information organ."[81] Grumbling that the Executive Committee had done little to organize them, soldiers disrupted one of the committee's first meetings. Pressed by demands for action, the Soviet sent representatives to Petrograd and Moscow to observe the political situation there. But there still remained a hunger for news, policy guidelines, and directives, while great confusion reigned among Saratov socialists over what the actual role of soviets should be, especially because the local soviet had become so unexpectedly influential. Some held that soviets should function as support organs of the Provisional Government; some saw them as watchmen over the bourgeois government; still others viewed them as temporary organs that should disband after lower-level factory committees and unions had been organized.

Following the example of the Petrograd Soviet, the Saratov Soviet voiced support for the Provisional Government, but encouraged it to enact basic social and economic reforms even before a constituent assembly was called.[82] The Saratov Bolsheviks, endorsing this expression of support for the new government, were in line with the party's Central Committee in Petrograd. On matters of local urgency the Saratov Soviet acted more authoritatively, so that its relations with the Public Executive Committee became strained. Some members of the Soviet's Presidium wanted to ignore the PEC altogether, but the Bolshevik Vasil'ev cautioned that the Soviet must work from within the committee "in order to influence it."[83] In March the Soviet had taken the initiative in reorganizing the police and the city's food-supply apparatus, prompting one deputy to argue that the government should actually subsidize the Soviet. Later, when the PEC requested an account of the Soviet's activities, it agreed to provide one, but only if the PEC submitted a similar report to the workers' and soldiers' soviet.[84] It displayed equal boldness dealing with the City Duma's reluctance to democratize itself.

81. *Saratovskii Sovet*, pp. 20–23, 37.
82. Osipov, *1917 god v Saratovskoi gubernii*, p. 49.
83. *Saratovskii Sovet*, p. 29.
84. Ibid., pp. 35–36.

In March the Soviet scored significant success in organizing the working class. A confusingly overlapping network of organizational units emerged, connecting workers to the Soviet, to the various parties, and to each other. Factory committees and to a lesser extent trade unions were the most important of these lower-level organs. At its very first meeting the Soviet had decided to organize factory committees; within two months all but the smallest enterprises in Saratov had elected them. The workers' initiative threatened industrialists and managers, who frequently refused to recognize the workers' organizations. One reason for management's suspicion of factory committees may well have been the initiative they took in organizing factory militias, which on their own accord arrested administrators who belonged to the Black Hundreds.[85] In some factories the committees completely overshadowed union organizations; elsewhere factory committees lacked purposeful initiative. But more often than not, they wielded considerable influence despite lack of authorization. As one activist recommended, the committees should "act on their own risk and responsibility without waiting for directives."[86] Trade union development attained unprecedented expansion as well, but the unions were overshadowed from the start by factory committees and played only a minor role in Saratov politics in 1917. The Saratov Soviet continued to devote more attention to factory committees than to unions. As we shall see in Chapter 4, factory committees were instrumental in achieving the eight-hour workday in individual Saratov enterprises, thus ensuring their popularity with workers.

As the Soviet was reaching agreements on labor disputes, the war issue became manifest. It soon became the most important political matter facing the Saratov Soviet and inaugurated a debate that strained relations among socialists within the Soviet. Because of the primacy of the war issue, developments in Petrograd directly influenced its interpretation at the local level. Most of the leaders of the Petrograd Soviet were internationalists. When Irakli Tsereteli returned to Petrograd from Siberian exile in mid-March, he propagated his theory of Siberian Zimmerwaldism, which sought to unify world socialism through the old International and thereby to apply pressure on the belligerent powers to conclude peace. The coalition of Mensheviks and moderate SRs that controlled the Petrograd Soviet and many provincial councils during much of 1917 accepted this view. Although opposed to the war in principle, the moderate socialist coalition argued that defense of one's country

85. *Izvestiia Saratovskogo Soveta*, no. 16, March 29, 1917, p. 2; *Saratovskii Sovet*, p. 58; E. D. Rumiantsev, "Fabrichno-zavodskaia militsiia i ee deiatel'nost' v Povolzh'e (mart–leto 1917 goda)," in *Ocherki istorii narodov Povolzh'ia i Priuralia*. No. 4, *Obshchestvenno-politicheskoe dvizhenie i klassovaia bor'ba na Srednei Volge (konets XIX–nachalo XX veka)* (Kazan, 1972), pp. 78–88, especially pp. 79–80.

86. *Izvestiia Saratovskogo Soveta*, no. 18, April 2, 1917, p. 2.

was justified in some instances. This blending of defensism with internationalism, known as revolutionary defensism, proved acceptable to most Russian socialists and became the policy of the Petrograd Soviet.

Saratov socialists accepted revolutionary defensism and adhered to the Petrograd Soviet's policy statements on the war; at first, however, they took a stand that was more conservative than revolutionary defensism. In early March, the Soviet's newspaper—like the local liberal papers—often called for "war to a victorious end." Even Saratov Bolsheviks, while remaining leery of defensism and eager to find out the position of their central committee, acquiesced to the formula. At Soviet meetings Vasil'ev cautioned that the local Bolsheviks must not make independent judgments, but must "wait for the decisions of the central organs." Although Miliutin suggested that defensism was wrong, he supported Vasil'ev. On March 19 Vasil'ev proposed that the Saratov Soviet accept the recent peace formulation announced by the Petrograd Soviet. Commenting on the text of the Petrograd Soviet's document, Vasil'ev noted that it should have emphasized "even more emphatically" the inadmissibility of a separate peace.[87] Soviet historians criticize these "errors" of the Saratov Bolsheviks, but in view of both local conditions in the spring of 1917 and the equivocal behavior of the party center in Petrograd, the Saratov Bolsheviks' actions made perfect political sense.

On March 14 the Petrograd Soviet requested the Saratov Soviet to organize a regional (oblast) conference of soviets, and in the meanwhile to function as a regional organizational and informational organ. Saratov's selection as a district center reflected the comparative success of the revolutionary underground here in the past and recognition of the Saratov Soviet's role in local politics after February. Convening on March 23, the conference had the distinction of being the first of its kind in the entire country. More than thirty delegates from sixteen urban centers and the village of Arkadak attended; most of the uezd towns in Saratov province sent delegates, as did the Astrakhan, Orenburg, Penza, Samara, Uralsk, and Cheliabinsk soviets. The delegates' registration forms indicate that seasoned revolutionaries controlled the soviets represented, and that only five had joined the revolutionary movement after 1910. Half of the representatives classified themselves as intelligenty; 41 percent listed themselves as workers, two-thirds of them in the metal-processing industry. A breakdown by party membership shows that Social Democrats had strong backing in the urban centers. Twenty-four delegates listed themselves as SDs, nine as SRs, one belonged to the Bund, and one listed no affiliation. The conference mandate commission

87. *Saratovskii Sovet*, pp. 31, 49.

did not differentiate between Menshevik and Bolshevik delegates, undoubtedly because many of the local committees were united at this time (Astrakhan, Orenburg, Penza, Tsaritsyn, Cheliabinsk). According to the Soviet historian A. I. Razgon, Mensheviks "represented not less than 40 percent" of the Social Democratic representation.[88]

Dealing with issues that would be discussed at the First All-Russian Conference of Soviets, which was to open in Petrograd on March 27, the Volga conference adopted resolutions on the war, on the soviets' relationship to the Provisional Government, and on local government. In commenting on the proceedings a member of the Saratov Soviet observed that "in general political matters, the conduct of the Petrograd Soviet apparently found universal approval."[89] Reflecting the revolutionary defensism of the Petrograd Soviet, the declaration passed on the war implicitly opposed Miliukov's recent statement that the "peace without annexations" formula advocated by the Petrograd Soviet was a "German formula." The Volga-area resolution declared that the war "must be liquidated in the shortest period and in the name of the interests of the revolution," and peace conditions must exclude any annexations or indemnities. The Petrograd Soviet was urged to promote international proletarian solidarity in the cause of peace and help convene a conference of international socialist parties. The local appeal likewise called upon the Petrograd Soviet to demand an open declaration from the Provisional Government denouncing aggressive military plans. The slogans "Down with the War" and "War to a Victorious End" were "equally recognized as inadmissible." Turning to the Provisional Government, the conference voiced the well-known "insofar as" (*postol'ku, poskol'ku*) proviso of the Petrograd Soviet. Recognizing the government as "that power which at the present time, under the control of the people, can retain and strengthen the achievements of the revolution," the Saratov conference of soviets agreed to back it "but only insofar as" it took into account the basic policy premises of the Petrograd Soviet, including the early convocation of a constituent assembly.[90]

Criticizing "antidemocratic" and "reactionary" institutions elected under old property qualifications, the conference endorsed the immediate democratization of local government by means of universal, direct, secret balloting.[91] It also elected a provisional oblast bureau consisting of the Saratov Bolshevik Lebedev, the Mensheviks Maizel' and

88. Razgon, "O sostave sovetov," pp. 88–95.

89. *Saratovskii Sovet*, p. 59.

90. *Saratovskii vestnik*, no. 68, March 28, 1917, pp. 3–4; *Saratovskii listok*, no. 68, March 28, 1917, p. 3; *Saratovskii Sovet*, p. 66; and *Izvestiia Saratovskogo Soveta*, no. 17, March 30, 1917, p. 2.

91. *Proletarii Povolzh'ia*, no. 1, March 29, 1917, p. 4; *Izvestiia Saratovskogo Soveta*, no. 17, March 30, 1917, pp. 2–3.

Guterman, and representatives from Orenburg and Astrakhan. The Volga-area bureau, however, did no more than fulfill informational functions until the fall of 1917. As Vasil'ev later explained, "each large town was preoccupied with its own concerns, and conditions in the Volga area were not appropriate for coordination [of policies] at that time."[92]

Political party organizations came into their own in March 1917. To do justice to the rich texture of local politics, it is necessary to mention not only the major parties but the secondary political groups as well. Among the more colorful were those that stood at the extremes of the political spectrum, the anarchists and the conservative monarchists. The few scattered references to Saratov anarchists suggest that they occasionally exerted considerable influence. In September 1917, in the wake of the Kornilov Affair, Saratov anarchist groups briefly published a newspaper that attracted the worried concern of the Saratov Soviet. They surfaced again in May 1918, when they participated in an attempt to overthrow Bolshevik power in town. More is known about the conservative right in Saratov, viewed so suspiciously by liberal and socialist elements. On March 2, it will be recalled, soldiers arrested monarchists, police officials, and Black Hundred leaders. Several days later the new revolutionary regime shut down the conservative newspaper *Saratovskii golos* (Voice of Saratov).[93] While temporarily keeping a low profile, rightist groups remained a constant, albeit minor, force in Saratov politics throughout 1917.

The Kadets were the most politically viable alternative to the socialist parties. As elsewhere, most members of the Party of People's Freedom, as the Kadets came to be known, tended to be professional people—lawyers, teachers, civil servants, doctors, office workers. Since they had participated legally in local and national politics before 1917, the party members had acquired a firm foothold in the Saratov PEC. Prominent Saratov Kadets included A. A. Tokarskii, B. S. Kanevskii, A. A. Nikonov, Iu. F. Krupianskii, A. M. Kogan, and V. R. Maltsev. A right Kadet, S. P. Krasnikov, edited one of the two leading prerevolutionary dailies, *Saratovskii listok*. During the war years the liberals had become increasingly critical of the government's poor image and inept handling of the war. Having come to power thanks to the rebellious Petrograd workers and soldiers, the liberals within the Provisional Government now channeled all of their efforts into setting right Russia's war machine. Advocating the postponement of fundamental reform until after the war, the

92. Z. L. Serebriakova, *Oblastnye ob"edineniia sovetov Rossii, mart 1917–dekabr' 1918* (Moscow, 1977), p. 25.
93. *Pochta*, no. 60, March 7, 1917, p. 3.

party sought to curb the revolutionary tide unleashed in the country at large. The Kadet tactical program, which opposed a return to monarchism, favored the enfranchisement of women, supported the Provisional Government, and called for a constituent assembly based on free elections. It also advocated "the continuation of the war to a victorious end."[94] The Volga regional conference of soviets that convened in Saratov had rejected the slogan "War to a Victorious End"; thus Kadet politics were at odds with mass opinion in the Volga area. When all is said and done, the party's firm commitment to the war cause determined its fate both at the national level and in Saratov.

Although they differed from the Kadets in the details of how a government should be formed, the Saratov Popular Socialists, an offshoot of the SRs, actually had drawn close to local Kadets in style and program. The Popular Socialists and the Trudoviks, who elected Kerensky to the Fourth Duma from Saratov, were virtually indistinguishable; in fact, the two parties actually merged in the summer. On March 14 the party elected its city committee, some of whose members had been prominent in the city government before February and held important posts afterward (especially in the various cooperative societies). P. S. Gusev worked on the editorial board of *Saratovskii listok* and N. I. Semenov became provincial commissar. Opponents of autocracy, they were respectable professional people and much like the Kadets, except that they saw a role for the Soviet. They differed in style, however, from the majority socialists, the moderate SRs, and the Mensheviks, who composed the political center in Saratov at this time.

One Bolshevik memoirist wrote that during February the SR party "was the largest and noisiest in the city."[95] The SR leader N. I. Rakitnikov, in contrast, reported to an SR congress that during the first days of the revolution the party was barely visible.[96] Both observations contain elements of truth. Saratov's heritage as a center of Russian populism now paid dividends. A public meeting sponsored by the SRs in early March attracted thousands of townspeople, especially from the foothills on the outskirts of town. Impressed with the enthusiastic turnout, the SRs held daily meetings in this region, which was inhabited mainly by unskilled workers and artisans. On March 12 the party committee began to publish a newspaper, *Zemlia i volia* (Land and Liberty), under the editorship of Rakitnikov, who enjoyed national standing within the party. A. V. Milachevskii, M. P. Tkachukov, and the SR leaders of the Military Committee occupied other important positions in the city organization. Still,

94. *Saratovskii vestnik*, no. 57, March 12, 1917, p. 1.

95. Kogan, "V te istoricheskie dni," p. 164.

96. G. A. Gerasimenko, *Partiinaia bor'ba v sovetakh Nizhnego Povolzh'ia 1917 g.* (Saratov, 1966), p. 10.

prominent SRs are missing from all accounts of the February Revolution in Saratov. They seem to have taken a minor role in the formation of the Soviet, and at first had no representation in the Public Executive Committee. In fact, they began to participate in new revolutionary institutions only after a party conference held at the end of March.

At the conference local SRs expressed a moderate stand on major political and social questions. Typical was the impassioned speech of Pontriagin, chairman of the Military Committee, condemning the eight-hour workday. "Soldiers in the trenches don't know the eight-hour workday," he snapped, "and a bad impression will be made on them when they find out about its introduction at the rear, in industries working for defense." In a resolution to the Petrograd Soviet, the conference members declared that it should not pressure the government to promote the convocation of a constituent assembly, "since the people are still not altogether prepared for elections." Until that time, the Soviet should cooperate with the Provisional Government. Overtures also were made to the Popular Socialists to join the SRs, "since tactically very little separated the parties."[97] Local SR opposition to any independent actions against landowners and their property contrasted sharply with the seditious SR appeals of 1905–7. Local SR agrarian policy now called for volost executive committees and peasants to come to terms over rented land. Only if landowners refused to reach an agreement with the peasantry should the estate owners' land be given to the peasants. At this time SR land policies harmonized with those of the Mensheviks, who rejected the call for an immediate seizure of land before convocation of a constituent assembly; soon advocates of the formation of a political bloc emerged in both parties.

In the spring of 1917 Bolsheviks and Mensheviks still belonged to united party organizations in slightly less than half of the towns represented at national party conferences. Within Saratov province a united SD committee existed in Tsaritsyn, and in Saratov itself party activists in both factions supported union. The formation of a separate Bolshevik committee in March 1917 can be attributed to the work of party activists during the war years. Though they wavered in their attitudes toward the war and their initial defensist sentiments, Saratov Bolsheviks eventually came to subscribe—if not wholeheartedly—to the Leninist antiwar platform. Yet traditional ecumenical feelings within the revolutionary underground in Saratov continued to create favorable conditions for cooperation. In March local Mensheviks had posed the question of merger. Some of the Bolsheviks, particularly such intelligenty as Miliutin and I. V. Mgeladze, supported union because they believed that a local Bolshevik group with insufficient intelligenty would have a difficult time organizing. This same rationale had led to the creation of a

97. *Saratovskii vestnik*, no. 63, March 21, 1917, p. 5.

united committee in Tsaritsyn. The Bolshevik workers who had orchestrated the Initiative Group in 1916, however—such men as K. I. Plaksin, M. I. Khrynin, and A. M. Martsinovskii—strongly opposed union.[98] Their proposals for merger eventually voted down, local Mensheviks established their own party organization.

Headed by D. A. Topuridze, the Menshevik Committee included I. A. Skvortsov, K. A. Tkachev, D. K. Chertkov, and I. Sudachkov.[99] Topuridze had returned to Saratov in March and was immediately co-opted into the Public Executive Committee and Soviet, and then elected to chair the local Mensheviks. Following the October Revolution, he abandoned Saratov for his native Georgia, where he served in the Georgian Menshevik government before emigrating. Described uncharitably by Lebedev as a "legal Marxist whenever that was convenient," Topuridze enjoyed broad popularity among Saratov workers.[100] As a group, Mensheviks soon exerted influence over the publication of the Soviet's newspaper. They also launched their own paper, *Proletarii Povolzh'ia* (Workers of the Volga Region), on March 29. Party registration got under way a few weeks later.

Bolshevik memoirists admitted the difficulty their local organization experienced emerging from the underground. The creation of a legal party consumed enormous energy in March. Returning from exile at the end of the month, Antonov observed that "even though almost a month had passed since the overthrow, emptiness and a feeling of despondency hovered over the rather spacious accommodations of the committee."[101] When the Bolsheviks sponsored their first meeting on March 4, only about fifty people showed up.[102] Somewhat pessimistic about the chances for the new order's continued survival, they voted in favor of assuming "semilegal" status.[103] The Bolsheviks selected Miliutin chairman of their committee and Rapoport secretary. Fenigshtein (Doletskii), Plaksin, Martsinovskii, Khrynin, Vasil'ev, and—when they returned from exile—Antonov and Lebedev also were elected to it. More confident a week later that the old order would not return, the Bolsheviks held a public meeting, and on March 23 their newspaper, *Sotsial-Demokrat,* went to press. On March 25, 150 party members adopted Antonov's organizational plan.[104] Within the garrison Second Lieutenant Sokolov and Kulikov, who sat on the Military Committee, formed a Bol-

98. Lebedev, "Fevral'–oktiabr' v Saratove," p. 239; *Saratovskii vestnik,* no. 68, March 28, 1917, p. 5.

99. *Proletarii Povolzh'ia,* no. 1, March 21, 1917, p. 1.

100. Lebedev, "Fevral'–oktiabr' v Saratove," p. 240.

101. Antonov-Saratovskii, *Pod stiagom,* pp. 96–97.

102. T. K. Chugunov, "Za vlast' sovetov," in *Za vlast' sovetov* (1957), p. 129; Martsinovskii, *Zapiski rabochego-bol'shevika,* p. 87.

103. M. G., "Iz istorii," *Kommunisticheskii put',* no. 18 (1927), p. 19.

104. Osipov, *1917 god v Saratovskoi gubernii,* pp. 55–56.

shevik military organization, independent of the city committee. The local party organ also took some preliminary steps to establish Saratov as the Volga district bureau of the Central Committee; after discussions of a possible merger with the Mensheviks broke down, a separate Bolshevik fraction crystallized in the Soviet. Nevertheless, the party committee was beset by more problems than Soviet writers acknowledge. In March a minority of local Bolsheviks sympathized with revolutionary defensism. The party's foothold in the factories remained shaky.

By the end of March tactical differences reflecting the Bolsheviks' willingness to implement their minimum program began to isolate them from their socialist comrades. The Bolsheviks' minimum demands included the establishment of a democratic republic, the eight-hour workday, and the confiscation of large landowners' estates.[105] Introducing these points at a meeting of the Soviet's Executive Committee on March 4, Vasil'ev clashed with the Menshevik faction, which agreed only to the call for a democratic republic. By the end of March the Bolshevik position in regard to the Provisional Government had hardened, further estranging the Bolsheviks from other socialists. At a time when most socialists accepted dual power, Khrynin, Miliutin, Antonov, and Lebedev articulated an increasingly critical attitude toward the Provisional Government.[106] Arguing that power remained in the hands of ideologues, even though workers and soldiers had overthrown the autocracy, a Bolshevik resolution criticized the bourgeois character of the Provisional Government and cautioned that as the revolution progressed it would "meet with opposition and should prepare for it."[107] By the end of March the local Kadet paper began to censure Saratov Bolsheviks for their inflammatory statements. "It is no longer a secret," the paper reported, "that the organs of the SD-Bolsheviks have created unrest in the army and among the working masses."[108]

What do these details of the first month of revolution in Saratov tell us about the Russian Revolution in general? Most striking is the quickness with which the local population responded to news of the revolution in Petrograd, creating a new political structure without any directives from the center. Equally noteworthy is the broad unpopularity of the monarchy and the old order in Saratov province. Writers have tended to emphasize the unexpected, accidental, and spontaneous nature of the

105. N. V. Afanas'ev, *Bor'ba partii bol'shevikov za ustanovlenie i uprochenie Sovetskoi vlasti v Saratovskoi gubernii* (Saratov, 1947), p. 5.

106. See, for example, Miliutin's statement regarding the "counterrevolutionary" nature of the Provisional Government at the all-Russian convocation of party workers in Petrograd at the end of March: "Protokoly Vserossiiskogo (martovskogo) soveshchaniia partiinykh rabotnikov," *Voprosy istorii* KPSS, no. 5 (1962), p. 116.

107. Antonov-Saratovskii, *Pod stiagom.* pp. 109–10.

108. *Saratovskii listok,* no. 67, March 25, 1917, p. 4.

revolution in Petrograd. To be sure, the population of Saratov was caught by surprise, but the enormous independent initiative shown by all layers of local society shows the extent to which the townspeople of Saratov had been tempered by years of revolutionary propaganda and activities. The new political alignment that emerged in Saratov reflected the extraordinary preparatory work of *all* revolutionary parties for the past generation as well as that of the liberal "bourgeois" parties, which had politicized society and weakened the autocracy by their implacable criticism of the tsarist regime.

The February Revolution in Saratov should not be viewed merely as a distant echo of events in Petrograd, but rather as a distinctive parochial revolution with its own interests and needs. The revolution in Saratov unfolded as a unique interaction between local structural conditions and larger events and issues. Realizing that the center could not save them from chaos and anarchy, Saratov leaders institutionalized the new revolutionary alignment of political power. Striving to work things out in the context of national issues, they responded soberly and cautiously to the task at hand, unaware or perhaps reluctant to admit to themselves that the revolution had dealt a death blow to the centralized state. In all of their actions, however, they had to take into account pressures from groups in society that heretofore had been disenfranchised. From the first days of March the aspirations of workers, peasants, and soldiers already shaped the revolution at the local level.

Despite the lack of bloodshed in Saratov, the arrest of more than 300 tsarist officials, police officers, and Black Hundred leaders suggests that violence could have colored the local revolution as in Petrograd had promonarchist groups chosen to resist. Of course, the garrison's enthusiastic acceptance of the new regime sedated any opposition, at least for the time being. In the district towns, as in Saratov, the political transition generally took place before directives came from the center. A variety of factors shaped these local revolutions. The relatively insignificant number of industrial workers and limited Social Democratic activity emboldened the police, who occasionally showed resolve to resist popular pressures. But, as in Saratov, soldiers played a paramount role in the district revolutions, and they continued to do so in the months that followed. Much of respectable society in the uezd centers had opposed the autocracy; in addition pressures from soldiers and workers ensured that "the democracy" would be represented in the new public executive committees taking shape side by side with the soviets. The villages expressed no regrets over the collapse of Romanov rule. Displaying the same penchant for independent initiative as the urban population, peasants elected their own committees to work toward what the revolution signified to them: an end to the exploitive system of rents and the transfer of land to those who tilled it.

Perhaps the most significant feature of the local revolution is the predominantly socialist orientation of the masses of people in the towns and surrounding areas. All too often discussions of the Russian Revolution have revolved around the question of tactical mistakes made by the liberals, which ultimately led to the Bolsheviks' coming to power. While the liberal parties represented the major challenge to socialist forces in Saratov, the Kadets' base remained restricted to a small group. After March the liberals' timid social programs, their suspicion of popular organs of the democracy, and their commitment to the war spelled their doom. Perhaps the real question that should be posed about Saratov politics, then, is how the radical wing of Russian socialism triumphed over the more moderate socialists who commanded such broad support in the spring of 1917.

Part of the answer to this question seems to lie in the ambivalence of the political structure created in March. In this regard the case study of Saratov may disclose something about provincial Russia in general. In Saratov and virtually everywhere else—in stark contrast with Petrograd—city soviets sent representatives into the various public executive committees that represented the Provisional Government locally and each of which stood as but one of several loci of power. As March progressed, the true significance of the local coalition within the PEC took on meaning: the overriding strength of socialist parties in Saratov in effect had created a situation in which the Soviet mustered far more power and prestige than even the most optimistic revolutionary could have expected a few weeks before. This emerging legitimacy of the Soviet in the eyes of the masses established an effective political medium for Bolshevik and left socialist aspirations.

Although class and social tensions were manifest in Saratov in March, they were overshadowed by a high degree of revolutionary camaraderie such as had long colored relationships among Saratov socialists. The Petrograd Soviet's acceptance of revolutionary defensism and its conditional support of the Provisional Government struck a responsive chord in Saratov, where prominent socialist leaders also adopted moderate views on such burning issues as the eight-hour day. Local Bolsheviks stood very close to other socialists on most tactical matters. During March and afterward, as the political parties formulated clearer positions on the key questions of the continuation of the war and support for the government, cooperation among socialists broke down. Perhaps more than anything else, Lenin's return to Russia in April led to an eventual split within Russian socialism. And, as we shall see, the repercussions of Lenin's political program proved equally important on the banks of the Volga.

CHAPTER 3

The Paradox of Revolutionary Politics: Saratov Organizations in the Spring of 1917

Late in the evening of April 3, the Menshevik leaders of the Petrograd Soviet, N. S. Chkheidze and M. I. Skobelev, left their offices for Petrograd's Finland Station, located in the Vyborg factory district. Little did they imagine that the man they were going to welcome home that evening after years of exile, V. I. Lenin, in his arrival address would rail at all of the tactical positions the Petrograd Soviet had formulated during the preceding month. Lenin aimed his forceful denunciations at his own party as well. Since mid-March, after the return to Petrograd from exile of such party moderates as L. B. Kamenev, J. V. Stalin, and M. K. Muranov, the Central Committee and the party organ *Pravda* had taken a noticeable swing to the right. Now advocating limited support for the Provisional Government, the party center rejected the slogan "Down with the War" as too adventuristic and inflammatory.

Lenin's homecoming coincided with the First All-Russian Conference of Soviets, which had convened in Petrograd on March 29. Addressing a caucus of Bolshevik delegates to the conference on the afternoon of April 4, Lenin enunciated his controversial April Theses. These propositions sharply separated him from the main-line Kamenev-Stalin group, which had gained control over the party leadership in recent weeks. Rejecting the "revolutionary defensism" of the Petrograd Soviet as totally unacceptable, Lenin called for open fraternization at the front. He argued that the events of February had represented the bourgeois-liberal stage of the revolution, and that Russia had entered a transitional period and already was moving toward social revolution. He opposed any expression of support for the Provisional Government. Ridiculing the prospects for reunification with the Mensheviks, he advocated an immediate struggle for the transfer of power to the soviets.[1]

Lenin's theses shocked his Petrograd comrades, many of whom dismissed the pronouncements as the delusions of a man who had lost touch with Russian reality during his many years in exile. In fact, the Petrograd Bolshevik Committee rejected Lenin's demands altogether. In an article in *Pravda*, Kamenev insisted that Lenin's ideas merely represented his "personal opinion" and were not binding on the party. Yet despite the initial sensation the theses had caused, by the end of April Lenin had swung the party over to his side. Between April 24 and 29, Bolshevik delegates from throughout the country had assembled in Petrograd for the Seventh (April) All-Russian Conference of the Bolshevik Party. At the gathering Lenin lobbied for the eventual transfer of power to the soviets, in contrast with those who still spoke in favor of vigilant supervision over the Provisional Government, and condemned the war effort as imperialist. Party delegates formally adopted Lenin's theses but rejected his appeal to break off relations with the Second International.

The April Conference had taken place in the wake of disturbing street demonstrations sparked by an unfortunate remark by the Kadet minister of war, P. N. Miliukov, during a press conference back in March, that Russia was fighting to gain parts of the Austro-Hungarian empire, Constantinople, and the Straits. Such imperialist-sounding statements outraged the Petrograd Soviet, which pressured the Provisional Government to publish a revised version of its war aims, denouncing postwar annexations and indemnities. On April 18 the Provisional Government forwarded this new declaration to its allies, but with a contradictory cover note from Miliukov, maintaining that there would be no slackening of Russia's war effort. When the text of the "Miliukov Note" became public, thousands of soldiers poured into the streets of Petrograd on April 20–21, carrying banners with the slogans "Down with Miliukov" and "Down with the Provisional Government." The first major crisis of the Provisional Government ended with its collapse and replacement by the First Coalition Government formed on May 5, which included representation from the socialist parties, with the notable exception of the Bolsheviks.[2]

1. For a description of Lenin's return to Russia and the impact of his April Theses, see Alexander Rabinowitch, *Prelude to Revolution: The Petrograd Bolsheviks and the July 1917 Uprising* (Bloomington, Ind., 1968), pp. 36–42.

2. Ibid., pp. 42–47; Rex A. Wade, *The Russian Search for Peace, February–October 1917* (Stanford, 1969), pp. 25–50; and William G. Rosenberg, *Liberals in the Russian Revolution: The Constitutional Democratic Party, 1917–1921* (Princeton, 1974), pp. 94–133.

The Miliukov Affair in part also explains the rapidity with which Lenin's celebrated theses became acceptable to the Bolshevik party at large.

In the new administration Aleksandr Kerensky, minister of war, emerged as the leading figure, soon overshadowing Prince L'vov, who still headed the government. Besides Kerensky, five other socialists accepted cabinet portfolios. Even though dissatisfaction with the previous government's stance on the war had brought about its downfall, the First Coalition Government, while paying lip service to the Petrograd Soviet's peace declarations, also failed to take any serious measures toward securing peace. In the following months the Bolsheviks' refusal to serve in a government with the bourgeoisie and their increasingly vocal support for Lenin's theses contributed to the drawing of hard party and class lines in political institutions everywhere in the country.

So it was in Saratov, where the adoption of Lenin's theses and the public reaction to the April Crisis struck the first—and perhaps fatal—blow to coalition government on the Volga. In Saratov two paradoxical political trends evolved in the spring and early summer of 1917. First, local socialists consolidated their position at the expense of the liberal parties and right; at the same time, however, a split developed between moderate and left socialists. Second, the Saratov Soviet consolidated its influence at the expense of both the City Duma and the Public Executive Committee, becoming for the working class and soldiers the most legitimate power in the city, eclipsing the PEC, which all but faded from the scene. As a result of elections to the Soviet in late May and its merger with the Military Committee, moderates came to dominate the Soviet. Having joined the middle classes in a coalition government at the national level, the moderate socialists sought to make the government's local bodies work too. This effort seems to have affected their attitude toward the Soviet itself, whose energies they now sought to curb. The ambiguous behavior of their leaders confused many workers and soldiers and led to their dissatisfaction with the political status quo. Differences between the moderate SRs and Mensheviks on the one hand and the more radical Bolsheviks and other internationalists on the other increasingly found expression at Soviet plenum meetings. As in Petrograd, workers and soldiers began to drift away from the Soviet. By the late spring of 1917 a disintegration of governmental services accompanied a breakdown of law and order, which in the long run strengthened the Bolsheviks' hand.

Western historians have neglected the rapid breakdown of the organs of the Provisional Government in the provinces and the administrative paralysis resulting from the weakness of the public executive committees. Between March and October 1917 the Provisional Government issued more than a hundred decrees, approximately half of which dealt with matters of local administration. Even a brief examination of the government's circulars reveals the true limitations of its authority. Dismayed by the failure of provincial organs to keep it informed, the Ministry of Internal Affairs urged local executive committees to report to it regularly. If the Saratov example is at all representative—and the language of the documents issued by the Ministry of Internal Affairs suggests that it is—the government's edicts on an array of important issues merely sanctioned what local administrations had already done. Other directives went ignored. As the Popular Socialist A. A. Vasil'ev said in April, "during the two months of its existence the Provisional Government has not repaired any broken ties between central and local organs."[3]

In Saratov as elsewhere the Soviet stepped into the political vacuum and soon generated tremendous political power. The Saratov Soviet's growing authority in the spring of 1917 can be attributed to its success in dealing with the most pressing issues facing the city's population, such as the threat of public disorder and dwindling, erratic food supplies. In March, it will be recalled, the Soviet had orchestrated the reorganization of the old tsarist police into a people's militia. The Soviet also had drawn up plans for establishing a food-supply assembly, which the townspeople elected in early April. The overwhelming majority of deputies came from "the democratic part of the population"; at the Food-Supply Assembly's first meeting, a "workers' group" numbering 200 people was formed. The assembly established its authority over all aspects of the acquisition and distribution of food in Saratov: it assumed the operation of food shops in town, sowed undeveloped city lots with potatoes, and took preliminary steps toward implementing a bread rationing system. With similar decisiveness the assembly dealt with shortages of tobacco, cigarettes, and sugar. Participation in the Food-Supply Assembly provided one more means of politicizing the heretofore disenfranchised lower classes, who came to acknowledge the Soviet as the institution most responsive to their needs.[4]

The Soviet's dogged determination to democratize the City Duma still further enhanced its popular image. Clashing repeatedly with the Duma over registration procedures, the Soviet sought to grant the franchise to soldiers residing within the city limits and rebuked the Duma for posting

3. G. A. Gerasimenko and D. S. Tochenyi, *Sovety Povolzh'ia v 1917 godu: Bor'ba partii, bol'shevizatsiia sovetov, Oktiabr'skie dni* (Saratov, 1977), pp. 79–81.

4. *Saratovskii vestnik*, no. 74, April 6, 1917, pp. 3–4. The Menshevik newspaper boasted that "workers elected from the poor regions displayed more energy and consciousness than those [wealthier] elements from the center." See *Proletarii Povolzh'ia*, no. 2, April 8, 1917, p. 4.

election-related announcements in the center of town, thereby slighting the heavily populated workers' quarters on the outskirts.[5] The Soviet also insisted on a grace period for late registration of voters, which ultimately added an additional 30,000 names to the lists of eligible voters. Because of the Duma's recalcitrance, the Soviet and PEC set up a control commission to report on the Duma's activities. Further, the newly elected Food-Supply Assembly demanded the resignation of the mayor, M. F. Volkov, for his alleged involvement with Black Hundred groups. Announcing its resolve to hold elections only if it were directed to do so by the Provisional Government, the Duma ignored the order to remove Volkov. But this snubbing of the Soviet and Food-Supply Assembly had more symbolic than actual significance. At an "emergency" meeting of the Duma, Volkov, unwilling to cooperate with the Soviet's control commission and unable to satisfy his accusers, offered his resignation. Refusing to accept the mayor's resignation, the majority of the Duma members passed a resolution calling the Soviet's control commission totally "unacceptable." A liberal Kadet deputy named Krupianskii, however, sensed the need for Volkov's dismissal. "I don't understand why control frightens you," he commented. "The Provisional Government isn't afraid of control from the [Petrograd] Soviet of Workers' Deputies. *We too must reconcile ourselves to this*" [emphasis mine]. More important, he insisted that Volkov resign because the "population is against him." One of the Duma representatives who sat on the PEC warned that Volkov must be ousted because he "is unable to work with the new democratic organizations and will hamper their activities." With the backing of the Soviet, the PEC ordered the mayor to resign. Faced with no other option, the Duma reluctantly agreed to dismiss him. This capitulation to the Soviet and Public Executive Committee served as a psychological deathblow to the Duma. Realizing that the Duma had lost its authority, many members stopped attending the infrequent meetings, which therefore were usually canceled for lack of a quorum.[6]

At the same time the Soviet won the upper hand over the Public Executive Committee. Composed of representatives of all major parties, the PEC experienced increasing difficulty reaching a consensus on pressing business. The fragility of the coalition within the PEC was evinced most clearly in its dealings with the Soviet. Liberals within the executive committee, for example, criticized the independent measures taken to

5. *Sotsial-Demokrat*, no. 21, June 2, 1917, p. 1, and no. 27, June 11, p. 3.

6. *Izvestiia Saratovskoi gorodskoi dumy*, pp. 101–2, 112–13; *Proletarii Povolzh'ia*, no. 5, April 22, 1917, pp. 3–4; no. 6, April 26, p. 3; *Saratovskii vestnik*, no. 87, April 22, 1917, p. 3. The Duma even had trouble mustering a quorum during crises. See *Izvestiia Saratovskoi gorodskoi dumy*, p. 127; *Saratovskii vestnik*, no. 131, June 16, 1917, p. 3; *Saratovskii listok*, no. 129, June 16, 1917, p. 3.

preserve order during local demonstrations protesting the Miliukov Affair. By the end of April, however, the "democratic elements" had established such a strong base within the committee that the majority voted to censure the Kadet spokesman who dared rebuke the Soviet.[7] During April and May the PEC underwent two changes. Responding to directives from the Provisional Government, it became the Provincial Public Executive Committee (PPEC). Next, at the end of May, when poor health induced provincial commissar Semenov to retire, a five-member collegium representing the major political parties replaced him. The Saratov Bolshevik committee, however, refused to take part in the coalition collegium, a decision that mirrored the degree to which Lenin's policy of nonsupport for the national coalition government had taken hold at the local level. The Saratov Bolsheviks' withdrawal from the PEC marked the end of their willingness to cooperate with the bourgeoisie and the beginning of their as yet restrained advocacy of an all-socialist government.

As it turned out, the Provincial Public Executive Committee merely functioned as an extension of the Soviet anyway. The new collegium included the Menshevik Topuridze, the SR Minin (both of whom belonged to the Soviet's Executive Committee), the Popular Socialist Maksimovich from the Military Committee, and the Kadet Kogan. Referring to the "chronic crisis" of the new coalition governorship, *Sotsial-Demokrat* reported that "members of the committee rarely attend" and "are little interested in their business."[8] Lebedev penned an editorial on the "death of the Provincial Executive Committee," labeling it "the fruit of the cooperation of the democracy with the bourgeoisie."[9] Semenov, now retired, lamented that the Public Executive Committee and Commissariat "are not ruling organs but madhouses."[10] *Saratovskii vestnik* gave notice of the repeated failure of the PPEC to assemble a quorum.[11] By the end of June, the committee's collapse was broadly recognized. The editors of *Saratovskii vestnik* complained that "at the last meeting of the Executive Committee the need to confer on the committee greater authority in the eyes of the population and greater capacity for work was discussed. . . . This question arose in connection with the fact that lately power not only in the city but throughout the province *has actually passed to the Soviet of Workers' and Soldiers' Deputies,* since the [Public] Executive Committee has not met for three weeks now."[12] For all

7. *Proletarii Povolzh'ia,* no. 8, May 3, 1917, p. 4.
8. *Sotsial-Demokrat,* no. 25, June 9, 1917, p. 3.
9. *Saratovskii vestnik,* no. 127, June 11, 1917, p. 4.
10. I. I. Mints et al., *Oktiabr' v Povolzh'e* (Saratov, 1967), p. 102.
11. *Saratovskii vestnik,* no. 127, June 11, 1917, p. 4.
12. Ibid., no. 138, June 28, 1917, p. 3; emphasis mine. See a similar statement in *Saratovskii listok,* no. 136, June 24, 1917, p. 3.

practical purposes, then, by late spring 1917 local power, diffuse as it was, rested in the hands of the Saratov Soviet. Psychologically, however, dual power took longer to pass from the scene.

But how representative were developments in Saratov? An examination of the alignment of political forces in the Volga provinces shows that the situation in Saratov was by no means an isolated phenomenon. The assistant to the provincial commissar of Kazan cabled the Ministry of the Interior that "public organizations show no noticeable activity, and even the Committee of Public Safety is dying out." From Mokshan in Penza province officials reported that "local authorities are powerless, local uezd committees are powerless. Local organs are idle." The Buguruslan Soviet in Samara province at its very first meeting discussed disbanding the town's public executive committee, "which is becoming well known for its inactivity."[13] In Tsaritsyn the soviet was recognized as the ruling organ in town by the end of April. After falling under the leadership of Bolshevik and Left SR radicals, the soviet acquired a national reputation for the unusually leftist character of its politics and soon found itself under attack in the national nonsocialist press.[14] Reacting to a resolution passed by the city soviet in early June calling for a transfer of power to the soviets, the provincial commissar of Astrakhan appealed to the Provisional Government for help.[15] In Glazovo (Viatka province) an executive committee of soviets of peasants', workers', and soldiers' deputies declared itself the ruling organ and demanded the liquidation of the public executive committee installed after the February Revolution.[16] The Nikolaev Soviet in Samara province on June 16 declared itself the highest political authority in the uezd and appointed its own district commissar. Soviets in Samara, Penza, and Syzran routinely replaced government organs during crises.

The vitality of local soviets was not restricted geographically to the Volga region. In his study of the Bolsheviks in Siberia, Russell E. Snow describes how soviet leaders entered public executive committees and even controlled them. The soviets became the de facto authorities in central Siberia during the late spring. According to Snow, "the Krasnoiarsk Soviet was the ruling authority in Eniseisk gubernia from the outset." In eastern Siberia, too, the executive committees of soviets soon ran things. In Tomsk and Novonikolaevsk, to take two slightly different examples reminiscent of the situation in Saratov, the leading members of

13. R. K. Valeev, "Krizis mestnykh organov Vremmenogo Pravitel'stva letom i osen'iu 1917 goda (Po materialam Povolzh'ia)," in *Oktiabr' v Povolzh'e i Priural'e (Istochniki i voprosy istoriografii)* [Kazan, 1972], pp. 120–21.

14. Donald J. Raleigh, "Revolutionary Politics in Provincial Russia: The Tsaritsyn 'Republic' in 1917," *Slavic Review,* 40 (1981), 198–202, passim.

15. Mints, *Oktiabr' v Povolzh'e,* p. 99.

16. Lepeshkin, *Mestnye organy vlasti,* p. 89.

the soviets and public executive committees "were the same men." Examining the situation in Latvia, Andrew Ezergailis concluded that "one peculiarity of the revolution in Latvia was that there was no counterpart for the *dual power* which, according to Lenin, existed in Russia. In the beginning there were as many as seven different councils claiming broad governing powers, but as the weeks went by, a process of elimination set in. By June the councils were in the hands of Bolsheviks." Ronald G. Suny, in recent essays on the revolution in Tiflis and Baku, reached the conclusion that soviet power existed except in name.[17] A. I. Lepeshkin observed that "soviets in this period often exercised effective control over the activities of the organs of state administration in the provinces and directed institutions of local government."[18] G. A. Trukan in his important study of the October Revolution in central Russia noted that "the state apparatus in the provinces was more disorganized than in Petrograd. State authority here turned out to be weaker and the pressure of the democratic forces more powerful."[19] In fact, at the Bolshevik April Conference some provincial delegates expressed more optimistic views of the role of local soviets and Bolshevik committees than their Petrograd comrades, prompting even Lenin to conclude that "in a number of local centers . . . the role of the soviets has turned out to be especially important. Single power [edinovlastie] has been created. The bourgeoisie have been disarmed entirely and have been reduced to complete subordination; wages have been raised, the workday has been shortened without a drop in production; food supplies have been guaranteed, control over production and distribution has gotten under way; all of the old powers have been replaced."[20]

At the same time that the Saratov Soviet emerged on top in the political contest with the Public Executive Committee, structural changes within the Soviet dramatically altered the political complexion of its leadership and rank-and-file deputies. The first convocation of the Saratov Soviet lasted from March 1 through May 26. During this period the number of deputies in the Soviet grew constantly while the executive organs expanded accordingly. The fluidity of the membership in the spring of 1917 makes it difficult to assess at any given time the size of the

17. Snow, *Bolsheviks in Siberia*, pp. 69–70, 87, 106, 108; Ezergailis, *1917 Revolution in Latvia*, pp. 16–18; Ronald G. Suny, "Nationalism and Social Class in the Russian Revolution: The Cases of Baku and Tiflis," in *Transcaucasia, Nationalism, and Social Change: Essays in the History of Armenia, Azerbaijan, and Georgia*, ed. Ronald G. Suny (Ann Arbor, 1983), pp. 246, 250.

18. Lepeshkin, *Mestnye organy vlasti*, pp. 99–100.

19. G. A. Trukan, *Oktiabr' v Tsentral'noi Rossii* (Moscow, 1967), p. 53.

20. Razgon, "O sostave sovetov," p. 107.

Soviet, its party composition, and the relative strength of the Workers' and Soldiers' sections. In the first weeks of March the largest industrial enterprises and those workplaces where revolutionary activity had been most constant since the turn of the century responded first to the call to elect deputies to the Soviet. Not surprisingly, local Bolsheviks enjoyed a dominant position in the Soviet's Executive Committee in March, and not only in Saratov but also in neighboring Samara and Syzran. As the smaller factories, dockworkers, and artisans organized, they too sought representation. By the middle of May, 209 factories, offices, party committees, unions, and factory committees had selected deputies to the council. This influx of new members from the nonindustrial proletariat, however, gradually altered the Soviet's composition and the alignment of political forces within it. Returning in mid-April from Petrograd, where he had attended the All-Russian Conference of Soviets, Vasil'ev observed that

> the election of office workers, students, small shop workers, bakery workers, and others lowered the qualitative makeup of the Soviet's deputies in comparison with the first half of March. Back then [industrial] workers and seasoned revolutionaries took part in the Soviet almost exclusively. Therefore the leadership of the Soviet at first fell into the Bolsheviks' hands. . . . Having returned from a trip to Petrograd . . . I found that the Soviet already was saturated with Mensheviks and SRs. . . . *Izvestiia* of the Saratov Soviet was edited by Maizel', who refused, by the way, to print correspondence from Petrograd about the All-Russian Conference of Soviets, about the return of V. I. Lenin, etc.[21]

At the end of March the Soviet had 392 deputies, of whom 248 belonged to the Workers' Section and 144 to the Soldiers' Section. The most striking characteristic of the 248 workers' deputies is that 193 were not affiliated with any political party, although they looked to the socialist parties for leadership. There were 28 Bolsheviks among them, 16 Mensheviks, 6 SRs, and 5 Popular Socialists.[22] Soldier deputies also tended to be nonpartisan at this time, although most contemporaries viewed them as supporters of the SR party. In contrast with the Military Committee, the overwhelming majority of soldier deputies elected to the Soviet in March came from the lower ranks. By mid-May the Soviet had grown to 532 members—322 workers and 210 soldiers—as Table 5 indicates. While party breakdown cannot be determined conclusively, the large percentage of nonparty deputies had been reduced and the number of SR deputies had increased among both soldier deputies and artisans.

21. *Saratovskii Sovet*, p. 782.
22. Razgon, "O sostave sovetov," pp. 116–17.

Table 5

Number and percentage of deputies in Workers' Section of Saratov Soviet, March 30 and May 13, 1917, by party affiliation

	March 30, 1917		*May 13, 1917*	
Party affiliation of deputies	*Number*	*Percent*	*Number*	*Percent*
Bolshevik	28	11.3%	53	16.5%
Menshevik	16	6.5	32	10.0
Socialist Revolutionary	6	2.4	30	9.3
Popular Socialist	5	2.0	5	1.5
Nonaffiliated	193	77.8	202	62.7
All deputies	248	100.00%	322	100.00%

According to the Bolshevik Antonov, the large number of nonaligned deputies represented "an undifferentiated mass whose mood was extremely revolutionary in regard to tsarism but at the same time was impregnated with the feeling of revolutionary defensism."[23]

The merger of the Military Committee with the Saratov Soviet at the end of May had the greatest impact on the nature of the Soviet's membership and on its political orientation, for it greatly increased the number of soldier deputies. The question of merging was first raised within the Soviet at the end of April, after the All-Russian Conference of Soviets called upon all separate workers' and soldiers' soviets to unite in order to minimize conflict.[24] The Soviet's Executive Committee and the Presidium of the Military Committee agreed to create a single organ—the Saratov Soviet of Workers', Soldiers', and Peasants' Deputies—but "with the observance of the principle of proportional representation."[25] Seats on the Executive Committee of the Soviet now would be divided among the parties, according to the size of their constituency among rank-and-file members.

Elections to the reorganized Soviet took place between May 25 and June 1. *Saratovskii vestnik* perceptively reported that although "the general results [of the elections] are not yet clear, it is already becoming obvious that the party composition of the Soviet is changing significantly."[26] The most reliable sources reveal that the Bolsheviks and Mensheviks had presented a single list of candidates for the election to the Workers' Section, which polled 155 votes. The SR list won 44 votes. The Bolsheviks received 85 or 90 of the 155 votes, the Mensheviks 65 or

23. Antonov-Saratovskii, "Saratov s fevralia," p. 188.
24. *Saratovskii Sovet*, p. 101.
25. *Khronika*, p. 59; *Sotsial-Demokrat*, no. 16, May 17, 1917, p. 2.
26. *Saratovskii vestnik*, no. 113, May 26, 1917, p. 3.

70.[27] In the Military Section, the SRs won an overwhelming 260 deputies, the Mensheviks 90, and the Bolsheviks 50.[28] But further changes in party affiliation took place immediately after the elections. The Workers' Section of the Soviet expanded to include 98 Bolsheviks, 97 Mensheviks, and 50 SRs; the reelected Executive Committee now consisted of 12 Bolsheviks, 12 Mensheviks, and 6 SRs.[29] At a meeting of both sections of the Soviet on June 24, deputies elected a new executive committee for both sections. The SRs received 150 votes and 13 members; the Bolsheviks 101 votes and 9 members; and the Mensheviks 87 votes and 8 members.[30] These figures are the best indicator of the actual size and party breakdown of the Soviet until new elections were held in September.

As party lines became more sharply drawn in the late spring and summer of 1917, an SR-Menshevik voting bloc took shape within the Soviet, which because of its numerical superiority could easily outvote the Bolsheviks. A pitched battle developed, for instance, over electing delegates to the All-Russian Congress of Soviets scheduled to open in July. In contrast with the Bolshevik recommendation that delegates be chosen in accordance with each party's strength within the Soviet, the SR and Menshevik proposal insisted on a "general mandate" by which the party that received the most votes would select all of the delegates, so that no Bolshevik deputies would be sent to the congress. The Bolshevik position was eventually adopted, but only after the other deputies abstained from voting to protest Bolshevik tactics.[31] At the first full plenum of the newly elected Soviet, however, the SRs insisted on choosing new delegates because the composition of the Soviet had changed so much in their favor. With the added strength of the Military Section, the SR-Menshevik mandate this time won an overwhelming number of votes. Now three SRs, one Menshevik, and one Bolshevik (Vasil'ev) were selected to go to the capital.

Acknowledging the strength of the moderate SR-Menshevik bloc in the Saratov Soviet, the Menshevik newspaper concluded that the SR and Menshevik platforms, which supported coalition with the bourgeoisie, were compatibly similar and that the Soviet now was "on the correct

27. Akademiia nauk SSSR, Institut istorii et al., *Revoliutsionnoe dvizhenie v Rossii v mae-iiune 1917 g.: Iiun'skaia demonstratsiia* (Moscow, 1959), ed. D. A. Chugaev et al., p. 201. *Sotsial-Demokrat*, no. 22, June 4, 1917, p. 3, however, cites 85 Bolsheviks, 70 Mensheviks, and 46 SRs.

28. M. Levinson, "Krest'ianskoe dvizhenie v Saratovskoi gubernii v 1917 g.," in *1917 god v Saratove* (Saratov, 1927), p. 81.

29. *Saratovskii vestnik*, no. 139, June 25, 1917, p. 3; also in *Sotsial-Demokrat*, no. 39, June 25, 1917, p. 4.

30. Gerasimenko, *Sovety Nizhnego Povolzh'ia*, p. 51.

31. *Saratovskii Sovet*, pp. 120–25; *Proletarii Povolzh'ia*, no. 14, May 24, 1917, p. 3.

path."[32] SR leaders from the Military Section, especially Pontriagin and Didenko, who had been prominent in the Military Committee, dominated Soviet meetings. Lebedev lamented that "remaining in the distinct minority we could no longer pretend to have a leading role in the Executive Committee and with Miliutin's departure from Saratov, Chertkov, an old, experienced Menshevik, a great orator and very intelligent man, was elected chairman of the Soviet."[33] Even though the Soviet held real power in Saratov, its authority and effectiveness appear to have declined at this time. Workers were beginning to complain that their interests were being overshadowed by those of the military, while garrison units were expressing dissatisfaction over the Soviet's support of the June offensive. The breakdown in cooperation among Saratov socialists, which by now had made its way to the floor of Soviet plenum meetings, contributed to the Soviet's unhealthy condition. Whether as the cause or the result of this malaise, the Saratov Soviet, like the Petrograd and Moscow soviets, began to meet less regularly in plenary session; the Executive Committee began to resolve the major problems facing the council.

Lenin's return to Russia in April and the Bolsheviks' subsequent adoption of his April Theses, followed by the co-optation of Mensheviks and SRs into the First Coalition Government at the national level, caused a critical rupture between the Bolsheviks and moderate socialists in Saratov, and open hostility between local Bolsheviks and conservative and liberal groups. But before we turn to a discussion of these political issues that undermined the post-February revolutionary solidarity among Saratov socialists, it would be useful to outline the main organizational trends within political groups and parties at this time. During the February Revolution and throughout most of March, conservative forces had maintained a low profile in Saratov. The progressively more militant articulation of radical slogans in Saratov in the spring of 1917, however, gave rise to a low-level resurgence of right-wing activity among former tsarist officials, the clergy, and Black Hundreds. By April the right had regained its courage and began to agitate against the new order. Earlier, in both Saratov and Tsaritsyn, the Orthodox bishops S. T. Illiodor and Germogen had become entangled with right-wing groups and had caused public scandals because of their ties with Rasputin. Now public opinion viewed some of the more active clergymen suspiciously. Bishop Palladii, of Saratov, was arrested in April for "counterrevolutionary agitation" and packed off to Petrograd.[34] Local newspapers frequently dis-

32. *Proletarii Povolzh'ia*, no. 18, June 7, 1917, p. 2.
33. Lebedev, "Fevral'–oktiabr'," p. 241.
34. *Khronika*, p. 44.

Troitskii Cathedral (built 1689–1695)

cussed the circulation of Black Hundred literature in town in May and June. Leaders of the Soviet received menacing messages from "criminal counterrevolutionary groups" bent on restoring the monarchy. A clandestine right-wing organization sent letters to Topuridze and other socialists in the PPEC, condemning them to death for their "harmful social activity."[35] Suspicions fell most often on former police officials as the perpetrators of these threats, and the Soviet resolved to imprison all tsarist police officials not serving in the army.[36] Although no major public disorders resulted from the conservative agitation, it nonetheless exacerbated social tensions.

For the Saratov Kadets, the spring of 1917 saw the weakening of the two institutions in which they had some political power: the City Duma and the Public Executive Committee. Once the political influence of these bodies could no longer be taken for granted, the Kadets began to pay greater attention to organizational matters. They held their first city meeting in April, elected a city committee led by Tokarskii in May, and channeled considerable energy into the garrison, where they formed their own military organization. In May *Saratovskii listok* became recognized as the Kadet newspaper. After the April crisis, which tarnished Miliukov's and the party's reputation, many provincial Kadet organizations abandoned their earlier quest for mass support and instead found new allies with other forces of "law and order." The enrollment into the party of large numbers of Octobrists, Nationalists, and other "prerevolutionary parties" (according to William G. Rosenberg, the historian of the Kadets) facilitated the party's shift to the right. In Saratov, for example, landed gentry flocked to the party, hoping that its prestige could help protect their property. The Kadet Central Committee labeled such people "March Kadets."[37] Even more harmful in the long run was the party's enthusiastic support of the Provisional Government and the war cause and its hostile attitude toward the Soviet, which shattered any hopes of acquiring a broad mass following along the Volga. As the months passed, townspeople responded with diminishing enthusiasm to the party's slogan, "Soldiers to the trenches! Workers to their machines! Farmers to their plows! Let's all unite, forget our quarrels, and remember one thing: everyone for victory!"

In contrast, the spring of 1917 marked the peak of local SR fortunes. With the reorganization of the Soviet and added strength of the Military Section, SRs constituted about half of the Soviet's membership. The party organization's newspaper, *Zemlia i volia* (Land and Liberty),

35. *Saratovskii listok*, no. 102, May 14, 1917, p. 4.

36. Ibid., pp. 1, 4; *Sotsial-Demokrat*, no. 15, May 14, 1917, p. 1; *Saratovskii Sovet*, p. 116.

37. Rosenberg, *Liberals in the Russian Revolution*, p. 121.

which had been the first local socialist paper to go to press after the February Revolution, soon became a daily, with a province-wide circulation of 30,000 copies. In April the party boasted more than 1,000 registered members in the garrison alone, and the city committee was the strongest in the Lower Volga region. Apart from its military organization, the party set up an "Open Saratov Military Organization of the SR Party," to which any soldier could belong without paying dues or joining the party. Within the city the party represented many of the unskilled so-called black workers *(chernye rabochie)*, artisans, craftsmen, students, and professionals. By the end of March party committees had begun to function in Balashov, Petrovsk, and Nikolaevsk. The well-known activist Rakitnikov chaired the local committee, which included A. A. Minin, V. M. Telegin, Tkachukov, and Didenko. Minin, Telegin, and Didenko all served on the Executive Committee of the Soviet. Rakitnikov not only headed the local committee but also chaired the Saratov uezd zemstvo board. In this capacity he likewise functioned as uezd commissar. In the new national coalition government made up of the bourgeoisie and moderate socialists, Rakitnikov accepted the portfolio of deputy minister of agriculture. Yet beneath the apparent success of the party in the spring of 1917 lay some structural and tactical fissures that would widen in the course of the year. Most local leaders belonged to the mainstream of the party, which at this time accepted coalition with the bourgeoisie, revolutionary defensism as its stance toward the war, and a policy of restraint in the countryside. Disregarding the endless stream of expressions of faith in the future constituent assembly, the editors of the local SR paper even admonished the Petrograd Soviet not to push for a speedy convocation of the assembly because the people "were not ready." The party's main bastion of rank-and-file strength in Saratov lay in the garrison, but antiwar sentiment gained more and more adherents in the barracks as the summer progressed. Soon the SRs found their main pillar of support crumbling. At the same time SR concentration on the interests of the peasant soldier did little to attract workers, who began to voice dissatisfaction with the Soviet leadership's slighting of workers' interests. Then, too, the party leadership was aware "that the horde of adventurers, careerists, and 'unsettled minds'" that had streamed into the party after the February Revolution "had introduced a strain of opportunism into its decisions."[38] Throughout 1917, "March SR" came to be used as a term of opprobrium. No firm commitments cemented these disparate types together; soon the same issues that had fractured the prerevolutionary party riddled this mass revolutionary party as well.

A split between the Bolsheviks and Mensheviks over fundamental

38. Oliver H. Radkey, *The Agrarian Foes of Bolshevism: Promise and Default of the Russian Socialist Revolutionaries, February to October 1917* (New York, 1958), p. 186.

tactical matters, to be discussed later in this chapter, paralleled the consolidation of separate party organizations in Saratov. The Mensheviks responded more slowly than the Bolsheviks to the matter of establishing a committee, in part because of the local leadership's commitment to unification. Nevertheless, the Saratov Menshevik Organization was the first independent Menshevik organization formed in the entire Lower Volga region. Until Lenin's radical position on the war and on the Provisional Government found adherents at the local level, Saratov Mensheviks had grounds for thinking a united committee possible. The left Menshevik leader Topuridze supported an internationalist position on the war, and Chertkov staunchly backed the cause of union. Holding their first organizational meeting on April 10, local Mensheviks elected a city committee led by Topuridze, Chertkov, and Maizel'. Given this late start, they lagged behind the Bolsheviks in publishing an independent newspaper and in developing district party committees within the city. Originally issued twice weekly, *Proletarii Povolzh'ia* did not become a daily until June. Analyzing their weaknesses at a city party meeting in early May, party activists pointed to financial difficulties, shaky ties with the factory district, and, despite enormous efforts, lecture and agitation activities that were less popular than similar Bolshevik endeavors. One speaker underscored the need for greater work in the garrison. By the beginning of May the Menshevik Military Organization had registered 300 members. In adopting an internationalist position on the war, they urged unification with other antiwar groups.[39] Similar internationalist sentiments were popular among the members of the Bund, the SD Jewish organization, chaired by Chertkov. Volga-area Bundist groups supported the tactical positions of the Petrograd Soviet's moderate leadership. They favored the unification of all groups except Plekhanov's Edinstvo (Unity), which favored the continuation of the war to a victorious end.[40] (The Saratov Edinstvo group, which crystallized at the end of May, controlled the editorial board of the daily *Saratovskii vestnik*. Workers from the railroad depots represented the major source of the group's limited support within the local working class.)

In contrast with the Mensheviks, the Saratov Bolsheviks set up a citywide organization in the first half of April, before the Moscow Bolshevik organization had fully emerged from the underground. In the rest of the province Bolshevik activities remained greatly circumscribed until later in the year. A Bolshevik organization began to operate in Balashov in March. By June small committees were functioning in Volsk, Nikolaevsk, and Novouzensk. The Saratov Bolshevik organization comprised five

39. *Proletarii Povolzh'ia*, no. 8, May 3, 1917, p. 2.

40. *Pervaia Povolzh'skaia oblastnaia konferentsiia Bunda: Protokoly* (Saratov, 1917), p. 8.

districts: the city, railroad yard, garrison, factory, and river-front districts.[41] The Bolsheviks' greatest strength at this time lay in the factory and railroad districts. They were weakest in the garrison and in the river-front districts. In April the organization opened a party school to train agitators and promote the party in underrepresented areas. Created in April, the Bolshevik Military Organization had enrolled 400 soldiers by June. L. M. Kaganovich, who years later surfaced as one of Stalin's henchmen, represented Saratov at the All-Russian Conference of Military Organizations.[42] For the most part, young inexperienced officers, many of whom were recent recruits to Bolshevism, made up the leadership of the committee. V. N. Sokolov, V. P. Kulikov, and P. G. Zhebrov appear to have had the greatest influence within the organization. Apparently not discerning the theoretical and tactical differences between Bolshevism and Menshevism, the young Bolshevik officers together with their Menshevik comrades published identical appeals in the Bolshevik and Menshevik newspapers, calling upon soldiers to join a united organization. A few days later at the Bolshevik city conference the party committee censured these independent steps of the Military Organization, and appointed Antonov to oversee future developments in the garrison.[43] Throughout the year, despite growing Bolshevik popularity in the garrison, the party organization could not rely on the leadership of its military organization. It bears repeating that unlike leaders in the city, who were seasoned and often well-educated Bolsheviks, those in the barracks who declared themselves party members were young and shaky in their understanding of Social Democracy. Moreover, these Bolshevized soldiers clearly shared special group interests with their comrades from other parties in the Military Committee. Military loyalties, as we shall see, played an important role in the October Revolution in Saratov.

Besides forming a military organ, the local Bolshevik committee strengthened itself in several other areas as well. The female Bolshevik activists E. K. Romanenko, E. N. Bogdanova, and E. R. Peterson formed a women's department in the city organization and recruited party members from among Saratov's working-class women. At the same time the Bolshevik party organization revived Maiak, which had suffered from benign neglect since the February Revolution.[44] Finally, the local Bol-

41. Antonov-Saratovskii, *Pod stiagom*, pp. 110–12.

42. See S. E. Rabinovich, "Vserossiiskaia konferentsiia bol'shevistskikh voennykh organizatsii 1917 g.," *Krasnaia letopis'*, no. 5/38 (1930), p. 109. See the report of a Saratov delegate to the All-Russian Conference of Military Organizations in Institut marksizma-leninizma pri TsK KPSS, *Bor'ba partii bol'shevikov za armiiu v sotsialisticheskoi revoliutsii: Sbornik dokumentov* (Moscow, 1977), pp. 249–50.

43. Vas'kin and Gerasimenko, *Fevral'skaia revoliutsiia*, pp. 63–64.

44. *Saratovskii vestnik*, no. 119, June 2, 1917, p. 3.

Political meeting, Saratov railroad station, 1917

shevik committee improved its publication, *Sotsial-Demokrat*. In many other provincial cities Bolshevik organizations had difficulty opening newspapers and often had to appeal to the Central Committee to send financial assistance and party workers.[45] This was true of neighboring Tsaritsyn, for instance; in April the Bolshevik Central Committee sent Ia. A. Erman there specifically to promote a newspaper. In Saratov lack of professional staff and funds had limited publication of the paper to three times a week. One memoirist recalled all of the technical problems that beset the staff, comparing the paper unfavorably with the more professional if less frequent Menshevik publication.[46] Having overcome these early difficulties, the paper became a daily in early June with a circulation of 10,000, which surpassed the Menshevik paper's circulation of 5,000 but still paled in comparison with the 30,000 copies of the SR organ.[47] Generally speaking, the expansion of *Sotsial-Demokrat* matched the rising fortunes of the local Bolshevik committee as a whole. At the April Conference Saratov delegates claimed a city organization of 1,600 party members.[48] In May the party had grown to 2,500 members; the committee's income from workers' dues, gifts, and lecture and concert fees had increased.

In filling out a questionnaire on their organization at the Sixth Bolshevik Party Congress in July, local Bolsheviks wrote that "the initial influence of the Bolsheviks in Saratov was strong."[49] But then structural changes in the Soviet, resulting in the increased influence of the Military Section, and new elections changed the Soviet so that its "general physiognomy . . . [became] SR-Menshevik." The Bolsheviks' hardened position on the war and on the Provisional Government also reduced their influence in the Soviet. Nevertheless, even though it seemed that the Bolsheviks "were suffering losses on all fronts," they "did not become despondent," according to Lebedev, but "felt that slowly and gradually our forces were beginning to strengthen." During the campaign for elections to the City Duma, Bolshevik strength began to grow. "All the hostile newspapers opened an intensive campaign against us and this especially

45. See, for instance, Kh. M. Astrakhan and I. S. Sazonov, "Sozdanie massovoi bol'shevistskoi pechati v 1917 godu," *Voprosy istorii*, no. 1 (1957), p. 90.

46. V. Babushkin, *Dni velikikh sobytii* (Saratov, 1932), p. 23.

47. Institut marksizma-leninizma pri TsK KPSS, "Zhurnal mestnykh partiinykh organizatsii 1917 g.: Dokumenty Instituta marksizma-leninizma pri TsK KPSS," *Istoricheskii arkhiv*, no. 5 (1959), p. 45.

48. K. T. Semenov and F. T. Misnik, "Aprel'skie tezisy V. I. Lenina—velikii obrazets tvorcheskogo marksizma," in *Kommunisticheskaia partiia—vdokhnovitel' i organizator pobedy Velikoi Oktiabr'skoi sotsialisticheskoi revoliutsii* (Moscow, 1957), p. 57; "Zhurnal mestnykh partiinykh organizatsii," p. 45.

49. Institut marksizma-leninizma pri TsK KPSS, *Shestoi s"ezd* RSDRP *(bol'shevikov), avgust 1917 goda: Protokoly* (Moscow, 1958), p. 369.

incited in the masses the desire to find out what exactly the Bolsheviks whom everyone was cursing represented."[50]

It is necessary to digress a bit to discuss the Polish refugees and prisoners of war in Saratov, since most of them expressed Social Democratic sympathies. During the war Saratov SDs had infiltrated the various legal societies organized to help refugees, including Poles, who had flooded Saratov province. After February prominent Polish SD activists emerged from the revolutionary underground in both Saratov and Tsaritsyn. Factionalism had characterized the Polish socialist movement from the beginning, and it is therefore not surprising that numerous groups appeared in Saratov. The party Social Democracy of the Kingdom of Poland and Lithuania (SDKPiL), which by now stood closest of all the Polish groups to the Bolsheviks, surfaced as the most forceful group among Saratov Poles. Ia. G. Fenigshtein (known also by his nom de guerre, Doletskii [Dolecki]), one of the leaders of the Saratov branch of the SDKPiL and a former activist in the Warsaw and Lodz committees, soon headed one of the neighborhood committees of the Saratov Bolshevik organization. Later elected to the Executive Committee of the Soviet, Fenigshtein became chairman of the Bolshevik fraction.[51] The nationalist-oriented Polish Socialist Party (PPS), its internationalist offshoot the PPS-Left, and the Polish Socialist Union (ZSP) also formed organizations in Saratov. The PPS operated a Polish cultural club and the SDKPiL and the PPS-Left both opened workers' clubs.[52] For the most part the more radical, internationalist groups displayed the greatest vitality.

In the final analysis, the local Bolshevik committee's adoption and practical application of Lenin's theses forced a split among local socialists. As in Petrograd, great confusion and bewilderment accompanied the acceptance of Lenin's political demands at the local level. "Upon Lenin's return to Russia," recalled Lebedev, "his [political] agitation, which at first was not even understood by us Bolsheviks because it seemed utopian, was gradually accepted by us and became a matter of flesh and blood."[53] Antonov described the impact of Lenin's arguments

50. Lebedev, "Fevral'–oktiabr'," pp. 242, 245.

51. Bronislaw Bronkowski (Bortnowski) and Jan Mizerkiewicz, both recently freed from prison, also merit attention. Remaining in Soviet Russia after the October Revolution, Bronkowski returned to Poland in 1929 as a member of the Central Committee of the Polish Communist party. In 1935 he became a member of the Executive Committee of the Comintern, only to fall victim to Stalin's purges. Mizerkiewicz left for Poland after the revolution and took part in the Polish Communist movement. Freed by the Americans from Buchenwald during the war, he then joined the Polish Workers' party. See A. Ia. Manusevich, *Pol'skie internatsionalisty v bor'be za pobedu Sovetskoi vlasti v Rossii, fevral'–oktiabr' 1917 g.* (Moscow, 1965), pp. 122–24, 141, 153.

52. Najdus, *Polacy w Rewolucji*, pp. 247, 374.

53. Lebedev, "Fevral'–oktiabr'," p. 242.

this way: "Comrade Lenin's arrival in Piter and his 'theses' made a tremendous impression on both the leadership and rank and file of our organization. We also became familiar with the discussion raging over Lenin's addresses—the polemic against him, Kamenev, and others. At first we were confused; some related altogether negatively to the 'theses' . . . others accepted only separate points, and only a few accepted them almost in their entirety."[54]

The adoption of Lenin's theses in Saratov destroyed all hopes for the unification of Bolshevism and Menshevism, and also brought the Mensheviks and SRs closer together. Still, individuals in both factions of Social Democracy continued to promote the cause of union throughout April and May. Despite the consolidation of a separate Bolshevik organization in Saratov in March, party members frequently discussed unification with the Mensheviks. It should be remembered that the Stalin-Kamenev group within the Bolshevik Central Committee in Petrograd had considered the possibility of a merger; hence what some Soviet historians call the equivocal position of Saratov Bolsheviks on the matter of unification more or less coincided with that of the party center. It likewise bears repeating that Saratov's working class tended to support the idea of a united party. After Lenin's return to Russia, and especially after the SRs and Mensheviks entered the First Coalition Government with the bourgeoisie, all chances for mending the differences had vanished, although this was not immediately understood at the time.

On April 12 the Saratov Bolshevik newspaper published Lenin's April Theses. Not taking a clear-cut stand on them, the accompanying editorial nonetheless suggested that acceptance of the theses would destroy all hope for union between the SD factions.[55] The merger was the focus of attention at the Bolshevik city committee's conference held on April 19–20. Before the conference convened, the Bolshevik organization's five district committees held discussions with rank-and-file members to assess working-class sentiment and explain the reasons for Lenin's strident stand. Before the opening of the city conference, the city district, one of the local committees, passed a resolution that probably reflected sentiments held by many within the Saratov party organization before Lenin's agitation had won converts. The city district committee declared that it would "welcome any steps taken toward the creation of a united Social Democratic revolutionary party"; but that union could take place only with "those groups grounded in international revolutionary socialism."[56]

During the Bolshevik city conference the local committee adopted a general strategy in regard to unification which already was less com-

54. Antonov-Saratovskii, "Saratov s fevralia," p. 180.
55. *Sotsial-Demokrat*, no. 5, April 12, 1917, p. 2.
56. Ibid., no. 6, April 16, 1917, p. 3; *Saratovskii vestnik*, no. 81, April 15, 1917, p. 3.

promising than the resolution passed by the city district committee. But because of the wide range of opinions expressed by Bolshevik intelligenty who dominated the proceedings, the door was not completely shut to unification with Menshevik Internationalists. Mgeladze stood out as the staunchest local Bolshevik supporter of union. He argued that union was possible with the moderate-oriented Petrograd Menshevik Organizational Committee and the group centered around *Rabochaia gazeta* (Workers' Paper, the official Petrograd Menshevik paper) even though it rejected "the position of Comrade Zinoviev, expressed in *Pravda*, about unification only with the so-called Zimmerwald Left, that is, with the left wing of the Zimmerwald Union of Internationalists."[57] As long as the Petrograd Menshevik Organizational Committee adhered to an internationalist position on the war, reasoned Mgeladze, union made sense. Lebedev strongly rejected Mgeladze's stand.[58] So did Antonov. Expressing reservations about a merger, Mitskevich and Miliutin nonetheless suggested that the two SD factions participate in a national congress in order to take into account the opinions of SDs throughout the empire, an idea that had enjoyed popularity among provincial committees back in 1905. (Earlier Mitskevich had favored the establishment of a united committee in Saratov.) After two days of debate the conference delegates passed a resolution stating that the imperialist war divided socialists into internationalists and national chauvinists, and that between the two "a bridge cannot be built." On the other hand, it argued that a merger should take place among all elements "that accept and conduct an internationalist policy, that is, reject 'civil peace' [*grazhdanskii mir*], take a position of irreconcilable class war, and lead the struggle for an immediate end to the World War." The resolution concluded with an expression of the Bolsheviks' determination "to achieve such a union, despite possible differences of opinion on several questions of proletarian tactics."[59] The conference furthermore agreed to participate in a joint newspaper venture that would unite all socialists who supported the

57. The Zimmerwald Conference, an attempt to restore the broken links among European socialists, met in 1915. At the conference delegates adopted the so-called Zimmerwald Manifesto, expressing abhorrence of the war policy backed by most European socialist leaders. See M. Gesler, "Saratovskaia bol'shevistskaia organizatsiia 10 let tomu nazad," in *1917 god v Saratove* (Saratov, 1927), p. 38. For a summary of Mgeladze's position see *Sotsial-Demokrat*, no. 8, April 25, 1917, p. 2.

58. Antonov-Saratovskii, "Saratov s fevralia," p. 179.

59. The resolution can be found in Gesler, "Saratovskaia bol'shevistskaia organizatsiia," pp. 38–39; *Sotsial-Demokrat*, no. 9, April 28, 1917, p. 2; Antonov-Saratovskii, *Pod stiagom*, pp. 114–15. Summaries can be found in D. Kin, "Bor'ba protiv 'ob"edinitel'nogo udara' v 1917 g.," *Proletarskaia revoliutsiia*, no. 6/65 (1927), p. 48. Those present at the conference decided to take part in a joint newspaper venture that would unite all those supporting the Zimmerwald and Kienthal conferences (including SRs). See *Sotsial-Demokrat*, no. 7, April 22, 1917, p. 3.

Zimmerwald and Kienthal conferences (Left SRs and Menshevik Internationalists).

All in all, the way was being paved for the formation of a left socialist bloc that would surface in Saratov in the fall of 1917. Be that as it may, a strong measure of uncertainty surrounded the local party organization's reaction to Lenin's April Theses and to the matter of unification with the Mensheviks. Most Soviet accounts oversimplify the true complexity of the interrelations among local socialists in the spring of 1917, painting everything in heavy strokes of black and white. The proposal passed by the Bolshevik city conference in April, calling for union with internationalists, kept the doors open to further discussion on the matter. Rank-and-file members continued to support union. In the beginning of May local railroad workers called for unification of all Bolshevik and Menshevik groups and elected a commission to look into the opening of a newspaper to represent the internationalist position.[60] Even though serious doubts about the utility of a merger between Social Democrats had surfaced, the various parties continued publicly to minimize their theoretical and tactical differences. At a meeting of representatives of all socialist parties held on April 29, a mood of camaraderie and cooperation on important matters pervaded the discussions. The socialist leaders had assembled to talk over the threat of counterrevolution and public disorder, which had intensified after the Miliukov crisis. The Bolsheviks present pointed an accusing finger at the bourgeoisie and at Black Hundred groups for fomenting local disturbances. The SRs Rakitnikov and Telegin similarly attacked bourgeois intrigues against the democracy, as did the Popular Socialist Miasoedov and the Menshevik M. E. Rozenblium. Although he took a cautious view of the role of soviets in the "bourgeois revolution," the Menshevik Chertkov voiced opposition to the creation of a coalition government. Before adjourning, the participants passed a resolution reaffirming the role of the Soviet in conducting organizational and political work among the masses, and called for more frequent meetings among leaders of the various socialist parties.[61]

Within two weeks, the relations between Bolsheviks and the moderate socialists had changed dramatically and sharp political debates now took place within Soviet plenums. Socialist leaders, however, continued to present a united front to the population at large. After particularly caustic arguments at the end of May, the various local party committees issued a joint declaration emphasizing that their differences remained "comradely."[62] It should be noted that the increase in tension followed the return of Miliutin, Alekseev, and Plaksin from the Bolshevik party

60. Antonov-Saratovskii, *Pod stiagom*, p. 127.
61. Ibid., pp. 291–95.
62. *Proletarii Povolzh'ia*, no. 16, May 31, 1917, p. 4.

Saratov railway shop workers, 1917

conference in Petrograd (at which Miliutin was elected to the Bolshevik Central Committee) and the local committee's formal adoption of Lenin's April Theses on May 11, which in effect marked its first public support for a transfer of power to the soviets. At the same time moderate socialists entered the First Coalition Government. Up until this point the nature of dual power at the national level had involved rivalry between two class organs—the middle-class government and the working-class Soviet. Now the differences had become blurred. Having been co-opted into the government, the moderate socialists would share responsibility for its successes and failures. At the national level the leaders of the Petrograd Soviet relinquished to the government much of the power it had held. At the local level, once the SRs and Menshevik committees accepted the formation of the government and agreed to support it, they began to assign a lesser role to the Soviet and actually sought to reduce its significance vis-à-vis governmental organs. Related to the acceptance of the new government, of course, was the issue of the war. Submerged beneath mass acceptance of revolutionary defensism lay the belief that the war soon would end and that the government was doing everything possible to conclude peace. When these hopes were shattered, the Bolsheviks benefited. For not only had they criticized the moderate socialists' participation in the coalition, but they also had taken a most relentlessly critical attitude toward the war itself.

These interrelated events did not proceed in a linear fashion in a direct march toward Bolshevism. Nevertheless, the combined effect of an expanding militancy among Bolsheviks and the moderate socialists' growing willingness to cooperate with the middle classes set the stage for later Bolshevik gains in Saratov. The local response to the Miliukov Note is a case in point. Mass attitudes in provincial Russia in the spring of 1917 are difficult to illuminate and probe, but the driving force behind the street disturbances that broke out in Saratov appears to have been increased dissatisfaction with the political status quo. Only two days before news of the Miliukov Note became known in Saratov, workers and soldiers had marched in a pro-government May Day celebration (which actually took place on April 18, in accordance with the New Style calendar, even though it had not yet been formally adopted).[63] A week later these same crowds rioted.

Locally, the Bolsheviks took the lead in condemning Miliukov, pressing the Soviet to convene a special session to discuss the foreign minister's alleged double dealing. The Executive Committee passed Vasil'ev's resolution denouncing the Miliukov Note.[64] At the next meeting of the plenum, deputies expressed concern over the effect the news would have on law and order in the city. The situation seemed particularly critical in the garrison and as a result Soviet deputies noted their apprehensions about the administrative ambiguity caused by the existence of both the Soviet and the Military Committee. Fears of street disorders proved well grounded. The local SR newspaper reported that "on April 25–26 in Saratov wineshops were broken into and the plundering of alcoholic beverages took place. The crowd, roused by pogrom agitators, had forgotten the difficult times that our homeland is living through; had forgotten their own brothers. . . ."[65] *Saratovskii vestnik* related that a drunken soldier had convinced a crowd that a certain shop owned by a merchant named Davydov was selling wine at a reduced price. Rushing to the store and discovering that the "unknown person in a soldier's coat" had lied, the public sacked the shop and seized the entire wine and food reserves.[66] The street disorders, which took several days to subside, called attention to the problem of political power in the city and contributed to the demise of the Public Executive Committee. According to press reports, former police officials and gendarmes had instigated the disorders. Without discussing their actions with the PEC, the Soviet and Military Committee banned "all street meetings and demonstrations,"

63. See *Saratovskii vestnik,* no. 78, April 12, 1917, p. 4, and *Sotsial-Demokrat,* no. 6, April 16, 1917, p. 2; *Proletarii Povolzh'ia,* no. 5, April 22, 1917, p. 1.

64. *Saratovskii Sovet,* p. 98; Osipov, *1917 god v Saratove,* pp. 73–74.

65. *Zemlia i volia,* no. 14, April 27, 1917, p. 1.

66. *Saratovskii vestnik,* no. 91, April 27, 1917, p. 3.

agreed to destroy all wine reserves in Saratov, forbade unwarranted arrests, and warned that all who violated these orders would be dealt with as "enemies of the people." Although the PEC later formally approved these measures, the Kadet members criticized the Soviet's actions as "an anarchistic display of power."[67] In response, the Bolsheviks as well as the SRs and Mensheviks blasted the "bourgeoisie" for their counterrevolutionary sentiments and actions.[68]

The Saratov socialists' united front against the street disorders and against "bourgeois" criticism of the Soviet crumbled with the formation of the First Coalition Government on May 6. In the Volga region as a whole the problem of the socialists' participation in the Provisional Government prompted passionate debates almost everywhere. Local Menshevik and SR committees endorsed the decisions of their central committees even though prominent individuals in both parties reluctantly backed the coalition. The Kazan SR Committee, for instance, which in the fall of 1917 became recognized as one of the strongest Left SR groups in the country, flatly rejected the party's willingness to enter the coalition, calling Kerensky's actions and Chernov's a betrayal of the party's revolutionary past. In Saratov, SR and Menshevik leaders supported the coalition. At a meeting called to discuss whether socialists should enter the government, the Executive Committee of the Soviet debated the very nature of the revolution and the role of the soviets in the new order. Adhering to resolutions adopted by the Bolshevik party at its April Conference, Saratov Bolsheviks insisted that the soviets represented real power and that they should move even more decisively in the future toward a strictly soviet solution to governmental power. In stark contrast, Menshevik and SR speakers expressed fear that the revolution would collapse without the participation of the bourgeoisie, and even argued that the Soviet's authority should be limited to the economic realm. According to B. N. Guterman, "the soviets should be centers of agreement. We are resolutely against any attempts to seize power on their behalf."[69]

The debate over the socialists' participation in the coalition government then shifted to the Soviet plenum. Repeating the commonly held Menshevik view that Russia was not ready for social revolution, Maizel' appealed to the delegates "to hold back the class struggle, or else Russia

67. Ibid., no. 92, April 28, 1917, pp. 2–3; no. 93, April 29, p. 4; no. 94, April 30, p. 5; no. 95, May 2, p. 5. Some of the rioters rallied around the slogan "Give Us Bread, Give Us a Tsar." The Bolsheviks accused landowners of instigating these disturbances. See *Sotsial-Demokrat,* no. 12, May 5, 1917, p. 1.

68. *Sotsial-Demokrat,* no. 12, May 5, 1917, p. 1; *Proletarii Povolzh'ia,* no. 8, May 3, 1917, p. 2.

69. Gerasimenko and Tochenyi, *Sovety Povolzh'ia,* p. 68.

will perish," and to support the new government wholeheartedly. In response Miliutin attacked coalition with the "counterrevolutionary bourgeoisie," insisting that the only way out of Russia's political impasse was a transfer of power to the soviets.[70] The subsequent vote on opposing resolutions was the clearest statement to date on working-class attitudes toward the government. By a vote of 153 in favor, 76 opposed, and with 11 abstentions, the plenum carried the moderates' resolution calling for support of the new government. Applauding the moderates' victory, *Saratovskii vestnik* reported that "apparently in the minds of the broad masses of the people, a turn is beginning to be noticed . . . the Soviet . . . voted its full support to the new government, having rejected the local Bolsheviks' resolution."[71]

Such a polarization of views on the new government and on the role of soviets ended cooperation among socialists in most other Volga-area soviets as well. On May 22 the Second Regional Congress of Soviets opened in nearby Samara. Among the 57 delegates were 30 Mensheviks, 15 Bolsheviks, and 12 SRs. Discussion revolved around the question of power; accordingly, the moderate socialists, arguing that the soviets should limit their activities to directing the working class's economic struggle, rejected the Bolshevik slogan "All Power to the Soviets" as too adventuristic and dangerous. Insisting that without the cooperation of the bourgeoisie a government of democratic elements would lead Russia to economic ruin, Menshevik speakers upheld the coalition with the middle class. The Congress also resolved to support the so-called Freedom Loan, floated by the government to fund the war, and passed a defensist resolution on the war.[72] Although the majority of delegates backed coalition with the propertied elements, a vocal minority of Bolsheviks pressed for adoption of a platform calling for a transfer of power to the soviets.

The irreconciliable differences between Bolsheviks and moderate socialists over support of the new government found analogous expression in all matters related to the war. Once again the Bolsheviks displayed increasing militancy as the spring progressed while the moderate socialists, having entered the new government, found themselves committed to the government's policies. As an illustration of changing Bol-

70. *Proletarii Povolzh'ia*, no. 11, May 13, 1917, p. 1. Typical of many passed throughout the country, the resolution called upon the democracy to show the government support "necessary for strengthening the gains of the revolution."

71. *Saratovskii vestnik*, no. 103, May 13, 1917, pp. 2–3. The Samara and Tsaritsyn soviets passed similar votes of support.

72. Gerasimenko and Tochenyi, *Sovety Povolzh'ia*, p. 75; Mints, *Oktiabr' v Povolzh'e*, pp. 100–101; F. F. Zakharov, *Samarskie bol'sheviki v Oktiabr'skoi revoliutsii* (Kuibyshev, 1957), p. 34.

shevik sentiments in Saratov at this time, one might turn to the local response to the Freedom Loan. By a vote of 189 to 21 a Soviet plenum agreed to back the loan. The large number of votes in favor suggests that many Bolsheviks initially supported it too. Yet all this changed, as one Bolshevik memoirist explained: "At first our organization had no idea of what to do; there was no unity of views among the majority of our members. But the confusion continued for several weeks only; then, on the basis of firmer directives from the center, Saratov Bolsheviks openly began to denounce the Freedom Loan to undermine the defensist Provisional Government, which had come out with the slogan of merciless struggle with dual power, that is, with the existence of the soviets."[73]

As we have seen, before Lenin's return to Russia the Saratov Bolsheviks had adopted the Petrograd Soviet's stand on the war, agreeing to bolster the rear and the front in order "to strengthen the achievements of the revolution."[74] In April, as the Petrograd Soviet battled with Miliukov over appropriate appeals to Russia's allies, the Saratov Bolsheviks adhered closely to the Petrograd Soviet's announcements. They adopted a resolution calling for a speedy end to the war "on the basis of peace without annexations or contributions and with the concession to each nation of the right of self-determination."[75] The SRs, Mensheviks, and Popular Socialists likewise accepted the Petrograd Soviet's platform. At a meeting of local railroad workers, deputies adopted by a vote of 154 in favor, 51 against, and 17 abstentions this very resolution introduced by Antonov on behalf of "both factions of Social Democracy."[76] Implicit in the resolution was not only a firm commitment to put a speedy end to the war by supporting the Petrograd Soviet's peace overtures but an equally firm one against conclusion of a separate peace. While the Bolshevik denunciation of the new coalition government appealed to industrial workers in the city's largest factories, these same workers clung stubbornly to the notion of revolutionary defensism. In the popular view, as long as Russia's war aims were no longer "imperialist," continuing the war meant safeguarding the fruits of the revolution in the face of German militarism; the idea of a separate peace amounted to an admission of failure and so went against the grain of national pride and esteem. Workers at the Zhest factory, to cite one example, while protesting the Freedom Loan and the entry of the socialists into the bourgeois government, called the idea of a separate peace "inadmissible and harmful to the cause of revolution."

73. E. Petrov, "Iz zhizni," *Vestnik Saratovskogo Gubkoma RKP*, no. 24 (1922), p. 11.

74. *Izvestiia Saratovskogo Soveta*, no. 18, April 2, 1917, p. 4.

75. *Saratovskii vestnik*, no. 78, April 12, 1917, p. 5.

76. *Sotsial-Demokrat*, no. 5, April 12, 1917, p. 2. See also *Proletarii Povolzh'ia*, no. 3, April 12, 1917, p. 2.

The issue of the war loomed large in the local response to the June demonstrations in Petrograd. At the beginning of the month Bolsheviks and anarchists had already begun to enjoy such a large measure of popular support in the capital that Petrograd Bolsheviks planned a public demonstration for June 9, which they hoped would turn into a mass demonstration on behalf of a call for a transfer of power to the soviets and against the new coalition ministry. Aware of Bolshevik plans, the Executive Bureau of the Petrograd Soviet banned all demonstrations, a decision endorsed by the First All-Russian Congress of Soviets, which recently had opened in Petrograd. Convinced that the Petrograd masses would support the coalition and reject Bolshevik agitation, the Executive Bureau in conjunction with the Congress later decided to stage a public rally of its own on June 18, and directed all provincial soviets to organize similar activities. Back in Saratov the Executive Committee experienced a deadlock, for the Mensheviks and SRs insisted on a Soviet-sponsored demonstration under the banner of common slogans issued by the Soviet. By a close margin they voted down the Bolshevik proposal calling for separate party slogans. When the Executive Committee turned to the problem of working out acceptable slogans agreeable to all parties within the Soviet, the moderates blocked the Bolsheviks' "All Power to the All-Russian Soviet of Workers' and Soldiers' Deputies," which amounted to a call for an all-socialist government. Because acceptable slogans could not be agreed upon, the SR-Menshevik majority in the Executive Committee decided to ban all demonstrations in Saratov.[77]

Requesting a change in the agenda of the June 20 Soviet meeting, the Bolshevik Fenigshtein attempted to debate the proposed demonstration within the plenum. He argued that growing mass indifference toward the Soviet necessitated the staging of some sort of political rally. The Menshevik Lin'kov spoke out against Fenigshtein's suggestion, maintaining that the Soviet had too much practical work to accomplish and also that the other parties found Bolshevik slogans unacceptable. When the matter of sponsoring a demonstration was put to a vote, the motion was defeated. Most of the deputies blocked Fenigshtein's efforts to speak again; the Bolshevik representatives accompanied by some SRs and Mensheviks (probably Left SRs and Menshevik Internationalists) quit the hall.[78] As an explanation of the moderates' behavior it is worth mentioning that much to the surprise of the Petrograd leaders, the demonstration on June 18 had turned into a massive show of support for the

77. *Saratovskii Sovet*, pp. 147–48; *Saratovskii vestnik*, no. 133, June 18, 1917, p. 4; *Proletarii Povolzh'ia*, no. 21, June 18, 1917, p. 2.

78. *Sotsial-Demokrat*, no. 36, June 22, 1917, p. 3. Some 104 deputies from the Workers' Section protested the Bolshevik walkout. See *Proletarii Povolzh'ia*, no. 23, June 28, 1917, p. 4.

Bolshevik platform. It was not altogether inconceivable that a similar turn of events, although on a lesser scale, would have taken place in Saratov. They simply didn't know.

The Bolshevik newspaper *Sotsial-Demokrat* announced that if the Soviet did not again place the demonstration on its agenda, the Bolsheviks would arrange a peaceful demonstration of their own in Saratov on the following Sunday. Accordingly, the Executive Committee of the Soviet adopted a resolution appealing "to our comrades the Bolsheviks not to organize a separate demonstration."[79] Fear that any public display could easily develop into unruly mob action colored the majority socialists' reluctance to stage a march. For several days enraged throngs of people had broken into cooperatives, threatened to loot the supplies of flour and sugar, and assaulted clerks. Rumors had apparently spread throughout town that after the co-ops closed, sales clerks illegally hawked reserves. Suspicion once again fell on former city and gendarme employees for instigating rumors and inciting the crowds.

At the same time that local Bolsheviks were backing resolutions unacceptable to the Soviet majority, they were voicing strong objections to the June offensive and the war effort in general. Vasil'ev stood particularly far to the left. At one Soviet meeting he advanced the slogan "Bourgeoisie to the Trenches"; the Menshevik newspaper chided him for his lack of "political foresight."[80] A few days later, Vasil'ev's perfervid antiwar speech created an uproar in the Soviet. By a vote of 241 to 130 the moderates defeated this call for an end to the war.[81] This vote was important not because the Bolsheviks lost but because radical slogans had mustered such surprisingly solid support.

The rupture between the moderate and radical socialists in Saratov also found expression in preelection campaigning for the Duma elections. Initially the Bolsheviks had agreed to form a bloc with the Mensheviks and SRs, but as the Bolshevik position on coalition government and on the war became more militant, the Mensheviks and SRs formed a separate bloc without them. The nonsocialist parties began their attacks on the Bolsheviks in April when an anti-Bolshevik leaflet, *On German Spies*, surreptitiously circulated in the city. Before long the editors of *Saratovskii vestnik* picked up on this theme, arguing that the Bolsheviks were working for Germany. In June the Kadet paper, *Saratovskii listok*, published what the Bolsheviks later blasted as Black Hundred–like articles against Bolsheviks and other internationalists.[82] The Bolsheviks, too,

79. *Sotsial-Demokrat*, no. 42, June 29, 1917, p. 3.

80. *Proletarii Povolzh'ia*, no. 23, June 28, 1917, p. 1. Antonov claims that the other socialists especially hated Vasil'ev because he was so sarcastic. See *Pod stiagom*, p. 125.

81. *Saratovskii vestnik*, no. 143, July 1, 1917, p. 3.

82. *Sotsial-Demokrat*, no. 26, June 10, 1917, p. 1.

eagerly engaged in the newspaper editorial war, especially after the formation of the coalition government. Censuring the "dictatorship of the majority over the minority" within the Soviet, for instance, *Sotsial-Demokrat* singled out the "Napoleonic tendencies" of the Menshevik leader Maizel'. Soon all of the papers were at war. The editors of *Proletarii Povolzh'ia* announced that the Edinstvo-backed *Saratovskii vestnik* had been friendly up until mid-June, but then had "declared war on the Mensheviks."[83] The Mensheviks lost no time responding in kind to the "Plekhanovites." The Kadet paper accused all of the socialist parties of tearing down Kadet posters and of other unfair practices.[84]

Campaigning for the City Duma elections in Saratov took place in an atmosphere of increased tension as political forces remained in flux. As in other towns, the local population had bestowed upon the Soviet more political weight than the Soviet leadership had anticipated. To the delight, confusion, dismay, and surprise of its leaders, the Soviet soon surpassed the Public Executive Committee in influence and authority. Viewed suspiciously and even disdainfully by broad elements of "the democracy," the City Duma, like all tsarist institutions elected under the old property qualifications, soon stopped functioning altogether. In the meanwhile, Lenin's return to Russia in April and the Bolshevik party's subsequent adoption of his April Theses provided the party with tactical guidelines that ultimately resulted in the drawing of hardened class and party lines within political institutions.

Marking a departure from their previous willingness to work within the coalition of fellow socialists and liberals, the Saratov Bolshevik Organization at the end of May refused to serve in the reorganized Provincial Public Executive Committee. Saratov's political leaders recognized the utter impotence of the committee, and accepted the evolution toward rule by the Soviet. The moderate socialists retained their cosmetic coalition with the bourgeoisie in the PPEC, but the major concern of Saratov's ruling elite by late spring 1917 was whether or not cooperation among socialists would continue. After the Soviet had merged with the Military Committee and had broadened its representation among the nonindustrialized working class, the Bolsheviks lost some of the ability to affect politics which they had enjoyed earlier. Nevertheless, the party's call for a soviet government and its rejection of the First Coalition Government set up in May clearly distinguished the Bolsheviks' program from others, laying the foundation for benefits that were to be reaped later. The Bolsheviks' growing antiwar stand also came to separate them from the

83. *Proletarii Povolzh'ia*, no. 22, June 22, 1917, p. 2.
84. *Saratovskii listok*, no. 144, July 5, 1917, p. 3.

majority socialists. Internationalist sentiments struck a surprisingly strong chord among some Saratov Mensheviks, Bundists, Polish socialists, and SRs, but an even more robust defensist spirit competed against internationalist feelings. By late June the illusion of socialist solidarity had been shattered, and the moderate socialists sought to apply the brakes to a social revolution that threatened to speed past them. Because of their commitment to coalition with tsenzovoe obshchestvo, the SRs and Mensheviks now placed their hopes on the City Duma, which would soon be reelected on democratic principles. But what they did not foresee was that the class-oriented Soviet would continue to muster more authority than a democratically elected duma, and that Saratov's working class and soldiers were beginning to listen more attentively to what the Bolsheviks had to say.

CHAPTER 4

The Meaning of the Newly Won Freedoms: Popular Organizations in the Spring of 1917

One of the most difficult objects of investigation in any revolutionary setting is the role of the common people. The vast array of ideological and emotional evaluations of the events of 1917 makes this a particularly tough problem to probe in the Russian context. During the revolution itself socialist jargon had split society into two antithetical groups: "the democracy," broadly defined as all political and social forces to the left of the Kadets, and tsenzovoe obshchestvo, or census society, as the propertied elements were called. In much of the existing historical writing about what these two groups expected from the revolution, heroes and villains abound. But it is the inarticulate, unscrubbed, ordinary sorts who receive the most diverse assessments. "The democracy," the people or *narod*, at one and the same time are labeled the manipulated mob, the revolutionary masses in step behind their progressive leaders, or an anarchistic, uncontrollable human tidal wave whose misguided rage washed away Russia's newly won freedoms. This chapter examines how Saratov's working class, the soldiers garrisoned in town, and the peasants in the surrounding countryside responded to the unprecedented freedoms introduced by the February Revolution. Without access to Soviet archives, the true complexity of the social texture of revolutionary politics in 1917 eludes investigation; much of what will be said here must therefore be viewed as inconclusive. Nevertheless, even a limited study of popular attitudes in Saratov adds a needed perspective to our understanding of the revolutionary process outside Petrograd and Moscow.

The attitudes of Saratov's factory workers toward the major political and social issues of the day lend themselves to partial analysis only. Most available information illuminates the behavior of industrial workers, and within that stratum, of those concentrated in the metalworks, railroad shops, and other large enterprises. A study of labor organizations, resolutions passed at factory meetings, the transactions of the Workers' Section of the Soviet, and less structured forms of behavior reveals a good deal about those issues that affected all workers. Because economic issues shaped working-class politics and attitudes in Saratov the most, an examination of the proletariat's efforts to improve its economic lot provides the most fruitful method of exploring working-class attitudes in general. Sources must be used with caution, especially with regard to the thorny question of the working class's relationship to census society and to the latter's political institutions. At the lowest level the most direct and often the only contact the proletariat had with "the bourgeois system" was at the workplace, in its dealings with the factory administration. The Saratov proletariat's sustained suspicion and mistrust of the factory management, sources suggest, paralleled a hardening of class lines toward the Provisional Government and political power in general.

Like workers virtually everywhere in urban Russia, the Saratov proletariat directed its first offensive in the economic realm at achieving the eight-hour workday. All sources illuminating working-class behavior in March and April underscore this almost universal demand. On March 10, the Society of Factory Owners in Petrograd signed an agreement with the Petrograd Soviet to institute the shortened workday in the capital. Without waiting for news of this precedent, workers at Saratov's Zhest factory "in a revolutionary manner" *(iavochnym poriadkom)*—illegally as far as the owners were concerned—declared the eight-hour day at their enterprise on the same day. Laborers in Saratov's butter creameries followed suit a few days later. Local Bolsheviks raised the issue of the eight-hour day within the PEC, which on March 18 ordered all factory owners to reach an agreement with the Soviet before March 22.

A variety of fears, however, prompted leaders to proceed cautiously in formally institutionalizing the eight-hour day in Saratov. Addressing the Executive Committee of the Soviet on April 3, a representative of the Petrograd Soviet confidentially reported on the introduction of the shortened workday in the capital. His account contributed to the reluctance of local leaders to act decisively. Describing how Petrograd workers "do not strain themselves . . . and take every opportunity to shun work," the visitor emphasized the possible negative effects of the reform, such as an estrangement between workers and soldiers and reduced production.[1]

1. *Saratovskii Sovet*, p. 80.

Although the Saratov Soviet's "conciliatory commission" had drawn up plans to introduce the change in all local enterprises, by the end of April the matter had not yet been completely resolved, in part because factory owners clearly opposed the shortened workday. Informing readers that the "bourgeois press . . . is continuing . . . the campaign to incite soldiers against workers," the Bolshevik's *Sotsial-Demokrat* described how "unknown characters in soldier's garb" were stopping people in the streets to discuss the eight-hour day, arousing soldiers and civilians against workers.[2]

Apprehensions over strained relations between workers and soldiers involved the Military Committee in negotiations concerning the eight-hour workday. In mid-April the MC invited representatives from all military units, factories, public organizations, and political parties to discuss the matter. Although they came to endorse the reform, speakers stressed the importance of initiating it "in a lawful manner" and of maintaining "harmony between labor and capital." Frank statements about the workers' spirited determination to reach independent solutions proved the most compelling reason for reaching an acceptable consensus rather than workers' dubious assertions that production had increased at enterprises in which the shortened day had already taken effect.[3] Noting that workers everywhere were introducing the eight-hour day illegally, "in a revolutionary fashion," representatives of local industry agreed "in the name of civil peace" not to raise again the question of abolishing the eight-hour day. The resolution passed at this meeting, markedly similar in tone to a decision reached at the All-Russian Conference of Soviets in Petrograd in early April, emphasized the urgency of producing defense-related materials and chided the press for encouraging rifts between soldiers and workers. Overtime work was deemed mandatory in some industries to placate industrialists and military leaders.

In the following weeks most Saratov factory workers reached agreements with their employers on the question of the eight-hour workday. The dynamics of the process entailed a mixture of tension and goodwill. In those cases in which local workers were pitted against industrialists in a struggle for the shortened workday, labor relations remained damaged, resulting in a heightening of suspicions and tensions by summer, for economic life deteriorated in Saratov at this time. Food reserves dwindled. Periodic shortages and long lines in front of local shops became more common, and Saratov newspapers offered little hope that conditions would improve. City authorities began to ration bread and sugar in June. Food riots broke out at the end of the month. The plundering of food shops resulted in a growing incidence of *samosud* or

2. *Sotsial-Demokrat*, no. 5, April 12, 1917, p. 1; no. 3, April 7, 1917, p. 2.
3. See, for example, *Saratovskii vestnik*, no. 87, April 22, 1917, p. 4.

vigilante activities as mobs of angry people beat up thieves and hooligans who happened to be apprehended. In some neighborhoods citizen groups formed night patrols to aid the militia against the sharp rise in thefts and murders.[4] An ever apparent housing shortage served as a sorry complement to the lack of goods. Flooded by refugees and soldiers, Saratov was hard put to house everyone. Renters charged that they were at the mercy of apartment speculators and greedy landlords. Toward the end of April the Saratov Soviet organized a union of renters, which soon signed up 12,000 members.[5] The relationship between renters and homeowners, *Sotsial-Demokrat* informed readers, is "one of those areas of our life in which a great many grudges, misunderstandings, and conflicts have built up."[6] In all areas the stark economic realities of war had created shortages and bottlenecks, making social services glaringly inadequate. Most of the estimated 1,500 school-age children of refugees crowded together in Saratov, for instance, were unable to attend school. Complaining about lack of underwear, linen, medical care, and even food, the administration of the local psychiatric hospital reported that the facilities built to handle 240 people now had to cope with 750 patients.[7]

Once the eight-hour day had been attained, workers complained most about wages, night work, child labor, poor medical care, and the nagging fear of losing their jobs. The proceedings of a congress of workers' deputies from twenty-six textile factories in Saratov, Samara, Simbirsk, and Penza provinces, held in Saratov in late June, provide insights into other grievances voiced by a stratum of local workers about whom sources are otherwise silent. While it is difficult to ascertain which workers represented Saratov factories, the reports suggest that the problems alluded to were almost universal. In addition to complaints about run-down machinery, poor working conditions, and rampant venereal disease, workers grumbled about the behavior of factory owners. Workers criticized their bosses' efforts to avoid military service, to sow dissent among workers and between workers and peasants or between workers and soldiers.[8]

The economic breakdown threatened Saratov workers with unemployment. Insufficient supplies forced some local industries to cut back their operations in April. Because of lack of raw materials, replacement saws

4. Ibid., no. 137, June 23, 1917, p. 3; no. 139, June 25, p. 3.

5. *Proletarii Povolzh'ia*, no. 7, April 29, 1917, pp. 2–3; also no. 11, May 13, p. 1.

6. *Sotsial-Demokrat*, no. 35, June 21, 1917, p. 3.

7. Information on the children of Saratov's refugees can be found in *Proletarii Povolzh'ia*, no. 7, April 29, 1917, p. 3. Overcrowding in the local psychiatric hospital is noted in *Saratovskii vestnik*, no. 111, May 24, 1917, p. 4.

8. *Zhurnal zasedaniia s"ezda rabochikh deputatov 26 fabrik sukonnogo proizvodstva Samarskoi, Saratovskoi, Simbirskoi, i Penzenskoi gubernii* (Saratov, 1917).

and other instruments, repair equipment, and nails, and a general transportation crisis, production at the Gering sawmill had dipped to less than 50 percent of the prewar level. A local foundry and machine-construction factory experienced an equally bleak drop in production and extensive layoffs. Three local printshops functioned at 40 to 70 percent of their prewar capacity, with a corresponding decrease in the number of workers employed there. The flour mills were hardest hit. Local peasants sent less and less grain to urban markets, a situation that reduced output and inflated flour prices.[9] The plight of Saratov's factories worsened in May, when eight small enterprises closed. According to a report in the Menshevik newspaper, "at the largest factories production is down, too. In addition, two flour mills are not working."[10]

Runaway inflation and a national transportation breakdown cut back on industrial output and aggravated unemployment. In Saratov the number of registered unemployed individuals (13 percent of whom were classified as skilled workers) reached 4,400 at the beginning of April. This figure shot up to 5,600 in May.[11] In June and July the number without work remained above 4,000. It seems unlikely, however, that the number of unemployed dropped because more jobs had become available. Since the jobless rates for unskilled laborers remained high, a return to the villages probably explains the decrease in registered unemployed workers. The Saratov Soviet had taken steps to alleviate unemployment, but the only documented successes it scored involved sending the unskilled jobless into the villages to hire themselves out.[12] In early May the Soviet commissioned Lebedev to work out a proposal to deal with unemployment. In accord with his plan to create more jobs, the Soviet set up a commission to investigate the causes for layoffs at each enterprise, and requested the minister of labor to take energetic measures at the national level to regulate production and organize insurance for those without jobs.

Often arguing that workers pressed for irresponsible and unreasonable gains, local industrialists faced serious problems keeping their enterprises running. Some factory owners, however, contributed to workers'

9. V. G. Khodakov, "Rabochii kontrol' v Saratovskoi gubernii v period podgotovki Velikoi Oktiabr'skoi sotsialisticheskoi revoliutsii (mart–oktiabr' 1917 goda)," in *Uchenye zapiski Saratovskogo gosudarstvennogo universiteta*, 47 (1956), 56.

10. *Proletarii Povolzh'ia*, no. 11, May 13, 1917, p. 2.

11. See *Khronika*, pp. 50, 60; *Proletarii Povolzh'ia*, no. 26, July 5, 1917, p. 3.

12. *Sotsial-Demokrat*, no. 44, July 2, 1917, p. 4. See also *Proletarii Povolzh'ia*, no. 26, July 5, 1917, and *Khronika*, p. 78. Unskilled workers threatened to drive away from work prisoners of war, reservists, and workers who had not registered to join the union of unskilled workers. The Soviet passed a resolution encouraging the unskilled not to coerce people to join their union and also advised them on the problems involved in enrolling prisoners of war in their union. See *Saratovskii Sovet*, p. 120.

discontent by rejecting the various labor organizations and mediating bodies that had been set up after February. Attacks in the socialist press fed strong suspicions that industrialists were purposefully resorting to industrial sabotage in order to get even with labor. Lebedev insisted that the "disorganizational activity of factory and plant owners" was primarily responsible for unemployment in Saratov.[13] Such sentiments, shared by many workers, mounted in the coming weeks, and by May several showdowns had taken place between owners and workers. Toward the end of the month some regions of the city had suffered bread shortages, caused not by lack of flour but by conflict over wages between the union of mill workers and the owners. While owners insisted that workers were responsible for the lack of bread because they had gone out on strike, the union pinned the blame on the owners for barring their employees from entering the mills in an effort to make them retract their economic demands.[14] In a similar incident, again brought about by workers' insistence on improved wages and labor conditions, workers at the Iuzhin oil press complained that the owner wanted to halt production even though the plant had a large reserve of sunflower seeds. The Soviet considered confiscating the enterprise after verifying the workers' claims.[15]

The strike movement in Saratov never assumed massive proportions in 1917, but as the realities of Russia's economic plight dampened hopes that the revolution in the short run would improve economic conditions, some Saratov workers gave vent to their discontent by going out on strike. Workers at the larger mechanized factories did not go out on strike at this time, probably because the eight-hour workday and wage hikes had come to these enterprises first. At lumber mills and other small enterprises in the province, however, strikes broke out in April.[16] Workers at the Egorov plant, for example, resorted to the strike after the factory management rejected their demands for higher wages. Skilled artisans who earlier had figured prominently in the local labor movement (recall *Nasha gazeta*) also appear to have been among the first Saratov workers to strike. Although the number of workers who went out on strike remained insignificant in April, the dynamics of labor conflicts at this time merit comment. Even though Zhest factory workers reached a settlement with the factory administration after submitting economic

13. *Khronika*, pp. 56–57.

14. *Saratovskii vestnik*, no. 112, May 25, 1917, p. 2.

15. *Saratovskii Sovet*, pp. 97, 118.

16. Fleer, *Rabochee dvizhenie v gody voiny*, pp. 52, 56. A multivolume Soviet document collection erroneously reports that there were no strikes in Saratov in April, May, or June. See Akademiia nauk SSSR, Institut istorii et al., *Revoliutsionnoe dvizhenie v Rossii v aprele 1917 g.: Aprel'skii krizis*, ed. L. S. Gaponenko et al. (Moscow, 1957), p. 478; and, in the same series, *Iun'skaia demonstratsiia*, pp. 295, 325.

demands, they expressed their determination to continue fighting for improvements. In another incident, a group of local seamstresses went on strike, stubbornly refusing to submit to their employer's threats. Confronted by their steadfastness, the owner backed down and entered negotiations. But since the women agreed to bargain only through representatives of their unions, the owner again refused to consider the workers' demands, apparently because he did not wish to recognize the union as a mediating agent.[17] Sources fall silent at this point on the outcome of this particular conflict.

In May and June the strike movement intensified. Apart from isolated strikes at industrial enterprises such as that at the Iuzhin oil press, broader strikes involving entire industries now broke out. Demanding better economic conditions, more than 3,000 stevedores declared a strike in May. A few weeks later mill and office workers from all of the city's flour mills went on strike, calling for a whopping 140 percent pay hike. Reporting that the workers had acted without the sanction of their union, the Menshevik leader B. N. Guterman argued that they should return to work immediately.[18] The Soviet encouraged workers to settle labor disputes through negotiations with industrialists and as a result many potential strikes were averted because settlements actually had been reached. Workers usually channeled grievances through their respective factory committees, unions, and conciliatory bodies, but when these institutions responded sluggishly or seemed ineffectual, workers acted independently, or turned to the Secretariat of the Soviet. In fact, an alarming trend appeared to be taking hold: workers were beginning to bypass all of their class organizations.[19]

During the period under review labor continued to be organized horizontally through trade unions and vertically through factory committees in each establishment. The local War Industries Committee also reorganized along more democratic lines in June, but it seems to have played no major role thereafter.[20] As we saw in Chapter 2, Saratov factory committees—as elsewhere—developed more political muscle than unions. Elected on the basis of general, direct, secret balloting, many committees

17. Osipov, *1917 god v Saratove*, p. 68.

18. *Izvestiia Saratovskogo Soveta*, no. 56, July 6, 1917, p. 2. For Antonov's account of the strike movement, see *Pod stiagom*, p. 128. At the very end of June the city's tram workers threatened to strike if they did not receive a pay raise. The Belgian-owned company refused to increase wages, however, because doing so would necessitate a fare increase. The Soviet eventually reached a settlement with the tram company. See *Saratovskii vestnik*, no. 143, July 1, 1917, p. 3; *Sotsial-Demokrat*, no. 43, July 1, 1917, p. 3, and no. 44, July 2, p. 3.

19. See *Saratovskii Sovet*, p. 75, and *Sotsial-Demokrat*, no. 28, June 13, 1917, p. 4.

20. See *Saratovskii vestnik*, no. 129, June 14, 1917, p. 4.

convened in the first days of March and in turn supervised elections to the Soviet and led the battle for the eight-hour day. By May local workers had elected eighty-five factory committees. An organizational bureau created at the end of March comprised organizational and inspection commissions that monitored local enterprises. Saratov factory committees purportedly set up the bureau because industrialists were beginning to ignore the factory committees.[21] Reorganized at the end of April, the Organizational Bureau included twenty-nine members, most of whom chaired factory committees at the largest industrial establishments. Bolsheviks may have occupied a majority of seats on the bureau.[22]

Seeking to prevent the industrialists' arbitrary firing of worker activists, the Organizational Bureau routinely intervened in factory personnel matters. When the Provisional Government on April 23 issued a decree on the role of factory committees, more modest in content than what the local Organizational Bureau in practice had achieved, Saratov industrialists challenged the activities of the local committees. Insisting that the April 23 law had not authorized factory committees to involve themselves so directly in hiring and firing matters, the industrialists questioned the legality of what had been going on in Saratov. The Organizational Bureau stood firm, however, filing protests at both the local and national levels against the factory owners and the government's April 23 decision. Quite indicative of provincial politics in 1917, the Organizational Bureau simply ignored the legislation passed by the Provisional Government.[23]

Factory committees involved themselves not only in personnel matters but also in fighting for a shortened workday, higher wages, better working conditions, and (later) workers' control over industry. Authoritarianism at the workplace had been a common feature of Russian industrial life, and the arbitrary actions of the bosses *(nachal'niki)* help explain the popularity of factory committees. Another reason for their success may have involved efforts to arm workers and establish factory militias. The formation of a workers' militia often took place contemporaneously with the election of factory committees and representatives to the Soviet. Although they fell under the supervision of the Saratov Soviet, these armed workers' groups were funded at the factory level. Of all the transitory armed workers' organizations that appeared in 1917, the factory militias remained the most important and served as a forerunner of the Red Guard.[24]

21. *Proletarii Povolzh'ia*, no. 3, April 12, 1917, p. 4.

22. Khodakov, "Rabochii kontrol'," pp. 59–60.

23. Ibid., pp. 59–61; "Professional'nye soiuzy," p. 156.

24. E. D. Rumiantsev, "Rabochaia militsiia: Krasnaia gvardiia Povolzh'ia v bor'be za vlast' Sovetov," candidate dissertation, Kazan State University, 1971, passim.

In addition to factory committees, sixteen trade unions had been chartered in Saratov by April.[25] The Saratov representative to the All-Russian Conference of Trade Unions reported that local unions had enrolled 26,000 workers. The metalworkers had formed the largest and most powerful union, with 3,000 workers.[26] A central bureau organized in May coordinated activities among unions and promoted the establishment of new ones. Chaired by a Bolshevik, E. V. Kosolapov, the bureau had a representative in the Soviet's Executive Committee. The bureau also handled conflicts between unions (which apparently quarreled over signing up the same workers) and disagreements between unions and factory committees. Unfortunately, sources do not shed much light on these disputes. Toward summer, however, they may have reflected the general drawing of partisan lines; evidence suggests that political parties tended to have bastions of strength in particular factories.[27]

While sources permit a rough sketch of the development and scope of labor organizations in 1917, it is more difficult to assess their real accomplishments. An examination of questionnaires sent to sixty-six Saratov enterprises at the end of April provides an unadorned glimpse at the status of factory committees and unions. Factory committees in 50 enterprises had signed up 10,000 workers. The committees still were struggling to move beyond the mere drawing-board stage in some establishments. Thirty percent of the workers surveyed held union cards. The most interesting data concern the scope and success rate of economic demands made by local workers through their class organizations. Workers at forty-one factories had submitted economic demands to their bosses. In twenty-one cases workers' demands had been satisfied completely; in ten cases they had been met in part; and in the ten remaining cases the outcome had been unsatisfactory. The questionnaires revealed that not all workers had achieved the eight-hour day.[28]

The organizational bustle that characterized Russia in the spring had created an overlapping, ill-defined, and often ineffective structure of uniquely Russian institutions. Some local organizations faded from the scene quickly while others managed to muster unusual authority. A case in point is the Executive Committee of Deputies of the Saratov Railroad Shop Workers, which actually functioned as a neighborhood govern-

25. *Khronika*, p. 50. Metalworkers, builders, lumberyard workers, sewing industry workers, shoemakers, domestics, dyers, and tobacco workers were among the first to organize. See V. Miller, "10 let professional'nogo stroitel'stva," *Kommunisticheskii put'*, no. 20 (1927), p. 73.

26. *Proletarii Povolzh'ia*, no. 27, July 6, 1917, p. 4.

27. I. I. Firfarov, "Piat' let bor'by," in *V boiakh za diktaturu proletariata: Sbornik vospominanii uchastnikov Oktiabria i grazhdanskoi voiny v Nizhnem Povolzh'e* (Saratov, 1933), p. 26.

28. *Sotsial-Demokrat*, no. 13, May 7, 1917, p. 3.

ment. One memoirist recalled that "not only railroad workers but the entire population of the surrounding region viewed it as the local organ of power."[29] A somewhat contradictory phenomenon became manifest at this time. On the one hand, Saratov workers moved toward localism, toward "occupational sectarianism" *(tsekhovshchina)* and factory patriotism, while on the other hand, the failure of the economy and its bleak prospects prompted them to press from below for high-level coordination to make things work.[30]

As a result, observers began to notice a growing organizational malaise toward the summer of 1917. It will be recalled from Chapter 3 that attendance at Soviet meetings dropped off in May and June, after the moderate socialists had entered the government. The same phenomenon cast a shadow over the proceedings of factory committees and unions.[31] Diane Koenker has documented a similar response among Moscow workers and Mark D. Mandel among laborers in Petrograd. In all three cities the alarming decline in workers' interest in their own class institutions coincided with the further drawing of partisan lines.[32] Several factors explain such developments in Saratov. The duplication of organizations had hampered their effectiveness and soon exposed both the inability of these organs to solve the massive problems confronting Russia and the shortage of able working-class leaders. At the bottom tiers people may have grown impatient with the endless meetings and political rhetoric that colored Russian political life after February. These proclivities represented not so much political apathy as a desperate reaction to what seemed an inexorable economic deterioration. Simply stated, working-class behavior at this point in the revolution was beginning to be shaped by the inability of factory committees and other institutions to effect change. Workers seem to have lost interest in attending meetings but were more and more prone to strike, ignoring labor leaders' appeals for moderation and discipline.

29. Petrov, "Saratovskii proletariat," p. 9.

30. Recent studies of the labor movement in Petrograd have called attention to the phenomenon of factory patriotism and of *tsekhovshchina*, or "occupational sectarianism." Rosenberg argues that Petrograd workers, highly stratified by profession and income, developed a syndicalist mentality as a result of the proliferation of workers' control organs. In contrast, Steve Smith, while accepting certain features of Rosenberg's argument, concludes that from the beginning there were strong pressures from below toward higher-level coordination and centralization. Evidence for Saratov suggests that occupational sectarianism developed in the few large factories and along the railroad lines, but that in the more numerous smaller enterprises it was not so important an issue. See William G. Rosenberg, "Workers and Workers' Control in the Russian Revolution," *History Workshop*, no. 5 (1978), pp. 89–97; and Steve Smith, "Craft Consciousness, Class Consciousness: Petrograd 1917," *History Workshop*, no. 11 (1981), pp. 33–58.

31. See *Sotsial-Demokrat*, no. 22, June 4, 1917, p. 3.

32. See Diane Koenker, *Moscow Workers and the 1917 Revolution* (Princeton, 1981), p. 177.

Saratov lumber mill

Within Saratov's diverse labor force partisan attitudes tended to develop first among metalworkers, railroad workers, and evacuated Latvian and Polish workers, and to a somewhat lesser extent among tobacco factory, lumber mill, and oil press workers. Such attitudes found expression in the numerous resolutions passed at factory meetings and rallies. Workers at the Zhest, Gantke, and Titanik metalworks, at the Derevo lumber mill, at the Levkovich tobacco factory, at local railroad depots, and at vegetable oil presses issued the most political resolutions in 1917. Office employees and skilled artisanal workers, who were widely dispersed in small establishments, passed fewer resolutions, although some (such as the tailors) were actively involved in politics. All of the workers' resolutions dating from March 1917 reflected the genuine popularity of the call for an eight-hour workday and of the political gains of the revolution—political amnesty, basic freedoms, and the speedy convocation of a constituent assembly. Only the Titanik factory, transferred from the Baltic and employing 450 workers, demanded an end to the war shortly after the February Revolution.[33] By April, however, perhaps because of the Miliukov Affair, calls for an end to the war appear to have rivaled economic concerns in frequency.

Several resolutions passed at the large metalworks in May expressed

33. This information is based on a reading of resolutions published in Saratov newspapers, on document collections, and on secondary works.

even stronger partisan sentiments, reflecting the extent to which appeals for an all-soviet socialist government had become acceptable (perhaps temporarily) to an important stratum of Saratov's working class. On May 11 the Saratov Soviet carried a Menshevik resolution calling for support for the new national coalition government comprising Mensheviks and Socialist Revolutionaries. On May 12 workers and employees at the Titanik factory condemned as a "great mistake the [call for] support for the Provisional Government voiced by the Soviet majority." Praising the (Bolshevik) minority that had cast a vote of no confidence in the coalition, the resolution went on to say that "together with this minority . . . we are convinced that all of the demands of the democracy will be realized . . . only when the revolutionary All-Russian Soviet of Workers' and Soldiers' Deputies stands at the head of the revolutionary people and army." A few days later workers at the Zhest factory issued an analogous resolution that labeled the local soviet's commitment to coalition government a mistake. Announcing their sympathy for the Bolshevik stance on this issue, the Zhest workers demanded a transfer of power to the soviets and protested the Freedom Loan.[34] Declaring their allegiance to the soviets, the 250 workers at the Levkovich tobacco factory likewise adopted a resolution condemning the coalition government and the Freedom Loan.[35] The tobacco workers, it will be recalled, had appeared repeatedly on the pages of *Nasha gazeta*. They also were the first in Saratov to organize an armed workers' militia.

Resolutions passed by Saratov workers reveal several interesting facts about the dynamics of the local labor movement. This was a period in which many workers began to differentiate among the various political parties. Nonetheless, the majority of workers remained nonpartisan in the spring of 1917. Those in the largest enterprises, however, tended to be Social Democratic. A small but important Bolshevik cadre agitated within the Titanik and Zhest plants; Menshevik worker-activists predominated at this time at Gantke. One of the clearest examples of growing partisan sentiment involved local railroad workers. Only two Bolsheviks had been elected to the seventeen-member (mainly Menshevik) Executive Committee of Deputies of the Local Railroad Shop Workers. But after reelections in late May, Bolsheviks held eight of the seventeen seats and one who recently returned from exile, Stepan Kovylkin, became chairman.[36] This rise in Bolshevik influence among railroad

34. Gerasimenko and Tochenyi, *Sovety Nizhnego Povolzh'ia*, pp. 77–78; Mints, *Oktiabr' v Povolzh'e*, p. 95. The Titanik factory resolution can be found in *Sotsial-Demokrat*, no. 16, May 17, 1917, p. 1, and that of the Zhest factory in *Sotsial-Demokrat*, no. 19, May 25, p. 4.

35. *Sotsial-Demokrat*, no. 18, May 21, 1917, p. 4.

36. Petrov, "Saratovskii proletariat," pp. 9–10.

workers is probably linked to the party's opposition to the formation of the coalition government.

As cooperation among the socialist parties began to break down on the floor of the Soviet, the workers' belief in fair play and unity began to disintegrate as well. Although shouted down while addressing workers at the Sotrudnik plant, the Bolshevik Mgeladze appears to have struck a responsive chord among some workers there. These workers, who characterized themselves as politically nonaligned, declared that they would walk out of future factory meetings if members of "other parties" were slandered.[37] It is also clear that even in the largest, politically active factories, levels of working-class consciousness varied from shop to shop. Singled out by Soviet writers because of their early move toward Bolshevism, the Zhest plant workers, under closer scrutiny, no longer appear to be so monolithic. On June 15 workers met to discuss how to use 10,000 rubles donated by the factory administration to improve labor conditions. According to a story in *Sotsial-Demokrat*, the debate "took on a terrible character." The "less conscious" workers wanted to divide the money evenly among themselves rather than put it at the disposal of the factory committees and trade unions.[38]

In April and May some Saratov workers already had issued resolutions expressing lack of faith in the Provisional Government and opposition to the Freedom Loan, and calling for a transfer of power to the soviets.[39] The Titanik workers passed the first resolution in Saratov in May, demanding "workers' control" over industry, an appeal that picked up dramatically in June and July. The Russian word *kontrol'* translates best as "supervision." Workers' control meant the establishment of safeguards to guarantee that the factory management did not deal arbitrarily with labor. Saratov workers established control commissions to supervise the flow of raw materials into the factories and the distribution of manufactured or processed goods. The growing popularity of workers' control at this time was yet another expression of workers' suspicion of their employers, and of fears of being locked out and laid off. In a four-month period, then, labor's demands evolved from relatively specific economic ones to insistence on workers' control over industry, which coincided with the first public articulation by Saratov workers of the slogan "All Power to the Soviets" and with votes of no confidence in the new coali-

37. *Sotsial-Demokrat*, no. 19, May 25, 1917, pp. 2–3.

38. Ibid., no. 33, June 18, 1917, p. 4.

39. The Titanik plant, for example, adopted a resolution condemning the Soviet's resolution supporting the coalition ministry and "greeted the minority, who insist on strict control over the Provisional Government." See *Saratovskii vestnik*, no. 136, June 22, 1917, p. 4. Similarly, the 250 workers at the Levkovich plant voted against supporting the Provisional Government and the Freedom Loan.

Gantke plant

tion government. There was a direct relationship between the Saratov proletariat's growing exasperation with the Provisional Government and impatience with the factory ownership and management.

Although the conclusions based on this glimpse at working-class attitudes must be viewed as tentative, the political aspirations of the Saratov working class appear to have been broadly similar to those that the French historian Marc Ferro describes as typical among Russian workers in general in the aftermath of the February Revolution: the eight-hour day, overall economic improvement, the guarantee of basic freedoms, and the convocation of a constituent assembly.[40] When the political pronouncements of Saratov workers are traced—and despite lack of information on such important questions as how local workers related to their fellow wage earners elsewhere—it becomes clear that the articulation of dissatisfaction with the coalition government and growing antiwar sentiments paralleled the consolidation of the moderate socialists within local political institutions. But political parties were to muster a following among workers only when they supported the economic and political goals workers themselves espoused. The Bolsheviks had much to gain.

40. Marc Ferro, *La Révolution de 1917*, vol. 1, *La Chute du tsarisme et les origines d'Octobre* (Paris, 1967), chap 4, passim; and "The Aspirations of Russian Society," in *Revolutionary Russia: A Symposium*, ed. Richard Pipes (New York, 1969), pp. 183–98.

Immediately after the February Revolution the soldier masses appear to have united behind and endorsed the defensist pronouncements of their commanding officers. As Allan K. Wildman so aptly put it, "unaccustomed to articulate expression and organizational behavior, they deferred to the leadership of their cultural superiors, adopting enthusiastically their revolutionary and socialist rhetoric on the naive assumption that it expressed their own inner promptings."[41] But it did not. Two things must be kept in mind to understand the quick radicalization of the soldier masses locally. First, dissatisfaction and antiwar sentiments had manifested themselves in some units before February. Second, as at industrial workplaces, authoritarian and arbitrary treatment had characterized relations between tsarist army officers and the soldiers. Customarily dealt with as inferior and increasingly feeling that their lives were being sacrificed recklessly, the endless stream of draftees nursed sundry grievances against officers. Once given the opportunity to express their feelings after the February Revolution, the soldier masses moved quickly beyond control. To the command structure, Pandora's box had been flung open.

Officers responded in a variety of ways to the new conditions in the army. Many commanding officers had come to question the government's prosecution of the war and had even supported the tsar's abdication, but they soon became alarmed over the evaporation of traditional codes of discipline and proliferation of soldiers' committees. The arrest of unpopular officers, censors, and army doctors during the February Revolution had set a dangerous precedent. Among local officers Colonel Korvin-Krukovskii, head of the Saratov ensign school, was most determined to reinstate military discipline locally. Coping well with the new revolutionary rhetoric for the time being, he remained committed to the old way. In the late spring he emerged as the champion of law and order, and later as a participant in the Kornilov Affair in August.

Nor did the middle-level officers have an easy time of things. Highly fragmented, power in the army both within the district and within the Saratov garrison was beginning to be based on voluntary recognition at best. A district military committee formed in Kazan in early April had introduced dual power in the district command structure, which encouraged already strong localist tendencies in Saratov and Samara. Acknowledging the authority of the Kazan committee in theory, local military committees ignored it repeatedly in practice.[42] In Saratov, the

41. Wildman, *End of the Imperial Army*, p. 378.

42. I. M. Ionenko and R. S. Tseitlin, "Kazanskii Voenno-okruzhnoi komitet (aprel'–oktiabr' 1917 goda)," in *Ocherki istorii narodov Povolzh'ia i Priural'ia*, no. 4, *Obshchestvenno-politicheskoe dvizhenie i klassovaia bor'ba na Srednei Volge (konets XIX-nachale XX veka)* (Kazan, 1972), pp. 89–93.

Military Committee strove to control the activities of the independent-minded soldier committees formed in the spirit of Order Number 1. But the Military Committee came under fire in carrying responsibility for prosecuting the war. Calling the war a "revolutionary struggle" had not made it more popular.

In the spring of 1917 ordinary soldiers were most concerned with preventing a return to the former command structure and with a resumption of the war on a major scale. The flurry of organizational activity among soldiers paralleled the workers' enthusiastic commitment to factory committees and unions, and was probably sparked by a similar desire to prevent arbitrary behavior on the part of their superiors. After the moderate socialists became part of the faltering state structure with the formation of the First Coalition Government in May, soldiers began to drift away from their revolutionary leaders and institutions, just as the workers began to lose interest in theirs. At the end of April soldier battalions still gathered to see off troops departing for the front. Six weeks later the same soldiers, ignoring appeals from the Soviet, refused orders to take part in the June offensive. This dramatic shift in attitudes can be traced in some detail.

Morale and discipline problems abounded in the Saratov garrison in the spring of 1917. As in the case of civilians, inadequate housing exacerbated discontent. Despite construction of additional military buildings, most soldiers remained cramped in dilapidated quarters. Typhus and other highly infectious diseases struck soldiers in March and afterward. The strained living conditions and new concept of discipline resulted in frequent outbursts of lawlessness, a problem compounded by criminal elements who, dressed in soldiers' garb, took full advantage of the permissive climate. Not surprisingly, vigilante-type (samosud) reprisals similar to those observed among the civilian population often befell the perpetrators of petty crimes in the garrison. Bleak news from the front, the presence of frontoviki recuperating in barrack hospitals, and contradictory but endless reports of desertion only made matters worse.

The disorder in the garrison often poured out into the streets of Saratov, adding an element of tension to relations between soldiers and civilians. Local newspapers reveal considerable resentment on the part of the townspeople toward the soldiers and contain numerous complaints about soldiers' harassment of civilians. Judging from the published protocols of the MC, young, recently drafted trainees appear to have been especially unruly. Their officers complained that after February the draftees refused to drill, demanded changes in training procedures, or simply insisted that they be sent home. Such sentiments even affected the elite cadet training school. Colonel Korvin-Krukovskii reported to the Military Committee that the ensigns had formed their own lower-level committee that met all day, decided nothing, and neglected training.[43]

The frontoviki were already infecting other soldiers with their rebellious attitude. Having formed their own committee as early as March 7, the frontoviki displayed greater recalcitrance toward authority in April and May than new recruits, and resorted to outright mutinous behavior in June and afterward. A young officer in the local cadet school, a Cossack by origin and monarchist by conviction, observed that "among them there were many cowards. Having been wounded at the front, they're now afraid to go back."[44] Bolshevik and Left SR agitators had become popular among evacuated soldiers in Samara and Tsaritsyn, and made some inroads within the Saratov garrison as well.[45] As Chapter 5 will show, the frontoviki were responsible for creating an extremely radical situation in neighboring Tsaritsyn, refusing to go to the front as early as April. They behaved similarly in Kazan. In Saratov the evacuated soldiers caused one of the most intransigent political crises confronting the Soviet after July.

The demands of national minorities within the armed forces further weakened military discipline in Saratov, intensifying the overall move of the country toward localism. Within the garrison Ukrainian and Muslim (mostly Tatar) soldiers and officers lobbied for the formation of national units. Jewish soldiers also set up a special military committee, while Armenian, Polish, and Lithuanian soldiers formed interest groups within the various nationalist committees that now existed among Saratov's civilian population. The Ukrainian and Muslim soldiers posed a particularly vexing problem in town because their demands became entwined with larger political issues. In mid-April, for example, Ukrainian officers, who constituted a significant portion of the leadership in the Saratov garrison, organized a Ukrainian club that announced its approval of autonomy for the Ukraine in a federated state and of the formation of separate Ukrainian military units. Citing as an example Latvian and Polish detachments that already existed in the Russian army, an estimated 4,000 Ukrainian soldiers stationed locally demanded the prompt formation of national Ukrainian regiments.[46] At the same time the Ukrainian Rada (national council or soviet) made similar requests to the Saratov Military Committee, while local Ukrainian organizations threatened to set up national units "in a revolutionary manner." On May

43. See, for example, *Protokoly Voennogo Komiteta*, no. 20, April 12, 1917, p. 22; no. 25, April 24, p. 2; no. 19, April 10, 1917, p. 19.

44. Golubov, "Saratov v 1917 g.," p. 7.

45. Mints, *Oktiabr' v Povolzh'e*, p. 135.

46. *Saratovskii vestnik*, no. 93, April 29, 1917, p. 3.

1 the Executive Committee of the Soviet rejected these demands as well as similar ones raised by local Muslim soldiers.[47] The issue was not solved decisively at this time and in May and June other nationalities likewise requested special privileges. The national government's acquiescence to the demand for formation of national units toward the end of June should be interpreted as a clear sign of its feebleness.

While sources underscore the intemperate behavior of young draftees, disaffection spread among older soldiers too. This stands out clearly in the attitude of the so-called over-fortys, who were sent back to the villages in the spring to take part in planting and haymaking. Their temporary return to the land increased the peasant soldiers' antiwar feelings, especially since they were suddenly summoned back to their units as part of plans for the June offensive. In response to the unpopular orders, the soldiers expressed concern over two matters. First, they felt that the villages needed them. In mid-June more than 1,000 Saratov garrison over-fortys petitioned the Petrograd Soviet and the minister of war to be allowed to remain in the countryside until after the harvest. "With our departure," they insisted, "there'll be nobody to harvest grain and we'll be threatened by hunger and total economic ruin."[48] Second, these soldiers had returned to the villages precisely when the revolution in the countryside entered a more radical phase. In fact they may have been partially responsible for it, since some had been elected to volost and village committees upon their arrival home. As summer approached, rumors spread throughout Saratov as throughout the rest of the country about a "black repartition" going on in the villages; events there now were unfolding regardless of directives from the government or from local commissars.

It is difficult to describe the daily operations of lower-level soldiers' organizations, but we know that soldiers turned to them to remove some of the remnants of privilege that had survived the first flood of revolutionary change. In early April the Military Section of the Soviet had supported soldiers' demands to abolish the *denshchiki*—soldiers assigned to do personal chores for officers—but the Military Committee refused to comply. On April 10 the MC issued a directive to the entire garrison, threatening that insubordination to officers and to the Military Committee and the unprincipled attitude of many soldiers toward service in general "would be punished according to the laws of wartime."[49] This attempt to restore discipline evoked so much ill will that the Bol-

47. *Saratovskii Sovet*, p. 103.

48. *Saratovskii vestnik*, no. 133, June 18, 1917, p. 4.

49. Vas'kin, "Iz istorii bor'by," p. 111; *Khronika*, p. 37. Such conflicts also occurred in other garrisons in the province. See *Saratovskii Sovet*, p. 87.

shevik Vasil'ev was emboldened to raise the question among soldiers of dismantling the MC. Shortly thereafter, the Military Committee tried to introduce an eight-hour day for soldiers, which would not necessarily have reduced the soldiers' duties and might actually have increased them, for soldiers' time would be accounted for more rigorously. A number of soldiers spoke against this proposal, arguing that the reform "was introduced by the committee [MC] without their [the soldiers'] knowledge and was detrimental to the interests of the soldiers."[50] Opposition was so strong that the matter was put off.

The publication of the Miliukov Note, coming so soon after the MC's unpopular announcement on April 10, irreparably damaged the committee's credibility. On the afternoon of April 20, an estimated 5,000 soldiers congregated on the slopes of Sokolov Mountain to discuss, among other things, the future of the Military Committee. Several days later soldier delegates voted to merge the Military Committee with the Military Section of the Soviet.[51] As part of the agreement, the Soviet expanded the number of soldier deputies within the Soviet. The Presidium of the newly elected Soldiers' Section, however, included most of the former leaders of the Military Committee, a fact that eventually resulted in the decline of the Soviet's influence over the garrison and a further erosion of SR popularity.

A move toward limiting the decentralizing impact of soldier committees and revitalizing the fighting capacity of the Russian army began with the formation of the First Coalition Government in May. After entry of the moderate socialists into the coalition ministry and the beginning of preparations for the June offensive, the army General Staff campaigned to check the further erosion of discipline. Former commander in chief General M. Alekseev and General A. I. Denikin organized a Union of Army and Navy Officers that aimed to restore the rights of officers. A branch was established in Saratov.[52] The junior officers who led the Saratov Military Committee supported these efforts to improve the army's fighting ability by purging the committee of undesirable elements. The leaders of the Military Committee also appealed to public organizations to help track down deserters. The leaders of the MC requested volost committees to register all soldiers arriving or departing from the villages and intensified this campaign after they took over the Military Section of the Soviet. On the evening of June 6 they ordered a roundup of

50. *Saratovskii vestnik*, no. 85, April 20, 1917, p. 5.

51. *Proletarii Povolzh'ia*, no. 6, April 26, 1917, p. 2.

52. Marc Ferro, *La Révolution de 1917*, vol. 2, *Octobre: Naissance d'une société* (Paris, 1976), p. 69.

deserters and draft dodgers. One person was killed and several were wounded in the resulting shooting, and more than 1,000 were arrested.[53] A shrill public outcry against the Military Section's actions prompted the Bolsheviks' *Sotsial-Demokrat* to inform the public that the entire Executive Committee of the Soviet had not discussed the roundup, and to place the blame squarely on the "military authority of the city of Saratov" (the Military Section of the Soviet).[54]

Cooperating with the city committees of the SR and PS parties, the leaders of the Military Committee strove to retain their hold on the garrison by involving soldiers in various party organizations. A "Military Club," "Union of Military Officials," "Union of Military Doctors," and other "educational" societies all tried to boost military morale and discipline. The Saratov SR organization promoted peasant unions and soldiers' *zemliachestva*, which were associations of peasant-soldiers from the same village or district.[55] After the Military Committee merged with the Soviet and soldiers began to listen to the Bolsheviks' position on the June offensive, the SRs formed a "Garrison Soviet of Peasant Deputies." Political attitudes were hardening in the garrison, however, and the Bolsheviks and left-wing members of the SR and Menshevik parties were emerging as the only groups that, in the popular view, supported the realization of the revolution's original goals. In the wake of the Miliukov crisis soldiers from the Fourth Machine-Gun Regiment already resolved to boycott all bourgeois papers.[56] A month later an editorial on the war appearing in *Saratovskii vestnik* noted that "almost on every corner" soldier orators "of the Bolshevik school" were "calling for an end to the war."[57] Although this appraisal could apply to other internationalists, it undoubtedly referred as well to a recent rise in Bolshevik fortunes.[58]

53. *Saratovskii vestnik*, no. 124, June 8, 1917, p. 3; *Sotsial-Demokrat*, no. 24, June 8, 1917, p. 4. *Saratovskii vestnik* later reported that only 200 were held and the rest were freed. See no. 126, June 10, 1917, p. 3.

54. *Sotsial-Demokrat*, no. 24, June 8, 1917, p. 4, and no. 28, June 13, p. 4.

55. V. V. Vas'kin, "Kontrrevoliutsiia v bor'be za armiiu v 1917 g.," in *Revoliutsionnoe dvizhenie v russkoi armii v 1917 godu: Sbornik statei*, ed. I. I. Mints et al. (Moscow, 1981), p. 149.

56. *Sotsial-Demokrat*, no. 9, April 28, 1917, p. 2; Osipov, *1917 god v Saratove*, p. 75; *Khronika*, p. 47.

57. *Saratovskii vestnik*, no. 115, May 28, 1917, p. 3. At the same time soldiers from the Eleventh Company of the 90th Infantry Division recalled their delegate from the Soviet because he voted for the Menshevik mandate and not for the Bolshevik one. See *Sotsial-Demokrat*, no. 19, May 25, 1917, p. 3.

58. A Saratov delegate to the All-Russian Conference of Bolshevik Military Organizations that convened in mid-June reported that "in many regiment and company committees members of our organizations are beginning to have significant influence. Soldiers are keenly listening to them and on several important questions our proposals are being adopted" (*Bor'ba partii bol'shevikov za armiiu*, p. 250). See also Rabinovich, "Vserossiiskaia konferentsiia," p. 109.

The moderate socialists' endorsement of the June offensive following their entry into the First Coalition Government changed soldiers' attitudes more than anything else, for it raised doubts among the rank and file that their leaders truly were working toward concluding peace. In early June the Kerensky government had ordered the transfer to the front of the Ninetieth and Ninety-first Reserve Infantry regiments, stationed in Saratov. Even before these orders had arrived the Saratov Bolshevik organization had published the party Central Committee's resolution denouncing the offensive, insisting that it "is connected with the support of an imperialist war and strengthens counterrevolution."[59] The Bolsheviks opposed sending the entire regiments to the front on the grounds that not all of the soldiers were prepared for combat. But the SR-Menshevik majority voted to uphold the government's order, and then went to the barracks to mobilize support for the offensive.[60]

An unpleasant surprise awaited Saratov's moderate socialist leaders. Crying out that they "did not want to listen to any orators," soldiers met the members of the Executive Committee with hostility.[61] That same day, soldiers resolved not to obey the government's orders, insisting that the "ten [capitalist] ministers must go."[62] Some soldiers did not reject the idea of going to the front per se, but rejected specific conditions of the order. Other soldiers expressed concern over lack of appropriate uniforms, equipment, and inadequate military training, while the wounded soldiers evacuated to Saratov complained that they were not well enough to see combat again. Soldiers also showed resentment toward those fortunate enough to have avoided the draft. Although local Bolsheviks opposed the offensive, they argued that because the party was in the minority and outvoted on this matter, and because Kerensky was a member of the authorized government, his orders should be obeyed.[63] Some independent-minded Saratov Bolsheviks, however, "have advised soldiers to disobey the minister of war's orders." The local party organization categorically declared that such statements "come from people who have nothing in common with our party."[64] It appears that the local Bolshevik committee was committed to avoiding excesses and to maintaining cordial relations with its moderate socialist comrades. But it also

59. Vas'kin, "Iz istorii bor'by," p. 116.

60. *Saratovskii Sovet*, p. 141.

61. P. N. Sobolev, *Bedneishee krest'ianstvo—soiuznik proletariata v Oktiabr'skoi revoliutsii* (Moscow, 1958), p. 79.

62. Vas'kin, "Iz istorii bor'by," p. 117. At a special meeting of the Executive Committee some moderates wanted to declare the soldiers "enemies of the people." See Gerasimenko, *Sovety Nizhnego Povolzh'ia*, p. 55.

63. *Saratovskii vestnik*, no. 129, June 13, 1917, p. 3; *Izvestiia Kazanskogo Voenno-okruzhnogo Komiteta*, no. 24, June 17, 1917, p. 2.

64. *Sotsial-Demokrat*, no. 29, June 14, 1917, p. 4.

bears noting that in nearby Tsaritsyn the Bolshevik- and Left SR–controlled garrison adamantly refused to go to the front, and that reports of anarchy there had attracted attention even at the national level. The militant mood in Tsaritsyn restrained the more moderate Saratov Bolshevik leaders, for the Tsaritsyn contagion already had spread to Saratov. One Saratov newspaper reported that an unknown Tsaritsyn Bolshevik who arrived in Saratov "comes out into the town squares at night after dark. He calls upon people to disobey the Provisional Government, and agitates against the war and the Mensheviks."[65]

Meanwhile, the Executive Committee of the Soviet sent a commission to Petrograd to discuss the offensive with Kerensky and with the Petrograd Soviet. Until word was obtained from the delegation, plans to prepare troops for the front continued, but authorities took the soldiers' concerns into account. A commission comprised of army doctors and ordinary soldiers examined 250 soldiers from each regiment and concluded that they were medically unfit for combat. The Executive Committee warned Bolshevik hotheads, however, that "decrees of the Soviet are obligatory for everyone, not excluding . . . the minority." Several days later the Military Section of the Soviet announced its support of the offensive, and on June 28 the Executive Committee, after word had come from the commission sent to Petrograd, voted to send the two regiments to the front.[66] Thereafter, the question of the war shaped attitudes most in the Saratov garrison.

Despite the different pace of political life in the district towns, local soviets or broadly representative executive committees led by socialists often had amassed considerable power in their hands by early summer. Although soviets had not been formed in the district towns during the 1905 Revolution, they were elected in most of the uezd centers by the end of March 1917, a fact that suggests the extent to which socialist ideas and propaganda had made inroads into the backwoods of Russia. It will be recalled that soviets of soldiers' deputies often appeared on the scene first, and then assisted the election of workers' soviets. In both Petrovsk and Volsk separate soldiers' and workers' soviets merged, but fell under the influence of the soldiers' sections. A peasant soviet was formed in May in Volsk. As was the case with soviets in the large towns, most uezd soviets had nonpartisan memberships, but populist parties, especially the SRs, dominated local politics as they had since 1905. Toward sum-

65. *Saratovskii listok*, no. 129, June 16, 1917, p. 3.

66. *Saratovskii vestnik*, no. 130, June 13, 1917, p. 3; no. 139, June 25, 1917, p. 3; *Khronika*, p. 78. The Bolshevik deputies in the Workers' Section walked out in protest when the Military Section agreed to send local soldiers to the front. See *Proletarii Povolzh'ia*, no. 23, June 28, 1917, p. 4.

mer some soviets became involved in disputes with the old dumas, or with groups of commanding officers. Usually the dumas did not have the popular authority to deal with everyday concerns, which instead had fallen under the jurisdiction of the soviets and executive committees. Elsewhere the dumas had to submit to reelection along democratic lines, as was the case in Khvalynsk. The Nikolaevsk Soviet of Peasant, Worker, and Soldier Deputies, after declaring itself the "highest political authority in the district" on June 2, dismissed the district commissar appointed by the Provisional Government and replaced him with a people's executive committee selected by the soviet and headed by the Bolshevik V. I. Ermoshchenko.[67]

The situation that developed in Kuznetsk serves as a revealing case study of politics in the uezd towns at this time. Here the local Executive Committee of Popular Authority (Ispolnitel'nyi komitet narodnoi vlasti), in which the "democratic elements" and SR party were firmly entrenched, eclipsed the authority of the town duma and uezd zemstvo, and negated the need for a powerful soviet to defend the interests of the working people, soldiers, and peasants. Elected to the committee were the town mayor, the owner of a local factory, a liberal lawyer and zemstvo activist, an office worker in a wine warehouse, and a revolutionary named F. Bobylev (probably an SR at this time), who chaired the committee. Having co-opted peasant representatives into its membership, the Executive Committee of Popular Authority introduced its own land reform. Ignoring the national government and Saratov PEC altogether, the Kuznetsk executive committee confiscated land from pomeshchiki, set rent prices, divided forestland and meadows. It then set up volost and village land committees "without the slightest regard for the national government or provincial center." For good reason, newspapers began calling the uezd the Kuznetsk "republic." The local executive committee democratized the duma and zemstvo, permitted private sale of grain, and forbade its export outside the district. As the chairman of the committee put it:

> We made arrests, and freed soldiers and civilians arrested by the tsarist authorities. We organized peasants' and workers' unions and determined the [length of] the workday. We called congresses. We traveled to the villages to settle land disputes. We sent one agitator after another into the countryside. We published a newspaper. . . . We registered the estates and property of the pomeshchiki. We seized the cloth mill from Aseev and imprisoned him. We even billeted soldiers in private homes.[68]

67. For information on Khvalynsk see *Saratovskii listok*, no. 136, June 24, 1917, p. 4. The situation in Nikolaevsk is discussed in Mints, *Oktiabr' v Povolzh'e*, p. 126.

68. F. Bobylev, "Kuznetskaia respublika," in *Fevral': Sbornik vospominanii*, pp. 37–39.

The insignificant size of the proletariat in most of these centers and lack of documentation make any detailed discussion of working-class attitudes impossible. In those towns that had factories, however, local workers pushed for the same benefits for which Saratov workers fought: mainly the introduction of the eight-hour workday and the right to set up their own committees. Workers won these improvements in March in Tsaritsyn. They came more slowly to other workers with the probable exception of railroad workers, many of whom had, as in Kuznetsk, formed armed guards during the February Revolution. The Balashov Soviet first discussed the eight-hour day in April. Apart from Saratov and Tsaritsyn, factory committees surfaced only in Volsk and Petrovsk in March. In Petrovsk factory and mill owners tried unsuccessfully to hold back recognition from the factory committees. Generally speaking, the economic vicissitudes of spiraling inflation resulted in the same fight for higher wages that occurred in Saratov.[69]

Few Bolsheviks played prominent roles at this time in the uezd towns. Occasionally individual party members requested aid from the Saratov Bolshevik Committee, but lack of personnel and money limited its ability to contribute to developments in the district centers during the first half of 1917. The situation in Volsk will be recalled, where a Bolshevik activist named Rubashkina who arrived in town to organize a local party cell found that there was not one Bolshevik or Bolshevik sympathizer. Eventually Rubashkina and a Bolshevik named Kukushkin formed a five-person SD cell (with Mensheviks). In early June she, Kukushkin, and the other Bolsheviks sat on the executive committee of the local soviet. About this time, however, the other political parties began to campaign openly against the Bolsheviks. Rubashkina appealed repeatedly to the Saratov committee for financial support and charismatic public speakers. They "sometimes promised Antonov or Vasil'ev," Rubashkina complained. "We decorated, put up announcements, filled an auditorium, but they never showed up! People felt deceived."[70] About the same time the SD group split into separate Bolshevik and Menshevik factions. In Balashov a Bolshevik named Bankvitser had served as the first chairman of the local soviet. From April, the other socialists promoted new elections to replace him. The majority of workers, who were nonaffiliated at this time, reelected Bankvitser, probably because of the decisive role he took in the arrest of the head of the tsarist police and the local marshal of the nobility back in February. Despite his success, Bankvitser's German name aroused suspicions after the abortive July uprising

69. Khodakov, "Rabochii kontrol'," pp. 54–57.
70. Rubashkina, "Vol'skaia organizatsiia," p. 81.

in Petrograd.[71] The few Bolsheviks in Atkarsk still saw no need to form a separate organization and continued to participate in a joint committee of socialists that included SRs.

The key to understanding politics in the uezd towns lies not so much in recounting these attempts at party building as in underscoring the tremendous impact of the local garrisons, some of which were as large as the towns in which they were located. In March and April rank-and-file soldiers expressed intense hostility toward unpopular officers who could not make peace with the various soldier committees. Everywhere the impact of Order Number 1 was visible. Soldiers in Petrovsk "strangely interpreted" the Declaration of the Rights of Soldiers issued by the Kerensky government, resulting in a "steep decline in discipline." In late March a "provocateur" tried to murder the regiment commander.[72] A representative to the Petrovsk Public Executive Committee reported to the Saratov Military Committee that "in the 145th Reserve Infantry Regiment discipline is lacking altogether; the officer corps and soldiers are completely at odds."[73] A delegate from the Atkarsk MC reported in Saratov that the Atkarsk garrison arrested most of the top command for its opposition to the new order and for rude behavior toward rank-and-file soldiers and lower-level officers.[74] A member of the local soldiers' committee of the Novouzensk regiment informed the Saratov Military Committee that "the [soldiers'] committee is powerless and asks for assistance. Recent recruits cannot be sent [to the front]. . . . Service is slipshod and inaccurate, those on guard duty sleep. Disorganization is massive." Further, a simmering unrest had been created among common soldiers in the Novouzensk garrison, who resented the privileges of cadre soldiers.[75] The civilian populations often had good reason to fear the soldiers. Reports flowed in to the Saratov Military Committee about raids on shops, banks, and warehouses for alcoholic beverages. The Saratov Soviet and Military Committee had to send an armed expedition to Pokrovsk to quell a "wine pogrom" remarkably similar to the one that occurred in Saratov. Another broke out in Novouzensk. While some of those detained in Pokrovsk were soldiers, others turned out to be thieves and former prisoners "dressed in soldier's garb."[76]

71. A. L. Bankvitser, "Vospominaniia," in *Ot fevralia k oktiabriu (Iz ankety uchastnikov Velikoi Oktiabr'skoi sotsialisticheskoi revoliutsii)* (Moscow, 1957), p. 30.

72. *Izvestiia Kazanskogo Voenno-okruzhnogo Komiteta*, no. 14, June 6, 1917, p. 3.

73. *Protokoly zasedaniia Prezidiuma Saratovskogo Voennogo Komiteta*, no. 3, March 13, 1917, p. 32.

74. Ibid., no. 4, March 16, 1917, pp. 32–33.

75. Ibid., no. 8, April 9, 1917, p. 35; *Saratovskii Sovet*, p. 87.

76. *Sotsial-Demokrat*, no. 10, April 10, 1917, p. 3; *Proletarii Povolzh'ia*, no. 8, May 3, 1917, p. 4.

Two points in regard to politics and popular attitudes at the district level stand out. Despite the elliptical nature of available information, it appears that local soldiers interpreted February as a way of getting rid of unpopular officers, injustices, and privilege. Soldier committees, which existed in all of the garrisons in Saratov province, had reduced the old command structure to memory. Clinging stubbornly to their newly won rights and taking the relaxation in discipline and order to excessive levels, soldiers held the civilian populations at their mercy. Second, the civilian populations in the uezd centers democratized administrative and executive bodies and set up their own control organs to prevent arbitrary government. Moreover, the peasant movement was beginning to shape politics and mass attitudes at the district level, not only because of the obvious link between the peasant soldier and villages but also because some district executive committees and soviets had large peasant representations. In early June the Nikolaevsk Soviet confiscated all but 10 of the 6,000 desiatinas constituting the estate of a local landlord named Shikhobalov; at approximately the same time the Balashov Soviet, probably owing to the agitation of radical SRs, passed a resolution calling for local peasants to seize landowners' estates.[77] But more on that later.

The Bolshevik V. P. Antonov concluded that "by virtue of objective circumstances we were not punished for our weak work among the peasantry. The spontaneity of the masses was on our side."[78] The peasant spontaneity about which Antonov spoke is evinced most clearly in the peasantry's disregard for the Provisional Government's successive agrarian programs. Delegates to the First Saratov Province Peasant Congress reported that peasants had reacted favorably to the news of the February Revolution and, depending on their proximity to Saratov or to smaller towns, had fashioned new local administrative organs, the volost (canton) executive committees.[79] Western historians have neglected these lower-level peasant organizations in part because of difficult and uncertain access to Soviet archives, which has made reliance on Soviet publications correspondingly greater. Basing his conclusions on massive archival data from the Lower Volga region, G. A. Gerasimenko has shown that after the February Revolution all social groups participated in the volost committees, although peasants made up the majority of members. Naturally the eldest men, former officials, rural intelligentsia, and others who held influence in the villages before February now served in the

77. For events in Nikolaevsk see Mints, *Oktiabr' v Povolzh'e*, p. 126; for Balashov, see M. Ia. Kosenko, "Iz istorii bor'by krest'ian Saratovskoi gubernii letom i osen'iu 1917 g.," *Uchenye zapiski Saratovskogo gosudarstvennogo universiteta*, vol. 68 (1960), p. 55.

78. Antonov-Saratovskii, *Pod stiagom*, p. 134.

79. *Saratovskii vestnik*, no. 77, April 11, 1917, p. 5.

V. P. Antonov-Saratovskii

volost committees. Beginning in April, when thousands of soldiers from urban-based garrisons returned to the countryside on Easter furlough or to work in the fields, however, the composition of the volost organs changed. Peasants took control of the committees and drove out non-peasant elements. By May, 70 percent of the committees in the Saratov area had undergone reelection. Lamented an editorial in *Saratovskii listok*: "There are even places where the committees are reelected almost every day."[80] According to the same newspaper, "right after the over-throw [of the tsar] power fell into the hands of the more energetic and bolder types. But not all of them remained in place. At the moment a process of reevaluating one's worth is going on. Many leaders already have left the scene, others are leaving, while still others are just arriving.

80. *Saratovskii listok*, no. 102, May 14, 1917, p. 4. For information on the composition of the volost committees see Gerasimenko, "Vozniknovenie volostnykh obshchestvennykh ispolnitel'nykh komitetov," pp. 63–65.

A veritable whirlpool of change is taking place."[81] The peasants' move to rid their organizations of nonpeasant elements found expression elsewhere as well. At a meeting of the Saratov uezd zemstvo in April peasants demanded the expulsion of deputies elected by census society. "Only the active interference of such members as V. O. Kokizova, S. V. Anikin, and N. I. Rakitnikov," reported *Saratovskii vestnik*, "convinced the peasants of the need to take the law into consideration and to retain the propertied members, especially since they would not have a decisive voice in any balloting."[82]

As organs comprising and representing peasant elements, the volost committees reflected the aspirations of the countryside at this time. Their membership is shown in Table 6. In early April a Provisional Government circular already spoke of the "large number of telegraph and personal reports about arrests and unwarranted actions of various village communes and volost committees, which deprive landowners, both large and small, of the possibility of fulfilling their obligations to the government."[83] The official decree recognizing these self-formed organs called for them to supply the army, maintain order locally, and preserve the property and official correspondence of the volost administration. Interpreting their roles more broadly than the government ever intended, however, many volost committees took over the functions of local zemstvos. The Atkarsk volost committee even worked out a detailed moral code for young people, exhorting them not to sing obscene songs, swear, smoke in public, or steal.[84] What disturbed the Provisional Government most, of course, was the committees' tendency to serve as the institutional vehicle through which the Russian muzhik battled for more land.

Even though the First Saratov Province Peasant Congress had voted in early April to postpone land reform until convocation of the Constituent Assembly, peasants began to seize property and work out a settlement on their own, under the guidance of village and volost executive committees. When one prominent landowner from Saratov province complained to the deputy minister of internal affairs that the local volost committee had decided to tax her land, the minister answered that "the volost committees do not have the right of compulsory taxation of land and property. You are not obliged to pay."[85] Several days later the Saratov provincial commissar issued a circular affirming that executive committees did not have the authority to take such measures. But the commisar's ruling was in vain.

81. Quoted in Vas'kin and Gerasimenko, *Fevral'skaia revoliutsiia*, p. 176.
82. *Saratovskii vestnik*, no. 134, April 20, 1917, p. 3.
83. *Sbornik tsirkuliarov Ministerstva Vnutrennykh del*, pp. 10–11.
84. G. A. Gerasimenko, *Nizovye krest'ianskie organizatsii v 1917—pervoi polovine 1918 godov (Na materialakh Nizhnego Povolzh'ia)* (Saratov, 1974), pp. 80–81.
85. Ibid., pp. 83–84.

Table 6

Number and party affiliation of volost committee members, May 1917, by uezd

Uezd	Volosts		Committee members				
				Party affiliation			
	Total number	*Number with data available*	*Total number*	*SR*	*SD*	*Kadet*	*Unaffiliated*
Atkarsk	32	24	354	99	—	—	255
Balashov	40	35	308	75	—	—	233
Kamyshin	25	17	470	75	2	29	364
Khvalynsk	26	18	135	15	—	—	120
Kuznetsk	13	5	261	51	4	—	206
Petrovsk	26	25	160	20	17	4	119
Saratov	18	12	176	29	—	—	147
Serdobsk	26	22	300	98	—	—	202
Tsaritsyn	8	3	110	10	1	2	97
Volsk	24	9	256	45	—	2	209
All uezds	238	170	2,530	517	24	37	1,952
Percent	100%	71.4%	100%	20.4%	1.0%	1.5%	77.1%

Source: Adapted from G. A. Gerasimenko, "Local Peasant Organizations in 1917 and the First Half of 1918," ed. Donald J. Raleigh, *Soviet Studies in History*, 16, no. 3 (Winter 1977–78), 28.

To slow down the move toward localism in the countryside and balance the independent activities of the executive committees, the Provisional Government issued an edict on April 21 calling for the election of land committees in the provinces. The committees would be responsible for collecting information on local land arrangements and land needs and for resolving land disputes until the implementation of land reform by the Constituent Assembly. Intended to stand between the volost executive committees and the estate owners, the land committees merely complicated the question of power in the rural areas. Without clearly demarcated functions, they remained unaccountable to the judicial apparatus until September. Furthermore, the April 21 decree had summoned the formation of committees at the provincial and uezd level, leaving the election of committees at the volost level optional. Convened by the SRs in May, the First All-Russian Congress of Peasant Deputies criticized the government decree and appealed for the routine establishment of land committees at the volost level. The congress also declared that the main function of the committees "should be not the preservation of the existing situation but positive action aimed at solving the agrarian question."[86] All land was to pass into the disposition of the land committees. In effect, the resolutions drawn up at the peasant congress gave the volost land committees full discretionary powers to interfere in and settle property disputes.

In mid-May local land committees began to appear in Saratov province. Even though moderate elements controlled provincial and district land committees, communal peasants directed the committees at the volost level. In half of the districts in Saratov province peasants began to form volost land committees at village meetings or in collaboration with the executive committees even before the uezd committees were set up. Between May and September more than 250 land committees were formed locally at the volost level. Despite prescribed norms, the committee size varied from three to ten or more members, and tended to have the same composition as the executive committees, thus ensuring that the organs would not apply the brakes to the disquieting peasant movement. A degree of social tension accompanied the formation of the land committees.

> On July 16 the Volsk Uezd Land Committee heard a statement by landowner N. A. Zorkin, who asked that members of the Union of Landowners be granted the right to elect and be elected to the land committees, and it rejected the request. On July 27 *Saratovskii listok* reported to its readers that the Union of Landowners had sent the Saratov Uezd Zemstvo a petition "to permit landowners to participate

86. Gerasimenko, "Local Peasant Organizations," p. 51.

> in election to the volost committees." The uezd zemstvo also "found this petition unacceptable." The political isolation of the prosperous elements of the countryside in the organization of volost land committees was very clearly noted at the congress of landowners of Saratov province. "In the volost land committees," N. A. Zorkin complained, "only those who want to receive land are represented, but those from whom they want to take land are not."[87]

Viewing themselves as watchmen over the government's regulations, the more moderate provincial and uezd-level land committees often clashed with the volost land committees, which promoted the communal peasants' aspirations to broaden the amount of land under cultivation. Technically the provincial land committee, which first convened between July 11 and 14, possessed the authority to abrogate decisions reached by lower-level committees. But as so often was the case in revolutionary Russia, the stark reality of the voluntary nature of power relationships revealed itself again. The Saratov Provincial Land Committee candidly admitted that the "limitations and uncertainty of its rights . . . makes it completely helpless in face of the real demands of life."[88] SR activists, who were growing further apart from party leaders in Saratov, probably served as the driving force behind the volost land committees' determination to transfer land to the peasants without further delay.

Under the threat of even more serious supply problems, the government established a state food-supply committee, with local counterparts, to regulate the flow of grain from the villages to the cities. By the end of March the government committee had already announced a grain monopoly with authority to set prices for grain and to establish the food committees at the provincial level. Prices for grain purchased from peasants were raised a staggering 60 percent on March 25, and food prices in the towns quickly rose. An April 11 law made local food committees responsible for grain under cultivation. On April 29 the government introduced rationing throughout the country, even in food-processing areas such as Saratov. The success of the government's food acquisition program and grain monopoly depended on the volost-level food-supply committees, but the volost committees lacked any authority to force peasants to turn over their grain. The government had not found a way to provide the committees with essential manufactured items that might serve as an incentive to the peasants. Food-supply committees at various administrative levels were founded in Saratov province in April (39), but most were set up in May (115) and June (56), and a few as late as July

87. Ibid., pp. 55–56. Also see his "Organizatsiia volostnykh zemel'nykh komitetov v Nizhnem Povolzh'e," *Povolzhskii krai,* no. 3 (1975), pp. 71–72.
88. Gerasimenko, *Nizovye krest'ianskie organizatsii,* p. 132.

(9).[89] In May, Minister of Food Supplies A. V. Peshekhonov ordered volost executive committees to relinquish their food-supply activities to the new volost food committees. According to government regulations, the volost food-supply committees were to comprise peasants, landowners elected by the uezd zemstvo assembly, zemstvo employees, and representatives of consumer cooperatives and other local bodies. Growing peasant ill will toward the landowners and zemstvo officials limited the ability of the food-supply committees to act. "As a result, volost food committees usually tended to become either appendages of already-existing peasant organizations or merged totally with those village-based bodies. . . . Volost food committees became more responsive to impulses from below than directives from above."[90]

The Socialist Revolutionary party also formed a confusing and overlapping series of party organizations in the rural areas during the spring of 1917. Conservative SR and Popular Socialist intellectuals gathered in Moscow urged the revival of national and regional peasant unions, which had flourished during 1905–6. Designed to promote the peasantry's interests in the broadest sense possible, the unions, in the opinion of their promoters, did not preclude the election of peasant soviets, which were viewed as exclusively political organs. But a more politically oriented group of Russian populists sought instead to establish peasant soviets. Meeting in more radical Petrograd between May 4 and 28, a national All-Russian Congress of Peasant Deputies endorsed the election of a national All-Russian Peasant Soviet and declared the peasant unions superfluous. As a result, a rival set of SR-backed peasant organizations existed simultaneously in parts of the country.

The moderate, centrist branch of the SR party remained strong in Saratov, and because it had much in common with the Popular Socialist promoters of the Peasant Union, the rift within local populism for the time being had a lesser impact locally than in such neighboring provinces as Kazan. Nevertheless, even in middle-of-the-road Saratov, signs of factionalism emerged. The Main Committee of the Peasant Union, selected in March, included several prominent Saratov SRs and PSs, such as A. A. Minin, V. D. Chenykaev, and A. S. Chumaevskii. Deputies to the First Saratov Province Peasant Congress elected a local union on April 7–8 and in May circulated 10,000 copies of the union's regulations throughout the province. Numerous peasant unions were set up in Saratov at all levels and even in the Saratov garrison. The Executive Committee of the Saratov Province Peasant Union, however, noted that some SRs related negatively to the organizations, especially after the

89. Ibid., p. 71.

90. Graeme J. Gill, *Peasants and Government in the Russian Revolution* (New York, 1979), p. 58.

ruling of the First All-Russian Peasant Congress. Riding about the countryside, these individuals called on the peasantry to abolish peasant unions and join local party organizations.[91] The Provincial Peasant Union censored these individuals acting independently, and sent SR and PS delegates into the villages to reestablish unions. This was one of the first indications that factionalism had split Saratov SRs. Once it became clear to local peasants that the peasant unions stood to the right of popular aspirations in the countryside, the unions began to disappear. By fall they survived in name only. In the period between March and October only thirty-seven peasant soviets were established in Saratov province, and this situation was common throughout Russia. Most rural-based soviets that appeared in the spring and summer months collapsed soon after their formation, in part because they duplicated the activities of village executive committees.[92]

The resolutions on the land question passed at a provincial peasant congress in April and at the Second Provincial Congress of Soviets in May provide further insights into the situation in the Saratov villages. More than 400 peasant deputies flocked to Saratov for the first congress. "The urge to organize at the present time literally has a spontaneous character," commented one observer. "It was enough simply to issue a call for the convocation of a congress to draw out delegates from various corners of the countryside." In harmony with a decision reached by the Saratov Province Food-Supply Committee, delegates decided that all unsowed land would be placed under the jurisdiction of local food-supply committees to be doled out to needy peasants according to prices set by the committees. The deputies also voted in favor of increasing the use of soldiers garrisoned in the rear for field work.[93] Passing a resolution forbidding the seizure of privately owned land before convocation of a constituent assembly, the deputies nonetheless resolved that "private ownership of land within the confines of the Russian republic is abolished forever." Using the familiar SR terminology, the same resolution decreed that the land belonged to the whole nation, that everyone has the right to its use on the basis of one's own labor, and that land "should pass from those who own it to the state without compensation." On the war question, the congress enthusiastically endorsed the peace program of the Petrograd Soviet.[94]

91. *Saratovskii vestnik*, no. 115, May 28, 1917, p. 5.

92. Gerasimenko, *Nizovye krest'ianskie organizatsii*, pp. 73–74, and "Vozniknovenie Sovetskoi vlasti v volostiakh Saratovskoi gubernii," *Povolzhskii krai*, no. 1 (1972), p. 62.

93. A. V. Shestakov, ed., *Sovety krest'ianskikh deputatov i drugie krest'ianskie organizatsii*, pt. 2, pp. 110–11.

94. *Saratovskii vestnik*, no. 77, April 11, 1917, p. 5; no. 78, April 12, p. 5; Shestakov, *Sovety krest'ianskikh deputatov*, p. 114.

The resolutions passed at the Saratov peasant congress are strikingly similar to those carried by peasant congresses in neighboring provinces. Peasant congresses held in May, however, tended to make far more radical demands than those that had convened earlier, probably because the All-Russian Peasant Congress raised hopes for an imminent land transfer. In Kazan, where peasants felt the land shortage to a greater extent than in Saratov, all arable land was placed at the disposal of volost committees. The Provisional Government circular criticizing the actions of the Kazan congress went ignored. A Simbirsk uezd peasant congress in May demanded an immediate transfer of all land to the peasantry. The Second Samara Province Peasant Congress approved a resolution that all land not worked personally would pass to volost land committees or executive committees for one year. Again, protests lodged by the government fell on deaf ears. Delegates from Samara province's various soviets, dumas, and commercial community were co-opted into the peasant congress, which began to call itself the Provincial All-Estate Congress (Gubernyi vsesoslovnyi s"ezd). Disbanding the local organ of the Provisional Government, the congress declared itself the legitimate authority in Samara province and circulated a telegram calling on the local population to obey the congress's decrees rather than those of the Provisional Government. Events in nearby Penza, which soon became known as the "Kronstadt of the countryside," also alarmed officials in Petrograd, in part because the local SR organization otherwise was considered moderate. In mid-May delegates to a provincial peasant congress placed all but allotment land at the disposal of the volost committees and abolished the right to rent out land. A representative of the Executive Committee of the All-Russian Congress of Peasant Deputies insisted that the resolutions passed by the congress had been formulated "under the influence of Bolshevik ideas" but failed to persuade the Penza peasant deputies to abrogate their decisions. For over a month the Provisional Government and leaders of the SR party sought to undo all of the resolutions passed by the Penza congress. They also failed. As the former provincial commissar reported to the Ministry of the Interior, the use of force against the peasants is "unlikely to bring any positive results."[95]

The extraordinary grass-roots impulse on the part of the Volga-area peasantry toward implementing land reform before the Constituent Assembly exposed the enormous gap separating rural activists from leaders in the towns and cities. This was the case in Saratov, too, where peasants pressed for more radical demands than their leadership. Although no

95. Descriptions of the Kazan, Simbirsk, and Samara congresses can be found in Mints, *Oktiabr' v Povolzh'e*, pp. 116–25. For information on the Penza congress see A. D. Maliavskii, *Krest'ianskoe dvizhenie v Rossii v 1917 g., mart–oktiabr'* (Moscow, 1981), pp. 230–39, and Ferro, *Octobre*, pp. 198–205.

second peasant congress convened in May, a Second Provincial Congress of Soviets representing the soviets of seven uezds opened in Saratov on May 5. Congress delegates passed a resolution "on land" introduced by the Bolshevik Miliutin. Encouraging peasants to seize land immediately, before the convocation of the Constituent Assembly, the resolution called for the nationalization of all land and for uezd and volost committees to work out the land settlement as soon as possible.[96]

Toward the end of spring the government's procrastination over the land question as well as its attempts to curb the power of the peasant volost executive committees generated disillusionment in the countryside. Once it became clear that the government had no power to enforce its decrees and that local urban leaders could do little but exhort the peasants not to press their demands until the Constituent Assembly, rural Russia embarked on its own revolution. Local peasants wanted to expand the amount of land under cultivation to create greater economic security. They could not understand why broad expanses of arable soil lay unplowed when the government and army needed more food. True, they could rent part of the landlords' estates, but at prices that seemed unreasonable or impossible to pay. Such practices may have been incomprehensible to the peasantry's sense of communalism. During the war, communes in the Lower Volga region sowed the allotment land of those households whose male workers had been drafted. Why should everyone contribute his share except the landlord? John Keep may well be correct in arguing that "civil war in the villages was virtually inevitable once the tsarist regime had collapsed."[97]

In Saratov province the "peasant movement broke out in five uezds in April and in all ten in June."[98] Based on specific socioeconomic grievances and conflicts, the movement reached high levels in the fertile interior districts of Atkarsk, Balashov, Serdobsk, and Petrovsk, where private ownership remained important. Clashes with landlords characterized peasant disturbances there. More diversified forms of production prevailed in the less fertile riparian and southeastern uezds, where disturbances appear to have been less frequent, with the exception of Saratov and Tsaritsyn districts. The large number of hired laborers and exploitive rent conditions also heightened rural unrest in these areas. Fewer rural disturbances flared up in those districts with large percentages of Germans, Mordvinians, and Tatars, who lived isolated from the Slavic population (Kamyshin, Kuznetsk, Khvalynsk, and Petrovsk).

96. *Khronika*, p. 53.

97. John Keep, *The Russian Revolution: A Study in Mass Mobilization* (New York, 1976), p. 112.

98. *1917 god v derevne: Vospominaniia krest'ian* (Moscow and Leningrad, 1929), p. 120.

G. A. Gerasimenko and V. V. Vas'kin have documented thirty-one peasant actions against landlord, state, and church ownership in March.[99] Since most unsowed land belonged to large owners from whom peasants rented, rent clashes were the most frequent form of peasant activity at this time, followed by disagreements over use of forest lands and efforts to restrict the landowners' access to prisoners of war. The Saratov Soviet may have unwittingly fanned the flames of social war in the countryside when it passed a resolution on March 17 calling for the transfer of all unsowed privately owned land to public organizations and an expansion in the use of soldiers and prisoners of war to work the idle fields. Conflicts broke out afterward between landowners and peasants over land rental rates, which volost committees usually settled in favor of peasants. At the same time peasants tried to curtail the landowners' and Stolypin peasants' use of prisoners of war, thereby reducing their sowed area and making the land available to the communal peasants. The decree of the Zhukovskii volost committee in Petrovsk district was representative of this trend. Noting that large numbers of prisoners of war were quartered in the district and that many peasant households were on the verge of economic ruin because of lack of farm hands, the Zhukovskii committee "authorized village committees to seize immediately half of the prisoners of war from all of the estates and to divide them among [peasant] households in need of work hands." Peasant committees also made it more difficult for estate owners to hire peasant workers by setting higher prices on day laborers and fixing modest fees for rental of farm equipment. Occasionally the committees replaced estate managers and stewards who related poorly to local peasants or refused to comply with rulings of the village committees.[100] In short,

99. Vas'kin and Gerasimenko, *Fevral'skaia revoliutsiia*, p. 200. How accurate are such figures? Historians naturally have tried to count the number of disturbances, but the breakdown of authority in 1917 makes this enterprise problematic. Depending on the level of unrest, the Provisional Government requested local authorities to report on the peasant movement at least once a month, but most did so more frequently. These statistics of the Main Land Committee were published in 1927; compilers cautioned users that the peasant movement in all probability was much broader. Although Soviet scholars have since documented additional cases of rural unrest, their compilations remain imprecise. Completely disparate features of the peasant movement are lumped together and such factors as the number of peasants involved and the intensity of the incidents are unknown. Despite all the shortcomings, there are no substitutes for these statistics; when combined with illustrative examples they probably present a fairly accurate picture of the scope and character of the peasant movement. In any event, all accounts maintain that Saratov province occupied a prominent place among the most turbulent Russian provinces. See V. P. Miliutin, ed., *Agrarnaia revoliutsiia*, vol. 2, *Krest'ianskoe dvizhenie v 1917 godu* (Moscow, 1928), pp. 94–95, 178; M. Martov, "Agrarnoe dvizhenie," *Krasnyi arkhiv*, no. 1/4 (1926), p. 184. Gerasimenko's more complete figures are higher than earlier compilations. See *Nizovye krest'ianskie organizatsii*, p. 98.

100. Vas'kin and Gerasimenko, *Fevral'skaia revoliutsiia*, pp. 205, 209–11.

peasants interfered in and restricted the estate owners' advantage in market relationships.

Seizure of estate owners' and other privately held land ranked first in terms of local peasant disturbances; forty-eight incidents were registered in April. Writing to her son, who was living in Saratov at the time, a local landowner expressed the frustration that many must have shared: "The peasants are demanding land, saying we stole it from them! They call it stealing when we bought it back in 1880 from a ruined pomeshchik and gave half of it back to the peasants free. We built them a church, school, and hospital, where my aunt served as a doctor, again free, not only for them but also for other neighboring villages in Volsk uezd."[101] Saratov peasants also continued to clash with landowners over land rental rates and to limit the pomeshchiks' use of prisoners of war and agricultural workers. The various encumbrances the peasant committees were able to place before the estate owners decreased the amount of land they were able to sow. Peasant committees established control over the unsowed land, leaving the landowner's family an amount it could farm with its own labor *(trudovaia norma)*. Peasants also began to seize pastureland and hayfields in April, undoubtedly anticipating the mowing of hay in May and afterward.

In May local peasants began to confiscate estates, removing prisoners of war and setting rental terms favorable to themselves. A report written by landowners from several black-earth provinces, including Saratov, to the Provisional Government and Petrograd Soviet reveals the dilemma in which the estate owners were trapped. "We meet," they declared,

> with the strongest opposition from village committees and commissars, who are acting illegally and carrying out undisguised propaganda for the abolition of every possible means of private ownership. . . . The general situation . . . at the present time is as follows:
>
> 1. Public organizations and their representatives, contrary to the law, fix the rent on land so low that it does not even cover the necessary payments due on the land.
> 2. Land is forcibly taken from its owners and handed over to the peasants. . . .
> 3. Wages for labor are arbitrarily set, interfering with freedom of labor and freedom of contract.
> 4. The sanctity of the home is being violated by searches and by confiscation of movable property. Landowners and their managers are deprived of liberty, without due process of law, for refusing to obey the unlawful demands of the committees and commissars.[102]

101. Golubov, "Saratov v 1917," p. 29.

102. Frank A. Golder, *Documents of Russian History, 1914–1917* (Gloucester, 1964), p. 380. A report similar in tone describing events in Balashov can be found in Launcelot A. Owen, *The Russian Peasant Movement, 1906–17* (New York, 1937), p. 183.

Attempts to establish control over estates and the actual sabotage of estates appear to have increased toward the end of May.[103] The peasantry's interest in establishing control over the use of land, resources, and equipment reflected the augmented ill will between peasants and estate owners, which paralleled workers' attempts to set up supervisory control over industrial production in the cities.

By June, when peasant disturbances had spread to all ten districts, the most widespread acts were the seizure of forest land, meadowland (hayfields), and arable land.[104] Although there was little peasant violence until fall, an unusually brutal incident received extensive newspaper coverage at this time. A confused sense of economic discontent and misplaced patriotism combined with ignorance and blind rage may have caused this attack. Near the railroad station at Rtishchevo, a mill owned by a German named Teilman mysteriously burned down. Rumors quickly circulated that Teilman himself had planned the fire in order to get even with local peasants who had quibbled with him over service charges. These accounts reached Teilman, who, given the excited mood of the local populace, tried to slip away from Rtishchevo until the bad feelings had subsided. But someone recognized him at the railroad station, and a group of soldiers held an impromptu trial and found him guilty. A soldier bashed Teilman in the head with a rifle butt. He was shot and bayonetted. His body was then scooped up on bayonet point and dumped on the railroad tracks. Threatened by the soldiers, the conductor was forced to drive the engine back and forth over the body. To the horror of those on the train, the soldiers then stuffed cigarettes in the corpse's mouth, set the body on fire, and began to dance.[105]

Saratov peasants also vented their hostility on the Stolypin peasants who had withdrawn from the commune to establish private farms. Evidence demonstrates that conflict between communal peasants and those who had left the commune, the *otrubshchiki* and *khutoriane*, made up a significant proportion of local peasant disturbances, although incomplete data and inexact measuring techniques prevent any precise assessments of how extensive such actions were. Gerasimenko and Vas'kin have identified four major disturbances aimed at the Stolypin peasants in Saratov and Astrakhan provinces in March and seventeen in April, mainly in Saratov, Balashov, Serdobsk, and Volsk districts. M. Ia.

103. According to Maliavskii, seizure of estates was not common in the country at this time, except in certain Volga and black-earth provinces. See *Krest'ianskoe dvizhenie*, p. 179.

104. Kosenko, "Iz istorii bor'by krest'ian," p. 60. Corroborating evidence can be found in K. G. Kotel'nikov and V. L. Meller, eds., *Krest'ianskoe dvizhenie v 1917 godu* (Moscow and Leningrad, 1927), pp. 94–95; *Iiul'skaia demonstratsiia*, p. 429; and *Saratovskii vestnik*, no. 146, July 5, 1917, p. 3.

105. *Saratovskii vestnik*, no. 136, June 22, 1917, p. 4.

Kosenko, who examined complaints from Stolypin peasants that volost and village executive committees had taken their land, documented 439 incidents from April through June.[106] Reporting to the First All-Russian Congress of Peasants, Saratov's Rakitnikov noted that local peasants "relate with great hostility toward the otrubshchiki. If a peasant went on *otrub* it would be such a blotch on his character, even if he were an SR, that he no longer would be picked for any office."[107]

The collapse of the central state apparatus and move toward localism had revived the village commune and worsened the political position of the Stolypin peasants. Deprived of their vote at village meetings, they could not influence the new executive committees, which became the administrative vehicle for the attacks on the more independent farmers. Communal peasants often aimed at the complete liquidation of independent peasant farms and in the meanwhile took their land, meadows, and forests. Some specific examples will convey the mood and scope of these actions. In late April representatives of ten villages in Saratov uezd agreed to divide the fallow land belonging to those peasants who had consolidated their strips. By August in this same district peasants had seized land from otrubshchiki in seventeen counties.[108] From Volsk district otrubshchiki complained that the executive committees had deprived them of all political and civil rights. Stolypin peasants from Atkarsk district wrote to the Saratov SR paper that "we argue with the communal peasants every time we meet and hate each other more than we do the Germans."[109]

Some Stolypin peasants appear to have willingly rejoined the commune, but others resisted the designs on their land. After visiting twelve volosts in Saratov uezd, the district commissar reported that local peasants who had earlier left the commune had reached agreements with their fellow villagers and returned their holdings to the collective fold. At the Sokurskii volost (Saratov uezd) peasant congress held in April, peasants voted to merge otrub and khutor holdings with the communal allotment land and afterward to divide the land according to number of males per household.[110] Conflicts of various degrees evidently predominated in relations between the two groups elsewhere, however, and

106. Vas'kin and Gerasimenko, *Fevral'skaia revoliutsiia*, p. 218; Kosenko is cited in T. V. Osipova, *Klassovaia bor'ba v derevne v period podgotovki i provedeniia Oktiabr'skoi sotsialisticheskoi revoliutsii* (Moscow, 1974), p. 102.

107. Quoted in Gerasimenko, *Nizovye krest'ianskie organizatsii*, pp. 62–63.

108. Osipova, *Klassovaia bor'ba v derevne*, p. 167.

109. These two examples can be found in G. A. Gerasimenko, "Vliianie posledstvii Stolypinskoi agrarnoi reformy na krest'ianskie organizatsii 1917 goda (Po materialam Saratovskoi gubernii)," *Istoriia SSSR*, no. 1 (1981), p. 42.

110. See Vas'kin and Gerasimenko, *Fevral'skaia revoliutsiia*, p. 219. Also see Mints, *Oktiabr' v Povolzh'e*, p. 128.

it was not unusual for Stolypin peasants to defend their interests vigorously.[111] Those who resisted the move back into the commune often joined together with landlords. At a Saratov uezd congress of landowners held in May, 135 of the 150 delegates were actually peasants. At a provincial congress of landowners that same month Stolypin peasants constituted the majority of deputies. The congress voted to "set for itself the task of creating a 'powerful organization' to defend the interests of the pomeshchiki." In the beginning of May a national congress of the All-Russian Landowners' Union, representing thirty-one provinces, assembled in Moscow. According to T. V. Osipova, "among the 300 delegates were many otrubshchiki and khutoriane."[112]

Saratov landowners and prosperous peasants fought a futile battle to hold on to their land. The Balashov branch of the Landowners' Union urged local authorities to take measures against "violent seizures of meadows and the removal of hay, with the assistance even of the cantonal [volost] committees and the militia!"[113] In late June the Balashov Landowners' Union cabled the Provisional Government three times, complaining of the volost committees' illegal seizure of haymaking areas. Asked to look into the matter, the uezd land administration, which sympathized with the peasantry, reported back to the government that accusations made against the peasants in regard to their purported use of force were exaggerated in 90 percent of the cases in order to "sow panic, create anarchy, and drown Russian freedom in a sea of blood and disorders."[114] Evidence reveals that toward the end of June the government sent soldiers and Cossacks to the more turbulent rural areas in Saratov province, where they arrested unruly communal peasants.[115] But peasants continued to ignore threats and appeals for restraint.

The local peasant movement at this time appears to have been self-generated, but the peasant soldier began to have an impact on the rural revolution. Deserters were already appearing in the villages by the spring of 1917; for the most part, however, they were not considered a radicalizing influence until later in the year. In some cases peasant deserters "bred disorganization in local life," but elsewhere peasants drove them away.[116] Much more important in familiarizing the peasantry with urban

111. See the complaint against the Stolypin peasants filed by communal peasants in a village in which the former controlled the local committee: Akademiia nauk SSSR, Institut istorii et al., *Ekonomicheskoe polozhenie Rossii nakanune Velikoi Oktiabr'skoi sotsialisticheskoi revoliutsii: Dokumenty i materialy*, vol. 3, *Sel'skoe khoziaistvo i krest'ianstvo*, ed. A. A. Anfimov et al. (Leningrad, 1967), pp. 361–62 (hereafter cited as Anfimov, *Ekonomicheskoe polozhenie Rossii*).

112. Osipova, *Klassovaia bor'ba v derevne*, pp. 98, 102.

113. Quoted in Owen, *Russian Peasant Movement*, p. 183.

114. Cited in Osipova, *Klassovaia bor'ba v derevne*, p. 185.

115. Maliavskii, *Krest'ianskoe dvizhenie*, pp. 179, 218.

116. *Saratovskii listok*, no. 102, May 14, 1917, p. 4.

developments, as has been suggested, were the approximately 20,000 soldiers who returned to the villages of Saratov and Astrakhan provinces on furlough during the spring. Officials reported that the land question took on new urgency under the influence of these soldiers.[117] Left SRs in the Kronstadt Soviet had sent a handful of agitators out into the Saratov countryside in May, but it is impossible to measure their impact on rural unrest.[118] Occasionally urban soviets also helped politicize the countryside. In June, for instance, the Balashov Soviet of Workers' Deputies supported the decision of local peasants to confiscate estate owners' land. At the same time some local peasants began to express antiwar sentiments.[119]

The February Revolution had unleashed an infectious but short-lived wave of euphoria and goodwill in Russian society. Striking a death blow to the age-old restrictions on popular initiative, the February Revolution had made Russia "the freest country in the world," ushering in an unprecedented level of mass participation in all aspects of public affairs. A flurry of organizational activity and the proliferation of new organizations characterized the spring of 1917. The population set up committees along political, occupational, national, social, sexual, and religious lines. But liberation had created an environment in which various social groups worked toward their own diverse priorities. As a consequence, the unanimous revolution soon yielded to political crisis and social polarization. For the country's ruling circles and Western-oriented political leaders, the revolution had swept away all of the frustrating administrative impediments that had made a scandal of the country's war cause. The middle-class government that ruled revitalized, revolutionary Russia was determined to mobilize all resources to win the war against German militarism. Reform had to wait. To ordinary citizens, however, the revolution had created propitious conditions for bringing about a better life. The deeply rooted feelings of injustice and suspicion toward the old order soon carried over to those in the post-February administration who sought to curb popular initiative and reform.

In Saratov the "democratic elements" fought to democratize such institutions as city dumas and zemstvos, which before 1917 had been the privileged domain of Russia's census society. Yet at the same time the formerly disenfranchised established their own unrepresentative class organs, which amassed considerable power. Among the overlapping network of popular organizations created in the first half of 1917, those elected directly by the people mobilized the most authority: factory committees and soviets, soldier committees, and volost and village executive

117. *Sotsial-Demokrat*, no. 8, April 25, 1917, p. 1.
118. *Saratovskii vestnik*, no. 116, May 30, 1917, p. 3.
119. See Anfimov, *Ekonomicheskoe polozhenie*, p. 360.

committees. All of these lower-level bodies tried to establish some means of control over factory administrators, officers, and estate owners, just as the Petrograd Soviet had served as watchman over the middle-class government and its institutions before the formation of the First Coalition Government in May. It bears repeating that the practices of the popular institutions had little in common with Western notions of representative political democracy. The common people may not have understood this concept at all, or viewed it with suspicion.

Social polarization complicated the tactical dilemma of the moderate socialists who entered the government in May. Many local SR and Menshevik leaders had feared that joining with the middle class would compromise their party programs and beliefs. They were right. This is particularly true of the SRs, who were enormously influential in Saratov province. While the fate of some SRs became linked to that of the coalition government, others who were more directly involved with the peasantry at the lower levels undertook to carry out programs advocated by the party since before 1905. The more moderate leaders of the party were hard put to deal with "our Bolsheviks," as they called their impatient comrades. Meanwhile, toward summer, workers and soldiers tended to ignore their own organizations once they advised restraint. Ironically, the impulse toward localism in the immediate aftermath of February, followed by an emerging organizational malaise, actually contributed to a further breakdown of the state apparatus and of law and order in general. As the year progressed, the atomization of political forms underscored the need for a return to a state of normality and to an administrative order that would make things work again. This is why extremist solutions to the question of political power presented themselves in Russia after the halcyon days of revolution had passed. The other alternatives simply had not worked.

CHAPTER 5

"Oh, Blind Leaders of a Blind People!": Summer Crisis in Saratov Province

On July 3–5, throngs of Petrograd workers and soldiers, exasperated by the government's renewed prosecution of the war and by their deteriorating standard of living, poured into the center of the capital. The demonstration, which threatened to topple the government, also was the result of weeks of Bolshevik agitation. Rank-and-file Petrograd party members from the city's factories and barracks had played a leading role in organizing the movement while the Bolshevik Military Organization and leftist elements in the Petersburg committee of the party encouraged it against the wishes of both the Central Committee and Lenin. As the eruption subsided, the rightist press launched an attack on the Bolsheviks, emphasizing charges that Lenin and other party leaders were German agents. To such damaging accusations were added an array of others, not only from elements of the extreme right but from liberals and moderate socialists as well. At the same time the government, under pressure from the liberals and the right, began an assault on the left. Bolshevik papers were ordered closed; party leaders were arrested; and Lenin, to avoid arrest, went underground—thus "proving" his alleged guilt.[1]

Historians rightfully argue that the abortive uprising of Petrograd workers and soldiers in the summer temporarily turned the scales in

1. For a discussion of the July Days in Petrograd, see Rabinowitch, *Prelude to Revolution*, pp. 135–228, and *The Bolsheviks Come to Power: The Revolution of 1917 in Petrograd* (New York, 1976), pp. 1–38.

favor of repressive measures against the left. But to fully comprehend the local impact of these distant disturbances in the capital, it is necessary to keep in mind the political and administrative crisis that had developed in provincial Russia by the summer of 1917, the main features of which were the extraordinary move toward localism and the increasingly disturbing voluntary nature of all power relationships. The emerging authority of the Saratov Soviet and the acknowledged weakness of the Provincial Public Executive Committee had magnified at the local level the importance of the nature of political power at the top. This was particularly the case after the SRs and Mensheviks risked compromising their party programs by entering the First Coalition Government in May. As far as provincial Saratov was concerned, then, the real significance of the summer crisis in the capital was that it further heightened the problem of political power. Party organizations were forced to react to the actions of their leaders in Petrograd, which were based on an altogether different set of circumstances. In this regard local history can shed new light on our understanding of the complex interaction of national and local events and of the revolutionary process at the provincial level.

Rumors about a Bolshevik uprising in Petrograd had circulated in Saratov before July 6, when Saratov newspapers provided the first full coverage of events in the capital. Cables from the All-Russian Executive Committee to the Saratov Soviet and from the central telegraph agencies to local newspaper offices informed the population that demonstrations had broken out on July 3; that the minister of justice had charged the Bolsheviks on July 4 with having accepted German funds; and that the government had seized the Bolshevik press on July 5. An editorial in *Proletarii Povolzh'ia* captured the tenor of most public reactions to the July Days published in Saratov at this time. While admitting that the complete details of the Petrograd demonstration were not yet known, the author concluded that even if the Bolsheviks were not shown to have instigated the uprising, "their agitation and demagogic tactics definitely shaped the movement."[2] Editorials in the socialist papers advised party members to remain cautious because no one could be certain of the nature of the Petrograd events or of their eventual outcome. Some lower-level Bolsheviks, however, ignored these appeals and organized a mass meeting in Theater Square on July 5, without the city committee's approval. When the majority of soldiers and workers present prevented the moderate socialists from speaking, the latter reassembled elsewhere and passed a resolution appealing to the populace to remain calm and to mobilize against anarchistic movements and the "disorganizational ac-

2. *Proletarii Povolzh'ia*, no. 27, July 6, 1917, p. 2.

tivity of demagogues."[3] The next morning a few local Bolsheviks abstained from voting when the majority of Soviet deputies accepted a resolution outlawing unapproved demonstrations, calling them "a serious threat to the cause of revolution and therefore inadmissible."

In blatant disregard of the Soviet's entreaty, a "Committee of Evacuated Soldiers" summoned soldiers to a demonstration that very evening. At dusk several garrison units and an unknown number of civilians assembled in one of the town's large squares. A Bolshevik soldier from Tsaritsyn lashed out against the June offensive, sharply rebuking the Military Section of the Soviet for not supporting the soldiers' desires to vote in the upcoming municipal elections. Speakers next decried the much-resented draft deferment of workers in defense-related industries. A bitter exchange between Vasil'ev and a recent returnee from the front followed. In response to the soldier's suggestion that Vasil'ev be sent to the front, the large number of pro-Bolshevik soldiers waved placards inscribed with Bolshevik slogans in support of Vasil'ev. The uncertain crowd movement caused widespread panic. Several people were hurt in the ensuing scuffle.[4]

Local pro-Bolshevik manifestations distressed moderate leaders of the Saratov Soviet and seriously complicated their relations with the Bolsheviks. Although the Executive Committee took the stand that Saratov Bolsheviks should not be blamed for the disturbances in the capital, SR and Menshevik spokesmen expressed great concern over how Saratov Bolsheviks interpreted the Petrograd events. Some moderates condemned the liberal press's attacks on local Bolsheviks, but others, especially SR members of the Military Section, voiced their hostility toward Bolshevik tactics.[5] When the Menshevik B. N. Guterman condemned the "defamation that the counterrevolution is conducting against the Bolsheviks," for instance, the SR officer M. T. Didenko replied that the Bolsheviks had "gone too far" in their denunciation of Kerensky.[6]

Tensions were strained even more the next time the Executive Committee met. Addressing a packed audience, Vasil'ev "brought the auditorium to the boiling point" by criticizing the government's actions against the Bolsheviks. Speakers from each faction then debated the future of the national government. On July 2 the Kadet ministers had resigned from the First Coalition Government, contributing to the resulting demonstrations in the capital. The Saratov Soviet now discussed whether the future government should be exclusively socialist or should

3. *Saratovskii vestnik*, no. 148, July 7, 1917, p. 4.

4. Ibid.

5. Antonov-Saratovskii, "S fevralia," p. 197.

6. See *Saratovskii vestnik*, no. 150, July 9, 1917, p. 3; *Saratovskii listok*, no. 148, July 9, 1917, p. 3; *Sotsial-Demokrat*, no. 50, July 9, 1917, p. 4.

include the bourgeoisie. Calling for a transfer of power to the soviets, the Bolsheviks demanded the creation of "truly democratic and revolutionary organs" both at the national level and locally, and argued that the further development of the revolution would diminish disagreements within "the revolutionary democracy," that is, among the internationalist wings of all of the socialist parties. (In fact, informal left socialist blocs of Bolsheviks, Left SRs, and Menshevik Internationalists had already become influential in Kazan, Samara, and some of the Ural soviets.) The SR-Menshevik rival resolution supporting the coalition ministry with the bourgeoisie, however, passed by a vote of 253 to 118.[7] (A similar vote on the First Coalition Government in May had yielded 153 votes in favor of coalition, with 76 votes cast against cooperation with the middle class and 11 abstentions.) It is impossible to say to what extent the emotionally charged atmosphere shaped the second vote in July.

Before the Soviet convened again to formulate an appropriate policy on the July Days, elections to the City Duma took place. Bolshevik memoirists insist that the timing of the elections put the party at a disadvantage, for anti-Bolshevik feelings had temporarily intensified. The nonsocialist press, and to some extent the socialist press as well, attacked Lenin and the Bolshevik party for instigating the abortive uprising in Petrograd. The radical character of Tsaritsyn politics also strengthened the arguments of Saratov political leaders who supported moderate policies. Events in Tsaritsyn had moved so far to the left that the Provisional Government and Saratov Soviet had felt compelled to send armed expeditions there.

Because sources reveal so little about voter behavior, it is difficult to judge the election results. Some 128,647 citizens had registered to vote during the preceding two months. About 47 percent (60,025) cast ballots, of which 58,444 were valid.[8] (During the last municipal elections held before the February Revolution only a small fraction of this number had met the property qualifications permitting them to vote.) Women constituted 60 percent of the voters in July, which was equal to their percentage of the population. Voter turnout was heavy among individuals over 40 years old and women under 30; it was light among homeowners, office workers, and soldiers.[9] It appears that soldiers were allowed to take part in the elections only if they resided within the city limits; perhaps one-third of the garrison forces did. In all, 4,260 soldiers voted.

7. *Saratovskii vestnik*, no. 150, July 9, 1917, p. 5.

8. *Proletarii Povolzh'ia*, no. 41, July 22, 1917, p. 3. See also *Saratovskii vestnik*, no. 159, July 20, 1917, p. 2; no. 151, July 11, p. 3; and *Sotsial-Demokrat*, no. 51, July 11, 1917, p. 3.

9. *Proletarii Povolzh'ia*, no. 83, September 5, 1917, p. 4.

Table 7
Number and percentage of votes cast and seats won in Saratov City Duma elections, July 1917, by party

Party	*Votes*		*Seats won*
	Number	*Percent*	
Popular Socialist	2,683	4.4%	5
Kadet	6,690	11.4	13
Union of Homeowners	1,862	3.1	4
SR-Menshevik-Bund	37,864	64.2	73
Edinstvo group	1,075	1.8	2
Poalai-tsion*	330	0.5	1
Zionist	1,305	2.2	2
Bolshevik	6,975	11.9	13

*Bloc of three Jewish groups.
Source: Saratovskii vestnik, no. 152, July 12, 1917, p. 1, and no. 159, July 20, 1917, p. 2.

As was customary in Russia at this time, voters cast ballots for party lists rather than for individuals. Each ballot contained a ranked number of candidates. Forming an electoral bloc, the Menshevik-SR-Bund ballot captured 64.2 percent of the total vote, giving them 73 seats (candidates 1–73 from their list) in the newly elected Duma of 113 members (see Table 7). Receiving 6,975 votes (12 percent), the Bolsheviks came in second, winning 13 seats in the Duma. With 6,690 votes (11.4 percent), the Kadets also won 13 seats. The Popular Socialists received 5 seats (4.4 percent of the vote); the Union of Homeowners, 4 seats (3.1 percent); the Zionists, 2 seats; and the Edinstvo group, 2 seats.[10] After weeks of negotiating, Chertkov, who in May had replaced Miliutin as chairman of the Saratov Soviet, was named president of the Saratov City Duma. The SR delegate L. A. Mukoseev eventually was chosen mayor. The results, reflecting the long-term effect of several decades of political agitation, show that 82.3 percent of the population who participated in the elections voted for the socialist parties that controlled the Soviet (the SRs, Mensheviks, Bolsheviks, Bundists, Popular Socialists, and members of the Edinstvo group).

An analysis of the data according to police district suggests that turnout was higher in the poorer, working-class neighborhoods located in Saratov's ravines and along the riverfront, and that the Kadets received their greatest support in middle-class areas. The Bolsheviks won their largest number of votes in police districts where the Bering factory settlement, tobacco plants, lumberyards, railroad yards, and other industrial

10. See *Saratovskii vestnik*, no. 152, July 12, 1917, p. 1, and no. 159, July 20, p. 2.

concerns were located.[11] On the eve of the elections the Polish Socialist Party (PPS)–Left and Latvian workers had both declared their support for "list number 8," the Bolsheviks. Railroad, flour mill, and lumberyard workers also tended to vote for the party. Not surprisingly, the city's influential consumer cooperatives publicly endorsed "list number 4," the SR-Menshevik-Bundist bloc.[12]

Occupational data are available for the candidate lists of several parties, and they corroborate other information about the social makeup of local political leadership. All of the Popular Socialist candidates belonged to the professional or clerical class (one-third were former zemstvo members); *Proletarii Povolzh'ia* described them as "a group of intellectuals with no class base or defined program." The Edinstvo candidates were divided almost evenly into professionals (lawyers, doctors, journalists, teachers) and skilled workers (mostly railroad workers). Twenty of the fifty Kadet candidates listed their occupation as "lawyer" and another eight listed "professional politician." The Kadets also put up for election a significant number of clerks and office workers. The Bolsheviks nominated a roughly equal number of professionals and workers, as did the Mensheviks. SR candidates came from various strata of the population and quite a few were zemstvo activists, professionals, and consumer society employees. No reliable occupational data exist for the Union of Homeowners' candidates, but *Proletarii Povolzh'ia* described them as a "Union of Slavin's Black Hundreds with Maslennikov's 'Progressists,'" while the Kadet newspaper more charitably referred to the union as an "organization of old, former Duma members."[13]

In the aftermath of the Duma elections, the liberal press in Saratov intensified its campaign against Bolshevik policies. Some Saratov citizens believed the spy charges against the Bolshevik leadership. According to Lebedev, it was unsafe for party activists to appear in the streets. "But worst of all," he admitted, "was that in our own ranks, many fainthearted ones could be found. The rapid growth of our organization not only stopped, but many withdrew, while others went into hiding." Antonov maintained that some soldiers of SR persuasion, driven "to fanaticism by their Neimichenko and Pontriagin," interrupted campaign meetings for the Duma elections and beat up Bolshevik agitators." While the moderate socialists did not endorse the spy charges openly, they called the July Days "a knife in the back of the revolution" and exhorted

11. Ibid., no. 151, July 11, 1917, p. 3.

12. Khodakov, *Ocherki istorii*, p. 281; *Proletarii Povolzh'ia*, no. 30, July 9, 1917, p. 2.

13. This information comes from *Saratovskii vestnik*, no. 140, June 27, 1917, p. 4; no. 144, July 2, p. 4; *Saratovskii listok*, no. 136, June 24, 1917, p. 3, and no. 140, June 29, p. 3; *Proletarii Povolzh'ia*, no. 25, July 4, 1917, pp. 1–2.

the Soviet to pass a resolution in that vein.[14] As it turned out, the Soviet's official response to the July Days was less emotional. On July 10 the Executive Committee of the Soviet drafted a policy statement on its attitudes toward the Petrograd events of July 3–5. Menshevik speakers condemned the defamation of the Bolsheviks by the "bourgeois" press while the SRs "devoted almost all of their attention to criticizing the Bolsheviks."[15] After orators pointed to the need to obtain more detailed information on who exactly had instigated the riots in Petrograd, members of the Executive Committee passed a six-point resolution. Moderate in tone, the document reflected the same degree of measured caution that local leaders had shown during the preceding days. Nonetheless, a substantial minority abstained from voting on each point. The Bolsheviks abstained on point 1 of the resolution, which called for a display of "universal support to the Kerensky government . . . that had been formed days before." Most SRs refrained from voting on point 4, protesting "against the slanderous campaign that the bourgeois press raised against the Bolsheviks" and calling for an end to "the fratricidal enmity among the various classes of the revolutionary democracy."[16] And even though the Soviet resolved to "struggle against counterrevolution," the Executive Committee turned a deaf ear to Bolshevik requests to clarify its position on several measures taken by the new government, such as the arrests of the Petrograd Bolsheviks and the banning of *Pravda* at the front.

Charges against the Bolsheviks multiplied in the days that followed. As in the capital, it became exceedingly difficult to find a press willing to publish Bolshevik materials. On July 23, *Sotsial-Demokrat* informed readers: "Comrades! Yesterday our newspaper could not be issued. We do not know whether we will be able to put out the next number on Tuesday. We have no press. Owners refuse to publish the workers' paper."[17] This was the last issue of the newspaper until August 27.

While Bolshevik memoirists agree that the July Days resulted in immediate setbacks for the party, evidence shows that the Bolsheviks were well on the road to recovery before the Kornilov Affair, at the end of August. A similar scenario holds true for Bolshevik organizations in Samara, Syzran, Astrakhan, and Simbirsk.[18] In completing a questionnaire at the Sixth Bolshevik Party Congress at the end of July, the Saratov

14. Lebedev, "Fevral'–oktiabr'," pp. 245–46; Antonov-Saratovskii, "S fevralia," p. 187.
15. *Sotsial-Demokrat*, no. 52, July 12, 1917, p. 3.
16. Ibid.; *Saratovskii vestnik*, no. 152, July 12, 1917, p. 3; *Saratovskii Sovet*, p. 163.
17. *Sotsial-Demokrat*, no. 61, July 23, 1917, p. 1.
18. Gerasimenko and Tochenyi, *Sovety Povolzh'ia*, pp. 130–37, and Tochenyi, "Iiul'skie sobytiia 1917 g. i nachalo krizisa melko-burzhuaznykh organizatsii (Na materialakh Povolzh'ia)," in *Nauchnye trudy Kuibyshevskogo gosudarstvennogo pedinstituta*, vol. 115, *Iz istorii Srednego Povolzh'ia i Priural'ia* (1973), pp. 60–67.

delegate commented that the July Days had caused dissatisfaction with the government among the mass of workers and soldiers. As for the Saratov workers, "the events at first influenced them, but then they became sympathetic." The rest of the population (except the soldiers) remained "hostilely disposed to our organization."[19]

The July Days in Petrograd greatly complicated the question of political power in Saratov. Affected by the leftward march of society in Tsaritsyn and by what they believed to be a premature and dangerous clamor for an all-socialist government, moderate socialists in Saratov and in certain other neighboring provincial centers now strove to revive the authority of the city dumas. In a sense, a resurgence of the Saratov Duma would have been to their advantage, for it was a representative rather than a class organ and the Bolsheviks made up only 12 percent of its membership. Restoring the authority of the Duma also appealed to some moderate socialist leaders' belief that cooperation with the bourgeoisie was essential. Besides, the Provisional Government had instructed local communities to reelect dumas to replace public executive committees. But such sentiments do not seem to have been shared by those of a more leftist bent or by some workers and soldiers. By this point in the revolution the class organs of the democracy were showing more vitality than representative democratic ones. Moreover, the Kadet ministers' resignation from the First Coalition Government had given rise to suspicions locally that liberals were out to sabotage the revolution.

A discussion of the City Duma's efforts to govern in the summer of 1917 reveals how close Russia had come to civil war and also exposes the seriousness of the administrative crisis facing the country at large. From the very start it became clear that the Duma suffered unmitigated problems. Although elections had ended on July 9, the first session of the new duma did not convene until July 24. One-fourth of the deputies failed to attend the opening meeting. A disagreement that broke out between the Kadets and socialists reflected another fundamental weakness of the Duma: moderate socialists controlled it, yet they could not decide whom to ally themselves with—the liberals or left socialists. At this first meeting, the Menshevik A. A. Gol'dshtein proposed that instead of the old tsarist oath, the delegates sign a declaration promising to "satisfy the needs and demands of the broad democratic strata of the population."[20] Arguing that the old oath was adequate, the Kadets rejected Gol'dshtein's text. Because a compromise could not be reached, the meeting adjourned to allow separate factional discussions. It is inter-

19. *Shestoi s"ezd*, p. 370.
20. *Proletarii Povolzh'ia*, no. 44, July 26, 1917, p. 2.

esting to note that SR and Menshevik speakers had pressed to keep this meeting closed to the public, perhaps because they had anticipated disputes with the liberals.

It soon became clear that mutual suspicion of Bolshevik tactics was not enough to unite the moderate socialists and liberals. When the Duma next met, sharp differences over the selection of a mayor disrupted the proceedings. Earlier, the Duma had agreed that if an SR were chosen mayor, then a Menshevik would become the president of the Duma. The center Socialist Revolutionary S. V. Milashevskii had been picked as mayor and the Menshevik Chertkov had been named president. Milashevskii's announced intention to retain the services of members of the former tsarist city administration, however, worried many other socialists. In the face of such opposition on this issue, Milashevskii turned down the post, leaving Saratov without a mayor until early August, when another SR candidate, the president of the consumer cooperatives and chairman of the uezd zemstvo, L. A. Mukoseev, assumed the position. Meanwhile, the Duma elected an administrative board comprising ten deputies, which rejected the Bolshevik and Kadet nominees. Weeks later disagreements over the election of the three remaining members of the administrative board were still crippling the Duma sessions.[21]

Largely because of this continual wrangling, the Duma accomplished virtually nothing. At most, it discussed but did not act upon such urgent social issues as food and housing shortages. According to Lebedev, "not one question that interested the masses was raised and resolved in its entirety. Naturally, the masses turned away from it as though they had forgotten about its existence."[22] While Lebedev can be said to have had a jaundiced eye, other sources reinforce his observation. A survey of other administrative organs reveals an equal degree of inefficacy. At a meeting of a provincial congress of uezd commissars at the end of July, speakers reported on their inability to maintain order in face of the social revolution erupting in the countryside. One delegate noted that Kronstadt sailors encouraged peasants to seize estates—not only those of the landlords but those of the wealthier peasants as well. He concluded that "in general soldiers make the village and town populations nervous."[23] In Petrovsk, Pokrovsk, and Nikolaevsk *no one wanted to assume the office of district commissar,* which remained temporarily vacant.[24] All of these problems appeared on the agenda of an oblast (regional) congress of

21. *Saratovskii vestnik,* no. 162, July 23, 1917, p. 3; *Sotsial-Demokrat,* no. 63, September 3, 1917, p. 3.
22. Lebedev, "Fevral'–oktiabr'," p. 246.
23. *Proletarii Povolzh'ia,* no. 47, July 29, 1917, p. 4.
24. Valeev, "Krizis mestnykh organov," p. 129.

public executive committees that convened in early August. Before the opening of the congress an incident took place that reflected the total paralysis of the Provincial Public Executive Committee. A. A. Tokarskii, a member of the committee, wrote that "because of illness I was unable to attend any meetings of the committee for a month. Resuming my duties after my recovery, I discovered that the committee had not met in the course of the month due to its members' absence. . . . Moreover, for the entire period there was not even one gathering of the Presidium." Tokarskii rebuked the new Provincial Commissar, the Menshevik Topuridze, for not convening the PPEC and for eventually doing so only after he had *"conferred with the Presidium of the Soviet of Workers' Deputies and received directives there."* In view of the influence the Soviet had over the PPEC and of its members' realization "that its role was spent," Tokarskii submitted his resignation.[25] Again, the situation in Saratov resembled that in neighboring towns and probably was widespread throughout much of Russia. Calling for the State Duma to establish stable power in the country, Rodzianko wrote in the central Kadet newspaper *Rech'* that

> new representatives of the government in the provincial and uezd centers are completely dependent on local party and class organizations, which authoritatively dictate their will to them. Judicial authorities are inactive. Committees and soviets under various names and of various and often self-willed origin, which constantly change their membership, rule locally. They know neither their rights nor their responsibilities. Deprived of governmental guidance and not restrained by anyone, they consider themselves to possess total state authority.[26]

When compared with the ineffectual City Duma and the largely ignored Provincial Public Executive Committee, the Soviet remained the only viable authority in the city. But this should not cloud the fact that a real paradox had taken shape, for workers and soldiers were growing indifferent to the Soviet as well. Continuing a trend set in June, Soviet plenums were called less frequently; decision making was left to the executive bodies. According to several recent studies, this phenomenon appears to have been common in much of urban Russia at this time.[27] The Executive Committee selected Antonov, Didenko, and Chertkov to form an executive bureau that met daily. After July 25 the Soviet held full plenums once every two weeks, while the Workers' Section met weekly. The Executive Committee now relied extensively on the work of the

25. *Saratovskii vestnik*, no. 173, August 5, 1917, p. 3; emphasis mine.
26. *Iiul'skii krizis*, pp. 318–19.
27. See, for example, Keep, *Russian Revolution*, pp. 119–39; Koenker, *Moscow Workers*, pp. 171–83.

three persons who sat on the Executive Bureau. The increased strength of the Military Section was revealed everywhere; with the July 20 issue, the official Soviet newspaper was called *Izvestiia Saratovskogo Soveta soldatskikh i rabochikh deputatov* (News of the Saratov Soviet of Soldiers' and Workers' Deputies).[28]

The reason for the indifference toward the Soviet may well have been that the advances of the revolution were coming to a stop. Euphoria had given way to anxiety over economic disruption and over what was rapidly becoming a hated war. The working class's growing apathy toward the Soviet worried some moderates, too, who expressed reservations about their backing of the middle classes and issued cautious calls for vigilance against "counterrevolutionary manifestations." In early August an SR, M. M. Struin, remarked that "if we look objectively at our work here, at the local level, then we must confess that at the present moment the Soviet is doing nothing to make its strength and authority felt." He went on to say that much of the Soviet's tedious business did not deal with the problems that demanded the most attention. The Menshevik Lavler elaborated on Struin's statement. "It's not that the significance of the Soviet is falling each day," he said, "but worst of all, that the workers themselves are no longer taking it into consideration . . . in part because of the impassioned factional bickering."[29] The question of working-class indifference to the Soviet's activities arose again when deputies discussed its newspaper. Because it had amassed a large deficit during the preceding three months, the Soviet decided to publish the paper only twice weekly.[30] One conclusion follows from all of this: in the summer of 1917 Saratov suffered from lack of any universally recognized, popular administrative body.

Historical writing has emphasized the difficult straits the Bolsheviks were in between the July Days and Kornilov's abortive conservative putsch at the end of August. The summer of 1917 was also a period of trial for the Saratov SRs and Mensheviks, and perhaps even more so. Although the SRs began the summer with the strongest party organization in the entire Volga region, by fall internal dissent had ripped apart unity and much of the SR's mass base had withered away. Centrist in its political leanings, the Saratov city organization had been spared some of the intensity of the factionalism that had broken the ranks of city committees in Kazan and elsewhere. But the SR officers who controlled the Military Section of the Saratov Soviet stood to the right of the rest of the local organization, and so contributed to its indecisiveness. They also

28. *Izvestiia Saratovskogo Soveta*, no. 62, July 20, 1917, p. 1.
29. Ibid., no. 70, August 8, 1917, p. 2.
30. *Saratovskii Sovet*, p. 178.

supported the reinstatement of the death penalty at the front and related measures introduced in late July. In the city the SRs ultimately lost the support of the garrison and of many workers. In the villages the SRs' reluctance to sanction the peasants' seizure of land strengthened the left wing of the party, which was beginning to have more in common with the Bolsheviks tactically than with its fellow populists. Calling attention to the apparent listlessness of the Saratov SRs, an editorial in the local Bolsheviks' *Sotsial-Demokrat* asked readers: "How can a party that can't organize itself organize a country?"[31]

As Chapter 4's examination of the railroad workers' committee between March and June showed, Menshevik strength within this traditionally Social Democratic stratum of the working class steadily eroded. By early summer Bolsheviks made up half of the committee's membership; by late August they occupied fourteen of its sixteen positions. At the beginning of July the Saratov Menshevik organization reached the zenith of its popularity, registering 3,000 members. By mid-August, however, the number of party card holders had dropped to 1,000. Similar losses were recorded in Samara and Simbirsk. Saratov's Chertkov candidly admitted that the Saratov organization "stood on the verge of collapse."[32]

How does one account for this malaise? It was not a matter of lack of Menshevik visibility, for between March and the end of July the local organization had distributed approximately 145,000 copies of various party brochures and leaflets. In some uezd centers the July Days, which had driven workers to the right, seem to have hurt the Mensheviks wherever they belonged to united committees with Bolsheviks. As regards waning Menshevik fortunes in Saratov, a delegate to a regional Menshevik conference held at the end of July mentioned a shortage of active party workers, poor ties with the center, lack of local Menshevik traditions, the strength of the SR party in the countryside, and the class makeup of the city.[33] While all of these problems clearly existed, Menshevik leaders were reluctant to admit how the party's tactical program affected its popularity. Evidence suggests that some Mensheviks actually abandoned the party during the so-called July reaction to join the Bolsheviks.[34] Conflicting tactical approaches to the questions of war and political power and of the correct relationship to the bourgeoisie separated the two factions of Russian Social Democracy at this time. At a July

31. *Sotsial-Demokrat,* no. 55, July 15, 1917, p. 1.

32. Quoted in Gerasimenko, *Sovety Nizhnego Povolzh'ia,* p. 74.

33. *Proletarii Povolzh'ia,* no. 43, July 25, 1917, pp. 1–2; no. 49, August 1, 1917, p. 2; no. 50, August 2, p. 3; no. 53, August 5, p. 2.

34. Fenigshtein reported on this during the city Bolshevik conference (July 15). See *Sotsial-Demokrat,* no. 57, July 18, 1917, p. 3. Also in Osipov, *1917 god v Saratove,* p. 119.

city conference, Saratov Mensheviks adopted a resolution declaring that "for the salvation of the country a provisional government with absolute authority is necessary to struggle against anarchy."[35] This position was bound to clash with the aspirations of much of the working class and could only result in the further deterioration of the party's base of support, a fact that election results to the Saratov Soviet in September demonstrated conclusively.

After the abatement of the July uprising in Petrograd, ties between the Bolshevik Central Committee and local committees became tenuous. This situation bred confusion and uncertainty in most Volga-area organizations. Equivocation and dismay seized hold of local committees. The Penza Bolsheviks, for instance, entered a joint committee with local Mensheviks following the July Days. In Saratov a week-long all-city party conference convened on July 12 to discuss the local organization's position in regard to Petrograd events and to prepare for the Sixth Party Congress, to be held in semilegal conditions at the end of the month. Perhaps more than anything else, this conference showed the effect Bolshevik actions in Petrograd had on Bolshevik outlook and actions in Saratov. Before the all-city gathering opened, the five separate district committees met to outline procedures. The Bolsheviks' "city district" passed the following resolution on the meaning of the Petrograd uprising.

> The crisis of the Provisional Government provoked by the withdrawal of the Kadets [from the First Coalition Government] gave rise to a disorganized uprising of workers and soldiers under the slogan "All Power to the Soviets." The majority of Mensheviks and SRs, instead of saving the Russian revolution by transferring power to the hands of the revolutionary democracy, not only made short work of the insurrectionists but turned all of their weapons against the proletariat's demonstration. With this campaign against us, with the Draconian laws of dictatorship concealed under the rubric "the saving of the revolution," they broke away from true revolutionary tactics. They subordinated the will of the free democracy to the interests of the bourgeoisie, to the interests of native and allied capitalists.[36]

Reflecting the position of the Bolshevik Central Committee, this policy statement became the basis for the Saratov organization's official perception of the July Days.

When the Saratov city conference opened, deputies postponed discussion of the party program in favor of hashing over urgent political topics.

35. Quoted in *Khronika*, p. 88.

36. *Sotsial-Demokrat*, no. 53, July 13, 1917, p. 3; Mints, *Oktiabr' v Povolzh'e*, p. 154; and Osipov, *1917 god v Saratove*, pp. 115–17.

Lenin's controversial flight from Petrograd prompted extensive deliberation. Most delegates endorsed Lenin's going into hiding, but a few older, seasoned Bolsheviks surprisingly refused to vote on the matter, "considering the circumstances of the affair unclear."[37] Mgeladze expressed majority sentiment when he argued that the masses had been driven to demonstrate in the capital because their basic demands had been ignored. More important, he concluded that Bolshevik tactics had not changed at all, that Bolshevik antiwar slogans remained in force. (He cautioned, however, that although "we are against the politics of the offensive . . . this does not mean that we are against the offensive itself.") It should also be mentioned that the Saratov (and Samara) Bolshevik committees did not jettison the slogan "All Power to the Soviets." At this time Lenin penned his pamphlet *On Slogans*, demanding that the slogan "All Power to the Soviets" be dropped because the soviets, now in the hands of moderate socialists who supported coalition with the bourgeoisie, were no longer revolutionary organs. But the Saratov conference rejected Lenin's arguments. Antonov insisted that Lenin's plea to break with the "socialist-chauvinists . . . would be an extremely harmful step."[38] In fact, Saratov Bolsheviks, addressing Soviet meetings during the last week of July, called for "the immediate transfer of power into the hands of the Central Executive Committee of the [Petrograd] Soviet."[39] Given the precarious but nonetheless leading position of the Soviet, it would have been foolish of the Saratov Bolsheviks to abandon this slogan and undermine their position further.[40]

The conference next assessed party activities since April and ways to improve recruitment. According to one report, membership had grown in June and Bolshevik Duma campaigning had met with sympathy, although the Bolsheviks had less funding than other parties. Even after the July Days, Bolsheviks controlled the Central Bureau of Trade Unions. A speaker representing the important factory district mentioned that after July the district suffered from lack of party workers, since most were busy in union and factory committee activities. In the railroad district the strength of the two SD factions was now equal and the Bolsheviks had not registered a loss in July. Actual gains were noted in the shore region, where Bolshevik activity first began in March. Workers there were considered the most "backward," but speakers maintained that the workers' "sentiments were always favorable to us. The workers themselves ask to organize meetings and gatherings, especially on political

37. Lebedev, "Fevral'–oktiabr'," p. 246; Antonov-Saratovskii, "S fevralia," pp. 182–83.
38. *Sotsial-Demokrat*, no. 55, July 14, 1917, pp. 2–3; no. 56, July 16, p. 3; no. 59, July 20, p. 3.
39. Gesler, "Saratovskaia bol'shevistskaia organizatsiia," p. 39.
40. They eventually did so, but only in late summer and for a very short time.

questions." The most pessimistic statements made at the conference concerned the party newspaper. Mgeladze sharply criticized party members' neglect of the paper, stating that they "do nothing for it. They don't give correspondence, they don't distribute it, foisting this off on somebody else's shoulders." The delegates agreed that in the future party members would be obliged to subscribe to *Sotsial-Demokrat* to ensure sufficient funds to continue publication. Because the post–July Days repression adversely affected funding in general, to say nothing of the effect of inflation, party leaders voted to raise and standardize dues.[41]

In view of the breakdown of party discipline in Petrograd (and Tsaritsyn, for that matter) during the July Days, the conference delegates decided to prepare potential members before registering them. In 1917 the party had become a mass organization and its ranks had swelled throughout the spring and early summer. Driving away the lightly committed, the July Days had revealed the potential problem of making a party card easily obtainable. The city organization now felt the need to review its membership roster. Reregistration was deemed necessary for all current cardholders and participation in Maiak became mandatory for those rejected for entry into the party but who wanted to reapply.[42] Shaken by the July Days, the Saratov organization took measures to recover and strengthen itself.

The worsening economic situation in the summer of 1917 may well have overshadowed the political crisis as far as Saratov's working class was concerned. Rural unrest, resultant food shortages, and the threat of even greater deficits in the future heightened the urban population's understandable anxiety. In the middle of June the Food-Supply Assembly had taken an inventory of all food reserves in Saratov and issued ration cards. Beginning on July 1, bread was distributed under this system. The Saratov Food-Supply Committee (the executive body of the Food-Supply Assembly) introduced an even more unpopular rationing system on August 1.[43] The reason for reducing rations further was not lack of grain in the countryside but rather the peasants' reluctance to market it in the cities because they could not exchange it for desired manufactured goods.[44] The threat of hunger was accompanied by the realization that the grain deficit adversely affected Saratov's grain processing and transportation industries. When authorities announced at the

41. *Sotsial-Demokrat,* no. 57, July 18, 1917, p. 3; no. 58, July 19, p. 3.

42. Ibid.

43. *Izvestiia Saratovskogo Soveta,* no. 60, July 15, 1917, p. 2, and *Sotsial-Demokrat,* no. 59, July 20, 1917, p. 4.

44. See *Proletarii Povolzh'ia,* no. 50, August 2, 1917, p. 4. On July 14 the Soviet discussed appropriate forms of agitation. See *Saratovskii Sovet,* p. 166.

end of July that the city had grain reserves to last for ten days only, the Soviet expressed concern that "after this the majority of transport workers and mill workers will be without work."[45] To avert labor problems, the Soviet encouraged owners to remodel their mills during any pause in production, thus preventing potential layoffs. Food shortages strained tempers in the uezd centers as well. Assessing the situation in town at the end of July, authorities in Volsk determined that there was enough grain to last only three days because peasants refused to bring it to market. Speculation and hoarding ran rampant. As a result of door-to-door searches, almost half of the population lost their coupons for bread and flour for up to three months. One Volsk inhabitant had stashed away 3,000 pairs of shoes.[46]

Grain and other essential consumer items became scarcer in August, especially for Saratov's poorer elements. On August 12, a joint meeting of representatives of the Soviet, trade unions, factory committees, and medical funds took the unprecedented step of appealing to the Provisional Government to register "the most essential items" and to "create in the province organs of control over production and distribution."[47] But whatever plans were thought up to eliminate such problems remained on paper. As the end of August approached, the already grave situation deteriorated further. Lines outside food and other stores became more commonplace and the slightest irritation promised to trigger disorders. A typical incident broke out at the Skorokhod Store. Irritated with the sales clerks, an estimated 2,000 women and teenagers waiting in line to buy shoes looted the store. Soldiers came to disperse the crowd, and the fire department hosed down those unwilling to leave. According to newspaper accounts, the angry citizens aimed their animosity at government employees and at other privileged citizens who received goods out of turn.[48]

The number of crimes related to the bleak economic situation seems to have shot up, as did a rise in vigilante-type justice. Perhaps only the smallest uezd centers were spared this misfortune. The housing crisis in Saratov worsened in the summer too. In an editorial in *Sotsial-Demokrat*, Lebedev called attention to the influx into Saratov of "village intelligentsia who did not trust their peasants." Apartment speculation accompanied the housing shortage.[49] Overcrowded living conditions had other ramifications as well. A city medical board had earlier voted

45. *Proletarii Povolzh'ia*, no. 50, August 2, 1917, p. 4.
46. *Delo naroda* (Petrograd), no. 114, July 30, 1917, p. 3.
47. *Khronika*, p. 98.
48. *Proletarii Povolzh'ia*, no. 58, August 11, 1917, p. 4; and no. 65, August 19, p. 4.
49. *Saratovskii vestnik*, no. 117, May 31, 1917, p. 3; no. 189, August 25, p. 3.

unanimously to close down one of the largest brothels, urging the city to provide housing and food for the 158 prostitutes who worked there.[50] Given the anxious mood of Saratov's workers and soldiers at this time, the visible decline in their living standard since February must have deepened their discontent with both the national and local government. As the examination of the attitudes of workers and soldiers suggested, these social groups had expected sweeping changes after February. By summer the gulf between reality and expectation had widened. All forms of authority came under suspicion.

As a result of the February Revolution the bargaining power of the working class had improved and some economic gains, such as the shorter workday, had been achieved. The deteriorating economy, however, canceled any betterment in the workers' standard of living. While the mechanism open to the proletariat for winning concessions had broadened considerably, the potential for workers to battle successfully against the propertied elements shrank as a result of the impaired economic situation. Labor relations remained strained. During the first half of the year workers' salaries throughout Russia had increased 50 percent, but rising prices prevented any gain in real wages. Data are less reliable for the second half of the year and it is not possible to study adequately wage-price spirals after July. Nonetheless, the gap between nominal and real wages probably continued to grow.[51] Shortages of raw materials and fuel and transportation problems led to decreases in production in some enterprises. Other industries shut down.

Because of the inauspicious economic outlook, Saratov workers joined workers elsewhere and went out on strike in the summer of 1917, demanding increased wages and better labor conditions. Workers also lodged complaints against threats of factory shutdowns because of shortages of raw materials. At the beginning of July the city's mill workers went on strike without the sanction of their union. Urging the workers to return to their jobs, the Soviet appealed to them to voice their grievances through the appropriate conciliatory bodies. But some Soviet deputies criticized these institutions, arguing that the workers' demands were not outrageous "considering the profits that owners recently made."[52] Despite their skilled status, Latvian workers complained in July that their living standard was much worse than that of the indigenous work force, which may help explain their affinity for Bolshevik propaganda.[53]

50. *Khronika*, p. 48.

51. P. V. Volobuev, *Proletariat i burzhuaziia Rossii v 1917* (Moscow, 1964), pp. 136, 221.

52. *Saratovskii Sovet*, pp. 156–57, 159–60; *Delo naroda* (Petrograd), no. 92, July 5, 1917, p. 2; Gerasimenko, *Sovety Nizhnego Povolzh'ia*, p. 62.

53. *Sotsial-Demokrat*, no. 47, July 6, 1917, p. 3.

With the exception of the mill workers' strike, local workers were relatively quiet during the first week following the July crisis. Yet demands for higher wages soon flowed once again into the appropriate channels. The Titanik workers demanded a 30 percent pay raise on July 10. Shortly afterward the sausage factory workers clamored for a 50 percent increase. In the latter case the factory owners had raised the price of sausage while the workers' monthly salary of 40 rubles remained well below the average wage earned by the local proletariat. The mill and sausage workers made their demands in view of the rise in profits that owners purportedly were drawing. Such mistrust of the propertied class extended to other aspects of labor–management relations too: the Bolshevik-dominated Central Bureau of Trade Unions abolished a union of restaurant, tavern, and cafeteria workers which was founded and controlled by proprietors.[54]

By the end of July production in some of the city's enterprises had fallen by as much as 50 percent because of lack of raw materials and fuel, the incapacity to replace worn-out equipment, and the unwillingness or inability of owners to switch to peacetime production.[55] During the month four flour mills, two butter creameries, and the Russian-Baltic plant shut their doors, throwing some 1,500 workers into the streets. At the end of July the mill workers again went on strike, this time prompted by the proprietors' intention to shut down production and lay off workers. Because of the immense suspicion between workers and factory owners, stemming from many industrialists' opposition to labor reforms earlier in the year as well as to the new political climate, the Organizational Bureau of Saratov Factory Committees took additional measures to establish some means of controlling the supply of raw materials and fuel flowing into the industrial enterprises and the distribution of manufactured products. In July, when the local furniture factory owner announced that the plant would have to shut down because of lack of demand for furniture, the Organizational Bureau investigated and ordered the factory to stay open. Soviets in the uezd towns also helped establish control commissions over local enterprises at this time.[56]

Saratov workers continued to press for economic improvement in August. During the month tram workers, hair dressers, barbers, hatmakers, and laborers from the Kolesnikov plant went on strike. The most serious strike involved the tram workers. After months of negotiations, the Belgian-owned company raised fares but continued to block an increase in workers' wages. The workers voted to strike. Fearing sabotage of equipment and personal attacks on the foreign managers, the Soviet pressured

54. *Khronika*, pp. 83, 87.
55. Ibid., pp. 92–93.
56. Khodakov, "Rabochii kontrol'," pp. 65–67.

the company to accept workers' demands.[57] Meanwhile, plant shutdowns and conflicts between owners and factory committees took place, and the administration of the Titanik plant announced that it would have to close the enterprise and lay off 100 Latvian workers because of "insufficient and irregular receipt of materials and a rise in the price of labor."[58] The administration flatly refused to submit to a factory committee request to look into the plant's financial records.

The deteriorating economy exacerbated unemployment. In June the city had registered 4,000 unemployed; in July this number had dropped to 3,500. Because many of the largest enterprises had curtailed production, unemployment would have gone up in the summer if workers had not returned to the villages. Even those who did not have ties in the countryside looked there as a possible escape from the dismal economic prospects in the city. Unemployed workers who asked the Food Supply Administration to help them obtain field work, however, found the administration's response limited, since soldiers were sent to the countryside "owing to the cheaper pay for their labor."[59] By August the number of unemployed fell to 2,238, perhaps because the demand in the villages was greater now, owing to the harvest. A closer look at the profile of the unemployed reveals a significant change since spring. Earlier, the majority without work had been unskilled workers, but now many of the unemployed—997—belonged to "intellectual occupations," and 836 individuals were from "private enterprises."[60]

While labor's economic demands found expression in strikes and efforts to establish control over factories, workers' attitudes toward the state and political power are more difficult to probe. Saratov workers passed very few political resolutions in July and August. In the post–July Days period, and in view of street excesses in Tsaritsyn, political agitators refrained from conducting mass meetings and demonstrations, while Soviet plenums convened rarely. In Chapter 4 it was suggested that workers' attitudes toward state power were reflected in their behavior toward factory owners. Before July the proletariat had become increasingly hostile toward the propertied class and had turned to the Soviet with their grievances. The proletariat's mistrust of the propertied elements continued unabated in July and August (recall the rise in demands for workers' control) but now some workers were ignoring the Soviet because of its timid policies. In this absence of recognized governmental authority, Bolshevik propaganda calling for strong-handed measures to

57. *Saratovskii vestnik*, no. 174, August 6, 1917, p. 4.

58. *Khronika*, p. 101; *Sotsial-Demokrat*, no. 63, September 3, 1917, p. 4.

59. *Sotsial-Demokrat*, no. 57, July 18, 1917, p. 4.

60. *Saratovskii vestnik*, no. 198, September 7, 1917, p. 3. Only 502 individuals among the 2,238 found employment. See *Khronika*, pp. 106–7.

end the war and to revive the economy must have struck a responsive chord.

The soldiers' political outlook changed dramatically in the anxious summer months, too. The garrison had stood solidly behind the SR party in early July; two months later the soldiers elected a majority of Bolshevik deputies to the Soldiers' Section of the Soviet. An article in the Kadet newspaper provided a candid glimpse at shifting attitudes in the garrison in mid-July. Describing a large meeting of soldiers at the city's covered marketplace, the author reported that "no one decided openly to defend the Bolsheviks, but the idea about putting an end to the offensive and declarations not to go to the front are still quite popular. . . . Also discussed was the 'desertion' of the Kadets from the government, which is interpreted as a counterrevolutionary act that had given rise to the [July] disorders. In short, the logic of the street is still much to the left of common sense."[61]

Judging from the published protocols of the Saratov Soviet and from the Soviet's newspaper accounts, the 3,000 evacuated frontoviki stationed in Saratov posed the greatest threat to public order. They took to the streets first when news of the July uprising in Petrograd reached Saratov; afterward they continued to challenge the imagination of Saratov's leaders. Considering the frontoviki carriers of a contagion that infected the vulnerable new recruits with whom they came into contact, many Soviet spokesmen believed that tensions would be relieved only when the local garrison was rid of the evacuees. But a medical commission investigating combat suitability reported that most evacuees were medically unfit to go to the front, a finding that created a real dilemma for the Soviet leaders. One of them suggested the creation of a disciplinary body comprised of commanders to restore discipline in the barracks, but Lebedev objected, arguing that only the Soviet should take such responsiblity upon itself. Another deputy described a recent meeting of unit commanders which left him with a "foul impression"—discontent over the continuation of the war had even penetrated the officer corps.[62]

Armed evacuated soldiers conducted garrison meetings in July without the Soviet's permission and usually in bold defiance of its objections. They demanded that the Soviet secure the return of weapons and ammunition that the local cadet training school had sequestered a few days before. The Bureau of the Executive Committee, however, was actually

61. *Saratovskii listok*, no. 153, July 15, 1917, p. 3. Strained relations between officers and soldiers occurred elsewhere in the province as well. In Kamyshin, for example, garrison troops attempted to assault their officers. See Mints, *Oktiabr' v Povolzh'e*, p. 169.

62. *Saratovskii Sovet*, pp. 164–65.

more concerned with retrieving weapons seized by the evacuated soldiers. One SR proposed that force be used to disperse the evacuated troops next time they gathered illegally, while Mgeladze suggested that the Executive Committee visit the barracks and appeal to the evacuated soldiers to disband their committee.[63] The Soviet resolved that "the army must closely rally around the soviets," and called separate military organizations "inadmissible."[64] Despite the reports of medical commissions, the Soviet's Executive Committee decided that the evacuated soldiers had to leave for the front.[65] The announcement that 7,000 soldiers from the rebellious Tsaritsyn garrison soon would be relocated to Saratov may well have forced this issue.[66] Moreover, the Soviet now had armed units at its disposal to help persuade the frontoviki to budge. On July 20, 300 Cossacks arrived in Saratov, where they remained in a state of military preparedness under Korvin-Krukovskii's command. That evening they broke up a large meeting of evacuated soldiers on Moscow Square.[67]

As several battalions from the Saratov garrison prepared to leave for the front during the last week of July, the Soviet and provincial commissar prohibited all public meetings. Ignoring such rulings altogether, evacuees persuaded a battalion getting ready to quit town to turn around and return to its barracks. In response, Korvin-Krukovskii and his Cossack units conducted a roundup of deserters, detaining 160 soldiers, 50 of whom were locked up for having gone into hiding on the eve of being sent to the front.[68] One of the young Cossack ensigns who took part in the arrests recalled that "we caught most of the deserters at the bazaar, where they were hawking stolen items, or in the taverns, where they were carousing after a successful 'job.' It's strange that these traitors nevertheless wore their uniforms. It turned out that among them were many who had been wounded and even St. George cavalrymen who shamefully wore crosses on their traitorous chests."[69]

Soldiers not only sought to avoid combat but also subjected the civilian population to their lawlessness. At one factory soldiers had driven workers away from their benches and tried to get jobs there themselves. Workers and office staff at the Nizhne-Dobrinskii mill complained to the Soviet that soldiers were "demanding under threat that they be given work and that we intercede on their behalf because they were working

63. Ibid., p. 170.
64. *Sotsial-Demokrat,* no. 60, July 21, 1917, p. 3.
65. S. Sh. Ovrutskaia, "Proval politiki kontrrevoliutsionnoi voenshchiny v iiule–avguste 1917 g.," *Istoricheskie zapiski,* 87 (1971), p. 360.
66. *Saratovskii vestnik,* no. 162, July 23, 1917, p. 3.
67. Ovrutskaia, "Proval politiki," p. 360.
68. *Saratovskii vestnik,* no. 164, July 26, 1917, p. 3; *Khronika,* p. 89.
69. Golubov, "Saratov v 1917 g.," p. 35.

for defense." Charges that soldiers looted gardens and fruit orchards inundated the Soviet and City Duma. A sign of the times was the appeal of the Polish Committee to Aid Refugees, which asked the Soviet "to take measures to protect fields of potatoes and carrots from the soldiers."[70] Reports from the uezd centers reveal that soldiers played the same disruptive role locally as in Saratov. In Kamyshin soldiers stole from private gardens and frequently raided the local railroad depot, "sacking the railroad cars, no matter what's in them."[71] To combat the disorders and its deepening loss of influence, the SR city committee revitalized the Garrison Soviet of Peasant Deputies, founded earlier in the year, which engaged speakers to educate soldiers on both political and personal questions. In early August a "Soldiers' University" began to function. Despite these efforts, newspapers reported an even larger number of crimes attributed to men "in soldier's garb."

As a result of the changed political climate after the July Days, efforts to restore discipline and to improve the fighting capacity of the army intensified nationally and locally. The reintroduction of the death penalty at the front by the new commander in chief, General Kornilov, set the tone for a series of measures taken by provincial authorities. A Union of Army and Navy Officers and an All-Russian Union of St. George's Cavalrymen, both of which articulated their support for the Provisional Government and for the continuation of the war to a victorious end, recruited members locally throughout July. In Saratov 300 individuals enrolled in the latter organization. Apart from these efforts, the army command isolated Cossack units from regular soldiers, since the Cossacks provided the small amount of armed force available to back up the decrees of the government. Attempts also were made to set up so-called death battalions, shock brigades, and the like, which rejected Order Number 1 and expressed their eagerness to fight. In Saratov military leaders enrolled civilians and regular soldiers in the "Saratov Regional Committee to Organize the Volunteer Army" and in the "Saratov Volunteer Guard." The Military Section of the Soviet created a special "Revolutionary Detachment of the Saratov Soviet," which attracted 3,000 signatures. A "Women's Volunteer Storm Detachment" signed up 500 women. Various death units and "Kerensky battalions" were organized in Volsk, Balashov, Pokrovsk, Kuznetsk, and Petrovsk. According to V. V. Vas'kin, school-age children and recent graduates constituted the majority of the civilian volunteers, while deserters could readily be found among the soldier members of these groups. Competing against the frontoviki for the common soldiers' loyalties, these special military

70. *Saratovskii vestnik*, no. 157, July 18, 1917, p. 3; no. 197, September 6, p . 3.

71. *Izvestiia Kazanskogo Voenno-okruzhnogo Komiteta*, no. 79, August 27, 1917, p. 3. See also no. 78, August 26, p. 4, and no. 70, August 17, pp. 5–6.

units appear to have had no significant impact on the further disintegration of the Russian army. In late August Saratov's newspapers already gave less and less coverage to the death battalions and by September many of these units had disbanded altogether.[72]

The July crisis in Petrograd also resulted in more pronounced anti-Bolshevik sentiments in the uezd towns, but did not damage the vitality of the soviets that had non-Bolshevik majorities. According to the Volga delegation's report to the Sixth Bolshevik Party Congress in July, the soviets remained powerful in the small towns after the July Days because "whatever their [social or political] composition, they had taken upon themselves the role of sovereign organs, and this saved them."[73]

Minor antiwar disturbances broke out in the Kamyshin, Petrovsk, and Balashov garrisons when news of the July crisis reached the district centers.[74] The soldiers' restlessness, combined with the spy charges made against the Bolsheviks, led to a purge of Bolshevik and even Menshevik elements from some soviets, especially in towns in which the SDs had belonged to united organizations. At the Volga-area Menshevik conference held in Saratov in late July, Menshevik delegates from Atkarsk, Kamyshin, and Rtishchevo noted that their party organizations had lost members after the Petrograd events.[75] In Kuznetsk and Volsk, Bolshevik chairmen of the local soviets were driven from office.[76] From Balashov, Bankvitser reported that the small Bolshevik organization "lay in shambles" and that young Bolshevik recruits had moved into the Menshevik camp. Bankvitser himself fled town after a garrison death battalion tried to hurl him under a train.[77] Officers gained control of the unruly soldiers' soviet in Kamyshin, but disturbances in the local garrison persisted unabated. In Atkarsk SRs received a sympathetic response from the public when they repeated the spy charges against Lenin.[78]

In virtually all of the small uezd towns the SR party continued to dominate local politics. SR newspapers, however, published by moderate party elements, purposely ignored the widening cleavages within the

72. Vas'kin, "Kontrrevoliutsiia v bor'be za armiiu," pp. 30–36, 38–41.

73. Gerasimenko and Tochenyi, *Sovety Povolzh'ia,* p. 145.

74. Ovrutskaia, "Proval politiki," p. 358.

75. *Proletarii Povolzh'ia,* no. 49, August 1, 1917, p. 2.

76. Gerasimenko, *Sovety Nizhnego Povolzh'ia,* pp. 63–64.

77. Bankvitser, "Vospominaniia," p. 30; Zhagar, "Put' k oktiabriu," p. 47; and V. V. Vas'kin, "Bor'ba bol'shevikov Nizhnego Povolzh'ia protiv formirovaniia kontrrevoliutsionnykh udarnykh chastei letom i osen'iu 1917 g.," in *Nekotorye voprosy otechestvennoi i vseobshchei istorii* (Saratov, 1971), p. 36.

78. V. Sushitskii, "Oktiabr'skaia revoliutsiia v Vol'skom i Atkarskom uezdakh," *Kommunisticheskii put',* no. 20 (1927), p. 109. See also *Delo naroda* (Petrograd), no. 96, July 9, 1917, p. 2.

party's ranks. As a result it is difficult to reconstruct the intraparty conflict at this time. A congress of soviets of Saratov province which met at the end of July passed a moderate resolution that, while recognizing the "critical situation" facing the country's leaders, emphasized the need for a "powerful revolutionary army" to defend Russia.[79] It is hard to believe in the face of later evidence that activists conducting party work in the garrisons and villages shared such sentiments.

The explosive situation that developed in Tsaritsyn merits special attention because it resulted in the direct military intervention of the Provisional Government and the Saratov Soviet, and strengthened the arguments of Saratov political leaders who supported moderate policies. In upholding the national government's efforts to maintain law and order, however, Saratov leaders were faced with a tactical and at times moral dilemma: keeping the lid on Tsaritsyn required them to revoke some democratic principles and to sanction orders that could be interpreted as "counterrevolutionary" by the Bolshevik-led townspeople of Tsaritsyn.

To a large degree Tsaritsyn's social structure and rapid growth in the decade after 1905 shaped the course of the revolution here, in Russia's "Chicago." It had a larger percentage of industrial workers than other cities in the Lower and Middle Volga region—some 12,000—and about 20,000 unskilled laborers, the majority of whom were hired by large woodworking enterprises or as stevedores or *burlaki,* the barge haulers, immortalized in I. E. Repin's painting *Haulers on the Volga.*[80] One of the largest armament works in Russia, the French factory (Diumo), employed more than 3,000 workers. Other industrial workers toiled in another major armament factory, various metal-processing enterprises, the Nobel oil refinery, the railroad lines, and the municipal tram system. Although a revolutionary tradition among Tsaritsyn workers had taken root before 1917, the economic vicissitudes of war contributed most to workers' dissatisfaction after 1914. Apart from this potentially volatile element of the population, a garrison of 15,000 to 20,000 soldiers was located in Tsaritsyn. In December 1916, on the eve of the revolution, soldiers had rioted and refused to carry out orders to punish deserters.[81]

It will be recalled that the city duma and representatives from various

79. See *Proletarii Povolzh'ia,* no. 55, August 8, 1917, pp. 2–3; for reports of local delegates, see *Izvestiia Saratovskogo Soveta,* no. 71, August 10, 1917, p. 1, and *Proletarii Povolzh'ia,* no. 53, August 5, 1917, p. 4.

80. I. Romanov and N. Sokolov, *Ocherk istorii revoliutsii 1917 goda v Tsaritsyne (Stalingrade)* (Saratov, 1932), p. 8. Commercial enterprises employed 25,000 workers and artisan crafts another 10,000. See M. A. Vodolagin, *Ocherki istorii Volgograda, 1589–1967* (Moscow, 1968), pp. 98, 103.

81. Romanov and Sokolov, *Ocherk istorii revoliutsii,* pp. 3, 11.

public organizations had formed a Temporary Executive Committee (TEC) on March 1. On March 3 a workers' soviet was convened and on March 5 a separate soldiers' council was elected. In the initial post-February period the TEC and duma shared power with the soviets. A local Bolshevik later argued, and his observation seems to ring true, that such a political situation emerged because the local "bourgeoisie were a bit more revolutionary and the Mensheviks and SRs were a bit more bourgeois than in other cities."[82]

Yet by late spring "dual power" had ended in Tsaritsyn and the soviet had become one of the first in the country to come under Bolshevik influence. As in many towns, Social Democrats founded a united party committee after February. But by the end of March relations between local Bolsheviks and Mensheviks already showed signs of strain, in part because of the return to Tsaritsyn of, in Trotsky's estimation, a "Bolshevik demagogue," Semen Konstantinovich Minin (not to be confused with the Saratov SR with the same surname). Arguments between the two SD factions now broke out over differing attitudes toward the war and over governmental orders to dispatch local troops to the front, many of whom were frontoviki. On April 12 soldiers' committees and regimental soviets denounced the Tsaritsyn Provisional Executive Committee and passed a resolution supporting Lenin's April Theses.[83] Shortly after this incident the separate soviets merged; from this time on the townspeople looked upon the Tsaritsyn Soviet as the center of revolutionary authority in the city. Further, the unpopular Temporary Executive Committee simply stopped meeting as the Soviet came to grapple with the most important social and economic issues facing the population.

Incited by the antiwar propaganda of all leftist groups, local troops took to the streets. One regiment refused to go to the front, demanding that those exempt from combat be sent first. Other soldiers rioted.[84] Even though the soviet met with success in taming such behavior, it was clear that the troops were disposed to act independently. So were the workers, among whom Bolshevik influence swelled, too.[85] Moreover, the local Bolsheviks' ready acceptance of Lenin's theses further strained their relations with local Mensheviks. When the local SD committee decided to publish a newspaper and chose only Bolsheviks for the editorial

82. S. K. Minin, *Gorod-boets: Shest' diktatur 1917 goda (Vospominaniia o rabote v Tsaritsyne)* (Leningrad, 1925), p. 11.

83. Raleigh, "Revolutionary Politics," p. 199.

84. G. T. Gavrilov, comp., *1917 god v Stalingradskoi gubernii (Khronika sobytii)* (Stalingrad, 1927), p. 27; Minin, *Gorod-boets*, pp. 24–25.

85. Vodolagin, *Ocherki istorii Volgograda*, p. 178.

board, the Mensheviks broke away to form a separate organization. Several days later the first issue of the Bolshevik paper, *Bor'ba* (The Struggle), went to press.[86] Within a month workers and soldiers passed a resolution against the Freedom Loan and in favor of a transfer of power to the soviets.[87]

Several factors explain the rapid, if broken, swing to the left by the population of Tsaritsyn. More than anything else the unusually high concentration of evacuees accounts for the notable degree of local radicalism.[88] Throughout the spring, the threat of being sent back to the front surfaced repeatedly; as the June offensive approached, the evacuees' antiwar feelings bordered on open mutiny. Then, too, SR city committee members did not have the hold over local soldiers that their comrades enjoyed in other towns. In fact, a sizable group of Left SRs had become popular in the garrison, particularly a certain Fedotov, who openly sided with Bolsheviks on important political issues.[89] Although it is more difficult to account for the behavior of Tsaritsyn workers, it appears that as elsewhere the metalworkers stood in the vanguard of the labor movement. But the main source of Bolshevik strength within the working class was the large number of port workers, stevedores, and lumbermill workers. Swept into the labor movement during the strikes of 1915–16, these workers now rallied behind the Bolsheviks, who consistently supported the shore workers' demands for higher wages.[90] The more precarious economic status of the less skilled and lower paid workers worsened toward summer, when economic life in the city almost became paralyzed as a result of a disrupted flow of goods through the port.[91] The threat of economic ruin hovering over Tsaritsyn created a psychological climate favorable to Bolshevik and other "internationalist" propaganda.

Tsaritsyn's tsenzovoe obshchestvo observed the growing radicalization of soldiers and workers with increased concern. An unfortunate

86. Minin, *Gorod-boets*, pp. 33–37; *Sotsial-Demokrat*, no. 23, June 7, 1917, p. 3.

87. *Khronika*, p. 63.

88. Recently published studies on the Russian army in 1917 suggest that evacuated soldiers had a similar impact wherever they were located. See T. F. Kuz'mina, *Revoliutsionnoe dvizhenie soldatskikh mass Tsentra Rossii nakanune Oktiabria (Po materialam Moskovskogo voennogo okruga)* (Moscow, 1978), pp. 50–51, 55; and Mikhail Frenkin, *Russkaia armiia i revoliutsiia 1917–1918* (Munich, 1978). According to Frenkin, sixty of the ninety-seven garrisons in the Kazan Military District were classified as being in a state of extreme trouble in June (p. 330). Frenkin also notes that from January to June the number of soldiers evacuated to rear garrisons grew, while the percentage returning to the front dropped substantially (pp. 302–3).

89. Ionenko, *Soldaty tylovykh garnizonov*, p. 112.

90. Romanov and Sokolov, *Ocherk istorii revoliutsii*, p. 33. Growing Bolshevik gains at Menshevik expense during April and May are discussed in the Menshevik newspaper *Proletarii Povolzh'ia*, no. 50, August 2, 1917, p. 3.

91. Ovrutskaia, "Proval politiki," p. 353.

incident on May 22 prompted the propertied elements and, to a lesser extent, the moderate socialists into launching an assault on the Bolsheviks. That day a mob of soldiers beat to death an allegedly drunken ensign who called the Bolsheviks "German spies."[92] Despite resolutions passed by factories, garrison units, the soviet, and the local Bolshevik committee condemning mob action, the death of the ensign became a cause célèbre for nonsocialist groups.[93] Local industrialists petitioned the city duma and Provisional Government to rid the city of "Bolshevik troops," while the duma asked the Petrograd Soviet to commission an investigation of the murder. An anti-Bolshevik campaign began immediately in the national press, where editorials referred to the "Bolshevik-instigated" murder and to the "Tsaritsyn Republic." On June 1–2 Kerensky ordered the commander of the Kazan Military District "to take decisive measures to establish order in the Tsaritsyn garrison." The Petrograd Soviet asked the Saratov Soviet to take "energetic measures concerning Tsaritsyn because the demagogy of Minin will inevitably result in a pogrom. On June 7, two delegations arrived in Tsaritsyn, one sent by the commander of the Kazan Military District, the other by the Saratov Soviet. After several days of deliberations both delegations blamed the bourgeois press for rumor-mongering, dispelled the notion of a "Bolshevik republic," and reaffirmed the Tsaritsyn Soviet's support of the policies of the Petrograd Soviet. The Kazan representative, however, prepared a separate report for limited government circles, contending that there was "complete disorganization in the garrison, and pressure from the garrison on all public organizations of the city."[94]

To some people the Kazan representative's clandestine report rang true; many local Bolsheviks stood far to the left of moderate elements within the party. Because of weak ties with the Central Committee in Petrograd, local militants pushed events. Nevertheless, evidence suggests that after the departure from Tsaritsyn of the two official delegations, the local Bolshevik committee coaxed the angry soldiers and workers not to riot. But preparations for the June offensive and pressing economic difficulties kept tempers in the city strained. This smoldering discontent flared up during the local reaction to the July Days. For several days public meetings, garrison councils, and factory committees passed resolutions supporting the Petrograd workers and demanding a transfer of power to the soviets.[95] In Tsaritsyn, unlike neighboring

92. Minin, *Gorod-boets*, pp. 48–51; Gavrilov, *1917 god v Stalingradskoi gubernii*, p. 43; Romanov and Sokolov, *Ocherk istorii revoliutsii*, pp. 41–42.

93. See, for example, *Tsaritsynskii vestnik*, no. 5456, May 27, 1917, pp. 2–3; Gavrilov, *1917 god v Stalingradskoi gubernii*, pp. 44–45.

94. Quoted in Ovrutskaia, "Proval politiki," pp. 353–55.

95. Gavrilov, *1917 god v Stalingradskoi gubernii*, p. 63. See also O. N. Znamenskii, *Iiul'skii krizis 1917 goda* (Moscow, 1964), p. 159; S. I. Zavarzin and E. N. Shkodina, comps.,

Saratov or Petrograd, for that matter, a full plenum of the soviet carried a resolution calling for a transfer of power to the soviets and for the speedy convocation of a constituent assembly.[96] To top things off, the Bolsheviks received the most votes of any party in elections to the city duma, winning 39 of 102 seats.

Given the reaction in Petrograd to the July Days, it is not surprising that this local call for a transfer of power to the soviets and Bolshevik success in the duma elections greatly alarmed the Provisional Government and moderate leaders in Tsaritsyn and nearby Saratov. Kerensky ordered the Tsaritsyn Bolshevik newspaper, *Bor'ba*, shut down, and the Saratov district court abrogated the election results to the city duma. The commander of the Kazan Military District, "in view of the continuing anarchy in Tsaritsyn," dispatched to Tsaritsyn a military detachment led by Colonel Korvin-Krukovskii from Saratov. The Saratov Soviet commissioned a delegation to accompany the detachment "to assist Korvin-Krukovskii in establishing order."[97]

Saratov Bolsheviks refused to take part in the Soviet's delegation and instead sent Antonov to Tsaritsyn as an independent observer.[98] Arriving in town before the military detachment, he learned that some local Bolsheviks wanted to lead an armed uprising against the government's forces. But after a long and at times inflamed debate within the local committee, Bolshevik moderates prevailed. They issued appeals for law and order to the townspeople and packed Minin off to Petrograd to attend the Sixth Bolshevik Congress. (He and Antonov were arrested in Kamyshin "under orders from Korvin-Krukovskii." Minin remained imprisoned in Saratov until he was freed by crowds of soldiers in the heat of the Kornilov crisis; Antonov was soon released through the intervention of the Saratov Soviet.)[99]

In an effort to nullify the need for the detachment from Saratov, the Tsaritsyn Soviet tried to rid the city of the more independent-minded troops. But the soldiers refused to go to the front "until the entrenched bourgeoisie go." A few days later Korvin-Krukovskii arrived in Tsaritsyn with a detachment of 500 Cossacks and 500 junkers, and with an agent of Kerensky, Korni-de-bad. Announcements heralding the arrival had been

---

1917 god v Tsaritsyne (Sbornik dokumentov i materialov) (Stalingrad, 1957), pp. 64, 67–70.

96. Gavrilov, *1917 god v Stalingradskoi gubernii*, pp. 64–65; Zavarzin and Shkodina, *1917 god v Tsaritsyne*, p. 65.

97. *Khronika*, p. 86.

98. *Saratovskii Sovet*, pp. 170–71; and *Izvestiia Kazanskogo Voenno-okruzhnogo Komiteta*, no. 67, August 11, 1917, p. 3.

99. Antonov-Saratovskii, "S fevralia," pp. 203–5; S. K. Minin, "Iz dnevnika S. K. Minina," *Partiinyi sputnik*, no. 7–8 (1922–23), p. 136; *Saratovskii vestnik*, no. 163, July 25, 1917, p. 3.

posted throughout the city, declaring that the expedition had been sent under orders from Kerensky "for the restoration of revolutionary order and discipline in the province and for the suppression of all anarchistic manifestations from the right and from the left."[100]

Even before his arrival, Korvin-Krukovskii had issued orders for the arrest of Minin and other popular Bolsheviks. Korni-de-bad intimated to the executive committee of the soviet that these were "only the beginning of the arrests."[101] In response the Bolsheviks labeled the expedition counterrevolutionary and walked out of the soviet. Nevertheless, Bolsheviks continued their efforts to calm garrison units that were itching for a showdown with Korvin-Krukovskii. At the same time, workers and soldiers, some of whom threatened to strike, demanded that the soviet take decisive steps to secure the release of Minin, Erman, and other arrested Bolsheviks.[102]

Despite some conciliatory gestures, Korvin-Krukovskii's actions remained highly suspect. He allowed a rightist newspaper, *Respublikanets* (The Republican), earlier closed by the soviet, to resume publication; its first issue called upon the townspeople to disband the soviet. Meanwhile, on July 29 the first echelons of the insubordinate 155th Regiment departed for the front, accompanied to the station by the well-armed troops of Korvin-Krukovskii. In his report to the commander of the Kazan Military District, Korni-de-bad observed that "Cossacks and machine guns . . . contributed more to the departure for the front than those verbal arguments with which we provided them."[103] Ridding Tsaritsyn of these soldiers may have temporarily eased tensions in Tsaritsyn, but the revolutionary-minded soldiers of the 155th Regiment quickly infected troops on the Rumanian front. Confidential reports written by government commissars noted the total lack of discipline, the agitation the soldiers conducted against the war, and the "abundant quantity of Bolshevik literature" they had brought with them. As the demoralized commander of the front put it, "all of these individuals had passed through the Bolshevik school of Minin in Tsaritsyn."[104]

It became increasingly apparent that Korvin-Krukovskii had no intention of subordinating himself to the Tsaritsyn Soviet. What little support he had from moderate socialists waned, and they, too, began to articulate their opposition to him. Saratov's Maizel' and Telegin condemned the

100. *Delo naroda* (Petrograd), no. 113, July 29, 1917, p. 3.

101. *Izvestiia Kazanskogo Voenno-okruzhnogo Komiteta*, no. 77, August 25, 1917, pp. 2–4.

102. Antonov-Saratovskii, "S fevralia," p. 205; *Khronika*, p. 92.

103. Gerasimenko, *Sovety Nizhnego Povolzh'ia*, p. 70; and Ovrutskaia, "Proval politiki," p. 370.

104. I. M. Ionenko, *Soldatskie massy v Oktiabr'skoi revoliutsii: Po materialam Povolzh'ia i Urala* (Kazan, 1982), pp. 20–22.

colonel's arrest of popular socialist leaders. Korvin-Krukovskii's failure to respond directly when the soviet called upon him to justify his actions caused further discomfort. By this time Maizel' and Telegin reported to the Saratov Soviet that their initial support of the expedition had been a mistake. Furthermore, a full plenum of the Tsaritsyn Soviet passed a resolution drafted by all three socialist factions. After censuring the end of freedom of speech and of the press, it expressed the view that since the detachment had arrived, "*the role of the soviet is amounting to nothing, that in fact an extraordinary situation bordering on a military dictatorship is being introduced into the city.*"[105]

In the late summer of 1917, particularly after the self-demobilization of the Russian army began and unemployed Saratov workers and outside agitators appeared in the villages, the local rural revolution began to converge with the urban one. As background, it should be recalled that at the First Congress of Peasant Soviets, held in Petrograd in May, delegates from all corners of the empire had presented strikingly similar demands. Foremost among them were the demand that the "right of private property in land [be] abolished forever" and the assertion that land "can be neither sold nor bought nor leased nor pledged nor alienated in any way."[106] Shortly afterward an SR party congress accepted these objectives in its party program but deferred their implementation until convocation of a constituent assembly. A July 8 decree of the Provisional Government, stating that any future land reform would be shaped by the principle that land would pass into the hands of those who worked it, also reflected peasant aspirations. But once again, actual reform was postponed until the opening of a national assembly.

With the formation of the First Coalition Government in May and the Second Coalition Government in July, socialist ministers came to fear responsibility for rural affairs. Ignoring the peasantry's extraordinary determination to implement land reform measures as soon as possible, the moderate socialists put off the enactment of their own party programs in order to cling to their alliance with the liberals. The Kadets, proponents of the idea of private property, favored state acquisition of privately owned land above a certain labor norm, with financial compensation to the large landowners. Opposing financial remuneration and private ownership, the Russian populists called for a redistribution of all land. It is difficult to imagine how these two contradictory programs could be reconciled without conflict. Deferring the perhaps unavoidable clash with the liberals over the land question proved to be an extravagant

105. Ibid., p. 374; emphasis mine. For a detailed account of the events see *Izvestiia Kazanskogo Voenno-okruzhnogo Komiteta*, no. 77, August 25, 1917, pp. 2–4.

106. W. H. Chamberlin, *The Russian Revolution* (New York, 1935), 1:248.

tactic. It cost the moderate socialists the support of part of the countryside, made the peasantry suspicious of the government, and turned their economic struggle into a political one by making their impulsive drive to acquire land illegal.

The number of peasant seizures of land swelled after the First All-Russian Peasant Congress, and in fact many peasants cited the declaration on land passed by the congress as justification for their behavior. As the government prepared for the Constituent Assembly, initially scheduled to open in August, the peasants under the aegis of village and volost committees or land committees continued their assault on estate owners and independent farmers. In an attempt to hold back the peasant movement that was running rampant across rural Russia, the Provisional Government had created a Main Land Committee that organized land committees at the local level. But these committees had soon come under peasant influence. As one local commissioner reported, since the formation of the land committee "agricultural lawbreaking has grown more common."[107] Many of the complaints landowners sent to the provincial authorities or Provisional Government in the summer of 1917 emphasized the driving force of the land committees behind peasant agitation.

The number of peasant disturbances in Saratov province shot up in June and the first half of July and then tapered off until September.[108] Statistics compiled by the government show that the peasant movement in Penza, Kazan, Saratov, Samara, and Tambov was among the most turbulent in the entire country in both June and July. The rhythm of rural unrest flowed with agricultural cycles and the peculiar time demands of farming; the forms the disorders took also had a logic of their own. Having seized land and repudiated rental agreements during planting season, the peasants now turned to taking equipment and livestock, felling trees, and mowing grass for haymaking. Now and then they committed acts of terror, perhaps to settle old scores. By mid-July thirty village clergy in the province had complained to the provincial commissar that peasants had seized church land.[109] Ukrainian peasants from Nikolaevsk—probably Stolypin peasants—cabled the Central Ukrainian Rada in Kiev that Russian peasants from the same settlement "torment us in all matters with the aim of driving us away from the village."[110] At the same time the Balashov Uezd Land Committee shot off an urgent telegram to Kerensky and Tsereteli, the minister of the interior, sharply criticizing the agrarian policy of the Provisional Government and warn-

107. Shestakov, *Sovety krest'ianskikh deputatov*, pt. 1, pp. 112–14.
108. Anfimov, *Ekonomicheskoe polozhenie*, 3:400–406.
109. *Saratovskii vestnik*, no. 157, July 18, 1917, p. 3.
110. *Proletarii Povolzh'ia*, no. 36, July 16, 1917, p. 4.

ing that the peasants' illegal seizures must be legalized and become government policy.[111] Leaders in Balashov informed authorities that "soldiers from the local garrison sent out to do agricultural work resolved to take away from landowners machinery for harvesting grain. Local authorities do nothing."[112] In the village of Lesnoi Karamysh in July the communal peasants' sustained conflict with the separators resulted in a bloody clash.

Several factors apart from the obvious economic considerations contributed to peasant lawlessness in the summer of 1917. Many of the approximately 20,000 conscripted soldiers sent to do field work in the villages of the Lower Volga appear to have remained there for haymaking and harvesting. Radical agitators from Kronstadt and Petrograd now made an impact, too, more so than the occasional deserter who wandered into the villages. Unfavorably dry climatic conditions also increased the local peasantry's push to take over landowners' pastureland and meadows in order to preserve the villages' livestock herds. The 1917 harvest was smaller than the previous year's and much lower than the 1913 yield.[113] By late summer, when the nature of the year's harvest became clear, the peasants proved reluctant to turn their crops over to the government grain monopoly. Threatened with shortages themselves, urban authorities cut back on grain shipments to the more industrialized provinces. Russia had broken apart into local economic units.

Viewing the peasant movement as part of the rising revolutionary tide and of the collapse of law and order in general, the Second Coalition Government tried to crack down on rural unrest. But the coalition ministry lacked both the will and the means to do so. Instead, the summer of 1917 saw the enactment of a series of uneven measures that had a marginal effect on the countryside. As commander in chief of the Southwestern Front, General L. G. Kornilov forbade peasant committees to seize equipment and livestock from landowners, while the L'vov ministry augmented prison sentences for those who ignored governmental instructions or called for agrarian uprisings.[114] The use of troops to pacify villages and to arrest peasant leaders and members of land committees took place, but rarely. More often, restrictive governmental regulations simply went ignored in places where officials found it impossible to pursue unpopular policies. At another level the government tried to

111. M. G. Fleer, "Vremennoe Pravitel'stvo v bor'be s agrarnoi revoliutsiei," *Krasnaia letopis'*, no. 2/17 (1926), pp. 14–15.

112. Kotel'nikov and Meller, *Krest'ianskoe dvizhenie v 1917*, pp. 153–54, 162–63.

113. *Saratovskii vestnik*, no. 209, September 22, 1917, p. 3. One extreme estimate put the 1917 harvest 50 percent lower than that of the year before. See *Proletarii Povolzh'ia*, no. 96, September 23, 1917, p. 4.

114. V. I. Kostrikin, *Zemel'nye komitety v 1917 godu* (Moscow, 1975), pp. 233–34.

undermine the authority of the land committees altogether. After cutting off financial support to the committees, the government made them responsible to the courts in early September. The regime also moved quickly on a decision made in late May to replace the hybrid executive committees with volost zemstvos. Election dates were set in most provinces for the second half of August and first half of September. Yet it bears repeating that such measures had a negligible effect. In mid-July the Saratov Provincial Land Committee (and provincial committees tended to be more moderate than lower-level ones) actually urged the government to initiate "the immediate realization in Saratov province of the land program of the Socialist Revolutionary party."[115]

The July uprising in Petrograd exacerbated the breakdown of central state power and strengthened the strong centrifugal pull of local forces that shaped the revolution along the Volga. The July uprising in Petrograd fueled partisan politics, calling attention to the various parties' attitudes toward the war and future government (i.e., should the socialists remain in coalition with the bourgeoisie). Strong feelings of camaraderie with other socialists continued to affect the behavior of Saratov Bolsheviks, who nevertheless supported an all-soviet, all-socialist government more resolutely than before. Fearful of mass excesses, local moderates found it increasingly difficult to back the war cause and to maintain their preeminence in the Soviet. Viewing their victory in elections to the City Duma as a vote of confidence and as a rejection of radicalism, SRs and Mensheviks sought to legitimize their rule by resurrecting the moribund City Duma. In the popular view, however, this tactic won little sympathy.

Instead, the moderate socialists' growing unwillingness to govern through the Soviet eroded the parties' heretofore widespread support. The ultimate ramifications this development would have on the outcome of the revolution were unclear to contemporaries at this point in the revolution. If it seemed that workers' and soldiers' attitudes were in a state of flux, it would be evident that by September the events of the summer of 1917 had played into the Bolsheviks' hands. Moreover, the inability of the successive governments to effect land reform had led to an upsurge in agrarian disorders, straining relations between town and country. The peasants' reluctance to market grain heightened social tensions in the city, where workers continued to battle for economic improvement and soldiers for an end to the war and for better living conditions.

Some sources for the second half of August convey an almost apoca-

115. *Saratovskii listok*, no. 153, July 14, 1917, p. 3.

lyptic sense of anguish and foreboding. In late August a Saratovite named E. Abramovich, a doctor by profession and a Menshevik by political persuasion, captured the anxious mood in a letter written to a friend in Minsk.

> As you see, my situation is not among the most pleasant. And there's nothing that can be done—such, apparently, is fate. . . . All around me life is boiling and through newspapers I follow how "a new life is being built." But newspapers rouse in me only spite, spite for myself, for Russia, for the whole world. For myself—for my weakness; for Russia—for her savagery and lack of culture; for the world—for its brutality. What does the future hold for us? Hunger, cold, general anarchy, spontaneous insurrections and pogroms, the collapse of the government, its financial bankruptcy, disaster at the front, German occupation, annexations and contributions, the loss of ports, the loss of seas, impoverishment, and a running wild of the masses and so on. . . . When I occasionally go out into the street or boulevard, when I see the strolling public in their foppish outfits, the overcrowded cinemas and *cafés chantants*, the frantically speeding automobiles with suspicious passengers, the loafing crowds of soldiers, it seems to me that I have come across a banquet during a plague. But still sadder thoughts seize me when I go to public meetings . . . and hear how "socialist" orators resort to unscrupulous demagogy, and "the revolutionary democracy," the greater part soldiers, with rapture greet the seductive slogans tossed at them. Oh, blind leaders of a blind people![116]

116. E. A. Abramovich, "Pis'ma E. A. Abramovicha k E. A. Gurvichu," *Katorga i ssylka*, no. 40 (1928), p. 149.

CHAPTER 6

The Revolution under Fire

After the abortive July uprising in Petrograd, conservative Russian statesmen, including prominent leaders of the Kadet party, encouraged Kerensky's commander in chief, General Kornilov, to assume a political role to arrest the growing anarchy in the country. One of their goals was to curtail the vast influence of the soviets in domestic affairs. Another was their determination to continue the war to preserve the country's national honor and to ward off a possible German conquest of Russia. For them, Kornilov was an ideal candidate for a position of authority. After being offered the post of commander in chief on July 18, he had predicated his acceptance on the adoption of a variety of measures aimed at strengthening military discipline at the front and order at home. Such behavior endeared Kornilov to rightist elements who hoped to manipulate the politically naive general. "I declare," Kornilov said in late August, ". . . that under the pressure of the Bolshevik majority in the soviets [*sic*], the Provisional Government acts in complete harmony with the plans of the German General Staff . . . undermining the very foundation of the country."[1]

Following Kornilov's appointment, the more conservative elements of Russian society took the offensive. On August 12–14 the Kerensky government convoked the Moscow State Conference to provide legitimization for the new coalition cabinet. Because the soviets and other popular

1. Quoted in M. Liebman, *The Russian Revolution* (New York, 1970), p. 210.

organs were underrepresented at the conference, the moderate socialists were uncertain how to relate to the gathering. While they equivocated, the Bolsheviks decided to attend the conference, condemn it, and walk out. As could be expected from the conference's makeup, the majority of deputies expressed staunch support for Kerensky and his program; after the Moscow State Conference adjourned, rumors of a right-wing coup circulated in Russia. In the meanwhile, Kerensky also appears to have concluded that his regime could be saved only by the curbing of democratic organs. Kerensky may have moved closer to Kornilov politically, but as Alexander Rabinowitch aptly put it, "each viewed himself (and not the other) as the strongman in a new authoritarian government." Their relationship deteriorated in the remaining days of August. Convinced that Kornilov had double-crossed him, Kerensky ordered the general's resignation on August 27, just as troops were preparing to march on Petrograd. To Kerensky's surprise, socialist forces in the capital rallied behind the government. The Petrograd Soviet insisted that Kerensky reject a proposal to negotiate with Kornilov, a position that Allied representatives and the Kadet party favored. At the last moment Kerensky decided to defend Petrograd. Fortunately for him it was already clear on August 29 that the threat of military takeover had subsided. Although saved by Russia's powerful socialist forces, Kerensky feared the vitality of the left even more than before. "Kerensky," argued Rabinowitch, "now behaved almost as if the Kornilov affair had not happened."[2]

Even before the Kornilov Affair, the Bolsheviks began to recover from the difficult straits they found themselves in after the July crisis. The conservative tone of the Moscow State Conference and the growing visibility of the political right at this time served as a tonic for the left. Workers in Saratov and Tsaritsyn protested the very opening of the conference by going out on strike. Within the Saratov Soviet the Bolshevik position on key issues was beginning to attract more votes than the size of the party's fraction warranted.[3] On the eve of the Kornilov Affair the Bolshevik newspaper *Sotsial-Demokrat*, which had been silent for six weeks, resumed publication. Party factions in neighboring towns experienced a similar comeback in August. On August 20, for example, the Astrakhan Bolsheviks finally broke from the local united SD organization, formed a separate committee, and launched a party newspaper.[4]

In view of such stirrings in the leftist camp in late summer, it is not surprising that Kornilov's attempt at a conservative restoration fueled

2. Rabinowitch, *Bolsheviks Come to Power*, pp. 116, 152.

3. An illustrative example is the vote taken on a Menshevik-sponsored resolution in support of the Stockholm Conference, which was an effort to achieve peace through an international conference of socialists representing all warring countries. See *Saratovskii Sovet*, p. 184.

4. Gerasimenko and Tochenyi, *Sovety Povolzh'ia*, pp. 149–51.

partisan politics in Saratov. As ambiguous news of Kornilov's maneuvers reached Saratov during the evening of August 27, the Soviet and Duma cautioned citizens against holding illegal street meetings and admonished them not to fall victim to rumors. When the Duma met on the morning of the 28th, factional fighting broke out as speakers from the various political camps blamed each other for Russia's political crisis. Even though they acknowledged the rise of "counterrevolutionary forces" in Russia, Saratov SRs called for the continued subordination of all political and administrative organs to the Provisional Government. An SR resolution summoning the population "to fight against all anarchy, from the right and from the left," provoked local Bolsheviks to introduce an alternative motion demanding "an immediate halt to the suppression of revolutionary parties and the rescinding of curbs on revolutionary newspapers." The resolution declared that the people must put an end to all "attempts at conciliation with the counterrevolutionary well-to-do classes and organize power . . . only from representatives of the revolutionary democracy." The Duma, as could be expected, adopted the SR resolution summoning the population to support the Provisional Government. But the Mensheviks amended the document to appease the Bolsheviks by dropping the phrase "threat of anarchy from the left."[5]

Discord also disrupted the Soviet Executive Committee's meeting that same day. In contrast with the appeals of moderate leaders, Antonov warned against unconditional support for the Provisional Government or for Kerensky, arguing that Kerensky's involvement in the conspiracy might not have been "altogether innocent." The Executive Committee then discussed preparations for a parade of garrison units, scheduled for the next day, to commemorate the six-month anniversary of the February Revolution. Taking into account the uncertain political climate and the provincial commissar's ban on street gatherings, the SRs and Mensheviks now spoke in favor of holding a military parade without civilian participation or political addresses. What happened next was a portent of new strains in Saratov's politics. The Bolsheviks, finding some of the slogans proposed for the next day's parade unacceptable, announced their intention not to participate in it. This decision sparked a vituperative exchange, which threatened to end in violence, between Vasil'ev and the SR officers from the Soldiers' Section. The representatives of the military on the Executive Committee stormed out of the hall, while the remaining members censured Vasil'ev.[6] It is interesting to note that similar strains surfaced precisely at this time in Petrograd and Moscow, and undoubtedly for the same reason: the Kornilov movement poisoned rela-

5. *Saratovskii vestnik,* no. 193, September 1, 1917, pp. 4–5; *Proletarii Povolzh'ia,* no. 76, September 1, 1917, p. 4.

6. See *Saratovskii Sovet,* pp. 186–89.

tions not only between census society and the democracy but also between radical and moderate socialists.

Subsequent events showed how far to the left the rank-and-file soldiers of the Saratov garrison had moved from the officers representing the soldiers in the Soviet. On the evening of August 28, the local garrison protested against the Kornilov conspiracy and demanded the release of Minin and other arrested Bolsheviks.[7] The next day, in blatant defiance of the provincial commissar's appeal and the Duma's ban on demonstrations, military units held anti-Kornilov rallies and a crowd of soldiers—many of whom had been transferred from Tsaritsyn a few weeks earlier—poured out into the streets of Saratov. Joined by workers' groups, they marched on the city prison and freed the Tsaritsyn Bolsheviks. Thousands of workers and soldiers waving banners inscribed with "Down with Kornilov" and "Long Live Kerensky" responded enthusiastically to the speeches Minin and Erman made upon their release from jail. To the dismay of the Soviet's leaders, young people distributed inflammatory proclamations issued by "The Saratov Free Association of Anarchist Groups," which summoned the townspeople "to an armed uprising and to the immediate seizure of land, factories, plants, houses, shops, and means of production."[8]

Later that day, the Soviet's Executive Committee agreed "to defend the revolution against Kornilov," but differed on whether to stand by the national government. SRs and Mensheviks continued to express their support of the Provisional Government, whereas the Bolsheviks lashed out against coalition rule. It should be pointed out that the general position of the Petrograd Soviet toward Kornilov was known in Saratov, for that day the Soviet had received a telegram from the All-Russian Central Executive Committee calling for all local soviets to support the Provisional Government.[9] Although agreeing on the need to prosecute Kornilov, the moderate socialists puzzled over what steps to take locally. Some clearly were uneasy about the demonstrations held that morning and the crowd's enthusiastic response to the release of Minin and Erman. These SRs and Mensheviks insisted that the two Tsaritsyn Bolsheviks "write letters to all socialist newspapers that their emancipation was unlawful and that they were ready to put themselves at the disposal of the legal authorities."[10] Afterward, the Executive Committee discussed formation of a workers' armed guard and agreed to set up a

7. Minin, "Iz dnevnika," p. 142.

8. See Medvedev, "Saratovskii Sovet," pp. 76–77; *Saratovskii vestnik*, no. 193, September 1, 1917, p. 5; *Sotsial-Demokrat*, no. 63, September 3, 1917, p. 3; R. Borisova, "U Volgarei," *Novyi mir*, no. 10 (1957), p. 166.

9. *Proletarii Povolzh'ia*, no. 73, August 29, 1917, p. 4.

10. *Saratovskii Sovet*, p. 189.

committee with representation from the three main socialist parties. The matter of organizing a special organ or committee to deal with the threat of counterrevolution also was posed, since deputies knew that the day before the Petrograd Soviet had formed a "Committee for the Struggle against Counterrevolution." The Saratov Soviet's Executive Committee tentatively decided to set up an "authoritative organ" comprising members of "local democratic organizations." All of the socialist fractions accepted this proposal.

Because the deputies had consented to establish a committee to combat counterrevolution under the Soviet's supervision, the SRs' and Mensheviks' unexpected departure from this strategy the next day strained even further the relationship between Bolsheviks and moderate socialists. That night SR and Menshevik Duma members advocated creation of an organ to combat counterrevolution which would be answerable to the Duma. Criticizing the Duma's proposal, Vasil'ev and Lebedev insisted that formation of a committee be postponed until the Soviet discussed the matter once again. When their request was voted down, the Bolshevik deputies, threatening to set up their own special committee, stormed out of the Duma hall, accompanied by cries of "Long live anarchy!" But the moderate socialists remained confused over who their real allies were. The suspicious behavior of the Kadet party's national leadership during the Kornilov crisis made the Saratov Kadets' insistence that the Bolsheviks be excluded from the committee against the counterrevolution ring false. The SR Minin expressed majority sentiment when he remarked that "we don't want [to work with] those who support Kornilov" (an obvious reference to the Kadets). Moreover, the majority of moderate socialists present rejected the Kadets' nominee to the committee, and the Kadets then withdrew from all Duma commissions. The moderate socialists had come to perceive the Bolsheviks as a threat from the left, but the moderates had failed to find common ground for cooperation with the liberals.[11]

When the Soviet's Executive Committee met on August 30, the threat of armed conflict locally complicated discussions over formation of a committee against counterrevolution. Sources suggest that the Kornilov movement contained a provincial component that has not been explored in the historical literature. Korvin-Krukovskii's military rule in neighboring Tsaritsyn had aroused suspicions in Saratov. Further, the All-Russian Central Executive Committee requested the Saratov Soviet "with all of its resources to help Tsaritsyn organize resistance to Ataman

11. This description of the Duma meeting was reconstructed from various newspaper accounts. See *Saratovskii vestnik*, no. 193, September 1, 1917, p. 4; *Proletarii Povolzh'ia*, no. 76, September 1, 1917, p. 1, and no. 80, September 2, p. 4.

Kaledin," whose forces were moving up the Volga. The Saratov Executive Committee demanded Korvin-Krukovskii's prompt departure from Tsaritsyn and declared Saratov to be in a state of emergency. The Executive Committee also decided to send to Tsaritsyn an armed detachment of soldiers and junkers, under the command of Neimichenko, Pontriagin, and the Bolshevik Sokolov. Because of this local military danger, the Soviet's Executive Committee eventually reached a compromise over the establishment of a committee to combat counterrevolution. In exchange for forming the committee under the Soviet, the Bolsheviks agreed to the representation outlined by the Duma. (The new committee mainly comprised representatives of organizations still under the influence of moderate socialists; the Bolsheviks nonetheless considered it a victory that the committee fell under the Soviet's jurisdiction.)[12]

Despite the emotional energies expended on establishing the Committee to Combat Counterrevolution, it met only once before disbanding. Afterward the Soviet once again functioned as the leading administrative organ in Saratov. Plenum meetings were called more often, at which Russia's political future was passionately debated. The tremendous impact of the threat of counterrevolution posed by Kornilov and by his supporters locally had resulted in a dramatic shift of many deputies toward the Bolshevik platform. When the Executive Committee met prior to a full plenum on August 31, moderates wanted to adopt a closed-door policy, but had to give in when it became clear that workers would "beat down the doors" if they were not allowed to observe the proceedings. A Soviet plenum then voted on rival resolutions, one drafted by the Bolsheviks, the other by the moderates. Even though the Bolshevik party was in the minority within the Soviet, its resolution won by a vote of 188 to 178.[13] This is the first time that a Bolshevik-sponsored policy statement on political tactics and power had captured a majority of votes at a plenum meeting. The document stressed the following points:

1. The main task of the democracy is the merciless struggle against all avowed and secret counterrevolutionaries, the close unification of real revolutionary forces, and the energetic rebuilding of Russia's economic and political order on new democratic principles.
2. Kornilov . . . and all participants in the counterrevolutionary conspiracies must be immediately arrested and brought to trial. The exile abroad of counterrevolutionaries is inadmissible. The State Duma and State Council must be abolished and all counterrevolutionary organs must be disbanded.

12. *Saratovskii Sovet*, pp. 190–91; *Proletarii Povolzh'ia*, no. 76, September 1, 1917, p. 4. See also Institut marksizma-leninizma pri TsK KPSS, *Perepiska sekretariata TsK RKP(b) s mestnymi partiinymi organizatsiiami* (Moscow, 1957), 1:185.
13. *Proletarii Povolzh'ia*, no. 80, September 2, 1917, pp. 3–4.

3. All attempts to conclude civil peace [*grazhdanskii mir*] with the counterrevolutionaries . . . must be rejected.
4. In the center and in the provinces organs of power capable of enjoying the complete trust of the revolutionary democracy, that is, of workers, soldiers, and the poorest peasants, must be formed as soon as possible.
5. The persecution of SD internationalists must be brought to a halt immediately, the arrested must be freed, and the suppression of revolutionary papers must be stopped.
6. All counterrevolutionary laws must be abolished, especially the death penalty . . . introduced under Kornilov, but only after it is used against its initiator.
7. The army must be reorganized on democratic principles. . . .
8. It is necessary to struggle decisively and unswervingly against the slanderous activity of the bourgeois newspapers and parties, aimed at the demoralization of the army and of the democracy. . . .[14]

Although of local provenance, the resolution reflected full awareness of the Bolshevik Central Committee's position, and called for convocation of a Second Congress of Soviets and for creation of a workers' armed guard.[15] The SR-Menshevik rival resolution contained some of the same points cited above, but it appealed to the population to accord full support to the Provisional Government, an idea conspicuously missing from the Bolshevik document. That same day the Petrograd Soviet passed a Bolshevik resolution similar to the one accepted in Saratov, but harsher in its condemnation of the Provisional Government. The Tsaritsyn Soviet carried a Bolshevik resolution on political power on September 8; the Astrakhan Soviet endorsed a Left SR resolution favoring Soviet power on September 2. Elsewhere in the region virtually every soviet passed resolutions condemning Kornilov. Particularly popular was the call for a transfer of power to the soviets and establishment of a "homogeneous government" (*odnorodnoe pravitel'stvo*) that excluded the propertied elements and included representation of all "democratically" elected institutions, such as trade unions, zemstvos, municipal dumas, and cooperatives, which were not nominally part of the All-Russian Executive Committee. Other soviets expressed their indignation with Kornilov while articulating their support of the Provisional Government and Central Executive Committee.[16] The wave of anti-Kornilov resolutions was not unique to the Volga area, then, but was manifested throughout most of the country. Democratic elements in most of Russia had rallied behind the Petrograd Soviet to prevent a conservative restoration.

14. *Saratovskii Sovet*, pp. 191–92.
15. *Proletarii Povolzh'ia*, no. 81, September 3, 1917, p. 4. The resolution can be found in Osipov, *1917 god v Saratove*, pp. 136–37.
16. Gerasimenko and Tochenyi, *Sovety Povolzh'ia*, pp. 153–57.

When we evaluate the response of Saratov Bolsheviks to the Kornilov threat, it is important to note that because some party leaders were still under arrest and Lenin could not be consulted directly, the only practical guide the party had was an ambiguous resolution on tactics adopted at the Sixth Congress in July. Adhering to these directives, Saratov Bolsheviks had joined other socialists to struggle against counterrevolution, but showed caution in cooperating with Mensheviks and SRs as long as they continued to support coalition with the bourgeoisie. In a sense, the Kornilov emergency both improved and exacerbated relations among Saratov socialists. The vote within the Soviet plenum on August 31 demonstrated that the growing factionalism had seized the SR and Menshevik ranks, and that left elements in both parties had come very close to siding openly with the Bolshevik position on critical issues. All in all, the Saratov Soviet's acceptance of a Bolshevik policy statement, with its implied call for an all-soviet socialist government, was the most salient indication to date of rising pro-Bolshevik sentiments locally.

The sympathetic response within the Soviet to Bolshevik resolutions continued during the first weeks of September as workers and soldiers elected new deputies to the council. The elections, which began on September 6, lasted one week. During this period it became clear that the moderate socialists' majority in the Soviet had melted away. When a full plenum convened on September 7 to reexamine the Bolshevik resolution passed on August 31, moderate socialists strove to amend the document. "It's necessary to save the country not only from Kornilov," injected the Menshevik Maizel', "but also from Wilhelm." However, deputies voted down the moderates' proposed amendment in support of coalition with the bourgeoisie at the national level. Arguing that "it is better to have an inexperienced officer-revolutionary in command than an experienced counterrevolutionary," Vasil'ev persuaded the deputies to reject pleas to block further democratization of the army. The plenum likewise defeated an amendment sponsored by the Mensheviks and SRs calling for a substitution of the proposed Second Congress of Soviets by the much-talked-about Democratic Conference. (A successor to the Moscow State Conference of August, the Democratic State Conference convened on September 14 to serve as a mediator between the Provisional Government and the nation until the Constituent Assembly was elected.) At the conclusion of the September 7 meeting the Saratov Soviet again overwhelmingly endorsed the Bolshevik resolution of August 31, this time by a vote of 139 to 28.[17] A few days later the entire SR Presidium of the Military Section resigned after soldiers passed a vote of no confidence in it.

17. Quoted in *Khronika*, pp. 110–11.

TABLE 8

Number of seats won and votes cast in elections to Workers' and Soldiers' sections of Saratov Soviet, September 1917, by party

Party	Total seats	Workers' Section		Soldiers' Section	
		Seats	Votes	Seats	Votes
Bolshevik	320	164	24,600	156	19,500
Menshevik	76	72	10,800	4	500
SR	103	43	6,450	60	9,000

Source: Compiled from V. P. Antonov-Saratovskii, *Pod stiagom proletarskoi bor'by: Otryvki iz vospominanii o rabote v Saratove* (Moscow and Leningrad, 1925), p. 145.

The appeal of Bolshevik resolutions in the aftermath of the Kornilov Affair foreshadowed the party's subsequent victory in elections to the Soviet, making the Saratov Soviet one of the first after Petrograd and Moscow to go Bolshevik. As a result of the balloting, the Bolsheviks won a majority in the Soviet. In the Workers' Section Bolshevik gains represented a loss for the Mensheviks, but not an overwhelming one. (At the end of June the Workers' Section had included 98 Bolsheviks, 97 Mensheviks, and 50 SRs.) A more stunning reversal was registered in the Soldiers' Section. In June the SRs had had five times as many deputies as the Bolsheviks. Now the Bolsheviks had captured 156 seats and the SRs only 60 (see Table 8). Reelections to soviets in Tsaritsyn, Samara, Nikolaevsk, and Syzran also gave majorities to the Bolsheviks. Even in towns where elections were not held, the Bolsheviks' position strengthened. In Astrakhan, for example, the local soviet's executive committee reorganized to take into account the changing composition of the rank-and-file deputies and now included all Left SRs and Bolsheviks.

The Soviet election results in Saratov reflected a revolution in local attitudes: by fall most Saratov workers and soldiers expressed sympathy for Bolshevik and other internationalist slogans. The fabric of local politics increasingly revealed the growing appeal of the call for the creation of an all-soviet, exclusively socialist government. And, while the mood of the masses had been shifting to the left before the threat of a counterrevolutionary movement, the Kornilov Affair had jolted public opinion, pushing it even further away from moderation. Lebedev admitted that the Kornilov Affair "with one stroke won back for us the sympathies of the masses." Antonov wrote that it had "electrified" the population. The Menshevik Maiskii noted a similar shift in public opinion elsewhere in the country. "I am hardly mistaken if I say that the present moment is in the hands of Bolshevism," wrote Maiskii. "General Kornilov rendered the latter a truly priceless service."[18] Maiskii argued that economic and

18. *Proletarii Povolzh'ia,* no. 97, September 24, 1917, p. 2.

financial ruin caused by the war had contributed to the growing Bolshevik tide, too. Yet, while Kornilov's conspiracy and the faltering economy surely deserve much credit for the public's swing to the left, one must not overlook the extent to which the political programs of the moderate socialists had been compromised. No matter how sympathetically one looks at the dilemma they faced, the moderates shared the blame for the growing emergency in the country at large. There was no easy or perhaps even entirely peaceful solution to Russia's political crisis after the Kornilov Affair. Paralyzed by both their theoretical conception of the revolutionary process and their understandable unwillingness to refute their policies since February, the leaders of the moderate socialist parties now more than ever before had to come to grips with the difficult question as to whether they should continue their cooperation with census society.

The suspicious role of prominent Kadet politicians in the Kornilov episode had brought about a short-lived period of camaraderie between the Bolsheviks and moderate socialists in Petrograd as well as Saratov. But the Bolshevik victory in elections to the local soviet doomed the renewed good feelings. At the very first plenum meeting held after elections were concluded, deputies passed a Bolshevik resolution stating that the much-acclaimed Democratic Conference "cannot inspire unconditional trust in the real revolutionary democracy."[19] From this point on the Bolsheviks could confidently count on carrying their policy statements through the plenums. The Soviet's executive organs were also in Bolshevik hands. The presidium of the Military Section included ten Bolsheviks and five SRs and was chaired by the Bolshevik second lieutenant Sokolov. On September 21 the Soviet selected a joint presidium on the principle of proportional representation, which gave the Bolsheviks a clear but not overwhelming majority. According to Lebedev, "the SRs wanted to elect Antonov chairman because he seemed to them more moderate [than Vasil'ev]. We did not object to Antonov and subsequent events would convince the SRs completely that 'between two evils 'tis not worth choosing' [*khren red'ki ne slashche*]."[20] Vasil'ev, Lebedev, and Pontriagin became chairmen of the Executive Bureau and the Bolshevik Kirill Plaksin now chaired the Workers' Section. The Executive Committee contained eighteen Bolsheviks, eight SRs, and four Mensheviks. At this same session Maizel' warned that the SRs and Mensheviks, because of their minority standing, would form an opposition "mercilessly critical of those measures that we consider incorrect."[21]

19. *Izvestiia Saratovskogo Soveta*, no. 83, September 19, 1917, p. 3.
20. Lebedev, "Fevral'–oktiabr'," p. 249.
21. Gerasimenko, *Sovety Nizhnego Povolzh'ia*, pp. 85–87.

Their base in the Soviet undermined, the moderates clung stubbornly to their Duma majority; the city council met more often in September than it had during the preceding months.

Because Antonov left with the armed detachment sent to Tsaritsyn, much of the Executive Committee's work fell on Lebedev and Vasil'ev. Assessing the political situation that developed in Saratov in September, Lebedev noted that the Bolshevik position got more difficult. "We were the ruling party, but we could do nothing because we had no power." Meanwhile, the masses of soldiers and workers became more impatient. A three-member Bureau of the Executive Committee, comprised of two Bolsheviks and the Menshevik Chertkov, spent entire days in the Executive Committee. "The masses turned to us to resolve problems whenever it was necessary 'to use power,'" wrote Lebedev, "but Chertkov was constantly on the alert with us. . . . It was felt that there must be some sort of major change, otherwise the masses would lose their faith in us and would take the initiative or else would cool."[22] Studies of the October Revolution ignore such political impasses, which developed in many provincial towns during late summer and early fall of 1917, and thereby fail to show the extent to which provincial developments came to bear on events in the capital. The form the political crisis took at the local level by fall, combined with the radicalization of the provincial urban population, attracted the attention of the Bolshevik Central Committee, and especially of Lenin, who now cited local affairs to add force to his own arguments. The government's impotence was certainly no secret to anyone. The Ministry of Internal Affairs even issued a circular to all provincial commissars in early September admitting that "the government and its local organs are powerless to preserve order."[23] Meanwhile, at the beginning of September, 126 provincial soviets sent messages to the All-Russian Executive Committee demanding it seize power and establish an all-soviet government.[24]

The growing clamor for the establishment of a soviet government at this time paralleled the total disarray of most Volga-area Socialist Revolutionary and Menshevik party organizations. As in the capital, SR organizations were deeply split among left, center, and right factions. By September the Left SRs could be considered a separate party, siding with the Bolsheviks on the most controversial issues, such as the establishment of an all-soviet government and immediate seizure of land by the peasantry. Factionalism struck Menshevik committees as well. Reacting to the popular mood, leftist elements in both parties joined with the Bolsheviks in urging the exclusion of the propertied elements from the

22. Lebedev, "Fevral'–oktiabr'," pp. 249–50.
23. Gerasimenko and Tochenyi, *Sovety Nizhnego Povolzh'ia*, p. 157.
24. Zakharov, *Sovety Srednego Povolzh'ia*, p. 149.

First Bolshevized Provincial Executive Committee, September 1917

new government. Fearing civil war and even greater social tension, the moderate Menshevik and SR leaders continued to shore up the coalition with the bourgeoisie. To repeat, to have done otherwise would have conflicted with their theoretical conceptualization that the revolution was still in a bourgeois and not a socialist phase, and also with the policies they had followed since February. Continued participation in a coalition government, however, discredited these parties even more in the eyes of the masses and deepened the splits in their own ranks.

In Saratov, home of the SR party, the local committee's activities decreased dramatically, a development that was reflected in the committee's appeal to members to support the newspaper *Zemlia i volia,* which was so short of funds that it was threatened with closure. Six months earlier the paper had boasted the widest circulation in the province. In Kazan the Left SR–led soviet passed a resolution calling for a transfer of power to the soviets. Left SRs likewise consolidated their position within the Astrakhan Soviet. Reacting to Kerensky's intent to form yet another coalition with the middle classes, the organ of the Penza Socialist Revolutionary committee queried: "What are you doing, Comrade Kerensky? We've been patient for a long time, we've been silent for a long time, but now we've had it!" In Syzran party membership plunged from 900 in June to fewer than 100 in September. Virtually everywhere along the Volga, as in much of the rest of the country, party committees experienced declining enrollments and growing inactivity. The same scenario holds true for local Menshevik organizations. Menshevik Left-Internationalists formed a separate organization in Saratov under the leadership of A. Dimant, who blamed the leaders of the moderate socialist parties and the revolutionary democracy itself for the Kornilov Affair. Separate Left-Internationalist factions broke off from the city organizations in Samara and Syzran as well. The Samara Menshevik Internationalists called for a transfer of power to the soviets. Even the centrist committees in Tsaritsyn, Saratov, and Samara articulated their opposition to further cooperation with the bourgeoisie.[25]

Leftist elements in Volga-area SR and Menshevik organizations, and in some cases centrist elements too, expressed hopes that the Democratic State Conference would create a homogeneous socialist government (*odnorodnoe sotsialisticheskoe pravitel'stvo*). On September 18 the Astrakhan Soviet carried a "Bolshevik" resolution on power which amounted to a local, hybrid interpretation of the party's program. According to the document—which reflected public opinion in much of the Volga region—power at the national level was to pass to the All-Russian Executive Committee of the Petrograd Soviet while at the local level

25. Gerasimenko and Tochenyi, *Sovety Nizhnego Povolzh'ia,* pp. 158–70.

power was to remain in the hands of soviets, unions, dumas, and other "democratically" elected organs (which might contain bourgeois elements). As it turned out, in a close vote the Democratic Conference accepted the idea of coalition, but then passed a confusing amendment calling for the exclusion of the Kadets from any future government. When Kerensky afterward formed a cabinet that included Kadets, Volga socialists expressed their dismay. The chairman of the Tsaritsyn Menshevik city committee called the conference's decision a mistake and later demanded that Mensheviks withdraw from the new government. Saratov's N. Kapitanovskii, a member of the Menshevik committee, concluded that "it's impossible to create an organ of power unconditionally authoritative for the entire population, for all classes."[26]

It may well have been too late to ward off civil war in Russia. Judging from the November election results to the Constituent Assembly, local public opinion had moved toward the political extremes at the expense of the moderate parties during the second half of 1917. While the ranks of radical Russian socialism swelled at this time, the Kadet party attracted an influx of recruits, too, many of whom had come to reject Russian populism. In general, the large percentage of nonparty elements began to dry up as people began to choose sides and change sides, and as parties realigned. Take this one unusual example. Considering itself "socialist" in orientation, a new Old Believers' Democratic party was organized in Saratov in the middle of September by disgruntled "left Kadets and right Popular Socialists."[27]

An examination of the economic background against which the Kornilov plot hatched and ran its course goes far toward explaining the burgeoning militancy of the local working class. It also shows the degree to which a new set of revolutionary processes, reflected in the rising visibility of extremist groups, now determined political outcomes. Newspaper accounts suggest that threats of hunger and unemployment were the greatest problems facing the civilian population of Saratov in the late summer and early fall of 1917. At this point in the revolution the issues of Russia's political future and economic recovery became tightly entwined.

The food crisis worsened in September because the agrarian movement had gained momentum. Saratov peasants became more reluctant than before to market their crops as the terms of trade became even less advantageous for them. The Saratov Food-Supply Commission informed the Food-Supply Ministry and the Democratic Conference that "Saratov

26. Ibid., pp. 167–78.
27. *Proletarii Povolzh'ia*, no. 90, September 16, 1917, p. 4.

is on the eve of disorders owing to lack of grain and flour. The hope of securing rye for the city from Samara province is vanishing because of bad transportation and exhausted reserves in the provinces."[28] Local governments throughout the country took care of their own needs first before filling government orders. While pressuring Samara to send grain southward, Saratov failed to supply other regions of the empire. As one local official admitted, Saratov had sufficient reserves to last until October only because the local "food-supply administration had categorically refused to fulfill ministerial orders for the month of July" and thereby "succeeded in avoiding the critical situation in which we would have otherwise found ourselves."[29] Agents of the city's food-supply administration sent to the countryside to purchase grain reported that their efforts were obstructed because "volost committees are not allowing peasants to sell grain."[30] At each administrative level, officials acted to ward off local hunger first.

Uncertainty over who had the authority to deal with food shortages contributed to the crisis. Elections to the Soviet had resulted in a break in the council's attempts to handle food supplies. In the meantime, the Duma sought to cope with shortages by creating its own food-supply department. But by the time the city's Food-Supply Assembly agreed to this move, the newly elected Soviet had convened and had set up a special food-supply department under the Soviet's jurisdiction. This department supervised the activities of the Food-Supply Assembly and of the Duma's new department. Vasil'ev served as go-between for the different bodies. By the end of the month the Soviet had taken several steps out of desperation. It ordered the Food-Supply Assembly to speed up its inventory taking and notified the Democratic Conference and the Provisional Government about the threatening situation in the provinces. The Soviet petitioned the national government to rescind the law doubling the fixed procurement price on grain, arguing that it was an inflationary measure, and tried to scotch rumors about an imminent pogrom. It locked up criminal elements and prevented soldier speculators from selling grain on the black market.[31] It also searched flour mills, warehouses, and private homes for caches of food.[32]

Taking advantage of the economic hardships to discredit the government, rightist agitators became more active than at any other time since February. Throughout September rumors about impending "counter-

28. Ibid., no. 98, September 26, 1917, p. 4.

29. *Saratovskii vestnik*, no. 209, September 22, 1917, p. 3.

30. *Proletarii Povolzh'ia*, no. 99, September 28, 1917, p. 3.

31. *Izvestiia Saratovskogo Soveta*, no. 85, September 26, 1917, p. 3.

32. P. S., comp., "Khronika Oktiabr'skoi revoliutsii v Saratove," *Kommunisticheskii put'*, no. 19 (1927), p. 36.

revolutionary pogroms" circulated widely in Saratov, and attracted attention in the national press as well.[33] Editors of *Proletarii Povolzh'ia* argued that it was necessary to organize dependable cadres of devoted people for the struggle with anarchy on the right, because in the "taverns of the upper bazaar region, at the open markets, the Stock Exchange, and the shipping exchange, agitation is being conducted by shady individuals without a doubt furnished with instructions by counterrevolutionaries from the merchant-industrial class."[34] The Saratov branch of the "All-Russian Central Committee of Onward for the Tsar and for Holy Russia" and related pro-monarchy groups that had threatened the lives of leading Saratov socialists in the spring and summer appear to have been responsible for this agitation in the fall of 1917. According to the report Maizel' submitted to the Duma, the pogrom was to be directed at local Jews.[35] Speculating that the rumors were exaggerated, Maizel' nonetheless cautioned that it was necessary to deal with them, as they could "create favorable ground for excesses." One Saratov Jew claimed that the "anti-Semitic mood is stronger here than it was in 1905, thanks to the flood of refugees."[36] Further, Topuridze reported that he had received "extremely threatening news" that elsewhere in the province, especially in the uezd towns, "gangs of criminal elements" had formed.[37] Bread shortages had sparked several days of violent rioting in neighboring Astrakhan.

At the other end of the political spectrum were local anarchist groups that now called for an armed uprising against the government, appealing to the townspeople to seize private houses and factories. The anarchists briefly managed to publish a journal at the end of September, *Golos anarkhii* (Voice of Anarchy), which provides interesting details about this otherwise elusive political force in Saratov politics. After the Kornilov Affair, three Saratov anarchist factions, including the Saratov Revolutionary Group of Anarchist-Communists, formed a Free Association of Anarchist Groups of the City of Saratov, which published *Golos anarkhii*. The association received subsidies from the "Samara Group of Anarchist-Communists."[38] Under the title "What the Bolsheviks Are Holding Back," the lead article in one issue criticized Bolshevik policies since February as too moderate and advocated instead decisive militant action. Other sources shed little light on the size and political role of the Saratov anarchists at this time, but the Soviet's concern over their agita-

33. *Delo naroda* (Petrograd), no. 158, September 19, 1917, p. 4.
34. *Proletarii Povolzh'ia*, no. 76, September 1, 1917, p. 4.
35. *Saratovskii vestnik*, no. 160, July 21, 1917, p. 3; no. 211, September 24, p. 5.
36. "Pis'ma E. A. Abramovicha," p. 149.
37. *Proletarii Povolzh'ia*, no. 97, September 25, 1917, p. 4.
38. *Golos anarkhii*, no. 2, September 21, 1917, pp. 1–8.

tion suggests that popular sentiments were becoming increasingly flammable.

Apart from food shortages, a swollen crime rate, speculation, and extremist agitation, epidemics of typhoid fever and venereal disease broke out in September. A laboratory report concluded that "typhoid is spreading in connection with the extreme pollution of the city, which forces the population to live in extraordinarily unsanitary conditions." Although the city provided free preventive inoculations, an epidemic of such proportions had not broken out in Saratov in twenty-two years.[39] Moreover, a "League for the Battle against Venereal Disease" was formed in Saratov in August.

It is probably safe to assume that economic insecurity and a declining living standard deepened Saratov workers' suspicion of the government and of its involvement with Kornilov. On August 28 the Menshevik M. I. Skobelev, minister of labor, had abrogated the factory committees' right to monitor hiring and firing practices, returning such prerogatives to the owners. A second ministerial circular forbade factory committees to meet during work hours. Reconfirming the rights of local factory committees, the Saratov Organizational Bureau condemned the Provisional Government's edicts. Coming on the eve of Kornilov's march on Petrograd, Skobelev's measures guaranteed an emotional response to the threat of counterrevolution. When news of Kornilov's intentions reached Saratov, factory meetings passed resolutions condemning him and counterrevolutionary activities. Most resolutions demanded the transfer of power to the soviets without further delay, and voiced disapproval over coalition with the bourgeoisie. On August 30 delegates representing more than 1,000 local railroad workers carried a Bolshevik resolution calling for "the merciless punishment of Kornilov . . . the immediate dispersal of the State Duma, State Council, and all counterrevolutionary organizations . . . the speedy arming of workers . . . the reorganization of power on the basis of union among workers, soldiers, and the poorest peasantry, [and] the taking of decisive measures for putting the economic life of the country in order."[40] During the first week of September Saratov workers continued to pass resolutions advocating the arming of workers, dissolution of the State Duma, and the transfer of power to the soviets. Typical was the resolution of 400 workers employed at the Bushkov lumberyards, who insisted on the reorganization of political power "with the aim of pulling the rug out from under the feet of the counterrevolution, which still is feeding on economic ruin, of putting the eco-

39. *Saratovskii vestnik*, no. 202, September 13, 1917, p. 3; *Proletarii Povolzh'ia*, no. 99, September 28, 1917, p. 3; and *Saratovskii listok*, no. 169, August 3, 1917, p. 3.

40. *Sotsial-Demokrat*, no. 63, September 3, 1917, p. 4; see also Osipov, *1917 god v Saratove*, pp. 134–35, and *Khronika*, p. 105.

nomic life of the country into order in a decisive manner, and of taking the most concrete measures in the struggle for peace." Workers at the Zhest factory urged the prompt closing of all bourgeois newspapers and the abolition of the death penalty after it had been used on Kornilov. Factory committees, trade unions, and medical funds in Saratov, Tsaritsyn, Volsk, and Petrovsk issued statements that they would ignore Skobelev's recent legislation limiting the rights of factory committees.[41]

The threat to the revolution posed by Kornilov made conditions favorable for the creation of an armed workers' guard in Saratov. Since February factory committees at some enterprises had formed various factory police units, workers' police, and armed guards *(druzhiny)* that reported directly to the Soviet. Now, responding to appeals and resolutions emanating from workers themselves, the Bolsheviks supported the idea of a Red Guard while the moderate socialists demurred, regarding the move as a threat to their own security. Lebedev appears to have spearheaded the process, using as models Red Guard units that had formed in Petrograd and Moscow. Because elections to the Soviet had not yet commenced (and it was therefore still in the hands of moderates), Lebedev took his plans to the factory committees, which endorsed them wholeheartedly. On September 3 he presented his proposal, which stressed that the armed workers would be totally subordinated to the Soviet and its Executive Committee for approval.[42] Only the most "dependable and prepared workers" with the recommendation of their factory committees, trade unions, or party organizations would be allowed to join the guard.[43] On September 7 a full plenum accepted the proposal worked out by Lebedev and the Executive Committee. Arguing that the soldiers already represented a reliable armed force, the moderate socialists opposed formation of a Red Guard.[44] Their intentions to strengthen the municipal police force instead, however, came to nought for lack of financial resources.[45]

That same day *Sotsial-Demokrat* appealed to workers to form armed guards to combat counterrevolution. "In Saratov, in view of the proximity of the Don [River] region, where counterrevolutionary actions are possible," read the call to arms, "*the creation of a workers' guard is*

41. V. G. Khodakov, "Rabochii kontrol'," pp. 70–71; Osipov, *1917 god v Saratove*, pp. 147–48.

42. A. V. Afanas'ev, "Iz istorii organizatsii Krasnoi gvardii v g. Saratove (sentiabr'–oktiabr' 1917 g.)," *Povolzhskii krai*, no. 4 (1975), p. 139. See also N. V. Afanas'ev, "Ustanovlenie Sovetskoi vlasti v Saratove," in *Iz istorii Velikoi Oktiabr'skoi revoliutsii i sotsialisticheskogo stroitel'stva: Sbornik statei*, ed. V. B. Ostrovskii (Saratov, 1958), p. 67; and Medvedev, "Saratovskii Sovet," p. 78.

43. *Saratovskii Sovet*, p. 196.

44. Afanas'ev, "Iz istorii organizatsii Krasnoi gvardii," p. 140.

45. *Saratovskii vestnik*, no. 203, September 14, 1917, p. 3.

A Saratov Red Guard unit, 1917 (staff headquarters in background)

especially important."[46] It bears repeating that because of Kaledin's maneuvers in the Don area, the resulting declaration of martial law in the Kazan Military District, Korvin-Krukovskii's shady behavior in Tsaritsyn, and the declaration of a state of emergency in Saratov province, the perceived threat of an armed counterrevolutionary movement was greater locally than in much of provincial Russia. As a result, Saratov workers responded enthusiastically to the call to arms. The Zhest factory contributed 3,000 rubles to the armed guard, and by the end of September 150 workers from the factory had joined the paramilitary organization.[47] By September 28 the Red Guard had enrolled 600 workers and by October 25 an estimated 2,500. A Bolshevik who recently had returned from exile, A. A. Fedorov, directed the units. The largest contingents were from the railroad workers, the Bering factory, and shore workers. Workers at the Mercury factory, the Levkovich tobacco plant, and butter creamery workers also formed armed units. The railroad workers had an independent branch of the Red Guard led by the Bolshevik I. P. Erasov, which was generally considered the best unit in Saratov.[48]

Most units appear to have conducted fairly regular training with the help of the Military Section of the Soviet, the Bolshevik Military Organization, and soldier instructors, many of whom, according to E. D. Rumiantsev, were frontoviki.[49] Shortage of weapons limited the size of the Red Guard. The Zhest factory, for example, announced that instead of the 150 workers enrolled in its contingent, it could have had 1,000 members if more weapons had been available. Requests for additional rifles and pistols were sent to the Moscow Soviet and then to Petrograd, but neither was able to help. Apart from the problems stemming from lack of arms, owners of small enterprises and the manager of the government stable created obstacles to the formation of armed workers' bands at their enterprises.[50]

The importance of the creation of a Red Guard in Saratov should not be underestimated. The overwhelming majority of units were set up at factories that were solidly pro-Bolshevik, and thereby provided the party with a reliable armed force. Local Bolshevik leaders simply could not count on the loyalty of the local garrison, not only because of the soldiers' recent conversion to Bolshevism but also because of their lack of discipline. During the October Revolution, Bolshevik leaders would turn

46. Afanas'ev, "Iz istorii organizatsii Krasnoi gvardii," p. 140; emphasis mine.
47. Afanas'ev, "Ustanovlenie Sovetskoi vlasti v Saratove," p. 68.
48. Petrov, "Saratovskii proletariat," p. 13.
49. E. D. Rumiantsev, "K voprosu o voennom obuchenii Krasnoi gvardii v Povolzh'e (osen' 1917 g.)," in *Sbornik aspirantskikh rabot*, no. 74, *Gumanitarnye nauki: Istoriia, pedagogika* (Kazan, 1973), p. 79.
50. Afanas'ev, "Iz istorii organizatsii Krasnoi gvardii," p. 142.

to their armed workers and special garrison units while seeking to keep the majority of troops off the streets. The Saratov Red Guardsmen likewise played a role in preserving order and in protecting property. In fact, they often were stationed at key points where soldiers already had been standing guard—hardly a vote of confidence in the garrison. When rumors about imminent pogroms and riots circulated in the city in September, "the Red Guard was summoned and it demonstrably marched through the streets; in a word, with its very presence it instilled absolute certainty that no pogroms would be allowed." Upon seeing the Red Guard maneuvering in front of the building where the Executive Committee of the Soviet met, the Menshevik leader Maizel' purportedly exclaimed, "This is the real revolution!"[51]

The formation of a Red Guard and the unprecedented disorder in the garrison may have made local workers more militant in their own economic demands. In Saratov and Tsaritsyn the strike movement picked up momentum during late September and early October, prompting the Kadet newspaper to call it "the most alarming fact of local life."[52] Usually owners' refusals to meet workers' demands for higher wages and better work conditions sparked the strikes. In September workers from Saratov's lumberyard, railroad yards, nail factory, flour mills, and metal-processing plants went on strike, and white-collar workers employed by city agencies threatened to walk out. The strikes at the city's flour mills and railroad shops were the most serious. Toward the end of the month mill owners formed a union of their own, which announced that as of October 1, 1,500 workers would be dismissed.[53] No settlement was reached with the Soviet or trade union before the end of September. The railroad strike, which broke out on September 24, was part of a national drive for higher wages. When the strike ended on other lines on September 26–27, Saratov workers voted "to continue to strike until the question had been completely settled."[54] Ignoring the call by Vikzhel (the All-Russian Executive Committee of Railway Workers), the local committee decided to inform all railroad stations of its decision to prolong the strike and to take over the leadership of those lines that might be encouraged to go out. Some Menshevik workers blocked the dispatch of the telegrams and three days later the local strike fizzled out.[55] Such militancy rarely had been displayed during the preceding months. In all, approximately

51. Lebedev, "Fevral'–oktiabr'," pp. 250–51.

52. Quoted in V. A. Osipov, ed., *Istoriia Saratovskogo kraia, 1590–1917: Khrestomatiia v pomoshch' uchiteliu istorii* (Saratov, 1967), 2:9.

53. V. G. Khodakov, "Bor'ba rabochikh Saratovskoi gubernii," p. 113.

54. *Khronika*, p. 119. For background to the national strike see William G. Rosenberg, "The Democratization of Russia's Railroads in 1917," *American Historical Review*, 86, no. 5 (1981), 983–1008.

55. I. Z. Erasov, "Nakanune oktiabria," in *V boiakh za diktaturu proletariata*, p. 6.

20 strikes involving more than 2,000 workers erupted in Saratov at this time.

The Kornilov Affair affected the soldiers' attitudes even more than those of workers. From early July evacuated soldiers as well as troops transferred from Tsaritsyn had created an easily ignitable situation in the Saratov garrison, which contributed locally to a growth in pro-Bolshevik sentiment in August. The rank-and-file soldiers' suspicion of the command structure had heightened just when it moved toward reviving the fighting capacity of the country's armed forces. At the First District Congress of Soldiers' Soviets of the Volga and Ural Regions, which took place in Kazan during the first three weeks of August, Bolsheviks, Left SRs, and Menshevik Internationalists had formed a left-socialist bloc that advocated the creation of an all-soviet government. Then came the Kornilov movement, which from the common soldier's point of view represented a return to former codes of discipline and a continuation of the hated war. Many soldiers also intuitively understood that a military dictatorship would have relied on the army to suppress the urban revolution. Sent under emergency orders to Tsaritsyn and Nikolaevsk "to defend the revolution" against Kaledin in the heat of the Kornilov episode, local soldiers returned to Saratov infused with a determination to protect their own interests. In the first week of September soldiers demanded more Bolshevik literature and complained that their SR Soviet deputies were not reporting on the Soviet's activities.[56] On September 7, 4,000 soldiers voiced their distrust of the Provisional Government, demanding an end to the war, the transfer of power to the soviets, the dissolution of the State Duma, and the release of all imprisoned Bolsheviks. On September 11, six regiments numbering about 4,000 soldiers combined passed a resolution expressing their distrust of the head of the Soldiers' Section of the Soviet, the SR Didenko, and insisting that he be sent to the front. Interpreting the troops' attack on Didenko as a rejection of the presidium of the Military Section in general, its members resigned. When the full Executive Committee of the Soviet met the next day, however, it resolved that the meeting of 4,000 soldiers "did not represent the mood of the organized garrison of 30,000," and then gave its full support to the presidium of the Soldiers' Section until its term ran out in three days. To compound the Soviet leaders' dilemma during their last hours in office, soldiers over forty years old began to call for their prompt demobilization.[57]

56. *Sotsial-Demokrat*, no. 64, September 7, 1917, p. 1.

57. *Saratovskii vestnik*, no. 205, September 17, 1917, p. 4; *Proletarii Povolzh'ia*, no. 90, September 16, 1917, p. 4; no. 94, September 21, p. 4; *Khronika*, p. 114; *Saratovskii Sovet*, p. 199.

The soldiers emerged from the Kornilov crisis radicalized, but not as stalwart Bolsheviks. Expecting expedient solutions to their demands, the soldiers challenged the Bolsheviks to implement their political promises. The uncertainty of party debates in Petrograd on tactics and the two weeks of discontinuity within the Soviet as it reorganized limited the Bolshevik leadership's ability to act swiftly and decisively enough for the soldiers. They became even more restless. The Fourth Machine-Gun Regiment is a case in point. Although a Bolshevik stronghold in the garrison since spring, it threatened to disobey orders if short furloughs were not granted. Bolshevik leaders patiently explained to the troops that the matter of leaves had to be decided by military authorities in Kazan, by the Central Executive Committee, and by the war ministry. Realizing the implications of the soldiers' frustrations, the Saratov Soviet cabled the center that the Soviet backed the local soldiers' demands in view of decisions to grant leaves within the Petrograd and Moscow military districts. "In the name of fairness the Soviet supports the granting of furloughs," read the cable. "A negative answer to the request for leaves would undoubtedly evoke undesirable excesses."[58]

By the end of September it seemed to much of the civilian population that the soldiers had de facto control of the city. Ignoring appeals published by the Soviet, soldiers plundered gardens, harassed citizens, hectored shop clerks, and contributed to the growing crime wave reported by the local press. With the advent of cold weather, the soldiers were itching to move from their dilapidated barracks into the city. A health commissioner reported that in the army hospital "it is so cold that water freezes; in the walls there are cracks two fingers wide, from insects there is no salvation, and the walls and ceilings are covered with dirt."[59] By mid-September the Soviet discussed the resettlement of soldiers each time it met. No easy solutions presented themselves, and since the townspeople feared the consequences of moving the soldiers into the city, no action had been taken by the end of the month. Pontriagin suggested that the school for daughters of the nobility be expropriated to billet soldiers. Neimichenko reasoned that it would be better to take over several large department stores that were about to shut down (owing to the lack of goods?).[60]

As October approached, the city in a practical sense found itself at the mercy of the soldiers. On September 29, 1917, the Saratov prosecutor of the court of appeals addressed the following letter to the minister of justice. His call for help is given in detail here because it so aptly captures the predicament of local civilian authorities:

58. P. S., "Khronika," no. 19 (1927), p. 36.
59. *Saratovskii vestnik*, no. 216, October 1, 1917, p. 5.
60. *Saratovskii Sovet*, p. 210.

Machine gunners, Thirty-second Division, Saratov, 1917

> I deem it my duty to inform you that the city of Saratov, and the whole Saratov district in general, finds itself at the present time in a very painful situation; in all probability the situation will shortly become even worse.
>
> The main evil against which there is no means to fight is the soldiers who . . . are the irresponsible masters of the situation. Crimes, lynchings, arbitrary arrests and searches, all kind of requisitions—all this in the majority of cases is being carried out by soldiers. . . .
>
> The *guberniya* authorities and public organizations are partly powerless to fight them, partly they do not fight evidently because they are afraid of losing their popularity. . . .
>
> At the present time two calamities are threatening Saratov: the general searches of all the inhabitants and the resettlement in the city of the soldiers from the barracks situated beyond the city.
>
> Having learned from the guberniya commissar that it has been decided to carry out within the next days a general search of the inhabitants of the city of Saratov, I deemed it my duty to intervene in a most emphatic way with reference to the existing laws. . . . The result of my intervention was that it has been decided to carry out the search only in the houses of those persons with regard to whom there is information that they concealed goods and products for . . . speculation. However, in spite of this, I am almost convinced that these searches will finally turn into pogroms. . . .
>
> On the other hand the guberniya commissar possesses neither authority nor power, and therefore, in his own words, he is not able to prevent the searches.
>
> The matter stands similarly with regard to the resettlement of the soldiers in the city: the soldiers have declared that they would appear in the city and would occupy the apartments they like. If they desire to do this, then I am convinced that no one will be able to prevent them.
>
> I have informed the commander of the troops of this, but probably Saratov cannot expect any help from this side.
>
> Matters are in no better shape in the uezd capitals and in the villages; the same demands . . . and the same complete absence of any kind of assistance to the judicial administration.[61]

Reports in the official publication of the Kazan Military Committee substantiate the Saratov prosecutor's observations and reveal that this situation was common throughout the district and probably in others as well. Soldiers sought to sequester town buildings in Glazovo, Penza, and elsewhere. In the Nikolaevsk garrison, the newspaper informed readers, "discipline is lacking, training is shoddy, and some of the soldiers walk about drunk." Soldiers in Petrovsk murdered an army officer sent from the Simbirsk Cavalry Reserves. During a search for deserters a few days later, shots were fired by a certain Telnov at the troops conducting the the towns had certainly influenced peasant rhetoric, as soldiers from the

61. Robert P. Browder and Alexander F. Kerensky, eds., *The Russian Provisional Government, 1917: Documents* (Stanford, 1961), 3:1644–45.

roundups. "One soldier was killed, another was wounded. The agitated soldiers then killed Telnov and roasted his body on a campfire." Reliable troops from Atkarsk were sent to Serdobsk to quell riots after the district commissar requested the government to declare martial law. In Balashov soldiers of the Ninety-seventh and Ninety-eighth regiments demanded to be demobilized and sent home. Soldiers there also seized the post and telegraph and released imprisoned Bolsheviks. In the Simbirsk and Syzran garrisons soldiers defiantly refused to go to the front. Throughout the Volga area the over-forty's challenged orders to return to their units. The situation in the army at this time proved fertile ground for the cultivation of Bolshevik ideas. Nevertheless, it bears repeating that the soldiers' sympathies remained highly impressionable and that their behavior created enormous problems for all civil authority even after power had passed to the soviets.[62]

The Kornilov Affair had the same jarring effect on political developments in Tsaritsyn. Even before Kornilov's threat, the unpopular policies of Korvin-Krukovskii had created a complicated political situation there. He upheld restrictions on public meetings, enforced censorship, and ignored requests from the Tsaritsyn Soviet to clarify his position. As in Saratov, monarchist groups became more active in town; the Bund soon complained that anti-Semitic feelings were on the rise. Industrialists began to ignore factory committees at a time when the townspeople faced growing economic difficulties. Sources suggest that the population experienced greater food shortages and a decline in real wages.[63]

The smoldering social unrest in Tsaritsyn even prompted the moderate socialists to reevaluate their previous acquiescence to Korvin-Krukovskii's measures. The SRs and Mensheviks demanded the detachment's withdrawal. On August 15 the Tsaritsyn Soviet declared the Moscow State Conference counterrevolutionary and called for a protest strike. On the eve of the strike, Korvin-Krukovskii arrested the entire strike committee. The next day 35,000 workers refused to go to work; most of the city's factories, stores, and offices closed and all activity on the docks and riverfront came to an abrupt halt. Workers' representatives declared that if the arrested were not released and if the detachment did not quit Tsaritsyn, the workers would continue their strike. This announcement prompted one Bolshevik to comment that "workers are not

62. *Izvestiia Kazanskogo Voenno-okruzhnogo Komiteta*, no. 93, September 16, 1917, p. 4; no. 94, September 17, p. 3; no. 102, September 30, p. 4.

63. Romanov and Sokolov, *Ocherk istorii revoliutsii*, pp. 51–52, 56, 63–64; Ovrutskaia, "Proval politiki," p. 372; *Izvestiia Kazanskogo Voenno-okruzhnogo Komiteta*, no. 77, August 25, 1917, pp. 2–3.

following the soviet, but are acting independently." On August 23 the soviet wired the minister of war that "it will be almost impossible to restrain the workers' excitement if the detachment is not recalled from Tsaritsyn immediately."[64]

The Saratov Soviet also reconsidered its attitude toward Korvin-Krukovskii and in the weeks before the Kornilov Affair it, too, concluded that the detachment had to be withdrawn from Tsaritsyn. The very discussion within the Soviet of an armed counterrevolutionary threat strained tempers in Saratov, and probably contributed to the sharp anti-Kornilov reaction in the city. On August 18 Telegin reported on his experience in Tsaritsyn to the Executive Committee of the Soviet. Following his sharp criticism of Korvin-Krukovskii, the Soviet adopted a resolution insisting on the speedy departure of the detachment from Tsaritsyn, the dismissal of Korvin-Krukovskii from the Saratov Soviet and as head of the local cadet school, and the release of Minin and other arrested Bolsheviks. Furthermore, the Soviet agreed that if Korvin-Krukovskii were shown to have overstepped his authority, he would be brought to trial.[65] One other reason for demanding the recall of the armed detachment was the upcoming elections to the Tsaritsyn Duma and Soviet. There was every reason to believe that Korvin-Krukovskii would interfere in the voting process.

While crowds in the streets were discussing the first reports on Kornilov's movements, voters cast ballots for deputies to the city duma. The Bolsheviks captured 45 of 102 seats. The SRs won 15 seats, the Mensheviks 11, the Union of Homeowners 6, the Popular Socialists 3, and the Kadets 2. All top offices in the duma went to Bolsheviks. Afterward the local party committee discussed whether it should seize power in Tsaritsyn. By a vote of 8 to 6, it decided not to assume power, but to include members of the other parties in the duma's ruling executive. Erman, who had been arrested only days before, became president of the duma, and Minin, soon freed by the crowds in Saratov, was selected mayor.[66]

The Tsaritsyn Soviet also formed a revolutionary staff of twenty, which included twelve Bolsheviks and was chaired by the Left SR Fedorov. Declaring itself the legitimate authority in the city, the staff sent a delegation to Korvin-Krukovskii to demand that he clarify his position in regard to Kornilov. On August 29 the colonel received several telegrams from his superior in Kazan insisting that he leave for Kazan on the next

64. Zavarzin and Shkodina, *1917 god v Tsaritsyne*, pp. 73–75; Ovrutskaia, "Proval politiki," pp. 375–76.

65. *Proletarii Povolzh'ia*, no. 68, August 23, 1917, pp. 3–4. See also *Saratovskii Sovet*, pp. 181–82.

66. Romanov and Sokolov, *Ocherk istorii revoliutsii*, pp. 57–58.

available ship. Two days later he received a second cable ordering him to leave for Kazan, this time warning that if he did not obey, he would be considered to have openly sided with Kornilov and A. M. Kaledin, whose Cossack forces threatened the Volga. Several hours later B. V. Savinkov, Kerensky's aide, ordered that Korvin-Krukovskii be brought to trial. Because Tsaritsyn's defenses had been weakened by the earlier removal of the 141st and 155th regiments, the threat from Kaledin was especially real. Moreover, Korvin-Krukovskii's reluctance to obey orders suggests that he was undoubtedly hoping that a military dictatorship would be installed. On September 4 a detachment arrived from Saratov and Korvin-Krukovskii subordinated himself to it.[67]

With the detachment's departure, political power in Tsaritsyn fell into the Bolsheviks' hands. In September they formed a Red Guard, despite objections from moderate socialists and difficulty in obtaining arms.[68] On September 8 the Tsaritsyn Soviet adopted a Bolshevik resolution condemning Kornilov.[69] The revolutionary staff now disbanded and surrendered its authority to the executive committee of the soviet. And, most significant, the Bolsheviks won a sweeping victory in the elections to the soviet conducted in September, receiving 111 seats while the other parties combined won only 58.[70] The Tsaritsyn Bolsheviks thus had an even greater degree of authority than the Saratov Bolsheviks, making their takeover in October almost anticlimactic.

Although political developments in the uezd centers did not take on the same intensity as in Saratov or Tsaritsyn, the Kornilov Affair had the same dramatic effect on mass attitudes. Most important, the "democratic" elements of the district towns interpreted Kornilov's march on Petrograd as a counterrevolutionary threat, and several changes resulted. The authority of local soviets increased. Factionalism and tactical disagreements seized many local SR committees. No longer discredited in the eyes of the townspeople, Bolshevik and Social Democratic committees emerged from the affair strengthened and revitalized. As in Saratov, their influence within garrisons now grew considerably.

News of Kornilov's threat to the Kerensky government reached the uezd centers shortly after the dispatches had been received in Saratov. As early as August 28, soviets in Balashov, Pokrovsk, and Petrovsk cabled the Saratov Soviet that they stood prepared "to defend the revolu-

67. Ibid., pp. 58–60; Ovrutskaia, "Proval politiki," pp. 378–79; *Izvestiia Saratovskogo Soveta*, no. 79, September 5, 1917, p. 2; Antonov-Saratovskii, *Pod stiagom*, pp. 131–32.

68. Romanov and Sokolov, *Ocherk istorii revoliutsii*, p. 60; *Khronika*, pp. 109, 114–15.

69. *Khronika*, pp. 111–12; Osipov, *1917 god v Saratove*, pp. 150–51; Gavrilov, *1917 god v Stalingradskoi gubernii*, pp. 213–14; Zavarzin and Shkodina, *1917 god v Tsaritsyne*, pp. 81–82.

70. Gerasimenko, *Sovety Nizhnego Povolzh'ia*, p. 85; Osipov, *Istoriia Saratovskogo kraia*, 2:9.

tion." The next day the Petrovsk Soviet informed Saratov that both local regiments were ready to fight against Kornilov. A Provisional Committee to Save the Revolution was formed in Pokrovsk on August 30. In almost all of the district towns soviets and public executive committees passed resolutions condemning Kornilov, but supporting the Provisional Government and the Petrograd Soviet. Typical was a resolution carried by the Volsk Soviet, which called for creation of a government "of representatives of socialist and revolutionary democracy, which would be responsible before the central organs of the soviets of workers', soldiers', and peasants' deputies." According to a Volsk Bolshevik, the local soviet remained SR-Menshevik in orientation, but the number of Bolshevik deputies increased after the Kornilov episode, especially among soldiers, as a result of an influx of newcomers. By the end of December the majority of deputies in the soviet were Bolsheviks and Left SRs.[71] The Balashov Soviet adopted a statement similar to the one passed in Volsk, marking a reversal in its tactical position of the preceding months.[72] After the July Days the Balashov Bolshevik organization had been driven into the underground. But now, in the wake of the Kornilov Affair, local Bolsheviks agitated openly and hosted Saratov's Vasil'ev, who lectured on the current political situation.[73] The Bolshevik organization in Atkarsk underwent a similar revival. The first issue of a Bolshevik newspaper in Nikolaevsk went to press on September 19. In Pokrovsk, a separate Bolshevik committee was formed. A Bolshevik organization comprised solely of soldiers emerged in Kuznetsk.[74]

In Serdobsk, radical activities intensified in September with the arrival of frontoviki and of the Left SR F. I. Serezhnikov, who became district commissar. The frontoviki organized public meetings and published a journal with an eclectic focus, containing articles written by SRs, Mensheviks, Anarchists, and Tolstoyans. Meanwhile, Serezhnikov encouraged local peasants to seize land. Political life in Serdobsk may have been representative of many small towns in the region. Some local SDs still considered themselves neither Menshevik nor Bolshevik, although certain individuals could be called "leftist" in their orientation. The much more important SR organization had broken up into four unofficial groups by September: right, center, left, and maximalist. A regimental committee formed by evacuated soldiers soon filled the existing political vacuum in Serdobsk. On October 12 the presidium of the regimental committee held a secret meeting during which it decided to organize an uezd executive committee. "The ineffectiveness and lack

71. Rubashkina, "Vol'skaia organizatsiia," p. 81.
72. *Khronika*, pp. 103–5; Gerasimenko and Tochenyi, *Sovety Povolzh'ia*, pp. 154–56.
73. Bankvitser, "Ot fevralia," pp. 31–32.
74. *Khronika*, p. 116; *Sbornik: Ves' Kuznetsk* (Kuznetsk, 1927), p. 75.

of authority of the zemstvo and city administration were glaringly obvious," recalled one Bolshevik; "in actuality there was no power in the district and the creation of the uezd executive committee was dictated by the logic of events." After the October Revolution the executive committee came to be recognized as the highest authority in the district.[75]

In sum, executive committees and soviets in the uezd capitals voiced fears that Kornilov's actions had posed a real counterrevolutionary threat. They also expressed support for the Provisional Government and Central Executive Committee of the Petrograd Soviet. Virtually everywhere, however, the coalition with the middle classes and propertied elements came under question. Although still comparatively small, Bolshevik and SD cells had recovered from the July setback, whereas factionalism now sapped the political strength of Russian populism. While the populations of few of these towns were to support the Bolshevik seizure of power in October enthusiastically, the post-Kornilov climate was one of great ambiguity and uncertainty in which the lack of decisive authority at the local level stood out more clearly, in effect creating conditions that in the long run contributed to a Bolshevik victory in Saratov in October.

The local peasant movement reached its culmination in September and October 1917. The attempt at a conservative restoration confirmed growing peasant suspicion of the government, which can be seen in the tone of the resolutions passed at the Second Peasant Congress of Saratov Province described below. In the type of political climate envisioned by Kornilov, one geared to prosecuting a war and preserving law and order, rural disturbances had no place. For the peasant, the Kornilov Affair augured the postponement of the transfer of land to those who worked it and also the institution of punitive measures against agrarian turmoil. But, essentially, peasant unrest developed according to a tempo of its own, and would have intensified at this time even without the Kornilov crisis.

Having equivocated on the land question since spring, the Socialist Revolutionary party's urban leaders now found that factionalism within their own ranks had torn the party apart. Ironically, this situation crippled the party's political effectiveness but had only a negligible effect on its popularity in the villages, since rural SR activists who worked closely with the peasantry had moved into the camp of populism's radical left wing. By September 1917 most Volga-area SR organizations—to a considerable extent owing to the vitality of the Left SRs—clashed with

75. Shchegol'kov, "Na zare: Sovetskaia vlast' v Serdobske (Vospominaniia ob Oktiabre)," *Kommunisticheskii put'*, no. 9/34 (1923), pp. 52–55.

their central committee's position on holding off the inevitable land transfer. With the exception of the Samara and Kazan organizations, however, urban SR committees along the Volga, admonishing the peasants to defer a land settlement until the Constituent Assembly, continued to adhere to the Provisional Government's directives. To the peasantry the Constituent Assembly was an academic question: everyone knew how the countryside would vote in a referendum on the land question. The self-demobilization of the army in the fall of 1917 and the return to the villages of disillusioned—and armed—soldiers fanned the flames of rural unrest. Work cycles also shaped peasant behavior. With the harvest in, the peasants now had spare time on their hands. Finally, the unrest manifested in September and October should be viewed as an attempt on the part of the peasants to protect themselves from the collapse of traditional market forces.

The size of the fall harvest contributed to the peasant movement as well, but it is difficult to gauge the extent to which reduced yields provoked rural radicalism. Although not uniformly mediocre, the harvest of 1917 was much lower in some provinces than 1916 yields. Calling the 1917 harvest "catastrophically bad," Keep noted that the harvest in Saratov had fallen 45 percent.[76] Khvalynsk and Kuznetsk uezds suffered the most disastrous harvests, while yields in Saratov, Volsk, and Kamyshin plummeted from 1916 figures. The average output in the remaining five districts was classified as satisfactory, but was nonetheless lower than the preceding year's harvest.[77] Yet it was precisely here in the other uezds that peasant radicalism was greatest, suggesting that other factors such as long-term clashes between peasants and landlords perhaps conditioned peasant attitudes the most.

Resolutions passed at the Second Peasant Congress of Saratov Province, held between September 10 and 14, reflected the militant mood in local villages and demonstrated how far removed the Petrograd and Saratov SR leadership's views were from those of the peasant. Even before the congress opened, various developments revealed the hostile attitude in the countryside. In the charged atmosphere created by the Kornilov Affair some local villages passed resolutions demanding the transfer of power to the soviets, the passing of land to the peasants, and sometimes workers' control over industry.[78] Soldiers and agitators from

76. Keep, *Russian Revolution*, p. 184.

77. S. Sh. Ovrutskaia, "Proval popytok eserov sderzhat' krest'ianskoe dvizhenie osen'iu 1917 goda (Po materialam Saratovskoi gubernii)," *Povolzhskii krai*, no. 3 (1975), p. 87.

78. Some of the resolutions can be found in *Obshchestvennyi krizis*, pp. 473–75; Akademiia nauk SSSR, Institut istorii, et al., *Revoliutsionnoe dvizhenie v Rossii v avguste 1917 g.: Razgrom Kornilovskogo miatezha*, ed. D. A. Chugaev et al. (Moscow, 1959), p. 595; also in Osipova, *Klassovaia bor'ba*, p. 212.

the towns had certainly influenced peasant rhetoric, as soldiers from the front began to return to the villages. Bolshevik propaganda made an impact in some areas as well. After the Sixth Bolshevik Party Congress in July, the Saratov Bolsheviks formed brotherhoods (*zemliachestva*) of persons from the same rural area who now lived in the city. These organizations actually became activated in September, when the party's central committee gave them more attention and its military organization provided them with agrarian literature.[79]

About 500 peasant deputies attended the Second Peasant Congress. Few belonged to the intelligentsia and most belonged to the 40–45-year-old age group, making the gathering more homogeneous and older than the first congress back in April. Reporters noted the intense, serious mood of the delegates and the absence of the holiday-like bustle and spirited animation of the earlier meeting. While the proceedings unveiled the limited strength of the Bolshevik party in the countryside, they also disclosed how similar Bolshevik and Left SR tactics had become. At the congress peasants passed resolutions on the nature of political power, on the land issue, and on the government's food monopoly and supply system. In each case deputies carried resolutions supported by the Left SRs. During the four days of meetings peasant speakers often expressed hostility toward the Bolsheviks, but not necessarily toward the Bolshevik program. Relentless cries of disapproval and contempt made it all but impossible to hear Bolshevik speakers, whereas the deputies listened attentively to the SR orator; but the resolutions the Bolsheviks and Left SRs introduced, demanding transfer of power to the soviets, were almost identical.[80]

Most of the reports from the districts dwelled upon clashes between rich and poor in the villages and called attention to the growing role of newly formed peasant soviets. (According to a delegate from Kamyshin uezd, even the poor elements among the German peasants requested "revolutionary" literature in their own language.) Locked into conflicts with the clergy, richer peasants, or landowners' organizations, peasant executive committees, land committees, and soviets continued to lead the peasant movement in the countryside. The driving force of the peasant committees behind the rural revolt challenges Soviet historians' argument that village executive committees lost their authority or that "Right SRs, kulaks, and the rural bourgeoisie" now controlled the zemstvos. In Tsaritsyn uezd, in fact, the Bolsheviks won the majority of votes in zemstvo elections in September.[81]

79. A. S. Smirnov, *Agitatsiia i propaganda bol'shevikov v derevne v period podgotovki Oktiabr'skoi revoliutsii* (Moscow, 1957), p. 146.

80. *Saratovskii vestnik*, no. 201, September 12, 1917, p. 3; no. 202, September 13, p. 4; *Proletarii Povolzh'ia*, no. 88, September 13, 1917, p. 3; no. 89, September 14, p. 3.

81. E. D. Popova, *Leninskaia agrarnaia programma i bor'ba bol'shevikov za krest'ianstvo v 1917 godu* (Leningrad, 1980), p. 113.

The resolution passed at the peasant congress on the current political situation starkly showed how radicalized the villages had become. Opening with the accusation that the "Kornilov uprising made it clear to everyone that the propertied classes are against the revolution," the resolution went on to say that "we therefore consider necessary the creation of a government of the people that would unswervingly fulfill the people's will and be responsible before the central organ of the united democracy."[82] The majority of the deputies opposed further coalition with the bourgeoisie, despite the position of the SR party leadership.[83] Saratov had been a stronghold of centrist SR sentiment. The shift to the left here should have warned the party's leaders that extraordinary measures responsive to peasant demands were necessary to prevent the party's total collapse.

The resolution on the land question passed at the congress incorporated the SR program in full. Private ownership was declared abolished; all land, forests, waters, and resources were deemed national property; all citizens were to have equal right to use these resources. Land was to be transferred to land committees and to be at their disposal until the convocation of the Constituent Assembly. As with the resolution on the current political situation, the Left SRs carried this one.[84] Related resolutions called for peasants to divorce themselves from any contact with the Union of Landowners and to support the SR party in elections to the Constituent Assembly. Abandoning the Peasant Union formed in April as "superfluous and even harmful," the congress voted to transform all peasant unions into volost soviets.[85] At first glance it seems surprising that the congress issued a statement criticizing the government's recent doubling of its fixed price on grain. A closer look, however, shows the extent to which the peasantry's animosity toward the higher prices reflected conditions in the villages. Deputies related how the price increases had upset their fellow villagers, since only the prosperous peasants had grain to sell anyway. The poorer peasants had to purchase grain themselves, and the new prices would make it even harder for them to survive.[86] The resulting resolution on the food-supply

82. *Saratovskii vestnik*, no. 203, September 14, 1917, p. 3; Shestakov, *Sovety krest'ianskikh deputatov*, pt. 2, p. 111.

83. M. Levinson, "Krest'ianskoe dvizhenie v Saratovskoi gub. v 1917 g.," in *1917 god v Saratove* (Saratov, 1927), p. 80.

84. The resolution can be found in *Proletarii Povolzh'ia*, no. 90, September 16, 1917, p. 4, and Kotel'nikov and Meller, *Krest'ianskoe dvizhenie v 1917*, p. 273. See also *Saratovskii vestnik*, no. 202, September 13, 1917, p. 4; *Proletarii Povolzh'ia*, no. 88, September 13, 1917, p. 3; and Levinson, "Krest'ianskoe dvizhenie," p. 81.

85. *Khronika*, pp. 112–13; also quoted in Iu. P. Suslov, *Leninskaia agrarnaia programma i bor'ba bol'shevikov Povolzh'ia za ee osushchestvlenie, mart 1917–mart 1918 gg.* (Saratov, 1972), p. 91; Gerasimenko, "Vozniknovenie Sovetskoi vlasti," p. 62.

86. *Proletarii Povolzh'ia*, no. 87, September 12, 1917, p. 4; no. 89, September 14, p. 3.

question championed the speedy return to the pre-August fixed prices and the government's guaranteeing of essential manufactured goods to the villages. Meanwhile, peasants were to continue to supply the government and towns with grain at the old prices.[87]

The resolutions carried at the peasant congress contributed enormously to the agrarian movement because local peasants accepted the decisions of the congress "as law."[88] The new wave of peasant uprisings flared up in Serdobsk uezd, triggering discontent in other districts. The largest pomeshchik latifundia were concentrated here, and a powerful Left SR organization controlled most important local administrative positions. Basing its decision on resolutions passed by village committees, the Chubarovsk volost food-supply administration took over all land within the county, doling it out according to need and ability to farm without hired hands. Despite condemnation from the district land committee, the peasants of Chubarovsk volost held tight; soon the movement spread to neighboring areas. The Menshevik newspaper reported that in Barkovsk volost peasants destroyed one-fifth of the landowners' and otrub estates. Topuridze ordered troops from Atkarsk to maintain order in Serdobsk, but apparently this effort scored no success. He also removed the Left SR Serezhnikov from his post as district commissar, insisting that he did not take appropriate measures to curb the local peasant movement. On September 29 a meeting of all public organizations met in Serdobsk to discuss the unusual situation. Those present passed a resolution placing all blame for the disorders on the Provisional Government's land policies and ordering the transfer of all private land to the volost zemstvos. Responding with dismay to the flow of events, the Serdobsk Union of Landowners petitioned Kerensky to put an end to the disorders, while the provincial food-supply authorities called for the firing of the entire Serdobsk uezd food-supply administration and the taking of legal action against its Left SR chairman.[89] A contingent of Cossacks was sent to Serdobsk, but to no avail. The presidium of the district executive committee cabled Saratov that "the measures taken by armed force did not achieve their aims. The only way to save the district from chaos is to transfer forests, lands, estates, and inventory to the land committees. Cable permission or else relieve us of our responsibility and authority."[90]

87. *Saratovskii vestnik*, no. 203, September 14, 1917, pp. 3–4; Ovrutskaia, "Proval popytok eserov," pp. 89–90.

88. See A. S. Smirnov, "Bol'sheviki i krest'ianskie s"ezdy v iiule–oktiabre 1917 g.," *Voprosy istorii KPSS*, no. 12 (1973), p. 69, and Levinson, "Krest'ianskoe dvizhenie," p. 79.

89. Ovrutskaia, "Proval popytok eserov," pp. 92–95.

90. *Saratovskii vestnik*, no. 213, September 28, 1917, p. 5; also in Kotel'nikov and Meller, *Krest'ianskoe dvizhenie v 1917*, p. 274.

After Serdobsk, the peasant movement gripped Balashov and Atkarsk uezds, which had also experienced a high incident of peasant terror in 1905. Whenever peasants sacked estates and resorted to violence—actions that increased in frequency at this time—they tended to treat contemptuously the symbolic reminders of their poverty. They seized and divided essential equipment and inventory, but destroyed fancy furniture, books, art objects, parks, and orchards. Distraught landowners flooded Topuridze and the Kerensky government with complaints. The Balashov Union of Landowners informed Petrograd that peasants were destroying estates, driving out landlords and their domestics, and burning threshing floors.[91] According to a Saratov editorial, "troubles are transferred from one volost to another, literally, an epidemic has infected the population, destroying its mental equilibrium and arousing lower instincts . . . local authorities telegraph about their complete impotence and urgently demand radical measures to liquidate the disorders."[92]

The anti-urban tone of the rural disturbances alarmed the civilian population of the towns because capricious grain deliveries exacerbated the already awful supply problem. Owing to deficits of manufactured goods, lamented *Saratovskii vestnik*, "the village categorically refuses to give products to the city." A spokesman for the Saratov Food-Supply Administration contended that the "dissatisfaction of the population of the city of Saratov is due mainly to the shortage of wheat flour. And therefore, to ward off possible excesses on this ground, it is necessary to direct all efforts to obtain it." One can easily imagine the frustration of local officials when they turned to the capital for directives. A local editorial complained that "in Petrograd offices they distribute assignments and supplies, and on paper everything goes well and smoothly. But in the province it's another story altogether; the village is confused and as a result there is chaos." And how did the peasant feel about this confusion? A local Menshevik who visited a village in Petrovsk uezd at this time reported on what may well have been typical peasant attitudes. Peasants hounded him with questions about what was going on in Saratov, about the government, and about the war. "Several peasants began to complain," he wrote, "that for a long time [the government] has not established order, that it has reached the point where one doesn't know who governs whom and to whom one must subordinate oneself."[93]

Topuridze and the emasculated local forces of the national govern-

91. O. Chaadaeva, *Pomeshchiki i ikh organizatsii v 1917 g.* (Moscow, 1928), p. 167.

92. *Saratovskii vestnik*, no. 214, September 29, 1917, p. 1; see also Kotel'nikov and Meller, *Krest'ianskoe dvizhenie v 1917*, p. 274.

93. *Saratovskii vestnik*, no. 209, September 22, 1917, p. 3; no. 211, September 24, p. 5; *Proletarii Povolzh'ia*, no. 96, September 23, 1917, p. 2.

ment took what few measures were possible to combat the disorders. Despite protests from the Saratov Soviet and the reluctance of SR leaders to resort to force, Topuridze sent small punitive Cossack units to defend landowners in the most volatile volosts.[94] Nevertheless, regardless of the exhortations and threats from the national government and from Topuridze, most peasant and land committees continued to implement land reform in a "revolutionary fashion." A Left SR delegate from Saratov to the All-Russian Congress of Peasant Deputies held a few weeks later related that Saratov peasants had lost faith not only in the central authorities but also in the "ruling organs of the democracy" over the land question.[95]

The political right's attempt to seize power nationally and Korvin-Krukovskii's blatant snubbing of popular organs locally radicalized politics along the Volga. Despite the potential menace of Kaledin's forces moving up from the Don, Saratov's workers and soldiers responded to the broader threat as if they were fighting surrogate Kornilovs, and in this regard the entire effort at a conservative restoration in the fall of 1917 served as a provocative conditioner, a dress rehearsal for the events of October. As a result of the Kornilov episode, the Saratov Soviet now fell into the Bolsheviks' hands. To the dismay of the good burghers of Saratov, armed local workers were prepared to fight against counterrevolutionaries, while Bolshevik slogans were enthusiastically echoed in the garrison. Compromised by their support of the coalition government, local SR and Menshevik organizations split apart as left elements sided with the Bolsheviks against further coalition with propertied Russia and centrist elements refused to repudiate the tactical policies they had pursued since February, perhaps still hoping that civil war could be staved off. Up and down the Volga and across the eastern tip of Russia's black-earth zone, workers' soviets, soldiers' soviets, executive committees, and party organizations called for a transfer of power to the Petrograd Soviet nationally and to democratically elected bodies locally. Even rural Russia rejected coalition with the propertied elements. The mood of provincial Russia did not determine the composition of the third and final coalition government created by Kerensky, but it did convince Lenin and other Bolshevik militants that the country was ripe for a transfer of power to the soviets.

Meanwhile, as the first autumn winds blew in from the Volga, a sense of despair and worry seized the population of Saratov. Newspapers had little good to report. Ignoring all appeals for restraint, local peasants

94. Lebedev, "Fevral'–oktiabr'," p. 247; Zhagar, "Put' k oktiabriu," p. 47.
95. Gerasimenko and Tochenyi, *Sovety Povolzh'ia*, p. 191.

completed their drive for the land, under way since March. Suspicious of government edicts and urban commissars and politicians, the peasantry responded approvingly to rural agitators who urged them to resolve the land question locally and to settle old scores. As the flow of grain from the countryside became more and more uncertain, food-supply authorities had to turn a deaf ear to appeals from Petrograd offices. Threatened with reduced food rations, with wage increases made worthless by runaway inflation, and with loss of their jobs, Saratov's working class went out on strike to better their ever precarious economic situation. It had not been safe to go out into the streets at night for some time, but now soldiers and suspicious individuals "dressed in soldier's garb" victimized civilians and their property during the day as well. With supplies running low, filth and neglect began to take their toll: epidemic diseases challenged public health authorities even more than before. Shops were closing, transportation was uncertain, and winter was just setting in.

The political situation was no better. The legitimacy and legality of governing bodies had been in flux since spring. All recognition of authority was voluntary at best as extremism of all sorts attracted adherents. More than at any other point in 1917, the country's political crisis confronted Russia's leadership face to face. The Kornilov Affair had not caused the strained situation in September. Rather, its historical significance lay in the fact that it forced the country's political leaders to make difficult choices, the results of which seemed increasingly unpleasant, unavoidable, and consequential.

CHAPTER 7

Saratov's October

"In the revolutionary air of Russia," wrote Vasil'ev in the middle of October, "a thunderstorm is brewing. Involuntarily and instinctively everyone feels the drawing near of decisive events."[1] Vasil'ev may well have expressed what many people felt, for both national and local non-Bolshevik newspapers daily fed readers rumors that the Bolsheviks had decided to seize power in conjunction with the All-Russian Second Congress of Soviets, slated to convene on October 24. The most striking thing about the October Revolution was that everyone expected it.

For many townspeople, however, forebodings of momentous events in the distant capital must have seemed secondary to the immediate problem of coping with everyday life. Urban Russia now experienced unprecedented shortages. Strikingly similar to moods in Petrograd, Moscow, and elsewhere, widespread demoralization locally, linked to a dismal economic situation and to a glaring decline in public services, gave no sign of easing off. There indeed was little to rejoice about. Neglect necessitated by wartime expenditures and conditions had overcome the city fathers' earlier efforts to make Saratov the pride of the Volga. The town's unsanitary condition now evoked sharper criticism than before. "Not only are the streets unswept," sighed the editors of *Proletarii Povolzh'ia,* "but garbage and litter are being dumped onto the

1. *Sotsial-Demokrat,* no. 74, October 12, 1917, p. 1.

streets from buildings." Typhus, the disease of poverty and filth, still claimed victims.[2] Occasional displays of mob action gave expression to the strained feelings harbored by Saratovites. On the morning of October 1, for example, prison guards fired at convicts trying to escape from the town jail. The ensuing commotion attracted a crowd of about 2,000 curious townspeople, who lynched one of the less fortunate escapees. Only with "great difficulty" did authorities "succeed in persuading the crowd to disperse."[3]

Dwindling food supplies exacerbated discontent. Several times in October Saratov actually remained without grain for a day or two because of snags in the transportation system and the peasants' reluctance to market their products. Although food had been scant at times in Saratov during the previous months, supplies had never before been totally exhausted. It is not surprising, therefore, that some people feared that the Soviet's decision to conduct a general search for hoarded food would touch off disorders. Anti-Semitic feelings, encouraged by right-wing agitation, had spread throughout the city on the eve of the Soviet's intended search. Whatever second thoughts the Soviet had, however, were soon dispelled. Threatening that if the Soviet did not act immediately "we ourselves will go and search," a group of angry working-class women from the city's mountain neighborhood burst into a meeting of the Soviet's Executive Committee. A member of the Duma later commented that "if there was dissatisfaction [about the searches], it came from where it was expected—from where the reserves were found." When the search was concluded, he noted with relief "that all of the . . . reserves were found not with Jews, but mainly with Christians."[4]

Although the city's food-supply commission confiscated tons of rye flour, the food crisis in Saratov did not abate. On October 2 city authorities, consumer societies, and mill owners fired off complaints to the national government that Saratov lacked grain because Samara refused to send supplies. "The mills have stopped," they reported, "and they'll have to lay off workers; this will cause disorders in the city." Shipments of grain arrived irregularly. On other days bakeries had to shut down because of lack of flour. When rumors of the evacuation of Petrograd circulated in Saratov at the beginning of October, groups of citizens conducted illegal searches; additional armed guards had to be posted throughout the city to maintain order. With no relief in sight, the food-supply institutions focused their attention on the peasants' unwill-

2. *Proletarii Povolzh'ia*, no. 119, October 21, 1917, p. 3; no. 111, October 12, p. 2; and *Saratovskii vestnik*, no. 218, October 4, 1917, p. 2.

3. *Proletarii Povolzh'ia*, no. 103, October 3, 1917, p. 3.

4. Ibid., no. 102, October 1, 1917, p. 3; and no. 103, October 3, p. 4.

ingness to relinquish grain. One report noted that only two of the ten uezds in the province were now shipping food to Saratov.[5] The unenviable situation in Saratov province attracted national attention, undoubtedly because, drought years aside, the very mention of Saratov normally conjured up images of fertile soil and comparative plenty. Minister of Supplies Prokopovich announced in Petrograd that "in Saratov . . . the number of starving people and of speculators is growing larger every day, becoming more and more menacing. The local committee and the Soviet of Workers' and Soldiers' Deputies are helpless to cope with the situation."[6]

Breakdowns in agricultural deliveries threatened to shut down still more flour mills and vegetable oil presses than in September. Shortages of fuel and raw materials of all sorts and partial demobilization of the army left others without work. Although fewer workers went out on strike in October, the strike movement nonetheless aroused widespread concern because it involved city employees, so that public services were even further endangered. At the last moment efforts were made to reach a settlement with the city employees' union, which thereupon agreed that the strike would not spread to the city hospital, drugstore, milk plant, water works, fire department, veterinary hospital, and vocational school. The support staff of three other Saratov hospitals walked off their jobs, however, and on the evening of October 7 the lamplighters went out on strike, plunging the town into total darkness. About the same time Saratov's restaurant workers announced a strike, while laborers at several factories producing consumer goods presented economic demands to their employers and made known their readiness to strike.[7]

There were also the truculent soldiers to deal with. Fluctuating throughout the year, the size of the local garrison had swelled to an estimated 65,696 by mid-October. This figure included a large percentage of frontoviki and at least one regiment transferred from the easily aroused Tsaritsyn garrison. The troops' weariness and snubbing of both military and civilian authority now matched their tenacious desire to move from the shoddy barracks into civilian dwellings in town. Torn between their fears of having soldiers quartered in the city and their knowledge that the barracks were substandard, Soviet and Duma leaders

5. *Proletarii Povolzh'ia*, no. 103, October 3, 1917, p. 3; *Saratovskii vestnik*, no. 217, October 3, 1917, p. 3; no. 218, October 4, p. 3; no. 221, October 21, p. 4.

6. J. Bunyan and H. H. Fisher, *The Bolshevik Revolution, 1917–1918: Documents and Materials* (Stanford, 1934), p. 50. This assessment matched that of Saratov delegates to the Second Congress of Soviets. See A. F. Butenko and D. A. Chugaev, *Vtoroi vserossiiskii s"ezd sovetov rabochikh i soldatskikh deputatov: Sbornik dokumentov* (Moscow, 1957), p. 76.

7. *Proletarii Povolzh'ia*, no. 115, October 17, 1917, p. 3; no 106, October 6, p. 4; no. 108, October 8, p. 4; no. 104, October 4, p. 4; *Izvestiia Saratovskogo Soveta*, no. 89, October 17, 1917, p. 2.

continued to equivocate. Meanwhile, army doctors confirmed the urgent need for major repairs in the so-called soldiers' suburb, reporting that "if the renovation is conducted slowly, then the sick will freeze to death in the winter."[8] A week later soldiers refused to go to the front because they had not received the boots and shoes they needed. Efforts to rid the town of the most recalcitrant troops came to nothing. The situation in the uezd towns and in other provincial centers in the Volga region was no better. Troops rioted in Volsk when they discovered that their rations contained rotten meat. Ignoring appeals from their soviet, soldiers in Balashov freed imprisoned soldiers.[9] In Petrovsk, soldiers and townspeople broke into the local jail and released prisoners. Reports of garrison disorders and illegal searches in Atkarsk, Kuznetsk, and Serdobsk also trickled into Saratov.[10] In Atkarsk, Kuznetsk, and Kamyshin soldiers and workers passed resolutions expressing disapproval of the Provisional Government or calling for a transfer of power to the soviets.[11]

The Saratov Soviet tried to cope with these problems. It cooperated with labor's various arbitration boards to end the strike of city employees. It concluded the strike at the Kolesnikov plant, and took measures to regulate food distribution and to use the Red Guard to curb violence and crime. With obvious reservations, the Soviet also agreed to quarter some of the garrison soldiers in the city "until the barracks are put in order."[12] Despite these actions, Saratovites still felt great anxiety over the growing lawlessness. Flashed the headlines of Saratov's middle-class *Saratovskii vestnik:* "Russia experiences complete anarchy and demoralization."[13]

Throughout October national and local newspapers discussed Russia's political future. The non-Bolshevik socialist press focused on the efficacy of continued coalition with the bourgeoisie. Now that the Bolsheviks and other elements of the radical left had won majorities in many provincial soviets, and in view of the much-talked-about collapse of SR and Menshevik organizations, the whole issue of coalition took on new urgency. The All-Russian Second Congress of Soviets, and elections to the long-awaited Constituent Assembly, scheduled for November,

8. *Proletarii Povolzh'ia,* no. 102, October 1, 1917, p. 3.

9. *Proletarii Povolzh'ia,* no. 103, October 3, 1917, p. 4; also in Bunyan and Fisher, *Bolshevik Revolution,* p. 27.

10. *Izvestiia Saratovskogo Soveta,* no. 89, October 17, 1917, p. 2; Akademii nauk SSSR, Institut istorii et al., *Revoliutsionnoe dvizhenie v Rossii nakanune Oktiabr'skogo vooruzhennogo vosstania (1–24 oktiabria 1917 g.),* ed. D. A. Chugaev et al. (Moscow, 1962), p. 359; *Izvestiia Kazanskogo Voenno-okruzhnogo Komiteta,* no. 105, October 7, 1917, p. 3.

11. *Khronika,* pp. 124, 126.

12. P. S., "Khronika," no. 20, p. 115.

13. *Saratovskii vestnik,* no. 222, October 8, 1917, p. 3.

further complicated the country's political crisis. It bears repeating that conflicting but persistent rumors that the Bolsheviks were planning an armed uprising against the government shaped popular attitudes at this time.

In this charged atmosphere right-wing groups in Saratov again attempted to discredit the left. Black Hundred activists distributed an inflammatory leaflet in the city's bazaars, along the riverfront, and in flophouses. Claiming that a new form of serfdom was being established in which workers would be the peasants' masters, those who wrote the leaflet sought to aggravate tensions between workers and soldiers and to instigate a pogrom aimed at the socialist intelligentsia. Although the right had no mass base of support, its agitation heightened fears and social tensions. "The spreading wave of pogroms that is covering the Russian revolution with disgrace," editorialized the official news organ of the Soviet, "threatens to seize even Saratov. Suspicious characters are trying to stir up the exhausted, tired, and hungry poor against the food-supply institutions and . . . also against organs of the revolutionary democracy . . . they are trying to instill in the soldiers mistrust . . . of the Soviet of Soldiers' and Workers' Deputies."[14]

Disturbed by the Bolshevik victory within the local Soviet, moderate socialist leaders had declared their determination to stand watch over the Bolshevik-dominated Executive Committee. As a companion policy, the moderates tried to give greater visibility and legitimacy to the municipal duma and even discussed the formation of neighborhood dumas. The institutional rivalry between the Soviet and the Duma camouflaged the more important political competition between the Bolsheviks and radical left on the one hand and the more moderate socialists on the other. The Duma's interest in strengthening the armed force at its disposal throughout October, moreover, reflected its concern over the possibility of an armed conflict. Soldiers from the local garrison could not be counted on; nor for that matter could the various factory militias or the Red Guard. Given these considerations, the Duma tried to register all privately owned firearms, perhaps with the aim of confiscating them for the police force, which was in dire straits. As one observer put it, "It's not our fault that our police are powerless, for they are not armed. Of 160 revolvers, 100 are good for nothing."[15] The police earned a very meager wage, which also made it difficult to attract capable personnel; as one of its last measures, the Duma allocated 1 million rubles to increase the size of the municipal police.

Despite the growing likelihood of armed conflict in the autumn of

14. *Proletarii Povolzh'ia*, no. 102, October 1, 1917, p. 3; *Izvestiia Saratovskogo Soveta*, no. 87, October 3, 1917, p. 3.

15. *Proletarii Povolzh'ia*, no. 121, October 24, 1917, pp. 3–4.

1917, the background to the October Revolution in Saratov should be seen as a political contest. As in Petrograd, October was a month of political debate; as in Petrograd, the Bolsheviks and other leftists now had a majority in the local soviet. But from its inception in the spring of 1917, the Presidium of the Petrograd Soviet had been comprised exclusively of Mensheviks and SRs, and the Bolsheviks played a role in the executive organs only toward fall. In contrast, the Presidium of the Saratov Soviet had always included a significant number of Bolsheviks. Now, months later, Bolsheviks controlled the local presidium and had the greatest number of elected deputies on their side. The local Bolshevik leadership had played a key role in the Saratov Soviet throughout the year, culminating in the September elections, which, if their results can be taken as a reflection of the mass mood, suggested that the political situation clearly favored the party. Without this majority in the Soviet, and without the support of leftist elements from the SR and Menshevik parties, the Bolsheviks would have been unable to come to power in Saratov.

The Bolshevik party organization in Saratov had grown from a handful of activists in March to 5,000 registered members in October.[16] Bolshevik sympathies were spread still more broadly among the working class and soldiers who were not party cardholders. Politically, the Bolsheviks stood for soviet power, for soviet democracy. They stood for an end to the war. The prestige of the Provisional Government had sunk to its lowest level by the end of September. While the country's powerful socialist forces had worked together to defeat Kornilov, Kerensky's failure to prosecute the insurgents and his continued support of coalition with tsenzovoe obshchestvo increased the appeal of the Bolsheviks' call for an all-soviet government.

As political debates intensified in Saratov in October, they often shifted from the floor of the Soviet and Duma halls to factory meetings and impromptu gatherings. Sometimes the verbal disputes resulted in violence.[17] One memoirist recalled that "with each day the conflicts became strained further and further. . . . Questions about the power of the soviets and of the Provisional Government were widely debated at all factories, plants, and workshops, where resolutions in favor of the soviets were decisively carried."[18] On October 11–13 the first conference of local factory committees took place in Saratov, which showed the overwhelming support the Bolsheviks enjoyed among the city's working class. The conference chose the Bolshevik Kirill Plaksin to represent

16. Medvedev, "Saratovskii Sovet," p. 81.

17. Antonov-Saratovskii, *Pod stiagom*, p. 146.

18. K. I. Plaksin, "Poslednye dni sushchestvovaniia men'shevistsko-eserovskogo soveta i Oktiabr'skii perevorot," in *Piat' let proletarskoi bor'by*, p. 45.

Saratov at the First All-Russian Conference of Factory Committees, held in Petrograd between October 17 and 20, at which Plaksin was elected to the presidium.[19]

The leaders of the SR and Menshevik parties who continued to support the Provisional Government, to place their hopes on the Constituent Assembly, and to believe that general conditions in the country at large made a socialist revolution premature were the tragic losers of 1917. Moderate socialist leaders feared the anarchistic temperaments of the masses brutalized by poverty, ignorance, and years of suffering during the war. The lawlessness of everyday life and the readiness with which the people seemed to fall victim to opportunistic slogans of the more radical left reinforced the convictions of the moderate leaders that Russia was unready for social revolution. In effect, the masses appeared to behave exactly as the moderates had feared: irresponsibly. The true complexity of the crisis the moderate socialist parties faced is placed in even sharper focus when the fate of their party organizations is considered. The move on the part of rank-and-file members (and leaders) into the Bolshevik camp, the vitality of the more radical wings within the SR and Menshevik movements, and the actual formation of a Left SR party indicate that many individuals had concluded that their party programs had indeed been compromised.

By mid-October the Saratov Menshevik and SR organizations were in dire straits. A prominent theme voiced at a provincial congress of Saratov Mensheviks, which convened in early October, was the crumbling away of the party's mass base and society's receptiveness to Bolshevik appeals. Delegates from the district towns reported that joint SD committees had all split into left- and right-wing factions. Moreover, the Mensheviks' financial resources had been exhausted. A suggestion to turn *Proletarii Povolzh'ia* into a provincial organ had to be scrapped for this very reason. Not long after the conference ended the treasurer of the Saratov committee, announcing that the party lacked funds to prepare for elections to the Constituent Assembly, asked activists to make personal contributions to finance the campaigning.[20] The local SR organization experienced similar difficulties, while the leftist faction became more powerful in the countryside. One speaker at the Menshevik conference admitted the "colossal influence of the SR Maximalists" in his district.[21] Other evidence suggests that moderate SR organizations in the uezd towns had lost support as a result of the party leadership's postponement of land reform and its sanction of the use of force to secure grain. The collapse of the party organization in Saratov persuaded some

19. Khodakov, "Bor'ba rabochikh Saratovskoi gubernii," p. 106.
20. *Proletarii Povolzh'ia*, no. 107, October 7, 1917, p. 4; no. 113, October 14, p. 3.
21. Ibid., no. 103, October 3, 1917, p. 4.

party leaders to reconsider their policies. In early October a leading SR, P. G. Kassandrov, agreed to accept the chairmanship of the local food-supply organization only if all private land was immediately transferred to land committees. While the Bolsheviks backed Kassandrov, most members of the consumer societies and food-supply organs rejected his conditions. On the very eve of the October Revolution, however, the Saratov provincial commissar petitioned the Kerensky government to sanction the nationalization of land without delay.[22]

The political impasse in Saratov moved toward a solution even before the confused Bolshevik Central Committee made plans for a seizure of power. On October 7 a full plenum of the Saratov Soviet adopted a resolution expressing complete mistrust of the new government Kerensky had formed a few days before. SRs and Mensheviks abstained from voting (rather than vote against the resolution), a fact that suggests they had reservations about Kerensky's inclusion of Kadet leaders in the Third Coalition Government. The Bolshevik resolution emphasized that compromise with the counterrevolutionary bourgeoisie had obviously failed during the Kornilov days and that further collaboration with the bourgeoisie could not settle the basic aims of the revolution—ending the war and concluding peace, putting the economic life of the country in good order, resolving the land question in the interests of the peasantry, and improving the lot of the working class. "A conflict between the government and the majority of the revolutionary nation is inevitable," read the Bolshevik resolution. "Therefore the Saratov Soviet . . . refuses to support the Provisional Government and calls upon the revolutionary democracy to rally around the Soviet in order, at the necessary moment, to repulse decisively and mercilessly all counterrevolutionary encroachments and to rally on behalf of a transfer of power into the hands of workers and peasants themselves, into the hands of the soviets of workers', soldiers', and peasants' deputies."[23] The plenum next selected representatives to the upcoming Congress of Soviets in Petrograd. Calling the opening of the congress "superfluous" on the eve of the upcoming Constituent Assembly, the SRs refused to participate in the balloting.[24] The SR Central Committee had directed provincial organizations to boycott the selection of deputies to the Second Congress of Soviets. As a result, Soviet deputies chose two Bolsheviks and one Menshevik to go to Petrograd. (The local Menshevik organization instructed its delegate to vote against any effort to create an all-soviet socialist government.) It is important to note that Kerensky responded to the Saratov Soviet's resolution of October 7 with a threat to send a punitive expedition there. In

22. Miliutin, *Krest'ianskoe dvizhenie v 1917 godu*, p. 79.
23. P. S., "Khronika," no. 20, p. 112; see also *Saratovskii Sovet*, pp. 211–12.
24. *Saratovskii vestnik*, no. 223, October 10, 1917, p. 3.

reply, "a meeting of soldiers from several regiments endorsed the resolution of the Soviet, announcing that in the event that punitive forces were sent, the soldiers would answer with bayonets and bullets."[25]

During October 1917 the Bolshevik Central Committee was often rocked by passionate debates over Lenin's call for an armed uprising. At the time Lenin launched his campaign to convince the party of the need to force a showdown with the government, most Central Committee members harbored strong reservations, especially since it seemed that the Second Congress of Soviets would form an all-soviet government anyway. Behind the belief of those Bolshevik leaders who opposed Lenin's tactics was the conviction that a transfer of power to the soviets by the Second Congress would simply be more legitimate. Even before the Bolshevik Central Committee discussed the question of an armed uprising, the party central apparatus canvassed the mood of the provinces, paying considerable attention to those locales where the Bolsheviks had won majorities in the soviets. That the Bolshevik Central Committee in Petrograd had not worked out a careful plan for a seizure of power (as Soviet historians argue) should not detract from the fact that there was considerably more organization and planning behind the Bolsheviks' coming to power than some Western writers admit. Miliutin, the first chairman of the Saratov Soviet, was sent by the Bolshevik Central Committee to meet with the Saratov Bolshevik organization as early as October 8. That same day another representative from the Central Committee, I. P. Zhukov, addressed a full plenum of the Syzran Soviet and later spoke before the Simbirsk Soviet.

Sources shedding light on Miliutin's visit must be used cautiously. According to the most reliable account, Miliutin detailed the impact of the Kornilov movement on political attitudes in Petrograd. Throughout September the party had stubbornly insisted on the calling of the Second Congress of Soviets, taking advantage of the Democratic State Conference to denounce publicly the moderate socialists' willingness to cooperate further with the bourgeoisie. Miliutin emphasized that the party must now conduct a "careful and restrained policy" and, referring to the July Days, must hold back the masses from independent disturbances of which the enemy might take advantage. He insisted that reports in the press about disagreements within the Central Committee were "complete lies," and that the party leadership was united. The slogan "All Power to the Soviets," he said, "remains for us intact. We are convinced that with the support of real live forces of the country, this slogan will be

25. V. P. Antonov-Saratovskii, "Oktiabr'skie dni v Saratove," in *Rasskazyvaiut uchastniki Velikogo Oktiabria* (Moscow, 1957), p. 291.

put into practice, despite the great difficulties."[26] The broad inference that one can make is that Miliutin, like Zinoviev, Kamenev, and other members of the Central Committee, and the local Bolshevik committee for that matter, fully expected the Second Congress of Soviets to assume power, and so they discussed how to meet efforts to block this move.

While Miliutin was in Saratov, Lenin met with the Bolshevik Central Committee on the evening of October 10. By a vote of 10 to 2 it passed a vague resolution "to place the armed uprising on the agenda." The next day—and surely before word had reached Saratov of the committee's decision—Saratov Bolshevik leaders assembled with representatives of Bolshevik organizations in Tsaritsyn, Volsk, Petrovsk, and the important railroad junction at Rtishchevo to talk over tactics in the event that armed opposition challenged the formation of an all-soviet government by the Second Congress of Soviets. Sources shed little light on what took place at this meeting, but there is little evidence to support the claim of Soviet historians that Volga-area Bolsheviks agreed to mobilize forces to prepare for an actual armed uprising.[27]

It soon became apparent that the majority of soviets along the Lower and Middle Volga backed the formation of an all-socialist government in conjunction with the Second Congress. On October 14–15, Saratov hosted a regional (oblast) congress of soviets, which was one of many local meetings held in preparation for the Second Congress. Like the Northern Regional Congress of Soviets, which had convened in Petrograd between October 11 and 13, the Volga congress endorsed the transfer of power to the soviets, but not before the opening of the Second All-Russian Congress. Forty delegates representing soviets in Saratov, Samara, Syzran, Simbirsk, Tsaritsyn, Astrakhan, and a number of district towns attended the congress. A party breakdown shows that eight Mensheviks, one "Menshevik sympathizer," four SRs, eight Left SRs, and nineteen Bolsheviks were present. While the Bolsheviks were two delegates short of a majority, Left SR support gave them a decisive edge. The Saratov congress opened on the morning of October 15, with reports from eight speakers who described the political climate in their districts. "All of the accounts were monotonous," *Proletarii Povolzh'ia* informed its readers. "All told of the ecstasy over the new majorities in the soviets, over the Bolshevik majority." The article continued that "the soviets are well prepared for the transfer of power into their hands." Saratov's Antonov then acquainted the delegates with the mood of local workers and

26. P. S., "Khronika," no. 20, p. 114.

27. Topaz, "Pobeda Velikoi Oktiabr'skoi sotsialisticheskoi revoliutsii," p. 152; Gerasimenko, *Sovety Nizhnego Povolzh'ia*, pp. 94–95; S. V. Terekhin, *Gody ognevye: Saratovskaia organizatsiia bol'shevikov v period Oktiabr'skoi revoliutsii* (Saratov, 1967), p. 12.

Sokolov with attitudes in the garrison. "The Duma," Antonov said, "is trying to draw the worker and soldier masses away from the Soviet." Sokolov noted such a "strong swing to the left on the part of the Saratov garrison that even anarchists found favorable soil for agitation [there]."[28]

Following local reports, the Tsaritsyn Bolshevik Erman addressed the delegates on the current political situation. Referring to state power in general, Erman declared that "the moment has now come when it is no longer possible to solve the question peacefully."[29] A Bolshevik named Deriabin then introduced the following resolution, which vividly demonstrated how uncompromising the Bolsheviks had become toward census society since February.

> The Russian Revolution has taken place under such conditions, international and national, that all questions raised by it can be resolved only at the expense of and against the propertied classes. . . .
>
> From the very beginning of the revolution the Russian bourgeoisie demonstrated that in essence they are counterrevolutionary. The right SRs' and Mensheviks' policy of coalition, their policy of compromise with the bourgeoisie, not only failed to resolve a single question raised by the revolution but led to the rule of a bourgeois dictatorship, to the Bonapartism of Kerensky-Kornilov. . . .
>
> The revolutionary wave is gathering force. The new government . . . , ruled by the counterrevolutionary Kadet party and relying on the bayonets of the reactionary strata of the Cossacks and on the leadership of the army . . . , is trying to challenge the masses to an open clash in order to drown this movement in blood. . . . The danger is great; the country already has slipped into a dark abyss.
>
> In view of the above, the Third Oblast Congress of Soviets of Workers' and Soldiers' Deputies declares:
>
> a. That it will show no support to this government, which is not responsible to the democracy and which is provoking civil war.
>
> b. That the only way out of the situation that has arisen is the immediate transfer of power to the soviets of workers', soldiers', and peasants' deputies.
>
> c. That only Soviet power, relying on the revolutionary army, peasants, and workers . . . , will pave the way to a democratic peace. . . .[30]

The rival Menshevik resolution called for the outlawing of all street movements and for support of the government. The Bolsheviks and Left SRs, by a vote of 28 to 12, passed the Bolshevik resolution. In protest, Menshevik and Right SR delegates, most of whom came from such uezd

28. *Proletarii Povolzh'ia*, no. 115, October 17, 1917, pp. 3–4; P. S., "Khronika," no. 20, p. 116.

29. *Proletarii Povolzh'ia*, no. 116, October 18, 1917, p. 3.

30. Osipov, *1917 god v Saratove*, pp. 173–74.

towns as Balashov, Novokuznetsk, Volsk, Khvalynsk, and Rtishchevo, withdrew from the congress.

Soon after their walkout, the moderate socialists denounced the congress and challenged its legitimacy. In explaining their behavior they argued that they did not want their presence to sanction "the important decisions of the congress, which are wrong and harmful for the cause of revolution and for 'the democracy.' " Voicing their confidence in the so-called Pre-Parliament and in the upcoming Constituent Assembly, they sought to undermine the authority of the rival Second Congress of Soviets.[31] The next morning Topuridze sent police to the meeting hall to shut down the congress. Soldiers from the Ninety-second Regiment, however, drove the police away and the congress again went into session.[32] The Volga deputies passed another resolution to the effect that "the provincial soviets call for preparations to repulse the counterrevolutionaries . . . because power again is in the hands of those pomeshchiki and conciliators who have threatened the country with civil war."[33] Before adjourning they issued a statement on the withdrawal of the SRs and Mensheviks from the congress, maintaining that this action "showed the complete incapability of the 'former leaders' of the working class to defend its interests."[34] Right after the gathering closed a mass meeting of evacuated soldiers voiced their support of the Bolshevik and Left SR resolutions passed at the oblast congress.

The political situation in provincial Russia at this time proved a decisive factor in Lenin's ability to persuade the Bolshevik Central Committee to act. On September 29 Lenin already had observed that "together with the Left SRs we now have a majority in the soviets, in the army, and in the country." In most provincial centers in the Volga and Ural regions, Bolsheviks, Left SRs, and Menshevik Internationalists had gained control of soviets, soldiers' organizations, and even town dumas. In Kazan, for example, Bolsheviks and Menshevik Internationalists united in a single organization during city duma elections in October; they also belonged to a joint military organization led by Left SRs. By mid-October most of the garrisons located in the Kazan Military District had subordinated themselves to local soviets that were in the hands of leftists. The

31. See *Proletarii Povolzh'ia*, no. 116, October 18, 1917, p. 4; no. 117, October 19, 1917, p. 4; *Saratovskii vestnik*, no. 230, October 18, 1917, p. 3; P. S., "Khronika," no. 20, p. 116. Antonov's memoirs mistakenly claim that this withdrawal took place on October 16, and that it was from the Soviet and not from the congress (*Pod stiagom*, p. 139). Gesler caught this error (*1917 god v Saratove*, p. 43). However, it was repeated in *Khronika*, p. 129.

32. Gesler, "Saratovskaia bol'shevistskaia organizatsiia," p. 43; Medvedev, "Saratovskii Sovet," p. 82.

33. *Proletarii Povolzh'ia*, no. 117, October 19, 1917, p. 4.

34. P. S., "Khronika," no. 20, p. 116.

Saratov Soviet removed Korvin-Krukovskii as head of the local military school and in every other respect acted as the highest authority in the garrison. Back in Petrograd, the Central Committee of the Bolshevik party on the evening of the 16th confirmed its resolution of October 10 and directed "all the organizations and all the workers and soldiers to prepare for the armed uprising most energetically." During discussions preceding the adoption of this second resolution, the committee assessed the mood of the provinces. Miliutin spoke at this momentous occasion, but it is impossible to ascertain whether he knew the results of the Volga congress of soviets. Nonetheless, he made an accurate reading of the local mood. Evaluating authority relationships in the provinces, Miliutin reported that "the slogan 'All Power to the Soviets' has reached full maturity, *especially in the provinces,* where here and there power actually already is in the hands of the soviets." Although Miliutin recognized that the question of power "is not decided by moods or bulletins, but by organized force," he spoke out fervently against an armed uprising, which smacked too much of illegality and aggression. Miliutin clearly linked a transfer of power to the Second Congress and, like several other Central Committee members, concluded that the party was not ready for provocative action. In character with his earlier position, he now reasoned that "we gained from the fact that there was no insurrection on [July] 3–5, and if there is not one now, it will not be the end of us."[35] Even after Lenin's resolution was carried by a vote of 20 in favor, 2 against, and 3 abstentions, Miliutin unsuccessfully tried to substitute the words "armed conflict" for "armed uprising." He opposed striking the first blow, and to a greater extent than many others saw the possibility of a defensive clash "resulting from objective conditions," which perhaps better than anything else described the situation in Saratov. (Afterward he, Nogin, and Rykov fought in vain to publish an appeal in *Rabochii put'*, the exact nature of which has never come to light.)

During the next ten days mounting tension between Saratov Bolsheviks and moderate socialists hamstrung what little authority remained in the city. Politically, the Bolsheviks competed against the moderate socialists and the liberals. The Bolsheviks' institutional rival was the Duma. In terms of national politics the contest revolved around support for the imminent Second Congress of Soviets (the Bolsheviks and left-wing factions of the other socialist parties) or for the Constituent Assembly (the moderate socialists, liberals, and some conservatives). As early as October 11 the Saratov Soviet carried a defiant resolution

35. *The Bolsheviks and the October Revolution: Minutes of the Central Committee of the Russian Social Democratic Labour Party (Bolsheviks), August 1917–February 1918,* trans. Ann Bone (London, 1974), pp. 100, 106, passim; emphasis mine.

affirming that it no longer would subordinate itself to decrees of the Provisional Government.[36] This challenge to the government's authority amounted to a declaration of Soviet power in Saratov. From this time forward, moderate socialist leaders did all they could to cripple the Soviet's activities. As in June, the Soviet had difficulty gathering a quorum, in part because of the moderates' hostility toward it.[37] Poor attendance at Soviet meetings in the summer, however, had reflected the workers' and soldiers' dissatisfaction with its moderate stance. It could well be that the Bolsheviks interpreted such indifference now as a similar rejection of the Soviet's timid policies.

The SRs' withdrawal from all executive organs of the Soviet on October 18, which the Mensheviks considered a grave mistake, increased the likelihood of an armed showdown in Saratov. Maintaining that they no longer could assume responsibility for "the Bolsheviks' tactics, which were destructive to the cause of the revolution," the city SR committee and provincial bureau presented a declaration to the Executive Committee.[38] While recognizing Bolshevik numerical superiority in the Soviet, the SRs accused them of introducing for opportunistic reasons resolutions and slogans that they were unable to carry out. The SR statement also condemned the Bolsheviks' calling of a second congress of soviets on the eve of the Constituent Assembly, and complained that "according to the example of the Petrograd and Moscow Bolshevik newspapers, the [local] party is defaming and accusing the SR party." Concluding with an announcement of the party's withdrawal from the Soviet's executive bodies, the SR declaration noted that rank-and-file deputies would remain in the Soviet to safeguard the party's main concern—the speedy convocation of a constituent assembly.[39] Although intended to focus attention on their rejection of Bolshevik tactics, the SR leaders' action merely gave the Bolsheviks carte blanche to do as they pleased within the Soviet. The moderates and liberals had cried wolf too many times before for people to listen seriously now.

Responding to the SRs' challenge, the Bolshevik Executive Committee on October 19 approved a "defensive plan" worked out by the Military Section, to be implemented in the event an armed uprising broke out in Saratov. It included provisions for the stationing of pickets throughout the city, the guarding of liquor warehouses, and, most important, the

36. Medvedev, "Saratovskii Sovet," p. 81.

37. *Proletarii Povolzh'ia*, no. 117, October 19, 1917, p. 4.

38. Gesler, "Saratovskaia bol'shevistskaia organizatsiia," p. 43.

39. The declaration can be found in *Proletarii Povolzh'ia*, no. 118, October 20, 1917, p. 3; and in *Saratovskii vestnik*, no. 233, October 21, 1917, p. 3. Vasil'ev erroneously dated the withdrawal to October 21. See M. I. Vasil'ev-Iuzhin, "Proletarskaia revoliutsiia v Saratove," *Sovetskoe stroitel'stvo*, no. 10–11 (1927), pp. 120.

issuing of orders forbidding soldiers to take up arms without the sanction of the Military Section. The next day the Executive Committee made several other important decisions. It reorganized the provincial food organs (former members—mainly SRs—retained only half of their seats), adopting stringent regulations to end grain speculation, including requisitioning of grain from all pomeshchiki and from large and middle landowners. Moreover, the Executive Committee encouraged the All-Russian Executive Committee to transfer all privately owned land to land committees and to introduce fixed prices on all essential consumer items.[40] As Vasil'ev said, they had to "show the government that the threat of hunger in the province has forced the Soviet to introduce these measures independent of the national government."[41] The move toward transferring all privately owned land to land committees induced the SRs to play their last trump. Despite their earlier decision to withdraw from the Executive Committee of the Soviet, they now turned to the Bolsheviks and proposed that the two parties issue a joint declaration placing pomeshchik-owned land at the disposal of the peasants. The Bolsheviks more than balked at the SR suggestion. As Bankvitser put it, "we told them to go to hell."[42]

Soviet historians generally argue that following the Central Committee's decision of October 10 to put the armed uprising on the agenda, provincial organizations set about preparing for an armed uprising, as Lenin urged. As we have seen, however, the Saratov Bolshevik Committee readied itself instead for a transfer of power to the soviets in conjunction with the Second Congress of Soviets. While the Saratov committee knew of Lenin's call for an armed uprising before the congress, it likewise understood that as of October 16, the Central Committee had taken no concrete steps toward the realization of this intent. The Saratov committee had begun to prepare for the possibility that trouble might break out in Saratov, but limited its actions to defensive measures. All turned to Petrograd for news and directives. As Antonov candidly admitted, "our party committee impatiently waited for guiding directives from our Central Committee. But there weren't any."[43]

As the opening day of the Second Congress grew close, newspapers gave even more attention than before to the possibility of a Bolshevik uprising in Petrograd. The non-Bolshevik press emphasized the much-talked-about dissension within the party's Central Committee. In addition to the anxieties stirred by such thoughts, reports circulated in

40. P. S., "Khronika," no. 20, p. 117.
41. *Proletarii Povolzh'ia*, no. 121, October 24, 1917, p. 4.
42. Bankvitser, "Ot fevralia," p. 33.
43. Antonov-Saratovskii, "Oktiabr'skie dni," p. 292.

Saratov that "shady individuals" were planning to burn the city down.[44] An article in *Saratovskii vestnik* captured the bewilderment and exasperation that many townspeople must have felt over such rumors: "What we are living through now reminds one very much of the last days of a convict sentenced to death."[45]

On October 24, talk spread throughout Saratov that Topuridze had received a telegram announcing the outbreak of disorders in Petrograd. The provincial commissar's office indeed had received an important message from the capital. The cable gave an account of Kerensky's speech before the so-called Council of the Republic in which he accused the Bolsheviks of plotting against the government.[46] In Petrograd, October 24 was a day of growing tension between the Kerensky ministry and its opposition. By early morning the Military Revolutionary Committee, created by the Petrograd Soviet to prevent Kerensky from moving the local garrison to the front, warned the populace of an impending Kornilovite plot against the Congress of Soviets. Elsewhere at this time a contingent of officer trainees occupied a Bolshevik newspaper office and smashed the print plates. By early afternoon Kerensky had proclaimed a state of emergency. Just before dawn on the 25th, "defensive" measures instigated by the Bolsheviks through the Military Revolutionary Committee began in earnest.

A second telegram arrived in Saratov in the early morning of October 25. Signed by Minister of Post and Telegraph P. N. Maliantovich, it announced the beginning of an armed uprising in Petrograd. The news reached Topuridze at 6:00 A.M. He promptly alerted the commander of the garrison to order the few reliable troops to guard the local telegraph and telephone stations.

If in the early morning of October 25 Topuridze knew little about the situation in the capital, everybody else in Saratov knew a great deal less. Until noon post and telegraph workers were the only ones who had seen the telegrams from Petrograd. As in the capital, these workers belonged to an active union still under Menshevik influence. Because of their political orientation the workers cabled other offices in the Saratov district, calling upon their fellow communications workers to ignore Bolshevik orders and, in the event the Bolsheviks seized power, to go out on strike. In this manner, news from the capital emanated from Saratov to a select few in other parts of the province.

Back in his office, Topuridze deliberated carefully about an appropriate course of action. Knowing that he had few loyal troops at his dis-

44. See *Proletarii Povolzh'ia*, no. 121, October 24, 1917, p. 3.

45. *Saratovskii vestnik*, no. 236, October 25, 1917, p. 1.

46. Antonov-Saratovskii, *Godovshchina*, p. 2; Plaksin, "Poslednie dni," p. 16; Gerasimenko, *Sovety Nizhnego Povolzh'ia*, p. 101.

posal, Topuridze decided to keep the news of an uprising in the capital from the Saratov Bolsheviks as long as possible and to try to obtain assistance from Cossack divisions stationed nearby. He also met with representatives from the Duma, zemstvo, food-supply organs, and judiciary—and with leaders of the local SR and Menshevik committees.[47] They remained in session for over four hours but nothing is known about what took place. Judging from subsequent events, it seems that they agreed to stall, hoping that loyal troops would suppress the Bolshevik uprising in Petrograd. They also worked out a plan of resistance in the event the Saratov Bolsheviks followed in the footsteps of their Petrograd comrades.

By now it was no longer possible to put off a meeting with local Bolsheviks any longer. Chertkov arranged an interparty convocation of SRs, Mensheviks, and Bolsheviks at 6:00 P.M. According to Antonov, Chertkov "enticed" the Bolsheviks to the meeting by informing them that important telegrams had reached Saratov. Insisting that the Bolsheviks "must have received information from their own [people]," Chertkov expressed ignorance of the cables' contents. But the Bolsheviks had received no messages or directives from the Central Committee, and Antonov and Vasil'ev so informed the gathering. During the first part of the meeting the Saratov Bolsheviks refrained from commenting on events in the capital. "Local Bolsheviks," declared Vasil'ev, "cannot politically or morally judge the Petrograders." Perhaps this reaction was due to Chertkov's intimation that government forces had quelled the uprising in Petrograd. After several others spoke, the SR Minin put the following question to the Bolsheviks: "Do you or don't you support your Petrograd comrades?" "We support them," answered the Bolsheviks. In response the SRs announced their total withdrawal from the Soviet. "Good riddance!" snapped Vasil'ev. "Then we'll go [too]," replied the Mensheviks. "And good riddance to you, too," Vasil'ev claims to have fired back.[48]

After the interparty meeting broke down, the Saratov Bolshevik Committee met. It decided to keep the Executive Committee of the Soviet on guard and to convene a full plenum of the Soviet the following day. The committee then disbanded to enable Bolshevik Duma representatives to participate in a scheduled Duma meeting.

The Duma went into session at 9:45 P.M., about an hour before the Second Congress of Soviets opened in Petrograd and before it had passed

47. N. V. Afanas'ev, "Ustanovlenie Sovetskoi vlasti," pp. 71–72; *Khronika*, pp. 134–35; M. I. Vasil'ev-Iuzhin, "Oktiabr'skaia revoliutsiia v Saratove," in *Piat' let proletarskoi bor'by*, p. 9.

48. Gesler, "Saratovskaia bol'shevistskaia organizatsiia," p. 44; Antonov-Saratovskii, *Pod stiagom*, p. 147; Antonov-Saratovskii, *Godovshchina*, pp. 2–3; Vasil'ev-Iuzhin, "Proletarskaia revoliutsiia v Saratove," pp. 120–21.

a resolution supporting an all-socialist government. "We all know. . . ," declared Chertkov in his opening address, "of the sad telegrams from Petrograd . . . the Bolsheviks have openly risen up against the Provisional Government and have begun a civil war." The majority of members opposed suggestions to adjourn for short fractional meetings. Some moderate socialists and Kadets expressed disapproval of their exclusion from Topuridze's private meeting earlier in the day—a clear indication that the groups opposed to the Bolsheviks were divided. Meanwhile, Vasil'ev insisted that the Bolsheviks had no intention of moving against the government. After considerable discussion the Duma agreed to create a "Committee to Save the Revolution," to include leaders from the SR, Menshevik, and Popular Socialist parties. At this point the discussion turned hostile. The Bolshevik Mitskevich suggested tauntingly that the committee should be called the "Committee against the Revolution." "You have betrayed the revolution," he accused, "and you are against the poor peasants. I spit on you." "He belongs in a psychiatric ward," responded several Duma members. With this exchange the meeting ended.[49] "I'll never forget," wrote Mitskevich, "that after the Duma meeting an SR ran up to me, grabbed me by the throat, and began to choke me."[50]

While the Duma was in session Antonov chaired a meeting of local Bolsheviks. Because events seemed to be leading toward a showdown, party leaders agreed to prepare troops and the Red Guard for action. Earlier in the month, after Miliutin's visit to Saratov, measures had been taken to mobilize forces for a potential conflict. Unsuccessful in obtaining arms for the Red Guard, the Bolsheviks had addressed a letter to the Central Committee, asking it for assistance. Local Bolsheviks also had stepped up their activity in the garrison, calling frequent meetings and sponsoring special lectures, but nothing appears to have been done in terms of concrete military planning. Now they decided to maintain constant communication with garrison troops and to hold discussions with the railroad workers' contingent of the Red Guard.[51]

That night, as Bolshevik forces in Petrograd took the Winter Palace, the townspeople of Saratov experienced one of their last peaceful evenings for some days to come. By the morning of October 26, Bolsheviks and moderate socialists had launched a flurry of activity. Nonetheless, both

49. The most detailed accounts of the Duma meeting of October 25 can be found in *Saratovskii vestnik*, no. 238, October 27, 1917, pp. 3–4, and in *Proletarii Povolzh'ia*, no. 124, October 27, 1917, p. 4. See also *Khronika*, p. 136; Antonov-Saratovskii, *Godovshchina*, p. 3; Vasil'ev-Iuzhin, "Proletarskaia revoliutsiia," pp. 121–22.

50. Mitskevich, "Vospominaniia o revoliutsii," p. 28. See also Lebedev, "Fevral'–oktiabr'," p. 255; and *Saratovskii vestnik*, no. 238, October 27, 1917, p. 3.

51. Antonov-Saratovskii, *Pod stiagom*, p. 147.

sides tried to stall for time: the Bolsheviks waited for directives from the Central Committee; the moderates pinned their hopes on a speedy rescue by Cossack forces. No one knew the outcome of the uprising in Petrograd. During the early morning Bolshevik speakers conducted agitational work in factories, and at the barracks they tried to persuade the soldiers to obey orders of the Soviet only. There was no call for action or any effort to spark a demonstration. Perhaps to intimidate the opposition, Bolshevik agitators pressed some 1,200 artillery troops into passing a resolution demanding the immediate transfer of power to the soviets, the transfer of land to peasants, the conclusion of a peace settlement, and the speedy convocation of a constituent assembly. The soldiers expressed their readiness to win by force any demands that were not met.[52]

The moderate socialists also were busy on the morning of October 26. The office of the provincial commissar—housed with the Executive Committee of the Soviet in the former governor's home—was the scene of considerable bustle. There, Duma members, city officials, the commissar of police, and heavily armed officers tried to make the most of one Bolshevik handicap: lack of Bolshevik cadres within the officer corps. Antonov even admitted that "in the garrison we had an overwhelming preponderance in a quantitative sense, but we were much weaker in a qualitative one."[53] Vasil'ev became suspicious when he entered the Military Section of the Soviet and discovered that the section's chairman and other members were nowhere to be found. It turned out that the SR Neimichenko had invited Bolshevik officers to a secret meeting, at which he sought to persuade them to form a special military committee. The chairman of the Soviet's Military Section was the twenty-year-old Bolshevik second lieutenant Sokolov. "I well knew that this sympathetic, sincere, and bold youth," Vasil'ev wrote, "was tied by personal friendship to Pontriagin, Didenko, Neimichenko, and other leaders of the SR military clique."[54] These personal bonds help explain subsequent events.

In the early afternoon a group of officers had appeared before the Soviet's Executive Committee with a proposal to form a special military committee. They insisted upon creation of a "neutral" revolutionary staff composed solely of military personnel, to be selected not proportionally, by party strength, but rather according to the candidates' "personal qualities." The staff would assume responsibility for the defense of the city and would not be subordinated to the Soviet or Duma.[55] Because the plan

52. *Khronika*, p. 139.
53. Antonov-Saratovskii, *Pod stiagom*, p. 148.
54. Vasil'ev-Iuzhin, "Proletarskaia revoliutsiia v Saratove," p. 123.
55. Antonov-Saratovskii, *Godovshchina*, p. 4; Antonov-Saratovskii, *Pod stiagom*, p. 150.

amounted to setting up military rule under the influence of moderate leaders, the Executive Committee recommended instead the selection of a military staff or committee under the Soviet's control. Confident that the Soviet plenum would reject the officers' proposal, Antonov, Vasil'ev, and the other Bolshevik leaders agreed to the officers' suggestion pending approval by the Soviet. Yet some Bolsheviks from the very beginning opposed even the tentative suggestion of cooperation with the military leaders.[56]

A full plenum of the Soviet assembled in the conservatory after ten o'clock that evening. Overflowing with delegates and curious bystanders, the hall now accommodated an estimated 2,500 citizens in all. Since a Bolshevik factional meeting beforehand had postponed the opening of the plenum, the general mood was anxious. After Antonov convened the session, Vasil'ev reported on events in the capital. Informing the audience that the Petrograd Soviet had seized power and that Lenin and Trotsky had formed a new government, Vasil'ev warned that compromise and coalition with the bourgeoisie were over, that one was either for or against the revolution. He also warmly greeted rank-and-file SR deputies who showed up at the meeting in spite of their party's withdrawal from the Soviet. Noting the strong possibility that Cossack regiments stationed in the province would march on Saratov, Vasil'ev stressed the need to create a revolutionary staff under the Soviet's jurisdiction. Antonov took the floor after Vasil'ev and presented a proposal for the structure and composition of the military staff. According to his provisions, it was to be coordinated by the Military Section of the Soviet but controlled by the Executive Committee. An enthusiastic wave of applause met this recommendation. When it came to selecting members, however, deputies opposed the candidacy of some leading SRs. Arguing that the staff's purpose was ill defined, that several nominees did not enjoy the support of the garrison, and that on the panel presented SRs outnumbered Bolsheviks, a soldier questioned the very need for the formation of such a body. Afterward, Soviet delegates rejected the candidacy of the SRs Didenko, Maksimovich, and Zaitsev. Antonov suggested that the Soviet deputies accept the slate of twenty candidates except for these three. When the Soviet deputies approved this plan, the SRs present announced that they would quit the Soviet. To the understandable dismay of the Soviet's Bolshevik leaders, Sokolov and Zhebrov, the two leading Bolshevik candidates on the list, likewise voiced their intentions to withdraw from the council. Their support of their fellow SR officers

56. Vasil'ev-Iuzhin, "Proletarskaia revoliutsiia v Saratove," p. 124; V. Leikina, "Oktiabr' po Rossii," *Proletarskaia revoliutsiia*, no. 49 (1926), p. 217; Bankvitser, "Ot fevralia," p. 34.

reflected a strong military camaraderie that crossed party lines, and also the fact that the Bolshevik Committee was correct in being suspicious of the nature of its support among the officer corps.[57]

For a moment after the departure of the disgruntled SR officers, the meeting lapsed into an embarrassing silence, broken by the unexpected appearance of some of the city's leading Mensheviks—Chertkov, Anisimov, Maizel', and Maiskii. Speaking on behalf of the group, Chertkov told the plenum that several telegrams had just arrived from Petrograd, informing Saratov that Kerensky at the head of loyal troops had crushed the Bolshevik uprising in the capital.[58] The Bolsheviks reacted to this announcement with disbelief. Catcalls, the stomping of feet, and a flood of vulgarity met Chertkov's insistence that he was not lying. "OK," responded Chertkov, "we fulfilled our obligation. We warned you. We announce that we will no longer participate in the Soviet." Antonov then took the floor. "I am answering on behalf of the Soviet. You are walking out, you are washing your hands like Pilate. So you're leaving. But remember that the workers and peasants will never forgive this. They will tell from generation to generation that in the greatest moment in our life, when we seized power and held off the furious attacks of the bourgeoisie, the Mensheviks and SRs abandoned us and went over to the enemy."[59] Applause and cheers indicated that the overwhelming majority in the crowd shared Antonov's sentiments. As the uproar subsided, reports arrived that the Duma was organizing a combat staff and was preparing an attack against the Soviet. In response, the plenum decided that the Bureau of the Executive Committee would take responsibility for defending the city. The garrison was ordered to stay put unless called into action by the Executive Committee. At 3:30 A.M. the Soviet adjourned. As the deputies were filing out of the conservatory building, a group of well-armed junkers could be seen making their way from the military settlement to the Duma building.[60]

In another part of town it was an evening of decision making for the Duma as well. Chertkov now suggested that the Duma turn itself into the center of authority in Saratov. At this moment a journalist read the contents of a telegram received from Petrograd, stating that Kerensky had

57. This discussion is reconstructed from accounts in *Saratovskii vestnik*, no. 239, October 28, 1917, p. 3; Antonov-Saratovskii, *Godovshchina*, pp. 4–6; P. S., "Khronika," no. 20, p. 118; Petrov, "Saratovskii proletariat," p. 18; *Saratovskii Sovet*, pp. 217–18; *Khronika*, pp. 140–41; V. Babushkin, "Istoricheskaia noch': Vospominaniia," in *Piat' let proletarskoi bor'by*, pp. 21–22.

58. Antonov-Saratovskii, *Godovshchina*, p. 5; *Proletarii Povolzh'ia*, no. 125, October 28, 1917, p. 4; Bankvitser, "Ot fevralia," p. 34.

59. Antonov-Saratovskii, *Godovshchina*, p. 6.

60. Petrov, "Saratovskii proletariat," pp. 18–19; Antonov-Saratovskii, *Pod stiagom*, p. 161.

marched on the capital but that the outcome of his venture was unknown. A one-and-a-half-hour break was agreed upon, during which Chertkov and the other Mensheviks dropped in on the Soviet meeting. After their unsuccessful experience there, the Duma reconvened and promptly resolved to create a battle staff composed of those officers rejected by the Soviet (Maksimovich, Didenko, Zaitsev, and others). The deputies declared the Duma the "only organ of power in the city and province." In addition, the Duma summoned the officer training school to be on military alert. It then prepared two appeals—"To All Citizens, Soldiers, and Officers" and "To All Citizens of the City of Saratov." Both documents announced that the Duma was the legitimate authority in the city and ordered the population to remain calm.[61]

Not all of the deputies went home when the Soviet adjourned in the early hours of October 27. The Executive Committee reconvened and selected a special bureau. Vasil'ev began work on a general appeal to the population and Antonov drafted a land decree. Both documents were ready in twenty minutes and were approved by the bureau. Declaring that the tragic situation in the country had forced the Petrograd workers and soldiers to remove the Kerensky government from office, the appeal to the townspeople of Saratov called upon all government and private office workers to remain at their posts and to obey orders of the Soviet. It likewise instructed soldiers and workers to follow directives issued by the Soviet only, and urged the population to remain calm. A caveat was added that any attempts to foment disorder would be mercilessly put down by armed force. The declaration assured Saratovites that preparations for elections to the Constituent Assembly would continue as planned. Moreover, the document announced that the Soviet had created a Military Revolutionary Committee (the special bureau of the Executive Committee) that had assumed power on behalf of the Soviet.[62]

The decree on land was based on the land policy of the SR party. Although strikingly similar to the land decree issued by the new Soviet government (Council of People's Commissars, or Sovnarkom) on October 26, the Saratov land decree was of local provenance. Placing all pomeshchik, monastery, church, and privately owned land at the disposal of peasant land committees, the decree expressed what the peasants most wanted to hear. But it also laid out regulations and obligations. Private individuals could not sell food reserves taken from confiscated estates. Live inventory was to be meted out according to need and equipment was to be placed under control of peasant organizations. Plunder-

61. Antonov-Saratovskii, *Godovshchina*, p. 8.

62. Ibid., pp. 7–8; Antonov-Saratovskii, *Pod stiagom*, pp. 160–61; Vasil'ev, "Proletarskaia revoliutsiia v Saratove," pp. 126–27.

Saratov Conservatory (built 1900–1902), where Soviet power was declared in 1917

ing of estates was strongly prohibited; peasant committees carried responsibility for cataloging all seized wealth, for preserving order, and for preventing excesses. Stipulating that the Saratov Soviet would settle conflicts, the decree gave local peasant bodies authority to resolve disagreements between communes. Finally, the Saratov Soviet's land decree ordered peasant committees to inform the Soviet of the amount of grain they were able to put at the disposal of the Soviet "to feed workers, the army, and the rest of the urban population."[63]

The Bureau of the Soviet took other important steps to consolidate power. It replaced Topuridze with Lebedev as provincial commissar and appointed emissaries to assume the responsibilities of the former uezd commissars. It prohibited newspapers and printshops from putting out anti-Bolshevik literature.[64] It designated a military officer, P. Shcherbakov, recommended by the soldiers themselves, to direct operations in case of an attack on the Soviet.[65] It also ordered Red Guardsmen and troops to take by force the telegraph and telephone stations that had been secured earlier by Topuridze. Finally, the Bureau decided to disconnect all phone lines not needed by the Soviet's Executive Committee.[66]

Townspeople who took to the streets on the morning of October 27 must have been confused by the contradictory signals bombarding them. Parading up and down the main thoroughfares of town, automobiles distributed leaflets informing the population that the Petrograd Soviet had assumed authority in the capital. In addition to the appeals issued by the Bureau of the Executive Committee of the Soviet, the Duma Committee to Save the Revolution had circulated its messages to the citizens of Saratov. Despite efforts of Red Guardsmen to intimidate them, workers at the government printing office ran off the Duma's two announcements. The first, "To All Citizens, Soldiers, and Officers," maintained that the Bolsheviks had risen up in Petrograd in order to subvert the Constituent Assembly and to seize power. The announcement reported the formation of the Committee to Save the Revolution and its Revolutionary Staff. All able-bodied men were enjoined to appear at the Duma building, while the garrison was instructed to obey commands only of the Committee to Save the Revolution. "All citizens," the decree concluded, "must recognize no other authority than that of the Provisional Government and of the Committee to Save the Revolution." The second

63. See Mitskevich, "Vospominaniia o revoliutsii," p. 28.

64. See, for example, *Saratovskii vestnik*, no. 239, October 28, 1917, p. 3; *Proletarii Povolzh'ia*, no. 125, October 28, 1917, p. 4.

65. Antonov-Saratovskii, *Godovshchina*, p. 7. See also *Saratovskii listok*, no. 238, November 5, 1917, p. 3.

66. Antonov-Saratovskii, *Pod stiagom*, p. 160; V. M. Korneeva, "Vospominaniia o deiatel'nosti Ispolnitel'nogo Komiteta v pervye dni Oktiabr'skoi revoliutsii," in *Piat' let proletarskoi bor'by*, p. 25.

Duma proclamation, "To All Citizens of the City of Saratov," reiterated the appeal for citizens to come to the Duma's aid. "All citizens who believe in the Provisional Government, which is leading the country to the Constituent Assembly," it read, "are obligated to fulfill their civil duty before the revolution and the country and to execute the present order immediately."[67]

For those who had viewed the Duma with suspicion all along, the moderate socialists' appeals issued in the name of the Duma came close to betrayal of the revolution. It is not surprising that so few responded to their appeal. In all, about 3,000 men, women, and students made their way to the Duma building. Apart from the leaders of the moderate socialist parties and some Duma members, cadets from the officer training school, officials, office workers, seminary students, shop owners, and students, including twelve- and thirteen-year-olds from the commercial school, answered the Duma's call to arms.[68] SR officers unsuccessfully made an effort to win the support of the artillerymen, since Pontriagin at least still continued to enjoy some popularity among them. Instead, Vasil'ev succeeded in neutralizing this important unit in the garrison.

On October 27 both sides took measures to be ready for an armed struggle if one broke out. Stressing the need to maintain order, Soviet agitators went to the barracks and factories. Bankvitser, the Bolshevik leader from Volsk, entrenched a small battalion of machine gunners around the Soviet building to defend the Executive Committee. The Red Guard also held impromptu meetings, while soldiers from the Ninety-second Regiment, after learning that the Second Congress of Soviets had resolved to take power, passed a resolution expressing their readiness to defend Soviet power in Saratov.[69] Although the Bolsheviks claimed the sympathies of the garrison, they would rely more heavily on the workers' Red Guard. For the moment Bolshevik leaders sought to keep all but a few dependable companies in their barracks and their firearms locked up.

Armed with machine guns, the Duma forces stationed themselves in the bell towers of the Church of St. Michael the Archangel. Toward evening a detachment of junkers confiscated a cache of rifles and began to stock an arsenal inside the Duma building. The cadets disarmed workers and soldiers, arrested supporters of the Soviet, and raided Vasil'ev's apartment. Other young officers went to nearby stores and to the closest markets, where they seized sacks of quinces and potatoes, carts, hay, and

67. Antonov-Saratovskii, *Godovshchina*, pp. 8–9, and in *Proletarii Povolzh'ia*, no. 125, October 28, 1917, p. 1; *Saratovskii vestnik*, no. 239, October 28, 1917, p. 2.

68. Vasil'ev-Iuzhin, "Proletarskaia revoliutsiia v Saratove," p. 128.

69. *Khronika*, p. 143.

firewood in order to construct barricades to shield the Duma building. Topuridze cabled to Baland and other railroad stations, ordering the Cossacks billeted there to come to the Duma's defense. A young officer who arrived at the Duma remembered that "the hall was packed with people of all ranks. . . . The Duma members themselves predominated. They were confused, scared, and listless. They ran from room to room giving orders and then changing them. When it comes right down to it, it was difficult to say who led the defense."[70] In another part of town troops loyal to the Duma arrested several members of the Soviet's Executive Committee as they returned by car from the railroad station, where they had tried unsuccessfully to establish contact with Moscow. (This attempt suggests that the Saratov Soviet was still waiting for directives from the capital and that it was not certain whether Kerensky had put down the Bolshevik uprising in Petrograd.) *Proletarii Povolzh'ia* informed readers that day that the Petrograd Soviet, demanding the transfer of power to the soviets, had declared the Provisional Government deposed.[71] Commenting on conditions in Saratov on October 27, *Saratovskii vestnik* reported that "throughout the day a multitude of all sorts of fantastic rumors circulated. However, life went on as normal. No excesses were observed. In the city all is calm."[72]

The night passed without incident, but by dawn on October 28 the Soviet had decided to force a showdown. In the early morning the Military Revolutionary Committee of the Soviet gave the order to surround the barricaded Duma building. About 3,000 soldiers and members of the Red Guard took up posts.[73] Rank-and-file Soviet members, including SRs, Mensheviks, and nonparty people, joined them.[74] By noon the Duma's forces had dwindled considerably. Only 30 of the 113 Duma members now remained inside. Defections were as heavy among the junkers and officers: the Duma's armed force had thinned to 300 cadets, about 100 officers, and several hundred private citizens.[75] A correspondent from *Saratovskii vestnik* remarked that by 4:00 P.M. it had become clear to the Duma supporters that "the forces were quite uneven."[76] Those peering through the windows of the Duma building in the late afternoon found themselves staring at enemy artillery entrenched along Sokolov Mountain near the Stock Exchange.

70. Golubov, "Saratov v 1917," p. 44.
71. *Proletarii Povolzh'ia*, no. 124, October 27, 1917, p. 1.
72. *Saratovskii vestnik*, no. 239, October 28, 1917, p. 3.
73. *Saratovskii listok*, no. 238, November 5, 1917, p. 2.
74. Plaksin, "Poslednie dni," p. 18.
75. *Khronika*, p. 148.
76. *Saratovskii vestnik*, no. 241, November 5, 1917, p. 2.

Neither side, despite serious preparations for battle, wished to fire the first shot. The Executive Committee eventually agreed to negotiate with the Duma that evening. According to Bolshevik memoirs, the Duma forces were hoping that the Cossacks would come to their aid. Only after Vasil'ev warned the Duma by telephone that shooting would break out if negotiations did not soon begin would the Duma agree to send a delegation to the Soviet. The capitulation document drawn up by the Executive Committee guaranteed the personal safety of the Duma's defenders, but demanded the "counterrevolutionaries'" disarmament. It called for cooperation in the normal functioning of the municipal economy, disbanding of the military staff and the Committee to Save the Revolution, and abrogation of the committee's appeals to the population.[77] Five representatives from the Duma soon appeared before the Executive Committee of the Soviet. At first they seemed reluctant to sign the terms of surrender, but the announcement that shooting had broken out persuaded the representatives to yield. They were given ten minutes to consult by telephone with those inside the Duma building, after which they accepted the Soviet's terms.[78] Several Executive Committee members led by Antonov then returned with the delegation to the Duma building. As Antonov and other members of the Executive Committee entered the meeting hall, however, those inside expressed their unwillingness to accept the Soviet's demands. At this point an agitated Duma member burst into the hall screaming, "They're attacking." Antonov stepped out into the street to persuade the troops to give the Duma more time to make up its mind.

Back in the former governor's home, where the Executive Committee of the Soviet was meeting, the sequence of events appeared to unfold differently. "No sooner had the delegation left," wrote Vasil'ev in his memoirs, "than a telephone ring was heard." Picking up the receiver, Vasil'ev found out from Pontriagin that the Duma demanded that its representatives return immediately. Informing Vasil'ev that the Duma had received a telegram that Kerensky had retaken Petrograd, Pontriagin added that the Duma had decided to hold out until morning and not to sign any document.[79] The conversation ended as Vasil'ev told Pontriagin that the Duma representatives had already agreed to surrender.

The Soviet probably did not take the stories about Kerensky's victory in Petrograd seriously because the telegraph office was now in the Bolsheviks' hands. With this in mind, Vasil'ev soon rang back to inquire

77. *Saratovskii Sovet,* p. 220; Antonov-Saratovskii, *Godovshchina,* p. 9; *Saratovskii listok,* no. 238, November 5, 1917, p. 2.

78. *Izvestiia Saratovskogo Soveta,* no. 93, November 12, 1917, p. 1; Antonov-Saratovskii, *Godovshchina,* p. 168.

79. Vasil'ev-Iuzhin, "Proletarskaia revoliutsiia v Saratove," p. 132; *Izvestiia Saratovskogo Soveta,* no. 93/97, November 12, 1917, p. 1.

whether the Duma had accepted the terms of surrender worked out by the Soviet. After speaking once again to Pontriagin and then with Didenko, he heard Antonov come on the line to say that the Duma had accepted the Soviet's demands. Minutes later Antonov left the Duma building. As Vasil'ev put down the receiver and informed the Executive Committee of what had taken place in the Duma, shots rang out, breaking several windowpanes. Seconds later the electric lights flickered off. As Antonov approached the Soviet lines, the crackling of rifle fire ripped through the dull patter of rain, forcing him to run for cover. The artillery flashed their fire. And while sources on both sides attest to the bravery of their supporters, not everyone's behavior was exemplary. Anticipation of battle and occasional snow flurries cooled the passions of many would-be heroes. Lebedev noted that when the first shot resounded, some Red Guardsmen fled their posts. "It was quite unpleasant to witness this scene," he remembered.[80]

Shooting continued all night. According to Vasil'ev, it was only after the firing had begun that he and two other members of the Soviet's Executive Committee learned that school-age children had remained inside the Duma building. Later, a leading female Menshevik activist named Lavler and another Menshevik approached Vasil'ev to inquire whether the Soviet would consider a cease-fire. Vasil'ev expressed his readiness to meet with representatives authorized by the Duma to work out a truce. Toward dawn, Pontriagin, Miasoedov, and B. S. Boiarskii appeared before the Executive Committee and informed it that the Duma was ready to submit to the Soviet. With his customary brassiness, Vasil'ev told them that the Soviet's capitulation demands had changed, that now all those who had taken part in resisting the Soviet were subject to arrest. "This is necessary and in the interests of their personal safety," argued Vasil'ev.[81] Eventually the Duma representatives accepted the Soviet's demands. Pontriagin even agreed to place himself under guard rather than chance being detected by angry soldiers while making his way back to the Duma.[82]

But the shooting continued after the Soviet issued an order to cease firing. The Red Guardsmen and artillery soldiers were reluctant to put down their firearms. It had rained all night, "poured from buckets," as Martsinovskii said, and the workers and soldiers understandably were antagonistic.[83] Two of their comrades were dead and ten others lay wounded. Moreover, stray shots kept coming from the side of the Duma.

80. Lebedev, "Fevral'-oktiabr'," p. 258.

81. Vasil'ev-Iuzhin, "Proletarskaia revoliutsiia v Saratove," pp. 134–35; Petrov, "Saratovskii proletariat," p. 22.

82. *Izvestiia Saratovskogo Soveta*, no. 93/97, November 12, 1917, p. 1.

83. A. Martsinovskii, "Pervye mesiatsy Oktiabr'skoi revoliutsii v Saratove," *Kommunisticheskii put'*, no. 20 (1927), p. 127.

Occasional outbursts from machine gunners in the bell towers of the Church of St. Michael the Archangel made the Soviet forces fear that the Duma would again stall for time. Taking advantage of the popularity he enjoyed in the garrison, Vasil'ev drove around to each contingent of soldiers, persuading them to stop shooting. It is likely that the soldiers would have continued firing had Vasil'ev not been on the spot. Once the Soviet forces lowered their rifles, Vasil'ev went into the Duma building to conclude the surrender.

Vasil'ev later wrote that he was surprised that so few people were still inside. He found many high school, commercial school, and seminary students, but only a handful of Duma deputies and leaders of the moderate socialists; the others had slipped away. "Neither Minin nor Didenko turned up among the arrested," wrote Vasil'ev, "and it seems that the first who tried to hide was the former provincial commissar, Topuridze."[84] There were also almost no members of the Kadet party present. In all, an estimated 298 junkers and 75 officers, including General Gorskii, head of the garrison, surrendered. Eight people inside had been wounded and another had died. "It is interesting to note," commented Lebedev, "that among those seized in the Duma was not one soldier, nor one worker, not even from the ranks of the Mensheviks and SRs."[85]

Those who had capitulated were in a dangerous position, for Vasil'ev could no longer guarantee their personal safety. As they made their way out of the Duma hall toward the former governor's home, where they were to be detained, they were met by hostile glances, abusive language, and calls of "Shoot them all" and "Into the Volga."[86] A young Cossack officer who had defended the Duma recalled that people on the street beat those who had surrendered, including General Gorskii, whose age did not save him from this indignity. Afterward a crowd of angry women "threw themselves upon us, scratching our faces with their dirty hands. Murderers [they yelled]." Another gang of soldiers approached with machine guns, prepared to mow down the cadets. Only the direct pleading of Vasil'ev, recalled the young Cossack, prevented them from being murdered by the mob,[87] which *Saratovskii listok* estimated to be 10,000 strong. Meanwhile, soldiers stormed into the building and helped them-

84. Vasil'ev-Iuzhin, "Proletarskaia revoliutsiia v Saratove," p. 139. Interestingly, some of the most vocal opponents of the Bolsheviks at this time came to join the party during the Civil War. Maizel' died on the front in 1918, a member of the Communist party. Chertkov also accepted Soviet power, as did the SR Minin, who died in Arkhangelsk fighting the British. See E. P., "Iz zhizni Saratovskoi organizatsii," *Vestnik Saratovskogo Gubkoma (RKP)*, no. 24 (1922), p. 12.

85. Lebedev, "Fevral'–oktiabr'," p. 261.

86. *Saratovskii listok*, no. 238, November 5, 1917, p. 2.

87. Golubov, "1917 v Saratove," pp. 47–48.

selves to the reserves of sausage, wine, canned meats, and bread. Other soldiers tore down the barricades formed by sacks of quinces and hungrily threw themselves upon them. As revolutionary justice had it, the Soviet charged the confiscated food items to those Mensheviks and SRs who had taken the goods from local merchants.[88]

A few days after the Saratov Soviet won the showdown with the forces of the City Duma, a local newspaper reported that "nothing unusual has happened. Instead of Topuridze, Lebedev has begun to rule."[89] But this appraisal was only partially true. The Soviet had but formally proclaimed the authority it had enjoyed among Saratov's working class and soldiers. To be sure, not everyone recognized this fact, and in some circles those who had defended the Duma were now hailed as heroes. What the paper failed to report was that the first shots of a civil war that was to last three tortured years had already been fired.

88. Martsinovskii, "Pervye dni Oktiabr'skoi revoliutsii," p. 128.
89. Quoted in Lebedev, "Fevral'–oktiabr'," p. 256.

CHAPTER 8

Regnat Populus: The Establishment of Soviet Power in Saratov Province

The Saratov Soviet's victory over the City Duma's forces touched off a rash of opposition to what, in effect, was amounting to Bolshevik rule. For five days following the siege of the Duma the non-Bolshevik papers fell silent. Then they began to vent their rage. The newspaper of the local Soviet of Peasant Deputies, published irregularly since the Saratov Province Peasant Congress in September, expressed its determined opposition to the Saratov Soviet's actions. "The Bolsheviks are the enemies of the people. They are undermining the elections to the Constituent Assembly." The publication's advice to its readers left no room for misinterpretation. To combat the Bolsheviks the population should "protest against their crude use of force, refuse to subordinate themselves to their orders, and disbelieve their promises."[1] "We are living under the power of darkness," cautioned *Saratovskii listok* when it resumed publication on November 5. A resolution signed by twenty-four organizations representing the city bureaucracy and government offices blasted the Bolsheviks and expressed support for the toppled Kerensky government. The Union of Newspaper Workers protested on behalf of 912 union members.[2] Under this onslaught of animadversions against Bolshevik power, most city employees went on strike during the coming weeks. A strike by telegraph and postal workers cut off Saratov from Petrograd for

1. *Izvestiia Saratovskogo gubernskogo Soveta krest'ianskikh deputatov,* November 4, 1917, pp. 1–2.
2. *Saratovskii listok,* no. 238, November 5, 1917, pp. 2–3.

almost two months and plunged several district towns into total ignorance of unfolding events. The Saratov Doctors' Union, announcing that it no longer would treat Bolshevik patients, expelled its two Bolshevik members. In the garrison, officers abandoned their units, a move that eventually forced the Soviet to commission the soldiers' committees to elect their own leaders.

The difficulties faced by the Bolshevik government in Petrograd in dealing with the other socialist parties in the days after the October Revolution broadly influenced the Saratov Bolsheviks' relationships with their own opposition. By an ironic twist of fate the moderates tried to overthrow Lenin's government precisely when the Bolshevik leadership may have been most willing to compromise and form an all-socialist coalition. The moderates' abandonment of the Second Congress of Soviets followed by their recourse to armed resistance gave Lenin, Trotsky, and other Bolshevik militants the ammunition they needed to convince their comrades that a coalition with the "counterrevolutionary" SRs and Mensheviks was as undesirable as participation in a ministry with the hated bourgeoisie. In the immediate aftermath of the Bolsheviks' coming to power in Petrograd, some SR and Menshevik leaders linked up with Kerensky, General Krasnov, and various Cossack units with the aim of crushing the Bolshevik government. Armed conflict raged in the streets of the ancient capital of Moscow during the first days of November. Under pressure from the All-Russian Executive Committee of Railway Workers (Vikhzhel) and other workers' organizations, a group of Left SRs, Menshevik Internationalists, and prominent Bolsheviks considered formation of a government that would include all groups to the left of the Kadets.

Although genuinely popular, the call for a "homogeneous socialist ministry" never amounted to anything. A Bolshevik–Left SR victory in Moscow and the collapse of the anti-Bolshevik military campaigns emboldened the party's leadership despite the resignation from the Central Committee and Council of Peoples' Commissars of such moderates as Zinoviev, Kamenev, and Saratov's Miliutin, who believed that the only way to avert civil war was to form an all-socialist ministry. Even though they were bargaining from a position of weakness, the SR and Menshevik spokesmen advocating coalition pretentiously opposed inclusion of Lenin and Trotsky in any new government. Their strong stand may well have been taken in the belief that no one would launch civil war solely as a matter of principle; if it was, they grossly underestimated the strength of Lenin's convictions.

The rupture of the SR party a few weeks later and the entrance of the Left SRs into the Sovnarkom helped immensely to strengthen the Bolsheviks' hand in the provinces. The events of October had exposed the extraordinary tension that had built up within the SR party by the fall of 1917. During the second half of November efforts to call the long overdue party congress resulted in the formation of a separate Left SR party. Although they disagreed with the Bolsheviks over numerous key issues, the Left SRs consented to join the government. In mid-November the All-Russian Peasants' Executive Committee, under Left SR leadership, merged with the Petrograd Soviet's Executive Committee. In December several Left SRs accepted government portfolios, lending a measure of stability to the new regime.

In Saratov the possibility of direct Cossack intervention helped solidify the anti-Soviet opposition; from the end of October until the last days of December the Orenburg Cossack Division, under orders from Ataman Dutov, maneuvered along the Lower Volga. Muffled communications, unreliable news, and false hopes guaranteed circulation of a host of rumors that left their mark on local developments. According to the diary entries of a Russian-born American who arrived in Saratov in October, rumors had it that Kerensky had returned to Petrograd and that reliable troops had crushed the Bolsheviks in Moscow and Kazan. Another rumor "hanged both Lenin and Trotsky." Yet another maintained that Cossacks had liberated Tsaritsyn and executed the Bolshevik leadership. The Saratov Bolsheviks' seizure of local banks set off a flurry of speculation that Lebedev, Vasil'ev, and Antonov had fled Saratov with millions of rubles.[3] All in all, the threat of a Cossack attack and lack of news naturally complicated the Soviet's relationship with the defeated Duma, which reconvened for the first time since the siege on November 9. Lashing out at the Bolsheviks' strong-armed behavior on the eve of elections to the Constituent Assembly, Chertkov emphasized that Miliutin, Kamenev, and Zinoviev had split with the Bolshevik Central Committee over its unwillingness to form a coalition ministry with the other socialists.

News of such conflict within the Bolshevik top leadership kept hopes burning locally that Bolshevik power would collapse and lent powerful impetus to those willing to challenge the Soviet's assumption of power. The Duma pressed for the release of the imprisoned junkers, who, if the anti-Bolshevik press is to be believed, suffered at the hands of their jailers. Vasil'ev promised the junkers' emancipation after the Cossack threat abated. A few days later the Duma members and city civil servants warned the Soviet that they would begin a five-week strike if the junkers were not set free. Arguing that the soldiers strongly opposed such a move, Antonov insisted that the Duma's demands simply could not be

3. Alexis V. Babine Diary, Library of Congress, Manuscript Division, Babine Papers, sec. 1 (1917–1919), pp. 16–35.

Meeting at Khlebnaia Square, November 1917

met.[4] Meanwhile, the Saratov Soviet prepared for an armed attack and also conducted negotiations with the Cossacks, who, as it turned out, wanted to avoid conflict as well.

Throughout November anti-Bolshevik elements in Saratov sought to discredit the Bolsheviks, whom they viewed as lawless usurpers. The majority of civil service employees and professionals responded positively to the Kadet A. A. Nikonov's call to "isolate the Bolsheviks from all imaginable cultural support."[5] An ephemeral "Soviet of Office Workers, Government Employees, and Workers of Private Organizations" assisted the Duma in orchestrating complaints against the Soviet. Although the moderate socialists and Kadets were united in their antagonism to the Bolsheviks, their lack of a broader basis for cooperation ruined their chances for success, as it had done in the past. When the Soviet invited all of the city employees and clerks to a meeting on November 21, an estimated 10,000 people held a counterdemonstration inspired by the SRs in Theater Square to condemn one-party rule and to demand freedom of speech and of the press. Emphasizing the legitimacy of the upcoming Constituent Assembly, the meeting called for the creation of a new national government *excluding the bourgeoisie.*[6]

Sustained opposition to the new regime and lack of directives from Petrograd thus characterized the first months of Soviet power in Saratov.

4. *Saratovskii vestnik*, no. 242, November 11, 1917, pp. 3–4; no. 247, November 17, 1917, pp. 3–4.
5. Antonov-Saratovskii, *Godovshchina*, p. 13.
6. *Saratovskii vestnik*, no. 251, November 23, 1917, pp. 3–4.

According to Antonov, the situation did not improve after the strike of the communications workers ended and ties were reestablished with the center. "Quite often," he recalled, "contradictory orders and directives came from the center. They evoked complete bewilderment locally."[7] Although things were not going well for the Saratov Bolsheviks, the crystallization of a Left SR party willing to support the Bolshevik government helped shift the tide in their favor and undermined the moderate SRs' confused efforts to end Bolshevik rule. Addressing the Soviet on November 9, a Left SR soldier named Stepin intoned that "we were not with you during the seizure of power, but since it's been accomplished, we're with you once again."[8] On December 3, after the creation of a separate party, Saratov Left SRs entered the Soviet's Executive Committee. The local Bolshevik organization expressed displeasure with Miliutin, Kamenev, and Zinoviev, who had resigned from the Bolshevik government at this time.[9] Threatened by the local challenge to Soviet rule, Saratov Bolsheviks sided with their central committee in condemning efforts to form a coalition with those very elements who seemed so dead set against October.

As the storm clouds of civil war moved closer to Saratov, the Soviet adopted a more militant attitude toward its opposition. In part it may have been responding to lower-level pressures. While the city employees denounced the government in Theater Square on November 21, for instance, a soldier inside the public theater declared that "all those who resist the new authority should be evicted from their apartments and shot."[10] On November 28 Red Guard and garrison units, armed to the teeth, barged into city hall and arrested the mayor and other top officials. Announcing the dismissal of the City Duma, Antonov and Vasil'ev ordered the city employees back to their desks. When they refused, Vasil'ev warned them that the Soviet would replace them with "some of its unemployed; we have four thousand of them." Soldiers then fired threatening shots into the air to intimidate the clerks.[11]

Apart from slamming shut the doors of the City Duma, the Saratov Soviet took other measures to stifle and demoralize its opponents. After it became known that communications workers had intercepted and diverted a sizable sum of rubles sent from Petrograd to the Saratov Soviet, and in view of large withdrawals from local banks, Bolshevik leaders sequestered the city's financial establishments. The Soviet also extended the duties of workers' control groups and organized laborers

7. Antonov-Saratovskii, *Godovshchina*, p. 34.
8. *Izvestiia Saratovskogo Soveta*, no. 94, November 17, 1917, p. 3.
9. Ibid., no. 93, November 12, 1917, p. 2.
10. *Sotsial-Demokrat*, no. 83, November 23, 1917, p. 4.
11. *Proletarii Povolzh'ia*, no. 136, November 29, 1917, p. 2.

who had not taken part in trade unions earlier. A member of the teaching staff at Saratov University remarked sardonically that "the long oppressed members of the university—janitors, messengers, laboratory hands, and the like—have raised their heads under the Bolshevik regime, are demanding economic equality with the teaching body. . . . The university library closes at 2 P.M. every afternoon to enable the staff to attend the rabble's 'emancipation' meetings."[12] The Soviet also took over the railroads, created a new militia, and gradually assumed total responsibility for the town's economic survival. The more power it wielded, the more impassioned the voices of opposition became. "Down with the autocracy of Lenin and Trotsky!" was answered with a decision made by the Soviet in early December (not unanimously) to shut down the non-Bolshevik press.

In this strained atmosphere the frightful level of lawlessness that had been rising gradually during the year now broke all previous bounds. Sources present a shocking scenario of besotted soldiers, responsible to no one, sauntering about the city, subjecting the civilian population to indiscriminate violence. A sympathetic Antonov pinned the blame for the troops' behavior on conditions: a subhuman living situation compounded by vile rations, rampant drunkenness, and pressures from the Ukrainian Rada to form separate national units. To be sure, taverns and cafés illegally but quite openly peddled vodka and moonshine. Some local businesses apparently survived the lack of regular supplies and wares by hawking liquor.[13] In middle-class neighborhoods citizens organized their own street militias to protect themselves against mob rule and to ward off the frequent robberies and assaults. Victimized too, the common people expressed their frustration by lynching thieves and criminals. As one observer described it, "the crowds are said to become perfectly frantic on such occasions and invariably demand immediate execution." In fact, it may well have been that working-class attitudes were turning against the armed soldiers who seemed to be the cause of the city's woes. One visitor to Saratov overheard a worker murmur to his companion that "soldiers are worse than dogs nowadays."[14] Taking advantage of the Soviet's efforts to discipline the garrison, anti-Bolshevik elements within the officer corps sowed discontent against the Bolsheviks. Angry soldiers in the artillery units (where certain SR leaders had remained popular in October) on several occasions made plans to disband the Soviet by force.[15] By early 1918 the volatile frontoviki, returning from the front to find themselves unemployed, posed one of the

12. Babine Diary, p. 25.
13. *Sotsial-Demokrat*, no. 98, December 20, 1917, p. 4.
14. Babine Diary, pp. 36–37.
15. Antonov-Saratovskii, *Godovshchina*, pp. 30–31.

greatest problems for local leaders. The Saratov Soviet also received reports from Volsk, Petrovsk, and Kuznetsk about trouble caused by frontoviki. In the midst of this turmoil, common soldiers made the most of the military doctors' willingness to declare soldiers unfit for duty. Doctors, who equated Bolshevik power with the existence of the local garrison, readily issued orders to send the soldiers back to their villages. Many draftees did not even bother with this formality and simply went home. There was no one to stop them.

During the second week of November the people of Russia elected deputies to the Constituent Assembly, which had become the rallying point of all those opposed to Bolshevism. Russia had opted for the "Belgian" or d'Hondt system of proportional representation, whereby voters cast ballots for political parties rather than for individuals. For every 55,644 votes a particular party captured, one delegate from its ranked list qualified to represent the province in the Constituent Assembly. Although cries of voter intimidation could be heard from every political party, all indications suggest that the normal aspects of the campaigning outweighed the abnormalities. While the Bolsheviks controlled the political climate in Saratov and Tsaritsyn, the actual voting machinery remained in the hands of the Bolsheviks' articulate opponents.

How would the local peasantry have responded if the elections had been postponed for several months and they had the option to vote for a slate of Left SR candidates? Antonov suggested in 1925 that if the elections had been put off even a month, the villages would have heard of the Soviet government's land decree and would have increased their otherwise negligible support for Bolshevism and for the Left SR party. The Soviet dissident historian Roy Medvedev has taken up the same point recently.[16] Such an assessment probably has some validity, since in the Constituent Assembly elections rural Russia backed the SR party, which by November had split into two parties. In Saratov, factionalism within the bulky SR organization had led to extensive bickering during the preparations of candidate lists for the Constituent Assembly; it was precisely at this time that the Left SR movement crystallized into a separate party. As a result of sustained disagreements over the naming of candidates, the Socialist Revolutionaries submitted their single list later than any other local party organization (October 19). Among the top contenders were two Left SRs, A. Ustinov and G. Ul'ianov. At the First All-Russian Congress of the Left SRs held in 1918, a Saratov representative reported that at the relentless insistence of the provincial Peasant Soviet

16. Antonov-Saratovskii, *Pod stiagom*, pp. 237–38; Roy A. Medvedev, *The October Revolution*, trans. George Saunders (New York, 1979), p. 111.

Table 9

Number and percentage of votes cast for delegates to Constituent Assembly in city of Saratov (including garrison), November 1917, by party

Ballot number and party	*Votes*	*Percent*
1 Kadet	11,971	19.9%
2 Menshevik	4,100	6.8
3 Union of Ukrainian and Tatar SR Peasant Organizations	1,097	1.8
4 Old Believers	1,003	1.6
5 Orthodox People's	1,924	3.2
6 Union of Landowners	1,764	2.9
7 Volga German	1,280	2.1
8 Popular Socialist	2,920	4.9
9 Society for Faith and Order	2,589	4.3
10 Bolshevik	22,712	37.7
11 Peasants of Petrovsk uezd and Mordvinians	116	0.2
12 Socialist Revolutionary	8,698	14.5
All parties	60,174	99.9%

Source: Saratovskii vestnik, no. 247, November 17, 1917, p. 3.

the left candidates were included on the ballot at the last moment.[17] Kerensky, incidentally, earlier had agreed to head the Saratov list, but only if radical elements were not represented.

Within the city of Saratov civilians cast 47,522 votes and the garrison 12,660 for a total of 60,182.[18] As Table 9 shows, the Bolsheviks captured more support than any other party, polling 37.7 percent of the total tally. The Kadets came in second place with 19.9 percent. The Socialist Revolutionaries polled only 14.5 percent and the Mensheviks 6.8 percent of the total. Conservative parties fared better than earlier in the year. Combined, the Kadet party and conservative groups won 32 percent of the local vote. If the soldiers' votes are excluded from the total Bolshevik count, the nature of local support for the party is placed in sharper focus. The Bolsheviks received 28.8 percent of the civilian vote and the second-place Kadets 24.1 percent.[19] Between July and November both Bolshevik and Kadet support roughly doubled, while the SRs and Mensheviks lost almost 25,000 votes to the left and the right. According to *Saratovskii vestnik*, 15,000 voters switched from the SR-Menshevik bloc to the Bol-

17. S. Sh. Ovrutskaia, "Politicheskoe bankrotstvo eserov na vyborakh v Uchreditel'noe sobranie (Po materialam Saratovskoi gubernii)," in *Nekotorye voprosy otechestvennoi i vseobshchei istorii* (Saratov, 1971), p. 44.

18. *Saratovskii vestnik*, no. 248, November 18, 1917, p. 2. These figures differ slightly from those in Table 9; the latter were compiled a day earlier.

19. Ovrutskaia, "Politicheskoe bankrotstvo," p. 45.

sheviks while 10,000 socialists moved into the bourgeois camp.[20] Fear of anarchy, economic collapse, and sustained inflation had driven many moderate elements to the right.

Fewer people participated in the November elections than in the July City Duma voting. Among the 115,540 eligible voters, 41.5 percent cast ballots, compared with a 46.8 percent voter turnout during the summer. Voter breakdown by precinct varied dramatically, from 20 percent to 47 percent. Turnout in working-class neighborhoods tended to be lower in November than in July, when the poorer regions generated more enthusiasm. Groups one would expect to be pro-Bolshevik appear to have responded with indifference to the fall elections.

Once again, consideration of the garrison vote makes the nature of Bolshevik strength stand out more clearly. In all, 12,660 soldiers took part in the elections, but it is impossible to tell how many local soldiers were eligible to vote or what percentage actually did. The Bolsheviks won 8,993 or 70.6 percent of the soldiers' votes. Coming in second place, the SRs captured 1,897 or 14.9 percent of the total. The only other parties to receive more than 200 votes in the garrison included the Union of Ukrainian and Tatar SR Peasant Organizations (701 votes) and the Kadets, who surprisingly enough captured 580 votes, while the conservative and religious parties fared miserably.[21]

Election results for the remaining uezds are incomplete. No statistics whatever exist for Kuznetsk, and only partial statistics are available for Balashov, Khvalynsk, and Tsaritsyn. In the district towns soldiers sustained Bolshevism in what was otherwise an indifferent or even hostile environment. Tsaritsyn again remained the exception; the election results there were similar to those in Saratov town. In Serdobsk, where the Bolsheviks polled only 33 percent of the garrison vote, Left SRs played an exceptionally important role, which, when taken into account, guaranteed a comparatively early consolidation of Soviet power. Left SRs also boasted a strong organization in Balashov. In Volsk, which in 1918 emerged as the center of an anti-Bolshevik uprising, the Bolsheviks appear to have mustered little enthusiasm. At the district level the same strengthening of the political extremes at the expense of the center appears to have been fairly common, but not to the same degree as in Saratov or Tsaritsyn. As will be shown below, however, when the total votes for the province are tallied, the Kadets captured a paltry 27,226 votes out of a total of over 1 million.

Across most of the country ethnically Russian rural communities voted heavily for the Socialist Revolutionaries. It bears repeating that the

20. *Saratovskii vestnik*, no. 248, November 18, 1917, p. 2.

21. Ibid., no. 247, November 17, 1917, p. 3; *Proletarii Povolzh'ia*, no. 134, November 18, 1917, p. 2.

formal split within the SR ranks came shortly after the elections and that the peasants cast their ballots for a party that was organizationally defunct. In much of Saratov province peasant voters had not yet heard of the October changing of the guard, or of the Second Congress of Soviets' endorsement of Lenin's land decree. Anti-Bolshevik sentiments thus often remained strong; judging by the total Bolshevik vote count for the province, however, the Bolsheviks must have appealed to a significant number of peasants—probably to those living near cities. For some reason, a higher percentage of rural people exercised their voting rights than of city dwellers. A vast array of factors, such as accessibility to news and proximity to towns, shaped voting behavior, too. In his excellent study of the Constituent Assembly elections, Oliver H. Radkey noted that in Saratov province whole villages often voted for a single party. Elsewhere, electoral behavior was much more complex. In the northeastern corner of Khvalynsk uezd, one of the remotest parts of the province, voting behavior in an otherwise representative village revealed not surprisingly that few voted for the Bolsheviks, but more important, that there was no unanimity among voters. As Radkey put it, "there were plenty of strays from the herd."[22]

As Table 10 demonstrates, the Socialist Revolutionaries captured 56.3 percent of all votes cast in the province, the second-place Bolsheviks 24 percent. Combined, the two parties won more than 80 percent of the votes, and the Kadets a mere 2.5 percent. Thus only the SRs and Bolsheviks received enough support to choose 11 and 4 delegates respectively to the Constituent Assembly. Everywhere more than half of the population went to the polls—except in the city of Saratov. Petrovsk uezd purportedly had a 93 percent voter turnout.[23] Authorities declared few votes invalid, but occasionally disgruntled SRs scratched off Kerensky's name from their ballot, thereby nullifying it. The predominant agrarian character of the province meant that local populists fared somewhat better than the national average, but apart from this peculiarity the election results are broadly representative of the country as a whole.

The election results in Saratov province reinforce Radkey's conclusions about voter behavior in the country at large. In addition to the overwhelming if inconclusive victory of socialism and the poor turnout province-wide for urban-based Russian liberalism, the Saratov returns underscore the insignificance of Orthodox and sectarian parties and the comparative vitality of the non-Russian national parties. Radkey concluded that "the correlation between the results of the elections and the lines drawn in the civil war is sufficient evidence in itself that the vote in

22. Oliver H. Radkey, *The Election to the Russian Constituent Assembly of 1917*, Harvard Historical Monographs 21 (Cambridge, Mass., 1950), pp. 65–69.

23. *Saratovskaia zemskaia nedelia*, no. 1, February 5 (18), 1918, p. 17.

TABLE 10

Number and percentage of valid votes cast for delegates to Constituent Assembly in Saratov province, November 1917, by party

Ballot number and party	*Votes*	*Percent*
1 Kadet	27,226	2.5%
2 Menshevik	15,152	1.4
3 Union of Ukrainian and Tatar SR Peasant Organizations	53,445	4.9
4 Old Believers	13,956	1.3
5 Orthodox People's	17,414	1.6
6 Union of Landowners	13,804	1.3
7 Volga German	50,025	4.6
8 Popular Socialist	10,243	0.9
9 Society for Faith and Order	6,600	0.6
10 Bolshevik	261,308	24.0
11 Peasants of Petrovsk Uezd and Mordvinians	6,379	0.6
12 Socialist Revolutionary	612,094	56.3
All parties	1,087,646	100.0%

Source: *Saratovskaia zemskaia nedelia*, no. 1, February 5 (18), 1918, p. 17.

November 1917 was an authentic expression of the will of the Russian people."[24] The results for Saratov did foreshadow the broad determinants of the subsequent civil war; in the towns the election results flowed along social lines. The collapse of the political center in Saratov and Tsaritsyn actually paralleled developments in Petrograd and Moscow, where the Kadets also polled more votes than the SRs. Thus Bolshevik strongholds likewise were centers of the Bolsheviks' class enemies. The Kadets did well in the towns but not in the garrisons, which backed the Bolsheviks and served as a critical link in establishing Soviet power in the villages.

The process of recognition of the new political order began in the district towns at the end of October, when the Tsaritsyn Soviet assumed power, and ended in January 1918, when soviets in the last remaining uezd centers consolidated their positions. In such centers as Khvalynsk and Petrovsk armed clashes between the local soviet and its opponents broke out. In Balashov, Atkarsk, Volsk, Serdobsk, and Kuznetsk groups opposed to the Bolsheviks obstreperously resisted Soviet power, but did not resort to violence. Usually the nonradical Socialist Revolutionary elements and the Kadet party, often ensconced in local dumas or zemstvos, struggled most stubbornly against Bolshevik activists. Protesting

24. Radkey, *Election*, p. 40.

Soviet power, city employees in Saratov had gone out on strike and in other ways sabotaged the spread of information from Saratov to the district towns. As a result, in the immediate aftermath of October the Petrograd Soviet and Bolshevik Central Committee occasionally knew more than the Saratov Soviet itself about the political climate in remote pockets of Saratov province. Moreover, the presence of Cossack divisions in Balashov, Rtishchevo, Balanda, and Elan certainly cooled the fervor of revolutionaries in those areas.

The almost simultaneous declaration of Soviet power in both Saratov and Tsaritsyn contributed immensely to developments in the rest of the province. The transfer in Tsaritsyn, unlike that in Saratov, was bloodless. Tsaritsyn's powerful Bolshevik organization discussed whether the soviet should seize power as early as October 19, the day after the SRs withdrew from the soviet. A minority of local hotheads clamored for doing so immediately, while the more careful majority voted to wait for Petrograd. On October 22 an estimated 15,000 townspeople and soldiers marched through the city, carrying banners inscribed with "All Power to the Soviets" and "Down with the Provisional Government." As in Saratov, telegraph workers interfered with cable traffic once reports of trouble in Petrograd began to arrive. On the morning of October 26, however, local newspapers published the first cryptic communiqués from the capital. The next day the soviet sanctioned the formation of a revolutionary staff—a move proposed at a conference of factory committees a few days before—to coordinate the transfer of power. Refusing to take part in the body, moderate socialists joined forces with the duma, district zemstvo, union of teachers, union of bank workers, post and telegraph workers, and peasant soviet to protest the Petrograd events, and to set up a "Committee to Save the Revolution." On November 1 the Revolutionary Staff of the Tsaritsyn Soviet assumed power. During the next few days, the staff and the moderate socialists' Committee to Save the Revolution refrained from provoking a clash. The absence of both Minin and Erman may explain the cautious behavior of the Tsaritsyn Bolsheviks. The local union of unions and railway employees condemned the animosities between the socialist forces, expressing hopes for the creation of a homogeneous socialist ministry instead of single-party rule. On November 4, after returning from the Second Congress of Soviets in Petrograd, Erman addressed the Tsaritsyn Soviet, which afterward passed a resolution establishing Soviet power. Although no showdown had occurred at this time, the conditions for a duel nevertheless had been drawn.[25]

25. For a description of the October Revolution in Tsaritsyn see Romanov and Sokolov, *Ocherk istorii*, pp. 69–84; Presniakov, "Iz podpol'ia na prostor," pp. 71–72.

Following Tsaritsyn, revolutionary forces next established Soviet power in Kamyshin. Here, as in Balashov, Atkarsk, Volsk, Kuznetsk, and Serdobsk, the staunchest opponents of Bolshevism resorted to instigating "wine pogroms," a tactic aimed at instilling in the common people fear of anarchy and disorder. The moderates hoped thereby to discredit their radical adversaries. A drunken orgy accompanied by shooting and looting broke out on November 8, when SR Maximalists supported a resolution on Soviet power. Beforehand, a representative of the Petrograd Soviet's Military Revolutionary Committee (MRC) had addressed the local soviet, informing it of the Petrograd events and introducing a resolution calling for a transfer of power to the soviets. Headed by the Left SR Golovanov-Vasin and an SR Maximalist named Polkovnikov, the Military Revolutionary Committee created by the Kamyshin Soviet mobilized Red Guard units and soldiers to restore order. An armed detachment arrived from Saratov to help the Kamyshin MRC battle with the zemstvo, duma, and district commissar, all of whom appealed to the peasantry to defy the Bolsheviks. Revolutionary elements immured their rivals and requisitioned all weapons. Afterward the soviet established commissions to deal with speculation and irregular food supplies. A local peasant congress recognized the new "worker-peasant" government in late November, an act that represented a major step toward securing Soviet power in the rest of the district. In mid-January 1918 an uezd peasant congress reaffirmed its support of the new government and liquidated all institutions of the Provisional Government. Agitators from Kamyshin, Saratov, and the capitals as well as local revolutionary-minded soldiers radicalized the peasantry. Although Kamyshin was a German town, sources simply do not permit an evaluation of the role nationality played in establishing the new order there.[26]

Revolutionary forces in Balashov recognized the government shortly after Kamyshin uezd had done so. In Balashov, Social Democratic elements had captured 2,000 of 7,000 votes cast in town duma elections before the October Revolution. A separate Bolshevik committee, however, was not set up until late October, even though Bolshevik activists had played prominent roles in local affairs since February. Stationed in Balashov until mid-November, detachments of the Second Orenburg Cossack Division blocked any efforts to raise the question of Soviet power. To the anti-Bolshevik townspeople of Balashov, the Cossacks must have seemed no better than the rabble in the local garrison, for what once had been the elite forces of the imperial army now looted the town's liquor warehouses, disarmed the garrison, and terrorized civilians.[27] The Cossacks departed for the Urals on November 11–12 at the

26. *Khronika*, pp. 154, 159, 165–67, 174; Mints, *Oktiabr' v Povolzh'e*, pp. 243–44.
27. *Saratovskii Sovet*, p. 230.

same time that elections to the Constituent Assembly took place. The Bolsheviks captured roughly two-thirds of the soldiers' votes and 39 percent of all votes cast (the SRs received 25 percent of the total vote and the Kadets 13.7 percent). On November 18 the workers' soviet discussed a resolution on Soviet power, which moderate socialists rejected. The next day the separate workers' and soldiers' soviets held a joint meeting, at which the tide turned in favor of the Bolsheviks. The combined soviets recognized the new revolutionary government and elected a Military Revolutionary Committee to deal with the opposition, comprising two Left SRs, two Bolsheviks, and one nonparty soldier. By early December the recently merged Balashov Soviet began to issue directives to volost peasant soviets. On December 12 a meeting of the Balashov Soviet of Workers' and Soldiers' Deputies and the Balashov Uezd Soviet of Peasant Deputies accepted resolutions on Soviet power passed a few days before at a provincial peasant congress.[28]

Soviet power was recognized in Atkarsk on December 16. Once again, radicalized soldiers proved the decisive factor both in town and in the villages where local peasants had declared war against landowners back in September. A Bolshevik organization had not been organized until October, and then only as a result of the direct involvement of Saratov's Vasil'ev and Antonov. As late as May 1918 only sixty-five Bolsheviks belonged to the local party organization.[29] However, the extent of the peasant movement in the villages of Atkarsk and the arrival of demobilized soldiers under the spell of a Bolshevik named Butakov electrified local public opinion. On December 16 the town soviet, which included peasant representatives, promulgated Soviet power in Atkarsk uezd. For the next few months former zemstvo members mobilized the considerable forces opposed to the new government. Red Guard units and armed soldiers, ready to resort to force to defend their revolution, maintained the shaky foundation on which Soviet power in the town had been erected.[30] As one participant in the events put it, "all of 1918 passed in a feverish struggle against [anti-Bolshevik] uprisings and in strengthening the party organization."[31]

Revolutionary elements set up Soviet power in Khvalynsk after a stubborn armed conflict that the radicals won only because outside help bolstered them. Not surprisingly, the district turned into a center of civil war in the summer of 1918 and afterward. A small town with few industrial workers and but a handful of soldiers, Khvalynsk remained fairly

28. Gerasimenko and Tochenyi, *Sovety Povolzh'ia*, pp. 267–68; Khodakov, *Ocherki istorii Saratovskoi organizatsii* (1968), pp. 328–29.

29. Terekhin, *Gody ognevye*, p. 40.

30. See A. A. Kondaurov, "Oktiabr'skie dni v Atkarske," in *Za vlast' sovetov* (1968), pp. 261–66; *Khronika*, pp. 155, 179, 197, 199.

31. Sushitskii, "Oktiabr'skaia revoliutsiia v Vol'skom i Atkarskom uezdakh," p. 110.

isolated from Saratov. No railroad line connected the town with the provincial center, and with the arrival of winter, Volga navigation had come to a standstill. A military secondary school with more than 300 students and 40 officers stood ready to combat the enemy. At first local revolutionaries, owing in part to their isolation and elliptical knowledge of the Petrograd events, did nothing to force a political showdown. The Petrograd Soviet sent D. V. Stepin and V. A. Kirpichnikov to Khvalynsk in November to promote Soviet power and to establish a Red Guard. Toward the end of the month a radical named Gerasimov from the small local garrison began agitating on behalf of the new government. Soon the soldiers articulated their readiness to accept Soviet power, and local workers and soldiers elected a soviet as a counterweight to the duma. In response, Khvalynsk liberals, Right SRs, and local antisocialist elements formed a "Committee to Save the Motherland and the Revolution," headed by a Menshevik named Bogoliubov. In the meanwhile the Petrograd Bolshevik Organization sent K. I. Ritsberg and E. A. Ritsberg-Afanas'eva to Khvalynsk to establish a Bolshevik cell.

When the Khvalynsk Soviet met on December 3, deputies chose Bolsheviks to replace SRs and Mensheviks within the executive committee. It also declared Soviet power in the uezd, a move that did not go unchallenged. The soviet then formed a Military Revolutionary Committee that tried to disarm the local junkers. When this move failed, the soviet cabled Saratov for help and dispatched Ritsberg-Afanas'eva to Petrograd to seek financial and military assistance. Shored up by an armed guard sent from the Syzran Soviet under directives of the Soviet government, the Khvalynsk Soviet repelled an armed attack instigated by junkers and officers on the evening of January 1–2, a few days after an uezd peasant congress recognized the government. Relying heavily on the demobilized soldiers, the soviet then spread Soviet power throughout the district. But anti-Bolshevik forces continued to resist.[32]

Armed force had to be brought in from Saratov to establish Soviet power in Petrovsk. Here a small Bolshevik fraction within the soviet first crystallized in October. As in many uezd towns, the garrison became radicalized after the Kornilov crisis and voted for the Bolsheviks in elections to the Constituent Assembly. Demobilized soldiers also proved ready to use force to defend the Bolsheviks. During the first half of November the Petrovsk Soviet gingerly proceeded to establish control over banks and printing presses. But in the second half of the month the town duma seized power and disbanded the soviet. Events remain blurred because at the same time a Black Hundred pogrom aimed at

32. Terekhin, *Gody ognevye*, pp. 45–46; Sushitskii, "Oktiabr'skaia revoliutsiia v Vol'skom i Atkarskom uezdakh," pp. 106–8; N. V. Afanas'ev, *Bor'ba partii bol'shevikov*, pp. 101–6.

radicals turned into a drunken orgy. Back on December 10 representatives of the Petrovsk Soviet had reported to the Saratov Soviet's Executive Committee that the soldiers from the Petrovsk garrison intended to loot the local liquor warehouse. (As the common soldier's sense of social justice had it, each soldier was entitled to a bucket of wine!)[33] Declaring Petrovsk under martial law, the Saratov Soviet on December 24 dispatched to Petrovsk Red Guard units under Ermoshchenko to quell the pogrom and reestablish the soviet. Antisoviet forces continued to demonstrate against the new government well into January. On January 7 what may well have been a sham district peasant congress recognized the government. The congress elected a new district executive committee that supervised the spread of Soviet power throughout the uezd. The creation of a revolutionary court at the end of January suggests that the opponents of the government continued to maneuver against it and that recognition of the Council of Peoples' Commissars had mere declarative significance.[34]

The massive level of the local peasant insurrection in the fall of 1917 and the strength of SR forces shaped events in Serdobsk. Once again, a radicalized garrison and a flood of frontoviki and demobilized soldiers created favorable conditions for the establishment of Soviet power. It will be recalled that since mid-October a district executive committee formed by the 161st Regiment Committee had represented the only authoritative center of power in the uezd. When news of the October Revolution reached town, SR activists struck an agreement with the district executive committee that it would continue to govern until it was replaced by the Constituent Assembly. Before long the committee began to send soldier-agents into the villages. One soldier reported to the Saratov Soviet that peasants in several villages he had visited enthusiastically greeted the Saratov Soviet's land decree but observed that "they don't know how to implement it. They demand lower prices on grain and on manufactured items."[35] According to the memoir of a participant in the Serdobsk events, absolutely no instructions came from Petrograd. Toward the end of November news began to trickle into Serdobsk that peasants in some volosts had begun to form soviets. Thus on November 29, the zemstvo in Sokolsk volost disbanded and transferred power to a newly elected soviet, which established a Red Guard. All circumstantial evidence points strongly to soldiers as the driving force behind such initiative. Under populist influence, the mood of the town population remained cautious but not altogether opposed to the creation of an all-

33. *Saratovskii Sovet*, p. 277.

34. Gerasimenko, *Sovety Nizhnego Povolzh'ia*, pp. 140–41; *Khronika*, pp. 155, 182, 193. 209; T. I. Gordeev, "Za sovetskuiu vlast'," in *Za vlast' sovetov* (1957), pp. 188–213.

35. *Saratovskii Sovet*, p. 236.

socialist government. (Well into December the few Bolsheviks in the district remained concentrated in the railroad yards at nearby Rtishchevo.) On December 12 representatives of volost zemstvos convened a congress in Serdobsk without the permission of the district executive committee, at which they set up a Committee to Defend the Constituent Assembly. On December 28 the first uezd peasant congress opened in Serdobsk. Although attempts to create a Bolshevik faction locally date from the congress, a Bolshevik activist admitted that even though many soldiers called themselves Bolsheviks, their theoretical understanding of the party's program was so crude that it was impossible to organize a faction. But shortly thereafter the arrival of yet another wave of revolutionary-minded frontoviki facilitated the establishment of Bolshevik cells in the villages. A second uezd peasant congress on January 10 elected a majority of Bolsheviks to a district executive committee that recognized Soviet power. The committee, however, had to contend with the determined Committee to Defend the Constituent Assembly.[36]

Demobilized soldiers and sailors tipped the scales in favor of Soviet power in Volsk, the only district town apart from Tsaritsyn with a significant number of workers. In the fall of 1917 SRs dominated the city duma and boasted a hardy following within the working class while Mensheviks appear to have been more powerful than Bolsheviks in the soviet. The democratized city duma and zemstvo had continued to function throughout the year, and officers relied on junkers in the local military school to curb unrest within the garrison. According to one newspaper account, the soviet's popularity had plunged throughout the uezd in the fall because it had had to resort to force to secure grain from local peasants.[37] On October 12 the Volsk Soviet had rejected a resolution on behalf of Soviet power introduced by Rubashkina and instead authorized its representative to the Second Congress of Soviets to vote against any attempt to establish an exclusively socialist government. On November 8 delegates to a meeting of local factory committees expressed their faith in the upcoming Constituent Assembly, and protested the seizure of power when the Bolshevik Kukushkin addressed the workers' deputies. In contrast, the Volsk garrison warmly greeted Kukushkin that same day. Election results to the Constituent Assembly shortly thereafter probably accurately depicted the alignment of political forces in town at that time. The SRs polled 5,750 votes, followed by the Bolsheviks' 2,256 votes, the Kadets' 1,825, and the Ukrainian refugees' 947. A variety of other parties attracted a total of about 2,500 votes. As elsewhere, Bolshevik strength lay in the garrison; the party captured a mere 6 percent of the civilian vote.[38]

36. See Shchegol'kov, "Na zare," pp. 54–57; *Stranitsy iz zhizni*, pp. 14–22.
37. *Proletarii Povolzh'ia*, no. 103, October 3, 1917, p. 4.
38. *Saratovskii listok*, no. 246, November 19, 1917, p. 4.

The Volsk Bolshevik organization became more powerful as soldiers and sailors streamed into town. Especially active was a Union of Sailors under the inspiration of a Kronstadt Bolshevik, S. N. Korzhevin. At the end of December reelections to the Volsk Soviet gave the Bolsheviks and Left SRs a majority, but at the same time the first uezd peasant congress rejected Soviet power. On January 8 a united congress of peasant and worker deputies passed by a vote of 109 to 24 with 8 abstentions a resolution backing the Bolshevik–Left SR ministry. The city administration continued to function, however, and during the coming months local workers in several bloody incidents clashed with peasants who refused to relinquish their grain. Here Soviet power remained precarious and went hand in hand with a bitter split between the town population and the peasantry.[39] Moreover, antigovernment elements mustered enough support to launch a major anti-Bolshevik uprising in the summer of 1918.

Lack of reliable information prevents any clear understanding of the spread of Soviet power to Kuznetsk, but according to Gerasimenko, events there followed the same pattern as in Atkarsk. Soldiers represented the only support the Bolsheviks could rely on locally. Until April 1918 no separate Bolshevik organization existed apart from the Bolshevik Military Organization in the 155th Reserve Infantry Regiment. Toward the end of 1917 only a few Bolshevik activists agitated within the SR-controlled soviet. The lack of any recognized administrative organ and the anarchistic behavior of the garrison colored the local transfer of power. In December 1917, after the Saratov Soviet had shut down the town's bourgeois papers, the staff of *Saratovskii listok* briefly published a new paper, *Saratovskoe slovo* (Saratov Word). An article appearing in it in mid-December reported on a violent "wine pogrom" in Kuznetsk, beginning in late November. If the account is to be trusted, hundreds were beaten and maimed during the drunken brawl that lasted several days. On January 18, 1918, the fourth uezd peasant congress passed a resolution acknowledging Soviet power and summoning the population to elect soviets. It seems probable that radicalized soldiers accounted for the reception of Soviet authority in the Kuznetsk countryside. While the town population undoubtedly remained opposed to Soviet rule, the citizens were unable to topple it.[40]

Recognition of Soviet power elsewhere in Saratov province and its environs merits a few words. In Pokrovsk, located across the Volga from

39. I. T. Cherkasov, "Bor'ba za sovety v Vol'ske," in *Za vlast' sovetov* (1968), pp. 245–50; Sushitskii, "Oktiabr'skaia revoliutsiia v Vol'skom i Atkarskom uezdakh," pp. 103–6; Rubashkina, "Vol'skaia organizatsiia SDRP," p. 81; V. E. Kokorin, "Vol'skaia krasnaia flotiliia v bor'be s kontrrevoliutsiei, in *V boiakh za diktaturu proletariata*, p. 37.

40. *Saratovskoe slovo*, no. 2, December 16, 1917, p. 2; *Sbornik: Ves' Kuznetsk*, p. 75; Terekhin, *Gody ognevye*, pp. 50–51.

Saratov, the soviet passed a resolution of support for the new government on November 7. At the Rtishchevo rail center the Bolshevik-led soviet seized power on December 30.[41] In Saratov uezd itself Soviet power was first decreed at the end of January, but of course lack of urgency accounted for this delay. On October 26 the Samara Soviet by a vote of 441 to 140 carried a resolution calling for a transfer of power to the soviets. The Bolsheviks, Bund, Menshevik Internationalists, and Left SRs endorsed the resolution. As in Saratov, moderate socialists initially were the staunchest opponents of the new government, but they were unable to subvert the local soviet. In Kazan the Bolshevik and Left SR military organizations merged in October and also swept elections to the city duma. On October 26 the soviet's Military Revolutionary Committee disarmed the small number of junkers and citizens who challenged the soviet's authority.

Elsewhere in the region—in the less industrialized towns of Simbirsk, Penza, and Astrakhan—revolutionary forces did not fare so well as those in Saratov, Tsaritsyn, Kazan, and Samara. On October 25 the Penza Soviet carried a resolution declaring that it would not subordinate itself to Bolshevik directives from Petrograd. In early November the Bolshevik Central Committee sent the activist V. V. Kuraev with a group of Bolshevik sailors to turn Penza red. Nevertheless, the Mensheviks polled almost twice as many votes in elections to the workers' section of the soviet on November 10 (42 to 24), and anti-Bolshevik sentiment continued to run high. In Simbirsk, Bolsheviks won a majority in the workers' section of the local soviet but failed to capture the soldiers' sympathies (there were few frontoviki in the garrison at the time). Throughout November Bolshevik agitators armed with Lenin's decrees on land and peace fought to popularize the new government in both provinces. The head of the Bolshevik organization in Penza made a surprising about-face and joined the Menshevik party in early December. Here the split within the SR organization and the emergence of a Left SR committee ultimately turned the tide in favor of the radicals on December 21, when the soviet recognized Soviet power. The Simbirsk Soviet had passed a similar resolution a few days before. Soviet power had come to Syzran, a district center in Simbirsk province, well before revolutionary forces in Simbirsk had subdued their opponents. Although Syzran was a relatively small city, the presence of 3,000 local workers and the large garrison of 30,000 bolstered Soviet rule and promoted its spread to Penza and Simbirsk and even to Khvalynsk in Saratov province.

The presence of Cossack units in Astrakhan delayed the acceptance of

41. *Khronika*, pp. 181, 186.

Soviet power until January 1918. Moveover, the local garrison—an important factor elsewhere—was comparatively small. The city duma in November created a Committee of People's Power, backed by the soviet and the local Bolshevik organization, which suggests the extent to which local Bolsheviks strove to avoid a rupture with their fellow socialists. Three district towns in Astrakhan province had already recognized the new government. As in Syzran, their action points to the impact of subjective considerations in the spread of Soviet rule. In late December the Astrakhan Bolsheviks withdrew from the Committee of People's Power and gave serious attention to arming and training a Red Guard. At the same time direct aid and instructions began to arrive from Saratov; the Astrakhan Soviet established a Military Revolutionary Committee, which in early January demanded that the Committee of People's Power disband by January 15. On the eve of a provincial congress of soviets, January 12, anti-Bolshevik forces bolstered by Cossack and Kalmyk units rose up against the soviet. For two weeks bitter civil war raged in the streets of Astrakhan before the forces of the soviet seized control. Thus Soviet power was recognized sooner in those Volga cities where the Bolsheviks had created party organizations early in 1917 (Saratov, Samara, Tsaritsyn) or where party organizations, united or otherwise, benefited from the strength of other radical groups (Kazan). Soviet power took longer to become established in those less industrialized centers where the Bolsheviks had formed separate organizations later in the year (Simbirsk, September; Penza, October; Astrakhan, August).[42]

The peasant soldier established Soviet power in the countryside. Despite prevailing anti-Bolshevik feelings in the villages, the Saratov Soviet's land decree, issued on the evening of October 27, plus the flood of self-demobilized soldiers back into the rural areas provided powerful ammunition that enabled the Soviet to neutralize the peasantry and shift the balance of forces in favor of the new regime. This was the case even in those remote regions where resistance to the Bolsheviks remained spirited. Usually in conjunction with resolutions passed at district peasant congresses, all of the uezd centers had recognized Soviet power by January 1918. Nevertheless, Soviet power rested on a shaky foundation that often had to be bolstered with armed force or intimidation.

On the eve of the October Revolution total disarray and anarchy had undermined any semblance of normality in the countryside. In late summer the Provisional Government had sought to replace volost executive committees with zemstvo assemblies, hoping thereby to trim the powers

42. Mints, *Oktiabr' v Povolzh'e*, pp. 219–40; Gerasimenko and Tochenyi, *Sovety Povolzh'ia*, pp. 228–63.

of lower-level land committees that seized the landowners' estates. Soviet historians often argue that the revitalized zemstvos applied the brakes to the rural revolution. Evidence does not convincingly show that the reelection of zemstvos curtailed the peasant movement. On the contrary, it took on new militancy in September and October. Snatching up inventory, equipment, grain, livestock, and manor houses, peasants also increasingly resorted to terror against landowners and Stolypin peasants.[43] Between October 7 and 21 alone Saratov peasants destroyed more than fifty estates.[44] In Serdobsk uezd, the most volatile district, various public organizations convened a special meeting to deal with the agrarian movement, at which delegates voted to place privately owned property at the disposal of the volost zemstvos immediately.[45] "A day doesn't pass," claimed *Saratovskaia zemskaia nedelia* (Saratov Land Weekly) "that news is not received of arbitrary actions on the part of naive peasants who take land from private owners."[46] The provincial commissar resorted to the use of armed force whenever possible but repressive measures helped little, in part because the demoralized, self-demobilized peasant soldiers returned to the villages at this time.[47] Their presence left an impact everywhere. An irate landowner who had arrested three people caught plundering his estate reported that "one was a second lieutenant. His father was a rather well-to-do peasant. The other was also a soldier."[48]

Disappointed with postponed reform and forced to cope with a disrupted market, local peasants now pressed to satisfy their urge for land. Deeply embedded in their elemental quest for social justice lay an odd need to rationalize their behavior. Folk etymology had traditionally created new forms and meanings of the unfamiliar language of urban Russia. Rumors had often abounded in the Volga provinces about the existence of documents proving that the peasants had been cheated of the land that rightfully belonged to them. In the fall of 1917—after local landlords, as part of a conservative revival following the July Days, tried unsuccessfully to curb the peasant movement—rumors circulated once again of mysterious documents, newly uncovered, that called upon the villagers to divide up the landowners' land. In Atkarsk and Serdobsk

43. Gerasimenko, *Nizovye krest'ianskie organizatsii*, pp. 172–75.

44. Antonov-Saratovskii, *Pod stiagom*, p. 143.

45. Gerasimenko, *Nizovye krest'ianskie organizatsii*, p. 199.

46. *Saratovskaia zemel'naia nedelia*, no. 2, October, 7, 1917, p. 1. Also quoted in Suslov, *Leninskaia agrarnaia politika*, p. 101. See a similar report cited in Levinson, "Krest'ianskoe dvizhenie," p. 79.

47. Chaadaeva, *Pomeshchiki i ikh organizatsii*, p. 169; Bunyan and Fisher, *Bolshevik Revolution*, p. 32. Levinson claims that repression helped little; see "Krest'ianskoe dvizhenie," p. 80.

48. *Saratovskii vestnik*, no. 234, October 22, 1917, p. 4.

uezds peasants spoke of a strange item called a "kalifesto." According to reports, a young man riding on "zemstvo horses" visited villages and read a document acknowledging that all land, inventory, and equipment of large estate owners and Stolypin peasants should be seized and distributed evenly among the villagers. "The peasants rejected attempts to explain the word 'kalifesto' as a bastardized form of the word 'manifesto,'" *Proletarii Povolzh'ia* noted. "They claim that they know what a manifesto is, but that this is something else, not a manifesto, but a kalifesto."[49]

In this chaotic environment news of the October Revolution and of the consolidation of Soviet power in Saratov spread unevenly. Ties between Saratov and the district towns and volost centers had been broken or interrupted; misinformation abounded. Even Soviet historians admit the extraordinary weakness of the Bolsheviks in rural areas. In most places uezd and volost zemstvos reacted negatively to reports that the Provisional Government had fallen. As Bolshevik agitators from Saratov and Petrograd sought to enlighten the peasants regarding the Saratov Soviet's land decree, SRs entrenched in the zemstvos agitated on behalf of elections to the Constituent Assembly. Many villages often learned of the revolution only after the elections had ended.

Ironically, on the same day that shooting had broken out in Saratov between the forces of the Soviet and the City Duma, the Provincial Land Committee, zemstvo board, and Peasant Soviet had finally reached an agreement calling for the speedy transfer of all land to land committees.[50] In the immediate aftermath of the showdown, the Peasant Soviet, which had emerged as the focal point of SR activities, passed stinging denunciations of Soviet power. It censured Bolshevik behavior and summoned the population to obey the directives of the Committee to Save the Revolution; it demanded the creation of an all-socialist government excluding the liberals and Bolsheviks; it argued that the soldiers at the front opposed the Bolshevik seizure of power; and it advocated the conclusion of peace and unconditional support for the Constituent Assembly.

Lenin's land decree, however, eventually undermined the appeal of the Saratov Peasant Soviet, and with its neutralization the SRs lost the villages. Approved by the Second Congress of Soviets on October 26, the decree transferred the land to the peasants. In early November a representative of the Petrograd Soviet arrived in Saratov with the text of the Bolshevik government's decrees on land and peace. Calling for an end to private ownership, confiscation of landowners' estates without remuneration, and a halting of the much-hated terms of renting and buying,

49. *Proletarii Povolzh'ia*, no. 102, October 1, 1917, p. 3.
50. *Izvestiia Saratovskogo Soveta krest'ianskikh deputatov*, November 4, 1917, p. 3.

Lenin's decree went further than the Saratov Soviet's October 27 document. By mid-November the Soviet began to circulate the new land decree while Saratov's Rakitnikov, who had served as deputy minister of agriculture under Kerensky, sent circulars to local zemstvos. The notices attacked Lenin's decree and presented the proposal worked out by local SRs on the eve of the opening of the Second All-Russian Congress.[51]

Outside activists from Petrograd also facilitated acceptance of the new regime in Saratov province. Within a month of the Bolshevik victory the Petrograd Soviet sent more than 600 agitators to provincial Russia to win support for Soviet power. Some forty-five Petrograd soldiers, sailors, and workers arrived in the Lower Volga provinces, fifteen in Saratov. Perhaps representative was the experience of one Ivan Korobkin, who agitated in Atkarsk uezd. "The peasants ask me," Korobkin reported to Petrograd, "what's a Bolshevik and what's an SR. . . . In general they don't know anything about politics here."[52] On November 12 the Saratov Soviet resolved, upon the advice of the Petrograd Soviet's visiting representative, to send to their home villages more than 300 soldier-agitators from the garrison. The Soviet commissioned them to organize elections of representatives to a provincial peasant congress slated to open on November 30, and to coax their fellow villagers to sell grain to the food-supply organs. Almost half of the 192 surviving reports submitted by these agents of the Saratov Soviet reveal massive hostility toward the Bolsheviks; some villages even refused to send delegates to the peasant congress.[53]

SR leaders tried to undermine the impact of the Bolshevik agitators. Contradictory and biased sources leave an incomplete picture of the confusion reigning at this time. Throughout the middle of November the Peasant Soviet, denouncing the "government of Lenin and Trotsky," met daily in the building of the local zemstvo administration. With the collapse of efforts to defeat the Bolsheviks with armed force, the Peasant Soviet passed resolutions calling for the creation of an all-socialist soviet ministry that would exclude the bourgeoisie and include those Bolsheviks who admitted that state power belonged to the Constituent Assembly. The canard that the Bolshevik leadership was a conglomeration of urban Jews already had become fabricated. One resolution introduced at a meeting of the Peasant Soviet crudely recommended the "removal of all yids from the Presidium," as their involvement in peasant affairs was "intolerable."[54] Another resolution articulated the necessity of preserv-

51. Sagrad'ian, *Osushchestvlenie*, p. 22.

52. Cited in Gerasimenko, "Vozniknovenie Sovetskoi vlasti," p. 64.

53. F. A. Rashitov, "Osnovnye etapy sovetskogo stroitel'stva v Saratovskoi gubernii v pervoi polovine 1918 goda," *Materialy k nauchnoi konferentsii aspirantov i molodykh nauchnykh sotrudnikov*, no. 1 (Saratov, 1965), p. 9.

54. *Saratovskii vestnik*, no. 248, November 18, 1917, p. 2.

ing civil rights and of concluding a speedy peace, but only in agreement with Russia's allies. Local SR leaders such as Pontriagin, arrested by the forces of the Saratov Soviet in late October and now released, regularly addressed the Peasant Soviet, leaving their mark on its resolutions. In regard to the problem of local political power, the Peasant Soviet advocated the creation of an authoritative provincial committee to be composed of delegates from the zemstvos, city dumas, Peasant Soviet, Saratov Soviet, and unions of post and telegraph and railroad workers, in short, in those very institutions (with the exception of the Saratov Soviet) still in the hands of moderate elements.[55]

Meeting in almost permanent session at this time, the Peasant Soviet resolved to open its own provincial peasant congress a week before the one planned by the Saratov Soviet. On November 21, however, two days before the peasant congress convened, the local SR organization held a city conference at which a left-wing SR resolution passed by a slim margin. This was an extraordinary development for middle-of-the-road Saratov. Committed to cooperating with the Bolsheviks in order to escape the political impasse and to avoid civil war, the Left SRs now offered their own plan for conciliation, which certainly undermined the Right SRs' upcoming peasant congress. The Left SR resolution welcomed the creation of an all-socialist ministry under the auspices of the All-Russian Executive Committees of the Petrograd Soviet and national Peasant Soviet. It also encouraged conclusion of a prompt peace settlement and the transfer of land to land committees. Urging the convocation of the Constituent Assembly in late November, the resolution demanded the reestablishment of all political liberties and an end to civil war.[56]

Thus when the peasant congress called by the Saratov Peasant Soviet opened on November 23, dissent within SR ranks guaranteed its failure. Addressing the Saratov Soviet, the Bolshevik Antonov reported that the SRs had summoned peasant representatives to Saratov selectively, purposefully avoiding rural communities that had responded approvingly to the Bolsheviks' land policies.[57] Only about a hundred deputies representing one-third of the volost land committees and uezd zemstvos attended this meeting. After the Saratov Soviet invited the peasant deputies to join the Soviet, forty or so peasants left the congress; those remaining denounced Bolshevik behavior and adopted a Right SR resolution on political power.[58]

The disgruntled, desperate members of the presidium of the SR congress appeared at the opening session of the rival "Third Peasant Congress of Saratov Province," which gathered on November 30, and tried

55. Ibid., no. 250, November 21, 1917, p. 3.
56. Ibid., no. 252, November 24, 1917, p. 3.
57. *Saratovskii Sovet*, p. 265.
58. Petrov, "Saratovskii proletariat," pp. 26–27.

unsuccessfully to convince the delegates that they had been deceived by the Bolshevik usurpers. The congress remained in session until December 4, during which time deputies approved Lenin's land decree, endorsed by the Second All-Russian Congress of Soviets on October 26, and dismissed the Peasant Soviet and the provincial food and land administrations. The congress elected a "Provincial Peasant Soviet" that voted to merge with the Saratov Soviet, which became the Saratov Soviet of Workers', Soldiers', and Peasants' Deputies.[59] Throughout the proceedings the Left SRs supported Bolshevik resolutions but spoke out against the Saratov Soviet's closing of the City Duma. Deputies elected forty members to the new enlarged Executive Committee of the Saratov Soviet, including four from each uezd and five from the Saratov garrison. Urging the creation of rural soviets to replace the organs of the Provisional Government that still functioned, the congress agreed to publish all of its decrees and to distribute them as broadly as possible throughout Saratov province. It should be noted that during the remainder of December peasants elected an additional thirty-four rural soviets.[60] The formation of village soviets amounted to the establishment of Soviet power.

The Third Peasant Congress's adoption of Bolshevik resolutions contributed singularly to the consolidation of Soviet power in Saratov province. Returning to their home villages, many peasant delegates spearheaded the election of soviets and calling of district peasant congresses. In December uezd peasant congresses in Balashov and Atkarsk voted their approval of the proceedings of the Saratov congress. In January district peasant congresses in Kamyshin, Petrovsk, Serdobsk, Volsk, and Kuznetsk recognized Soviet power.

How representative of the mood in the villages was the Third Peasant Congress? No clear answer emerges from the contradictory, partisan sources. Close to 200 deputies representing all ten districts participated in the gathering, making it more representative than the SR congress, but by no means indicative of the mood of the entire countryside. More than half of the volosts in the province had sent deputies to Saratov (105), whereas 65 "refused to do so for political reasons," and 10 were unable to do so for a variety of technical reasons.[61] Judging from the politicized rhetoric of the conference, conflict in the villages as evinced in the high incidence of clashes between communal and Stolypin peasants helped facilitate recognition of Soviet power. Some delegates complained to the

59. G. A. Gerasimenko, "Ustanovlenie Sovetskoi vlasti v uezdakh Nizhnego Povolzh'ia," in *Iz istorii Saratovskogo Povolzh'ia* (Saratov, 1968), p. 81.

60. G. A. Gerasimenko and V. P. Sem'ianinov, *Sovetskaia vlast' v derevne na pervom etape Oktiabria* (Saratov, 1980), p. 45.

61. Ibid.

Saratov Soviet that a local official and "kulaks" had forced them to vote for SRs during elections to the Constituent Assembly. Other speakers insisted that "kulaks" had prevented the poorer rural elements elected locally from attending the Saratov congress.[62]

Poor peasants and hired agricultural hands had fallen under the spell of the seductive slogans thrown at them from the extreme left. The loyalties of the large stratum of middle peasants were probably split by a variety of local and subjective factors, but many of these peasants, as Oliver Radkey concluded, moved into the Left SR camp.[63] Again and again sources show that the younger and middle-aged peasants who had served in the army almost exclusively voiced Bolshevik or Left SR sentiments at this time. Returning to the villages armed and angry, they had both the conviction and the might to shape local developments. As Radkey so colorfully said, it was not the "white bearded village elder or patriarch honoring the Mother of God," but rather the young or middle-aged peasant returning from war "accustomed to violence and not loath to use it, who . . . dictated the course of affairs in the village. Age conferred no distinction . . . but only physical debility, and a flowing beard served no other purpose than to be pulled by an angry soldier."[64] One poignant example from Saratov province captures the essence of the situation in the villages. A memoirist writing in the early 1920s recalled that

> in the neighboring village of Likhomanovo a sailor named Iakob Smirnov showed up. . . . Arriving at the local village meeting, he uttered . . . such awful words that all of the muzhiks feared him. He said the hell with the tsar, God, icons, the church, and rich people. He said that we have to seize everything from them and divide it among the poor, that now power was ours, power of the poor. They described him to me as being "terribly frightening, tall, with big fists. Everyone was afraid of him. He could do anything."[65]

A few days after the Third Saratov Province Peasant Congress closed, a "Fourth Congress of Soviets" opened in Saratov, representing about half of the district soviets in the province. According to local reports, town soviets had consolidated power but faced intractable opposition from propertied elements, Right SRs, and Mensheviks. The congress elected a new executive committee, expressed its determination to implement the

62. *Saratovskii Sovet,* p. 269.

63. Oliver H. Radkey, *The Sickle under the Hammer: The Russian Socialist Revolutionaries in the Early Months of Soviet Rule* (New York, 1963), p. 138.

64. Ibid., p. 279.

65. V. Bunarov, "Oktiabr'skaia revoliutsiia v derevne," *Kommunisticheskii put',* no. 9/34 (1923), p. 72.

various decrees passed at the recent peasant congress, and summoned the creation of Red Guard units in the localities.[66] The editors of *Proletarii Povolzh'ia* considered the congress illegal, not only because of the absence of delegates from Tsaritsyn, Balashov, Serdobsk, Petrovsk, and Atkarsk but also because Vasil'ev and Antonov secretly opened the gathering early, apparently to prevent an incident with the old regional bureau, which still contained a significant number of moderate socialists.[67] Undoubtedly the true extent of the use of force and intimidation at this impassioned time will never be known.

The rump Fourth Congress of Soviets of Saratov province adjourned in the wake of the Left SRs' entry into the national government and the local committee's merger with the Saratov Soviet's Executive Committee. Soviet power became recognized in much of Saratov province precisely during this brief coalition between the Bolsheviks and Left SRs, that is, between December 1917 and March 1918, when the government signed the Brest-Litovsk Treaty with Germany, thereby formally ending Russia's involvement in World War I and rupturing the fragile alliance between the revolutionary populists and the Bolsheviks. The recognition of Soviet power can be seen in the steady growth in the number of soviets. In Saratov province peasants elected eleven volost soviets in October, seven in November, and thirty-four in December. Most soviets were formed in January and February 1918: ninety-five were established in January and sixty-two in February. All of this activity corresponded closely with the situation throughout the European part of the country.[68]

As in urban Russia, a variety of tensions colored the early months of Bolshevik rule in the countryside, which did nothing to dull the edge of social struggle. Peasants from Berezovsk volost in Petrovsk uezd complained to the Saratov Soviet that soldiers from the Petrovsk garrison (probably draftees from other provinces) forced grain from them. A delegation from another village requested weapons in order to secure surpluses from village kulaks. Another speaker reported that in his county peasants welcomed the resolutions of the Third Peasant Congress except for the Stolypin muzhiks, who refused to subordinate themselves to the soviets.[69] In sharp contrast some delegates from the Saratov Soviet sent to the villages reported that they were met with hostility, that Bolshevik newspapers were not permitted, that Bolshevik soldiers were not believed.[70] These conflicts indicated that the tensions between urban and

66. *Izvestiia Saratovskogo Soveta*, no. 107, December 12, 1917, p. 3.
67. *Proletarii Povolzh'ia*, no. 142, December 9, 1917, p. 4.
68. Gerasimenko and Tochenyi, *Sovety Povolzh'ia*, pp. 291–94.
69. *Saratovskii Sovet*, pp. 277, 279–80.
70. *Sotsial-Demokrat*, no. 101, December 24, 1917, p. 4; no. 103, December 30, p. 3.

rural Russia, which are central to an understanding of this period, had not been resolved. Toward the middle of 1918 the Bolshevik rulers created committees of village poor and urban grain detachments to exacerbate class war in the countryside in order to feed the starving cities. The peasants had their land, the Bolsheviks their power. But both claims remained fragile.

Soviet power thus spread across the flat steppes and rolling hills of Saratov province in an uncertain political climate characterized by factionalized armed opposition, anarchy, and rumors that the Bolsheviks had been suppressed in Petrograd. The balance of political forces in the capital and the shifting response of the moderate socialists complicated the dilemma of local leaders who defied Bolshevik authority. Still, as the first two months of Soviet rule show, once the local junkers had been subdued and Cossack forces left the region, chances for any armed toppling of the Soviet without outside help seemed slight. Ironically, the leaders of the SR and Menshevik organizations who had challenged the Bolsheviks had relied on the rifles and artillery of Cossacks and junkers, who for the most part stood in a different political camp altogether.

At first glance the recognition of Soviet power in Saratov province seems to have had greater symbolic value than practical significance. To be sure, the October Revolution was but part of a social and political process that, one could argue, did not stabilize until the civil war drew to a close several years later. But a closer look shows that recognition of Soviet power in Saratov province had marked a major realignment in political forces. Despite the unbending opposition to the new order, the local Bolsheviks could galvanize the working class into action on their behalf and for the moment benefited from the heady, evanescent mood in the garrison. Behind Bolshevik leaders stood a mass of followers who were willing to defend those who promised land, peace, and bread. In stark contrast, the fissiparous tendencies so endemic to Russian radicalism and social thought crippled the potential power of the Bolsheviks' contenders. Riven by factionalism and weakened by indecisive leadership, the opposition parties proved unable to present a united front. As a result, they lost the people. Even SR, Menshevik, and Kadet leaders writing in emigration years later admitted this. Cries to rally behind the Constituent Assembly as well as intensified solicitude lavished on the peasants and an articulated readiness to end coalition with the bourgeoisie now fell on deaf ears.

Nevertheless, the acceptance of the new political order in the province at large seems inconceivable without the ubiquitous presence of the soldier masses and the fortuitous formation of a Left SR party that entered the Lenin government. Not for nothing the Bolsheviks' enemies began to call the party "the party of the rear garrisons." Virtually in every district town and in the villages, too, radicalized soldiers proved to be the decisive factor in the recognition of Soviet power. From the uezd centers emissaries went into the villages and neutralized the peasantry by appealing to their great leveling instincts. Everywhere the soldiers made their presence felt. The tremendous role the Left SRs played also needs to be emphasized even though sources do not permit an assessment of how large a following the more radical wing of Russian populism actually had at this time. Strong in those uezds with the most volatile peasant movement, the Left SRs accepted the October Revolution, thereby giving considerable legitimacy and authority to the Bolsheviks at a critical moment. As a Left SR named Ezhov reasoned, "if the Constituent Assembly supports coalition, the Left SRs will not support the assembly. When they say all power to the Constituent Assembly and down with the Bolsheviks, they mean power to the Right SRs and Mensheviks and a struggle against the soviets."[71]

Even though the loci of power and main transportation and communication networks had fallen into the Bolsheviks' hands, it was a tottering Soviet regime that entered 1918. The considerable opposition to the new order constantly reminded Bolshevik leaders of the still unresolved nature of political power. While some Saratov Bolsheviks moved in an increasingly militant direction toward one-party rule, others lamented the collapse of revolutionary solidarity and the early signs of civil war. (In late December at a Bolshevik city conference a few spokesmen even advanced the argument that the October Revolution was not a socialist one, which of course had strong implications for the question of political power in general.) Sponsored by Saratov SRs, a demonstration on December 31 on behalf of the upcoming Constituent Assembly turned into street disorders and bloodshed, which prompted the declaration of martial law in Saratov. After the government closed down the Constituent Assembly when it convened in Petrograd a few weeks later, city dumas in Saratov, Khvalynsk, Volsk, Balashov, and Serdobsk cabled their protests to Petrograd. For the most part, though, the population of Saratov reacted apathetically to the news of the shutting down of the ephemeral Constituent Assembly. People had simply had enough. Probably few realized that Russia would face an even more tortured period in the years ahead.

71. *Saratovskii Sovet*, p. 286.

CHAPTER 9

Conclusion

The tsarist government's capacity for successful reform has been the topic of sustained historical debate. Much of this controversy has centered upon the extent to which the strains of the Great War caused the Revolution of 1917. This examination of Saratov suggests that Russia's sociopolitical evolution had greatly limited chances for the survival of a Western-style parliamentary system. Kept weak by the autocracy historically and only partially brought into the political structure after 1905, the Russian middle class and Russian liberalism as a political force had a negligible impact on the lower classes before the outbreak of war in 1914. In contrast, several generations of educated Russians who had turned to revolution offered a different political ethos to the masses. The revolutionaries' idealism, exaggerated belief in their own historical mission, widely accepted view of the state as a moving force in history, and exasperation over the government's unwillingness to integrate them into the existing polity drove a minority within the movement to accept the efficacy of violent revolutionary change. True social revolution erupted in Russia in 1917. It was not accidental. It was not solely the child of the war. It was not out of character with the country's political and social development.

Concentrating almost exclusively on Petrograd and to a lesser extent on Moscow, Western historical writing on the revolution until recently has ignored popular moods and attitudes in the country at large. For this reason alone, provincial Russia needs to be brought into our understanding of the revolution. When we look beyond the confines of Petrograd, it becomes clear that many interpretations of 1917, when translated into a local setting, are glaringly inadequate. This investigation of Saratov challenges those a priori evaluations of October that explain what happened in terms of Lenin's and Trotsky's unscrupulousness (and their opponents' fateful mistakes) or in terms of conspiracy, historical accident, or political manipulation. This investigation belies the arguments of historians who maintain that the Bolsheviks came to power in October because of the discipline and conspiratorial nature of the party itself, which imposed its will on a reluctant, indifferent, or politically immature people. This investigation also brings into question Soviet historians' image of a tightly knit, centralized party and of a meticulously planned insurrection in October. Such interpretations often color one's assessment of the course of Soviet history and less consciously weigh upon attitudes toward the Soviet Union today. Moreover, Western monographs and general histories tend to suggest that provincial Russia was nothing more than a torpid partner to developments in the capital cities.[1] If this work on Saratov draws attention to revolutionary politics in provincial Russia, raises questions about standard accounts of the revolution, and contributes to a broader understanding of what took place in 1917, it has served its purpose.

The tsarist political system with all of its shortcomings had provided rich soil for the growth of an opposition movement. The autocracy had alienated much of the professional middle class. It had failed to satiate the peasants' hunger for land. It had hampered workers' attempts to mitigate the social ills of industrialization and the arbitrariness of authority relations at the workplace. Then came war. The socioeconomic disequilibrium and extraordinary movement of people caused by it and the government's suspicion of public initiative during the war furthered discontent, exacerbating antigovernment feelings even within official circles.

Dealing a death blow to the centralized state structure, the February Revolution swept away all of the impediments that had kept the Russian masses out of the country's political life; now an array of other considerations led to October. The moderate socialists' theoretical conceptualization of the revolution as bourgeois-democratic undermined their party programs after February: in Saratov it caused them to abandon the legitimacy of the popular organs set up in 1917; and it eventually led to a rupture between party leaders and the rank and file, who came to share the Bolsheviks' call for an all-soviet government. Although riddled with

1. See, for example, Basil Dmytryshyn, *USSR: A Concise History* (New York, 1971), p. 73.

compromises, retreats, setbacks, and confusion, the Bolshevik party offered the most consistently plebian program to the Russian people, and rode to power at the top of self-legitimized popular organs—soviets, factory committees, trade unions, Red Guard detachments, soldier committees, and the rest. In Saratov as in Petrograd, Moscow, and Baku, the Bolshevik platform of land, peace, and bread and the slogan "All Power to the Soviets" appealed increasingly to common people, whose expectations often had soared to unreasonable levels while their economic situation deteriorated. The Bolsheviks' combination of tactical flexibility with a militant class interpretation of Russian political life (in the inclusive Russian sense of the upper classes, *verkhi*, pitted against the lower elements, *nizy*) proved successful in a fluid setting characterized by economic ruin, growing anarchism, and a tottering structure of voluntary authority relationships. The October Revolution *was not so much a Bolshevik Revolution as a triumph of all radical groups* that had broken decisively with those elements that supported further coalition with the bourgeoisie—Bolsheviks, Left SRs, SR Maximalists, Menshevik Internationalists, and anarchists. This convergence of purpose explains the spread of Soviet power throughout Saratov province.

Two broad political contests actually took place in 1917. The first involved the competition between Russian socialism and Russian liberalism. It found expression in the system of dual power that surfaced after the February Revolution. The second involved the competition between radical socialism and moderate socialism. It found expression in the battle over whether or not an all-socialist government could rule Russia. To understand the dynamics of the move toward a class solution to the question of Russia's political future posed by the February Revolution, it is necessary to weigh the impact of popular attitudes in Saratov toward political power and toward the new plebian institutions formed after the fall of the autocracy. For the first time since the Revolution of 1905, the people were brought into politics; what is most striking about their behavior is the degree to which socialist ideas and rhetoric had shaped it during the preceding generation. This conclusion raises further doubts about the viability of a democratic representative government for Russia. Ronald G. Suny has noted that "despite frequent claims of detachment and objectivity, scholars often make their judgments about the revolution and the Soviet Union against the standard of quite different European and American experiences."[2] It is time for us to explore the implications of the fact that Russia's political evolution differed from our own.

The unresolved question of Russia's political future acquired an in-

2. Ronald G. Suny, "Toward a Social History of the October Revolution," *American Historical Review*, 88, no. 1 (1983), 32.

stitutionalized form in the compromise system of dual power embodied in the parallel existence of the Provisional Government and the Petrograd Soviet, which soon spoke out on behalf of the newly formed popular organs established throughout the country. When translated into a provincial setting, the dual authority fashioned in Petrograd took on new shape. The weakness of Russian liberalism was much more apparent in Saratov and throughout much of provincial Russia in general, where political power had already been concentrated in the hands of local soviets in April. The dilemma posed by this unexpected situation could remain unresolved as long as the forces of "the democracy" and of the propertied elements appeared to be working for the same common goals. Why was this, and why did the truce ultimately break down?

First, the Provisional Government and its provincial counterparts, the public executive committees, claimed to be the legitimate heirs to the Imperial Duma, pending convocation of a constituent assembly. The Petrograd Soviet did not challenge this fundamental interpretation of the revolution. Second, at the local level the socialists had entered the public executive committees from the very beginning, and often played the most important role in them of the various political groups. In Saratov, socialists took over the public executive committee, which became an extension of the Soviet. Socialist sympathies prevailed overwhelmingly at the local level and it was tacitly understood that any permanent solution to the problem of political power would reflect this reality. (In the July Duma elections, the socialist parties polled 82.3 percent of the popular vote.) Third, the moderates believed that Russia could not sustain social revolution until objective historical conditions had ripened.

But Lenin's return to Russia in April and the collapse of the Provisional Government over the Miliukov Affair, which pushed the Mensheviks and Socialist Revolutionaries into a coalition with the liberals, exposed the fragility of the compromise. Now only the Bolsheviks maintained that Russia could move immediately to establish a socialist government without the participation of the country's propertied elements. Insisting that his party should not support the Provisional Government, Lenin lobbied for a transfer of power to the soviets; this turned out to be one of the most important tactical positions taken by a political party in 1917. The leaders of the moderate socialists, seeking to prevent social war, saw their historical mission as that of harmonizing the discordant political voices raised throughout the country. Entering the coalition ministry, they believed that they were saving war-torn Russia from a counterrevolutionary restoration and from the demagogic appeals of the Bolsheviks. In retrospect, however, the moderate socialists' co-optation into the bourgeois government blurred the meaning of dual power at both the national and the local level and failed to resolve the differences they had with Russian liberalism. More important, it forced the Rakitnikovs, Chertkovs, and Topuridzes eventually to reject their own revolutionary programs, revealing the extent to which many of the moderate leaders had come to accept nonradical, compromise—democratic—politics. The Russian political center remained socialist, but in becoming respectable it had lost its revolutionary fire.

Ironically, after their entry into the government the moderates tried to curb the power of the soviets in internal affairs. In striving to revive the prestige of the Duma, the moderates sacrificed their mass support and took the country one step closer toward civil war. As various election results in Saratov strongly suggest, once the failure of the Kornilov Affair indicated that a peaceful resolution to the question of political power was unlikely, some of the less radical socialists moved into the liberal camp, while the more militant elements within these parties now embraced Bolshevism or formed separate factions that agreed with the Bolsheviks that only a transfer of power to the soviets could save Russia. A vote for Bolshevism in local terms stood for an all-soviet socialist government, but since only the Bolshevik party and splinter groups from the other parties advocated a transfer of power to the soviets, it perhaps is not surprising that the new regime eventually turned into an exclusively Bolshevik one. It was Chertkov, a local Menshevik leader, former chairman of the Saratov Soviet and president of the City Duma, who led the struggle in Saratov against a transfer of power to the soviets.

In view of the deep social tensions within Russian society and of the strength of socialist sentiments among workers, soldiers, and peasants, it is possible that a broadly based socialist regime that included representation from democratically elected local bodies, municipal and government workers, shopkeepers and people from cooperatives (*odnorodnoe sotsialisticheskoe pravitel'stvo*), could have been established in Russia even without war. It is difficult to imagine the Bolsheviks' coming to power and creating essentially a one-party government, however, if Russia somehow had withdrawn from the war or had avoided it altogether. The war split apart Russian socialism and led to the terrible economic situation that magnified social tensions. Moreover, without war there would have been no Saratov garrison, and the soldiers, after all, played an enormous role in establishing Soviet power. The ambiguous political structure set up in March combined with efforts to continue fighting, on the one hand, and the Bolsheviks' rejection of it and of the Provisional Government, on the other, contributed immensely to the events of October. The collapse of the First Provisional Government in April had exposed both the divisions between upper- and lower-class

Russia and the tactical differences within the socialist camp, which became more pronounced during debates over the June offensive and further strained as a result of the July uprising in Petrograd and the move toward Soviet power in Tsaritsyn. Meanwhile, the democratic elements had begun shifting to the left as the coalition government failed to end the war and halt the ongoing economic ruin. In early August the Bolsheviks began to recover from temporary setbacks caused by the abortive July uprising, while the Menshevik and SR organizations experienced growing apathy and disillusionment within their ranks. Left-wing factions in both groups, often composed of the rank and file, moved willy-nilly toward a Bolshevik government by accepting the need to break decisively with the bourgeoisie.

Efforts to suppress Bolshevism in July, followed by the failure of a military restoration in August, shattered hopes for a liberal or peaceful solution to the question of Russia's political future. Force failed to curb the revolutionary tide and the disintegration of state power; instead the threat of counterrevolution revitalized the soviets, whose deputies across much of Russia now elected Bolshevik and other leftist representatives. Isolated from the lower classes, the liberals remained politically vulnerable. Dissension ripped Russian socialism apart. In the popular view the Bolsheviks became inseparably associated with Soviet power, whereas the moderate socialists, clinging stubbornly to coalition with the bourgeoisie and to their belief in the righteousness of a revolutionary war against the Central Powers, lost credibility.

Although they faced determined opposition from moderate leaders, the Saratov Bolsheviks controlled the Soviet's executive bodies in September. Throughout the month workers and soldiers passed resolutions demanding a transfer of power to the soviets, the dissolution of the State Duma, and the arming of workers. Across Russia people expected a promulgation of Soviet power at the upcoming Second Congress of Soviets; others feared a Bolshevik coup in the name of the soviets beforehand. In either case, the strength of the Bolsheviks and other leftist groups within the context of the soviets was manifest. The Bolsheviks won in Saratov because they stood for Soviet power and in this regard enjoyed institutional legitimacy. Once Soviet power was challenged, civil war began in earnest.

What has this study told us about the nature of local Bolshevism? Saratov Bolshevism bore the telltale marks of local conditions. Since the turn of the century a strong measure of comradeship had united the opposition movement in Saratov and weakened the impact of partisan politics, which were a pervasive element of émigré politics. Interaction among local activists, party centers, émigré groups, and exiles had created a fluid relationship. Conditioned by the peculiarities of the Volga underground, Saratov Bolshevism had developed a healthy respect for local needs, which affected its response to party tactics in general.

In his two-volume investigation of the Petrograd Bolsheviks, Alexander Rabinowitch stressed the historical significance of the "dynamic relationship that existed in 1917 within the top Bolshevik hierarchy, as well as between it, the ostensibly subordinate elements of the party, and the masses."[3] Rabinowitch also called attention to the relatively flexible structure of the party as it emerged from the underground and to its tactical responsiveness to the prevailing mass mood. As in Petrograd, the price of the same uneven but ultimately large growth in membership of the Saratov Bolshevik organization was a proportionate increase in problems of control at all levels. The problem of control was evinced in the tactical debates taking place within the Saratov committee itself and in its relations with the center and neighboring party organizations. At the provincial level the Saratov Bolsheviks' efforts to contain their Tsaritsyn comrades' radical inclinations strained relations between leaders in the two cities. At the regional level the Saratov Bolsheviks failed to establish an oblast committee because of the rivalry between the Saratov and Samara organizations. (Samara's Kuibyshev as well as Tsaritsyn's Minin considered Antonov too conciliatory.) To be sure, the Saratov committee strove to adhere to policy guidelines formulated in Petrograd. But first it had to ascertain what they were and decipher the mixed signals it sometimes received from the center before adapting the measures to local conditions. The party center presented a far from confident image to provincial leaders, and the many debates that rocked the Central Committee (over Lenin's April Theses, the June demonstrations, the July Days, the vitality of the soviets, political power, and later the question of an insurrection) complicated politics along the banks of the Volga. At times the Saratov committee ignored directives from Petrograd (e.g., it refused to drop the slogan "All Power to the Soviets" after the Sixth Party Congress in July deemed it inappropriate.) Likewise, the Tsaritsyn Bolsheviks came close to effecting a purely local seizure of power; the Astrakhan Bolsheviks remained part of a united Social Democratic organization until October; and the Samara Bolsheviks actively participated in the deliberations of the city's public executive committee until late fall.

Much has been written about the rapid radicalization of the Petrograd masses. This study has shown that the deepening of the revolution in Saratov, as in Baku, did not lag behind developments in Petrograd to any

3. Rabinowitch, *Bolsheviks Come to Power*, p. 312.

great extent. In fact, the early consolidation of power in the hands of the Saratov Soviet and simultaneous collapse of the Public Executive Committee suggest that provincial populations often had to deal with one of the most important issues of the Revolution before it was resolved at the national level. Events in Tsaritsyn show that given the right circumstances, provincial populations could be as leftist in their political orientation as inhabitants of the capital. Petrograd Bolsheviks captured only 10 percent of the votes in elections to the city soviet in July 1917 but more than 50 percent in September elections. Scoring similar successes at approximately the same time, Saratov Bolsheviks, too, benefited from the perceived threat of counterrevolution and from the tottering economy and breakdown in law and order.

Because of the failure of traditional pillars of authority before 1917, workers, soldiers, and peasants had placed considerable hope in the ability of their own, unrepresentative class institutions to effect change. Even though many questions remain unanswered regarding Saratov's working class, some recent findings on the political behavior of the Moscow and Petrograd proletariat appear to hold true for Saratov workers, who became radicalized in 1917 by participating in a frustrating struggle to improve their economic position. The crumbling economic structure caused by the war turned workers against the government and eventually against those socialist parties that supported it. Profound suspicion toward the propertied elements and industrialists expressed itself in workers' efforts to better their economic situation already in March, and as crisis after crisis broke out, workers came to perceive Soviet power as a rational solution to their economic straits and to political impasse.

Not to be viewed as a monolithic social group, Saratov's work force responded variously to the political climate of 1917. Skilled workers—and not "dark," semipeasant unskilled types—were the first to become radicalized. Workers evacuated from Russia's Baltic and Polish provinces as early as April advocated Soviet power. But one must not ignore skilled local workers in the metal-processing industry, in the railroad yards and on tram lines, and in the large mechanized food- and lumber-processing plants, who contributed to the Saratov labor movement many militant working-class activists. Unskilled workers toiling in the abovementioned industries, especially in those in which revolutionaries had carried on underground agitational work the longest (flour milling, tobacco processing, vegetable oil, and transportation), also became swept into the labor movement and by fall helped swell Bolshevik ranks. In Tsaritsyn, for example, lumber workers and dock hands fell under the influence of their more militant comrades in the large metalworks and of the unruly frontoviki.

The Saratov garrison and within it the frontoviki particularly played a greater role than the working class in turning the tide in favor of Soviet power locally. The impact of the garrisons was even more important in the uezd towns, where Soviet power was first recognized by radicalized soldiers. Strong before February, antiwar feelings gradually infected the entire Saratov garrison once institutional vehicles for expressing soldiers' aspirations were set up and the old command structure ceased to exist. The continuation of the war soon became the most important issue as far as the masses of soldiers were concerned, and after the moderate socialists, especially the Socialist Revolutionaries, entered the coalition ministry in May, the door to victory was left wide open for any group that denounced the war. The garrison's conversion to Bolshevism began when the SR party joined the liberals in pressing for the continuation of the war to a victorious end. To those in the barracks and trenches there was little difference between a revolutionary war and an imperialist one. The June offensive and the conservative resurgence in July and August meant a revival in discipline and the postponement of any hopes of returning to the countryside to share in the division of land. Visits to home villages for furloughs or for field work, combined with the impact of the frontoviki and of a swell of deserters, deepened the soldiers' discontent. Spreading tales about horror and carnage at the front, the evacuated soldiers now refused to fight. There was no one to make them. The soldiers were, as one government report put it, "the irresponsible masters of the situation."

Although the Saratov garrison did not turn into a Bolshevik stronghold until fall, the move to the left deprived the opposition of any potential armed force and strengthened at a critical moment those groups that advocated a transfer of power to the soviets. Bolshevik popularity among soldiers remained tenuous, however. Saratov Bolshevik leaders, fully aware of the fragility of their hold over the garrison and the lack of cadre within the officer corps, avidly promoted a workers' Red Guard. As the events of the October Revolution in Saratov and the uezd towns show, the Bolshevik leaders' apprehensions over the reliability of the soldiers was warranted. Their Bolshevism was only skin deep.

Because the economic life of Saratov was based on the production, processing, and distribution of agricultural products, the peasant movement also left its mark on local developments. The magnitude of the Saratov peasant uprising sharpened political debates in the towns, resulting in a rupture between the peasants' self-propelled move toward satiating their land hunger and the call of the populist leaders for restraint. By fall the peasants' reluctance to sell grain had created food shortages in Saratov and upset deliveries to more industrialized provinces.

The broad forces that shaped agrarian relations and attitudes in

Saratov province since the mid–nineteenth century explain what took place in the villages in 1917. The cumulative impact of the activities of several generations of revolutionaries, strained economic relationships, and the vitality of the commune account for the immediate move on the part of the peasantry against the economic advantages of the estate owners and Stolypin peasants. Launching their assault against the landowners already in March, the peasants quarreled over rents and the use of prisoners of war for farmwork. They seized forestland. The chronology and scope of the peasant movement in Saratov challenges widely accepted views in Western historical writing, which date the beginning of the agrarian movement from April and May.[4]

In the Saratov countryside the February Revolution led to the spontaneous establishment of peasant organizations that promoted the interests of the communal peasants. Examination of the varied activities of the peasant executive committees shows that the mood of the countryside was far less cautious and patient than that of the urban-based leaders of the populist parties. In this regard subsequent developments in the Saratov villages underscored the weakness of the SR party's leadership. Once the moderate socialists entered the coalition government they became accountable for its hesitant agrarian program. Government efforts to curb the power of the peasant executive committees by establishing land committees and food-supply committees failed. Local activists and often government officials themselves, becoming increasingly sympathetic to the peasants' demands, pressured authorities to resolve the land question promptly. The failure to do so had the same consequence as the government's inability to end the war: it alienated a large element of the population and seriously challenged the hold the populist parties had over the villages. In the less remote rural areas populism split apart, and local-based militants now reached the same conclusion that many workers and soldiers had come to accept: only an all-soviet socialist government could end the war, distribute land, and set the economy right. Left SRs carried resolutions at the Second Saratov Province Peasant Congress, held in September, calling for an immediate transfer of land to those who tilled it and the establishment of an all-soviet government.

Despite the separate sets of demands, aspirations, and attitudes of Russian workers, soldiers, and peasants, then, a combination of factors brought the lower classes together, providing, as Michal Reiman so aptly put it, a "dividing line for . . . social upheaval."[5] The class organs created by the February Revolution—soviets, factory committees, trade unions,

4. Like most Western historians, Ferro notes that the agrarian movement "had started in May." See *Révolution de 1917*, 2:217.

5. Michal Reiman, "Spontaneity and Planning in the Plebian Revolution," in *Reconsiderations on the Russian Revolution*, ed. Ralph C. Elwood (Columbus, O., 1976), p. 12.

military committees, soldiers' committees, armed guards, peasant committees, volost committees, and rural soviets—created a rival form of political representation outside conventional middle-class politics. Virtually all of these bodies viewed the legitimate institutions with distrust and suspicion, and sought to set up some sort of supervision or control over them. As the year progressed and the successive governments failed to solve the pressing socioeconomic problems, people came to believe that the propertied elements were acting in their own best interests. By the fall of 1917 the wide strata of workers, soldiers, and peasants had concluded that only an all-soviet government could solve the country's problems.

APPENDIX

Additional Results of Elections to the Constituent Assembly

Table A-1

Number and percentage of votes cast for Bolshevik, Socialist Revolutionary (SR), and Kadet delegates to city dumas and to Constituent Assembly, Saratov province, 1917, by town

	Bolsheviks				*Socialist Revolutionaries*				*Kadets*			
	Duma		*Constituent Assembly*		*Duma*		*Constituent Assembly*		*Duma*		*Constituent Assembly*	
Town	*Number*	*Percent*	*Number*	*Percent*	*Number*	*Percent*	*Number*	*Percent*	*Number*	*Percent*	*Number*	*Percent*
Atkarsk	—	—	260	14%	1,097	37%	560	28%	218	7%	503	27%
Balashov[a]	—	—	3,489	39	3,780	50	2,233	25	756	10	1,194	14
Khvalynsk	—	—	1,009	24	2,574[b]	20[b]	708	16	901	16	840	18
Saratov	6,975	12%	13,719	29	37,864[c]	64[c]	6,801	—	6,690	11	11,471	24
Serdobsk	—	—	—	—	974[d]	37[d]	676	22	—	—	258	8
Tsaritsyn[e]	13,130	50	14,463	47	4,360	14	4,468	14	292	0.1	2,889	9
Volsk	—	—	584	6	6,357	64	3,682	37	830	8	1,840	18

Note: Figures are exclusive of garrison votes unless otherwise noted.
[a] Figures include garrison votes.
[b] SRs formed bloc with Popular Socialists in duma elections.
[c] SRs formed bloc with Mensheviks and Bund in duma elections. Mensheviks polled 3,907 votes.
[d] SRs formed bloc with Social Democrats in duma elections.
[e] Duma elections in Tsaritsyn took place in August.

Sources: S. Sh. Ovrutskaia, "Politicheskoe bankrotstvo eserov na vyborakh v Uchreditel'noe sobranie (Po materialam Saratovskoi gubernii)," in *Nekotorye voprosy otechestvennoi i vseobshchei istorii* (Saratov, 1971), pp. 45–46, 50; *Saratovskii vestnik*, no. 152, July 12, 1917, p. 1, and no. 159, July 20, p. 2.

Table A-2

Number and percentage of votes cast for Bolshevik and Socialist Revolutionary delegates to Constituent Assembly by garrisons in Saratov province, 1917

	Bolsheviks		*Socialist Revolutionaries*	
Garrison	*Number*	*Percent*	*Number*	*Percent*
Saratov	8,993	71%	1,897	15%
Military Suburb (Saratov)	5,581	80	695	10
Tsaritsyn	2,150	78	500[a]	18
Atkarsk	1,808	84	360[a]	16
Volsk	1,722	42	1,338	32
Pokrovsk	1,241[a]	73[a]	290[a]	17[a]
Serdobsk	648	33	1,173	58

Note: No information is available on the votes cast by the garrisons at Balashov, Kamyshin, Khvalynsk, Kuznetsk, and Petrovsk.

[a]Estimated.

Source: S. Sh. Ovrutskaia, "Politicheskoe bankrotstvo eserov na vyborakh v Uchreditel'noe sobranie (Po materialam Saratovskoi gubernii)," in *Nekotorye voprosy otechestvennoi i vseobshchei istorii* (Saratov, 1971), p. 48.

Table A-3

Number of votes cast for Socialist Revolutionary (SR) and Bolshevik delegates to Constituent Assembly in Saratov province, 1917, by uezd

Uezd	*SRs*	*Bolsheviks*
Atkarsk	69,054	43,315
Balashov	101,635	33,639
Khvalynsk	50,128	7,767
Kuznetsk	42,983	16,272
Petrovsk	60,384	15,582
Saratov	49,057	25,350
Serdobsk	100,586	11,355
Tsaritsyn	18,318	19,333

Note: No data are available for Kamyshin and Volsk uezds.

Source: Adapted from G. A. Gerasimenko, "Local Peasant Organizations in 1917 and the First Half of 1918," ed. Donald J. Raleigh. *Soviet Studies in History,* 16, no. 3 (Winter 1977–78), 73.

Selected Bibliography

Chronologies and Special Bibliographies

Anikeev, V. V. *Deiatel'nost' TsK RSDRP(b) v 1917 godu: Khronika sobytii.* Moscow, 1969.

Dmitrenko, S. L., et al., eds. *Velikaia Oktiabr'skaia sotsialisticheskaia revoliutsiia: Khronika sobytii.* 4 vols. Moscow, 1957–61.

Gavrilov, G. T., comp. *1917 god v Stalingradskoi gubernii (Khronika sobytii).* Stalingrad, 1927.

Gerasimenko, G. A., et al., eds. *Khronika revoliutsionnykh sobytii v Saratovskom Povolzh'e.* Saratov, 1968.

Kabytov, P. S., and E. D. Rumiantsev, comps. *Velikaia Oktiabr'skaia sotsialisticheskaia revoliutsiia v Povolzh'e (Rekomendatel'nyi ukazatel' sovetskoi literatury 1917–1976 gg.).* Kuibyshev, 1977.

P. S., comp. "Khronika Oktiabr'skoi revoliutsii v Saratove." *Kommunisticheskii put'*, no. 19 (1927), pp. 29–36; no. 20 (1927), pp. 111–25.

Serdiuk, I. I. *Revoliutsionnoe dvizhenie i bor'ba za Sovetskuiu vlast' v Saratovskoi gubernii, 1861–1920: Ukazatel' literatury.* Saratov, 1963.

Sineskov, N. A., comp. *Ukazatel' materialov po istorii revoliutsionnogo dvizheniia Stalingradskogo kraia 1905–1922 gg.* Stalingrad, 1930.

Sokolov, N. N., ed. *1917 god v Stalingradskoi gubernii: Khronika sobytii.* Stalingrad, 1927.

Sokolov, S. D., ed. *Materialy dlia ukazatelia po revoliutsionnomu dvizheniiu v Saratovskom krae, 1861–1921.* Saratov, 1928.

Sushitskii, V. A. *Materialy dlia ukazatelia po revoliutsionnomu dvizheniiu v Saratovskom krae, vyshedshei v 1928 godu, 1861–1921.* Saratov, 1930.

Documentary Materials

A. K. "Materialy o zabastovkakh v Saratove v 1901 godu." *Vestnik Saratovskogo Gubkoma RKP,* no. 7 (32) (1923), pp. 94–95.

Abramovich, E. A. "Pis'ma E. A. Abramovicha k E. A. Gurvichu." *Katorga i ssylka,* no. 40 (1928), pp. 142–50.

Akademiia nauk SSSR, Institut istorii, et al. *Ekonomicheskoe polozhenie Rossii nakanune Velikoi Oktiabr'skoi sotsialisticheskoi revoliutsii: Dokumenty i materialy.* Vol. 3, *Sel'skoe khoziaistvo i krest'ianstvo,* ed. A. M. Anfimov et al. Leningrad, 1967.

——. *Krest'ianskoe dvizhenie v Rossii, iiun' 1907 g.–iiul' 1914 g.: Sbornik dokumentov.* Ed. A. V. Shapkarin. Moscow, 1966.

——. *Krest'ianskoe dvizhenie v Rossii v gody pervoi mirovoi voiny, iiul' 1914 g.–fevral' 1917 g.: Sbornik dokumentov.* Ed. A. M. Anfimov. Moscow, 1965.

——. *Revoliutsiia 1905–1907 gg. v Rossii: Dokumenty i materialy.* 15 vols. Moscow, 1955–63.

——. *Revoliutsionnoe dvizhenie v Rossii nakanune Oktiabr'skogo vooruzhennogo vosstaniia (1–24 oktiabria 1917 g.).* Ed. D. A. Chugaev et al. Moscow, 1962.

——. *Revoliutsionnoe dvizhenie v Rossii posle sverzheniia samoderzhaviia.* Ed. D. A. Chugaev et al. Moscow, 1957.

——. *Revoliutsionnoe dvizhenie v Rossii v aprele 1917 g.: Aprel'skii krizis.* Ed. L. S. Gaponenko et al. Moscow, 1958.

——. *Revoliutsionnoe dvizhenie v Rossii v avguste 1917 g.: Razgrom Kornilovskogo miatezha.* Ed. D. A. Chugaev et al. Moscow, 1959.

——. *Revoliutsionnoe dvizhenie v Rossii v iiule 1917 g.: Iiul'skii krizis.* Ed. D. A. Chugaev et al. Moscow, 1959.

——. *Revoliutsionnoe dvizhenie v Rossii v mae–iiune 1917 g.: Iiun'skaia demonstratsiia.* Ed. D. A. Chugaev et al. Moscow, 1959.

——. *Revoliutsionnoe dvizhenie v Rossii v sentiabre 1917 g.: Obshchenatsional'nyi krizis.* Ed. D. A. Chugaev et al. Moscow, 1961.

——. *Velikaia Oktiabr'skaia sotsialisticheskaia revoliutsiia, Oktiabr'skoe vooruzhennoe vosstanie v Petrograde: Dokumenty i materialy.* Ed. G. N. Golikov et al. Moscow, 1957.

Amosov, P. N., et al., eds. *Oktiabr'skaia revoliutsiia i fabzavkomy: Materialy po istorii fabrichno-zavodskikh komitetov.* 2 vols. Moscow, 1927.

Antonov-Saratovskii, V. P., ed. *Saratovskii Sovet rabochikh deputatov, 1917–1918: Sbornik dokumentov.* Moscow and Leningrad, 1931.

The Bolsheviks and the October Revolution: Minutes of the Central Committee of the Russian Social-Democratic Labour Party (Bolsheviks), August 1917–February 1918. Trans. Ann Bone. London, 1974.

Browder, Robert P., and Alexander F. Kerensky, eds. *The Russian Provisional Government, 1917: Documents.* 3 vols. Stanford, 1961.

Bukhbinder, N. A. "Proklamatsii i listi Tsentral'nogo Komiteta i provintsial'nykh s.-d. organizatsii po povodu sobytii 9-go ianvaria 1905 g." *Krasnaia letopis',* no. 1 (1922), pp. 287–88; no. 2 (1922), pp. 16–226.

Bulkin, F., comp. "Soiuz metallistov i departament politsii." *Krasnaia letopis',* no. 5 (1923), pp. 252–67.

Bunyan, J., and H. H. Fisher. *The Bolshevik Revolution, 1917–1918: Documents and Materials.* Stanford, 1934.

Butenko, A. F., and D. A. Chugaev, eds. *Vtoroi vserossiiskii s"ezd sovetov rabochikh i soldatskikh deputatov: Sbornik dokumentov.* Moscow, 1957.

Chernyshev, I. V. "Otchet komiteta po okazaniiu pomoshchi golodaiushchim, sostoiavshego pri I. V. E. Obshchestve za 1906–1907 prodovol'stvennyi god." *Trudy imperatorskogo Vol'nogo Ekonomicheskogo Obshchestva,* no. 1–2 (1908), pp. 130–52.

Dubrovskii, S. M., ed. *Krest'ianskoe dvizhenie v revoliutsii 1905–1907 gg.* Moscow, 1956.

Fabriky i zavody g. Saratova v sanitarnom otnoshenii. Saratov, 1911.

Gokhlerner, V. M., comp. *Listovki Saratovskikh bol'shevikov, 1902–1917.* Saratov, 1979.

Golder, Frank Alfred, ed. *Documents of Russian History, 1914–1917.* Gloucester, 1964.

Gratsianov, P. K. *Agronomicheskaia organizatsiia Saratovskoi gubernskoi zemleustroitel'noi komissii v 1911 godu.* Saratov, 1912.

Institut marksizma-leninizma pri TsK KPSS. "Adresa mestnykh organizatsii RSDRP (1917–1918 gg.): Dokumenty Instituta marksizma-leninizma pri TsK KPSS. Adresnaia kniga TsK, RSDRP(b)." *Istoricheskii arkhiv,* no. 5 (1956), pp. 31–45; no. 6 (1956), pp. 36–66.

——. *Bol'sheviki v gody imperialisticheskoi voiny 1914–fevral' 1917 gg.: Sbornik dokumentov mestnykh bol'shevistskikh organizatsii.* Moscow, 1939.

——. *Bor'ba partii bol'shevikov za armiiu v sotsialisticheskoi revoliutsii: Sbornik dokumentov.* Moscow, 1977.

——. *Bor'ba za sozdanie marksistskoi partii v Rossii. Obrazovanie RSDRP. Vozniknovenie bol'shevizma (1894–1904): Dokumenty i materialy.* Moscow, 1961.

——. *Perepiska sekretariata TsK RSDRP(b) s mestnymi partiinymi organizatsiiami: Sbornik dokumentov.* Vol. 1, *Mart–oktiabr' 1917 g.* Moscow, 1957.

——. *Perepiska V. I. Lenina i rukovodimykh im uchrezhdenii RSDRP s partiinymi organizatsiiami 1903–1905 gg.: Sbornik dokumentov v trekh tomakh.* Ed. M. S. Volin et al. Moscow, 1974, 1975, 1977.

——. *Protokoly Tsentral'nogo Komiteta RSDRP(b): Avgust 1917–fevral' 1918.* Moscow, 1958.

——. *Sed'maia (Aprel'skaia) vserossiiskaia konferentsiia RSDRP (bol'shevikov): Petrogradskaia obshchegorodskaia konferentsiia RSDRP(b), aprel' 1917 goda: Protokoly.* Moscow, 1958.

——. *Shestoi s"ezd RSDRP (bol'shevikov), avgust 1917 goda: Protokoly.* Moscow, 1958.

——. *Tretii s"ezd RSDRP, aprel'–mai 1905 goda: Protokoly.* Moscow, 1959.

——. *Vtoroi s"ezd RSDRP, iiul'–avgust 1903 g.* Moscow, 1932.

——. "Zhurnal mestnykh partiinykh organizatsii 1917 g.: Dokumenty Instituta marksizma-leninizma pri TsK KPSS." *Istoricheskii arkhiv,* no. 5 (1959), p. 45.

Karpov, N., ed. *Krest'ianskoe dvizhenie v revoliutsii 1905 goda, v dokumentakh.* Leningrad, 1926.

Kokshaiskii, I. N. *Gorod Saratov v zhilishchnom otnoshenii.* Saratov, 1922.

——. *Predvaritel'nye dannye perepisi naseleniia goroda Saratova i ego prigorodov.* Saratov, 1916.

Kotel'nikov, K. G., and V. L. Meller, eds. *Krest'ianskoe dvizhenie v 1917 godu.* Moscow and Leningrad, 1927.
Kratkie otchety sanitarnykh vrachei Saratovskogo gubernskogo zemstva v 1909–1910. Saratov, 1910.
Lomov, G., et al. "Pis'ma v redaktsiiu zh. 'Proletarskaia revoliutsiia.'" *Proletarskaia revoliutsiia,* no. 2 (49) (1926), pp. 276–79.
Maksimov, A., ed. *Tsarskaia armiia v period mirovoi voiny i Fevral'skoi revoliutsii: Materialy k izucheniiu istorii imperialisticheskoi i grazhdanskoi voiny.* Kazan, 1932.
Mal'kov, A. A. *Estestvennoe dvizhenie naseleniia Saratovskoi gubernii za period 1914–1925 g.* Saratov, 1926.
Martynov, M., ed. "Agrarnoe dvizhenie v 1917 godu po dokumentam glavnogo zemel'nogo komiteta." *Krasnyi arkhiv,* no. 1 (14) (1926), p. 124.
Materialy dlia otsenki zemel' Saratovskoi gubernii. Pt. 1, *Zemlevladenie.* Saratov, 1906. Pt. 2, *Eksploatatsiia pashni v chastnovladel'cheskikh khoziaistvakh i krest'ianskie vnenadel'nye arendy.* Saratov, 1905.
Materialy k opisaniiu Saratovskoi gubernii: Geografichesko-statisticheskie svedeniia o gubernii. Saratov, 1875.
Materialy k voprosu o nuzhdakh sel'sko-khoziaistvennoi promyshlennosti v Saratovskoi gubernii. Saratov, 1903.
Miliutin, V. P., ed. *Agrarnaia revoliutsiia.* Vol. 2, *Krest'ianskoe dvizhenie v 1917 godu.* Moscow, 1928.
Milovzorov, A. F. *Krest'ianskoe i chastnovladel'cheskoe khoziaistvo Saratovskoi gubernii posle goda voiny.* Saratov, 1916.
Nevskii, V. I., ed. *1905: Sovetskaia pechat' i literatura o sovetakh.* Moscow and Leningrad, 1925.
Ol'minskii, M. S. "Tri pis'ma (G. Petrovskogo, Ia. M. Sverdlova i V. P. Antonova-Saratovskogo)." *Proletarskaia revoliutsiia,* no. 4 (1922), pp. 275–77, 282–89.
Osipov, B. A., ed. *1917 god v Saratovskoi gubernii: Sbornik dokumentov, fevral' 1917–dekabr' 1918 gg.* Saratov, 1957.
Otchet ob agronomicheskikh meropriiatiakh Saratovskogo uezdnogo zemstva za 1914–1915 god. Saratov, 1916.
Otchety o deiatel'nosti uezdnykh sanitarnykh vrachei Saratovskogo gubernskogo zemstva v 1912–1913 godakh. Saratov, 1914.
Pervaia Povolzh'skaia oblastnaia konferentsiia Bunda: Protokoly. Saratov, 1917.
Proekt smety raskhodov i dokhodov po spetsial'nym kapitalam Saratovskogo gubernskogo zemstva na 1909–1916 gg. Saratov, 1908–16.
Protokoly Saratovskoi voennoi okruzhnoi konferentsii Kazanskogo okruga. Saratov, 1917.
"Protokoly vserossiiskogo (martovskogo) soveshchaniia partiinykh rabotnikov." *Voprosy istorii KPSS,* no. 5 (1962), pp. 106–25.
Protokoly vtorogo brigadnogo s"ezda Saratovskoi mestnoi brigady (10–11 sentiabria, 1917 g.). Saratov, 1917.
Protokoly zasedanii Saratovskogo Voennogo Komiteta. Saratov, 1917.
Protokoly zasedanii Saratovskogo Voennogo Komiteta: Protokoly zasedanii Presidiuma Saratovskogo Voennogo Komiteta. Saratov, 1917.
Saar, G. P. "Okhrannoe otdelenie o deiatel'nosti Saratovskoi organizatsii RSDRP." *Kommunisticheskii put',* no. 9 (34) (1923), pp. 199–214.

Saratovskaia gorodskaia duma. *Izvestiia Saratovskoi Gorodskoi Dumy.* Saratov, 1917.
Saratovskaia gubernskaia uchenaia arkhivnaia komissiia. *Materialy po krepostnomu pravu: Saratovskaia guberniia.* Saratov, 1911.
Saratovskoe dvorianskoe deputatskoe sobranie: Otchet Saratovskogo dvorianskogo deputatskogo sobraniia. 3 vols. Saratov, 1908–14.
Saratovskoe oblastnoe sel'skokhoziaistvennoe soveshchanie: Materialy. 2 vols. St. Petersburg, 1911.
Sbornik svedenii po Saratovskoi gubernii za 1905 g. Vol. 2. Saratov, 1905.
Sbornik tsirkuliarov Ministerstva Vnutrennykh del za period mart–iiun' 1917 goda. Petrograd, 1917.
Shestakov, A. V., ed. *Sovety krest'ianskikh deputatov i drugie krest'ianskie organizatsii.* Vol. 1, 2 pts. Moscow, 1929.
Spiski naselennykh mest Saratovskoi gubernii. Vol. 7. Saratov, 1914.
Statisticheskii ezhegodnik Rossii za 1916. No. 1. Petrograd, 1918.
Statisticheskii sbornik po Saratovskoi gubernii. Saratov, 1923.
Tomarev, V. I., and E. N. Shkodina, eds. *1905 god v Tsaritsyne (Vospominaniia i dokumenty).* Volgograd, 1960.
Troinitskii, N. A., et al., eds. *Pervaia vseobshchaia perepis' naseleniia Rossiiskoi imperii, 1897 g.* Vol. 38, *Saratovskaia guberniia.* St. Petersburg, 1904.
United States. *Russia: The Volga River and Caspian Sea.* Confidential report. Washington, D.C., 1919.
Ustav obshchestva potrebitelei g. Saratova. Saratov, 1915.
Varzar, V. E. *Statisticheskie svedeniia o stachkakh rabochikh na fabrikakh i zavodakh za desiatiletie, 1895–1904 gg.* St. Petersburg, 1905.
——. *Statistika stachek rabochikh na fabrikakh i zavodakh za trekhletie 1906–1908 gg.* St. Petersburg, 1910.
——. *Statistika stachek rabochikh na fabrikakh i zavodakh za 1905 g.* St. Petersburg, 1908.
Zavarzin, S. I., and E. N. Shkodina, comps. *1917 god v Tsaritsyne (Sbornik dokumentov i materialov).* Stalingrad, 1957.
Zhurnal zasedaniia s"ezda rabochikh deputatov 26 fabrik sukonnogo proizvodstva Samarskoi, Saratovskoi, Simbirskoi, i Penzenskoi gubernii. Saratov, 1917.

1917 Saratov Newspapers

Golos anarkhii. Anarchist paper published in the fall of 1917.
Izvestiia Saratovskogo Gubernskogo Soveta krest'ianskikh deputatov. Official organ of the Saratov Peasant Soviet, published in the fall of 1917.
Izvestiia Saratovskogo Soveta rabochikh i soldatskikh deputatov. Official organ of the Saratov Soviet.
Pochta. Conservative Saratov daily.
Proletarii Povolzh'ia. Newspaper of the Saratov Menshevik Organization.
Saratovskaia zemskaia nedelia. Irregular publication of the Saratov zemstvo.
Saratovskie gubernskie vedomosti. Irregular publication of provincial authorities.
Saratovskii golos. Conservative boulevard daily, closed down in 1917.

Saratovskii listok. Saratov daily associated with the Kadet party.
Saratovskii vestnik. Saratov "bourgeois" daily, later associated with the Edinstvo moderate socialist faction.
Saratovskoe slovo. Published in December 1917 by the staff of *Saratovskii listok.*
Sotsial-Demokrat. Saratov Bolshevik paper.
Zemlia i volia. Daily of the Saratov Socialist Revolutionary party.
Zhizn'. Conservative Saratov daily published through the first half of 1917.

Other Newspapers and Newspaper Reprints

Izvestiia Kazanskogo Voenno-okruzhnogo Komiteta. Paper of the Kazan District Military Committee.
Izvestiia Petrogradskogo Soveta rabochikh i soldatskikh deputatov. Daily paper of the Petrograd Soviet and later of the Central Executive Committee.
Kommunist. Contemporary Saratov newspaper; organ of the Communist party.
Nasha gazeta. Legal Social Democratic paper published in Saratov in 1915 (nine issues). Subsequently reprinted in 1935 as *Nasha gazeta, no. 1–9, 1915,* ed. G. I. Lomov et al. (Saratov, 1935).
Ol'minskii, M. S., ed. *"Vpered" i "Proletarii": Pervye bol'shevistskie gazety 1905 goda.* 3 vols. Moscow, 1924.
Pravda. Central Bolshevik party organ published in Petrograd.
"Stat'i iz Saratovskoi 'Nashei gazety' 1915 g. (Prilozheniia k stat'e Antonova-Saratovskogo)." *Proletarskaia revoliutsiia,* no. 14 (16) (1923), pp. 216–54.
Tsaritsynskii vestnik. Tsaritsyn "bourgeois" paper.

Published and Unpublished Memoirs

Akimov, I. "Kak my dobivalis' svobody pechati u eserov (Vospominaniia)." *Kommunisticheskii put',* no. 9 (34) (1923), pp. 214–15.
Antonov-Saratovskii, V. P. *Krasnyi god.* Moscow and Leningrad, 1927.
——. "Oktiabr'skaia revoliutsiia v Saratove." *Kommunisticheskii put',* no. 34 (1925), pp. 77–86.
——. "Oktiabr'skie dni v Saratove." *Proletarskaia revoliutsiia,* no. 10 (1922), pp. 278–98.
——. "Oktiabr'skie dni v Saratove." In *Rasskazyvaiut uchastniki velikogo Oktiabria,* pp. 290–307. Moscow, 1957.
——. "Otbleski besed s Il'ichem." *Proletarskaia revoliutsiia,* no. 3 (26) (1924), pp. 183–91.
——. *Pod stiagom proletarskoi bor'by: Otryvki iz vospominanii o rabote v Saratove.* Moscow and Leningrad, 1925.
——. "Saratov s fevralia po oktiabr' 1917." *Proletarskaia revoliutsiia,* no. 2 (25) (1924), pp. 144–71; no. 4 (27) (1924), pp. 178–210.
——. "Saratovskie bol'sheviki vozglavliaiut bor'bu." In *Pervaia russkaia . . . Sbornik vospominanii aktivnykh uchastnikov revoliutsii 1905–1907,* pp. 72–80. Moscow, 1975.
——. "Saratov v gody Imperialisticheskoi voiny (1914–1966 gg.) i 'Nasha Gazeta.'" *Proletarskaia revoliutsiia,* no. 16 (1923), pp. 7–81.
——. "Vospominaniia o V. I. Lenine." *Voprosy istorii,* no. 4 (1955), pp. 40–44.
——, ed. *Godovshchina sotsial'noi revoliutsii v Saratove.* Saratov, 1918.

Argunov, A. A. "Iz proshlogo partii Sotsialistov-Revoliutsionerov." *Byloe*, no. 10 (22) (1907), pp. 94–112.
Argunov, P. "Iz vospominanii o pervoi russkoi revoliutsii." *Katorga i ssylka*, no. 1 (74) (1931), pp. 142–62.
Babine, Alexis V. Diary. Library of Congress, Manuscript Division, Babine Papers, sec. 1 (1917–19).
Babushkin, A. V., et al., eds. *Za vlast' sovetov (Sbornik vospominanii starkyh bol'shevikov)*. Saratov, 1968.
Babushkin, V. F. "Provokator Platonov." *Vestnik Saratovskogo Gubkoma RKP*, no. 17 (1922), pp. 28–30.
——. *Vragi (Vospominaniia)*. Saratov, 1932.
Bankvitser, A. L. "Vospominaniia." In *Ot fevralia k oktiabriu (Iz ankety uchastnikov Velikoi Oktiabr'skoi sotsialisticheskoi revoliutsii)*, pp. 29–40. Moscow, 1957.
Batov, M. "Moi vospominaniia." *Partiinyi sputnik*, no. 9–10 (1923), pp. 73–80.
Bazhenov, N. "Kak u nas proizoshlo agrarnoe dvizhenie: Zapiski krest'ianina." *Russkoe bogatstvo*, no. 4 (1909), pp. 97–120; no. 5 (1909), pp. 92–111.
Bekker. V. *Vospominaniia o Saratovskoi gubernii Statskogo sovetnika*. Moscow, 1852.
Bock, Maria (Stolypina). *Reminiscences of My Father, Peter A. Stolypin*. Trans. and ed. Margaret Patoski. Metuchen, N.J., 1970.
Bogdanova, E. N. "Iz lichnykh vospominanii." *Vestnik Saratovskogo Gubkoma RKP*, no. 3 (28) (1923), pp. 46–47.
——. "Stranichki vospominanii: Oktiabr' v Saratove." *Vestnik Saratovskogo Gubkoma RKP*, no. 25 (1922), pp. 128–30.
——. "Uchastie zhenshchiny v stroitel'stve sovvlasti Saratova (Iz vospominanii)." *Kommunisticheskii put'*, no. 23 (85) (1927), pp. 45–47.
Breshkovskaia, K. *Hidden Springs of the Russian Revolution*. Stanford, 1931.
Bunarov, V. "Oktiabr'skaia revoliutsiia v derevne: Vospominaniia." *Kommunisticheskii put'*, no. 9 (1923), pp. 72–75.
Ch. "Saratovskaia organizatsiia s 1909 po 1917." *Vestnik Saratovskogo Gubkoma RKP*, no. 3 (28) (1923), pp. 50–51.
Chernov, V. M. *The Great Russian Revolution*. Trans. and abr. Philip E. Mosely. New Haven, 1936.
——. *Zapiski Sotsialista Revoliutsionera*. Vol. 1. Berlin, 1922.
Chernyshevskii, N. G. *Polnoe sobranie sochinenii*. Vol. 1. Moscow, 1939.
Cheudakhin, P. A. "Kak voznikla v 1917 g. RKP v Balashove." *Vestnik Saratovskogo Gubkoma RKP*, no. 8 (33) (1923), pp. 91–92.
Chugunov, T. K. "Iz istorii Saratovskoi organizatsii, 1902–1907." *Vestnik Saratovskogo Gubkoma RKP*, no. 3 (28) (1923), pp. 44–46.
Druzhinin, N. M. "V Saratove v 1905 g. (Vospominaniia)." *Povolzhskii krai*, no. 5 (1977), pp. 69–88.
——. "V Saratove v 1905 g. (Vospominaniia)." *Voprosy istorii* KPSS, no. 10 (1979), pp. 99–110.
Ezhov, A. "Moi vospominaniia o Maiake." *Vestnik Saratovskogo Gubkoma RKP*, no. 6 (31) (1923), pp. 69–70.
——. "V Saratove (1907–1917 gg.)" *Kommunisticheskii put'*, no. 10 (1923), p. 189.
Fevral': Sbornik vospominanii o 1917 g. Kniga pervaia. Saratov, 1922.

Fisher, G. M. *V Rossii i v Anglii: Nabliudeniia i vospominaniia Peterburgskogo rabochego (1890–1921)*. Moscow, 1922.
Fomina, M. "Pamiati Varvary Alekseevny Koshelevoi." *Katorga i ssylka*, no. 4 (53) (1929), pp. 193–94.
Golubov, M. A. "Saratov v 1917 g.: Vospominaniia pomoshchnika Kursovogo ofitsera Saratovskoi shkoly praporshchikov." Manuscript dated Innsbruck, Austria, 1955. Columbia University, Butler Library.
I. B. "Iz istorii Saratovskikh profsoiuzov 1905 goda." *Kommunisticheskii put'*, no. 39–40 (1926), pp. 119–22.
Illarionov, M., et al. "Krest'ianskoe dvizhenie v sele Nikolaevskii Gorodok Saratovskoi gubernii v 1905." *Proletarskaia revoliutsiia*, no. 12 (47) (1925), pp. 194–204.
Ipatov, A. D., ed. *Bylye gody: Vospominaniia starykh rabochikh tabachnikh fabrik g. Saratova*. Saratov, 1937.
Ivanov, F. "Pod rukovodstvom rabochikh bol'shevikov." *Vestnik Saratovskogo Gubkoma RKP*, no. 3 (28) (1923), pp. 43–44.
Kanatchikov, S. *Iz istorii moego byt'ia*. Moscow and Leningrad, 1929.
Kh. I. "Pamiatnik bortsam revoliutsii v Saratove." *Sovetskoe iskusstvo*, no. 2 (1926), pp. 62–64.
Koblents, S. "Iz istorii Saratovskoi organizatsii (1902–1907). (Iz besedy so starym podpol'nikom T. K. Chugunovym)." *Vestnik Saratovskogo Gubkoma RKP*, no. 3 (28) (1923), pp. 44–46.
——. "Zabastovochnoe dvizhenie 1901 goda: Iz besed s rabochimi zh. d. masterskikh." *Vestnik Saratovskogo Gubkoma RKP*, no. 3 (28) (1923), pp. 72–73.
Kudelli, P. "Svetloi pamiati Anny Il'inichny Elizarovoi-Ul'ianovoi." *Krasnaia letopis'*, no. 1 (1936), pp. 201–5.
Kuznetsov, L. I. "Rabota v podpol'e (Vospominaniia)." *Vestnik Saratovskogo Gubkoma RKP*, no. 5 (30) (1923), pp. 81–82.
Lalova. "Kusochek vospominanii (O krasnykh dniakh oktiabria 1917 goda v gorode Saratove)." *Kommunisticheskii put'*, no. 58 (1926), pp. 48–49.
Lebedev, P. A. "Fevral'–oktiabr' v Saratove." *Proletarskaia revoliutsiia*, no. 10 (1922), pp. 238–56.
——. "K istorii Saratovskoi organizatsii RSDRP (1901–1902 g.)." *Proletarskaia revoliutsiia*, no. 15 (1923), pp. 227–51.
Lepshinskii, P. "Iarkii svetoch bol'shevistskoi pechati: Pamiati M. S. Ol'minskogo." *Staryi bol'shevik*, no. 2 (5) (1933), pp. 7–14.
Liadov, M. N. *Iz zhizni partii v 1903–1907 godakh (Vospominaniia)*. Moscow, 1956.
——. "Moi vstrechi." In *Vospominaniia o II s"ezde RSDRP*, pp. 52–80. Moscow, 1959.
——. "Zabastovka na zavode 'Sotrudnik' Beringa." *Vestnik Saratovskogo Gubkoma RKP*, no. 6 (31) (1923), pp. 70–72.
Lushnikov, G. "Vospominaniia o vozniknovenii v Saratove sotsdemokraticheskoi rabochei gruppy, 1896–1899 gg." *Kommunisticheskii put'*, no. 10 (35) (1923), pp. 169–85.
M. G. "Iz istorii Saratovskoi bol'shevistskoi organizatsii (1916–1918 g.)." *Kommunisticheskii put'*, no. 17 (80) (1927), pp. 34–36; no. 18 (81) (1927), pp. 19–22; no. 19 (82) (1927), pp. 20–22.

Martsinovskii, A. "Pervye mesiatsy Oktiabr'skoi revoliutsii v Saratove." *Kommunisticheskii put'*, no. 20 (1927), pp. 126–30.

——. *Zapiski rabochego-bol'shevika*. Saratov, 1923.

Minin, S. K. *Gorod-boets: Shest' diktatur 1917 goda (Vospominaniia o rabote v Tsaritsyne)*. Leningrad, 1925.

——. "Iz dnevnika Sergeia Konstantinovicha Minina za 1917 god." *Partiinyi sputnik*, no. 7–8 (1922–23), pp. 137–42.

Mitskevich, S. I. "Vospominaniia o revoliutsii v Saratove." *Rabotnik prosveshcheniia*, no. 8 (1922), pp. 26–30.

Pervoe maia: Sbornik vospominanii. Bk. 2. Saratov, 1922.

Petrov, E. "Iz zhizni Saratovskoi organizatsii RKP." *Vestnik Saratovskogo Gubkoma RKP*, no. 24 (1922), pp. 10–12.

Petrov, Z. S. "Stranichki iz istorii Saratovskoi organizatsii VKP(b)." *Kommunisticheskii put'*, no. 5 (1928), pp. 41–45; no. 7 (1928), pp. 63–64; no. 9/10 (1928), pp. 91–93.

—— and V. Sergeev. "Partrabota na vodnom transporte 1906–1908." *Vestnik Saratovskogo Gubkoma RKP*, no. 2 (28) (1923), pp. 47–50.

Piat' let proletarskoi bor'by, 1917–1922. Saratov, 1922.

Piatnitsky, O. *Memoirs of a Bolshevik*. New York, n.d.

Polveka nazad: Vospominaniia uchastnikov revoliutsionnykh sobytii 1905 goda v Saratovskoi gubernii. Saratov, 1955.

Presniakov, I. "Iz podpol'ia na prostor." *Partiinyi sputnik*, no. 9–10 (1923), pp. 68–72.

Rakitnikova, I. I. "Revoliutsionnaia rabota v krest'ianstve v Saratovskoi gubernii v 1900–1902 gg." *Katorga i ssylka*, no. 10 (47) (1928), pp. 7–17.

Ruban, D. "Oktiabr'skaia revoliutsiia i bor'ba za sovety v Novouzenske." *Vestnik Saratovskogo Gubkoma RKP*, no. 5 (30) (1923), pp. 79–80.

Rubashkina, G. "Vol'skaia organizatsiia SDRP (bol'shevikov)." *Vestnik Saratovskogo Gubkoma RKP*, no. 5 (30) (1923), pp. 80–81.

Samsonov, M. B. "Otryvok iz vospominanii M. B. Samsonova." *Kommunisticheskii put'*, no. 32 (1927), pp. 87–89.

Sapronov, T. "Tri mesiatsa na Volge (1916 g.)." *Proletarskaia revoliutsiia*, no. 8 (43) (1925), pp. 216–37.

Saratovskii krai: Istoricheskie ocherki, vospominaniia, materialy. Saratov, 1893.

Shchegol'kov. "Na zare: Sovetskaia vlast' v Serdobske (Vospominaniia ob Oktiabre)." *Kommunisticheskii put'*, no. 9 (34) (1923), pp. 51–62.

Sokolov, I. S. *1905 god na Riazano-Ural'skoi zheleznoi doroge: Po vospominaniiam uchastnikov i materialam Saratovskogo gubernskogo arkhiva*. Saratov, 1925.

Stalingradskii, G. "Kak vooruzhalis' stalingradskie rabochie: Iz istorii Krasnoi gvardii." *Partiinyi sputnik*, no. 11 (1927), pp. 20–32.

Stanchinskii, A. "S. D. podpol'e v Saratove i zhurnal 'Saratovskii Rabochii,' v 1899 g." *Proletarskaia revoliutsiia*, no. 14 (1923), pp. 87–108.

Studentsov, A. *Saratovskoe krest'ianskoe vosstanie, 1905 goda (Iz vospominanii raz"ezdnogo agitatora)*. Penza, 1926.

Sukharev, G., et al., eds. *Za vlast' sovetov: Vospominaniia uchastnikov revoliutsionnykh sobytii 1917 goda v Saratovskoi gubernii*. Saratov, 1957.

Sushitskii, V. "Oktiabr'skaia revoliutsiia v Vol'skom i Atkarskom uezdakh." *Kommunisticheskii put'*, no. 20 (1927), pp. 102–11.

Sushkin, G. G. "Oktiabr', noiabr' i dekabr' 1905 g. na Riazano-Ural'skoi zheleznoi doroge." *Katorga i ssylka*, no. 12 (73) (1930), pp. 145–59.
——. "V tiur'me 1905 goda." *Katorga i ssylka*, no. 8–9 (1930), pp. 149–56.
Tomarev, V. I., and M. Ia. Kleinman, eds. *Za Sovetskuiu vlast': Sbornik vospominanii uchastnikov revoliutsionnykh sobytii v Tsaritsyne.* Stalingrad, 1957.
1917 god v derevne: Vospominaniia krest'ian. Moscow and Leningrad, 1929.
1917 god v Saratove. Saratov, 1927.
Ul'ianova-Elizarova, A. I. "Iz aftobiografii Anny Il'inichny Ul'ianovoi-Elizarovoi." *Proletarskaia revoliutsiia*, no. 6 (1935), pp. 133–34.
Vasil'ev, M. I. [Vasil'ev-Iuzhin, Misha]. "Iz vospominanii o piatom godu." *Proletarskaia revoliutsiia*, no. 3 (38) (1925), pp. 136–38.
——. "Oktiabr'skaia revoliutsiia v Saratove." In *Pobeda Velikoi Oktiabr'skoi sotsialisticheskoi revoliutsii: Sbornik vospominanii uchastnikov revoliutsii v promyshlennykh tsentrakh i natsional'nykh raionakh Rossii*, pp. 44–62. Moscow, 1958.
——. "Proletarskaia revoliutsiia v Saratove." *Sovetskoe stroitel'stvo*, no. 10–11 (1927), pp. 119–41.
V boiakh za diktaturu proletariata: Sbornik vospominanii uchastnikov Oktiabria i grazhdanskoi voiny v Nizhnem Povolzh'e. Saratov, 1933.
Vlasov, P. "Vospominaniia o 1905 godu v Saratove." *Staryi bol'shevik*, no. 2 (1932), pp. 215–20.
Zhagar, A. "Put' k oktiabriu: g. Balashov, Saratovskoi gubernii." *Kommunisticheskii put'*, no. 58 (1926), pp. 45–48.

Secondary Materials

Afanas'ev, A. V. "Iz istorii organizatsii Krasnoi gvardii v g. Saratove (sentiabr'–oktiabr' 1917 g.)." *Povolzhskii krai*, no. 4 (1975), pp. 135–48.
Afanas'ev, N. V. *Bor'ba partii bol'shevikov za ustanovlenie i uprochenie Sovetskoi vlasti v Saratovskoi gubernii.* Saratov, 1947.
——. "Ustanovlenie Sovetskoi vlasti v Saratove." In *Iz istorii Velikoi Oktiabr'skoi revoliutsii i sotsialisticheskogo stroitel'stva: Sbornik statei*, ed. V. B. Ostrovskii, pp. 53–87. Saratov, 1958.
Alava, Hamza. "Peasants and Revolution." In *The Socialist Register*, ed. Ralph Miliband and John Saville, pp. 241–77. London, 1965.
Amal'rik, A. S. "K voprosu o chislennosti i geograficheskom razmeshchenii stachechnikov v Evropeiskoi Rossii v 1905 godu." *Istoricheskie zapiski*, 52 (1955), 142–85.
Anfimov, A. M. *Rossiiskaia derevnia v gody pervoi mirovoi voiny (1914–fevral' 1917 g.).* Moscow, 1962.
Astrakhan, Kh. M., and I. S. Sazonov. "Sozdanie massovoi bol'shevistskoi pechati v 1917 godu." *Voprosy istorii*, no. 1 (1957), pp. 87–98.
Avgustovskii, K. V. "'Soiuz russkogo naroda' (Iz zhizni Saratovskogo otdeleniia)." *Sovremennyi mir*, no. 9 (1907), pp. 59–73.
Babikov, I. I. "Krest'ianskoe dvizhenie v Saratovskoi gubernii nakanune pervoi russkoi revoliutsii." *Uchenye zapiski Saratovskogo gosudarstvennogo universiteta*, 55 (1956), 172–218.
Babushkin, V. F. *Dni velikikh sobytii.* Saratov, 1932.

Bartlett, Roger P. *Human Capital: The Settlement of Foreigners in Russia, 1762–1804*. Cambridge, Eng., 1979.
Bas, I. *Bol'shevistskaia pechat' v gody imperialisticheskoi voiny*. Moscow, 1939.
Berkevich, A. B. "Krest'ianstvo i vseobshchaia mobilizatsiia v iiule 1914 g." *Istoricheskie zapiski*, 23 (1947), 3–43.
Bondar', N. A., and I. N. Steshin. *Saratov*. Saratov, 1951.
Bonnell, Victoria E. "Radical Politics and Organized Labor in Pre-revolutionary Moscow, 1905–1914." *Journal of Social History*, 12, no. 2 (1979), 282–300.
——. "Trade Unions, Parties, and the State in Tsarist Russia: A Study of Labor Politics in St. Petersburg and Moscow." *Politics and Society*, 9, no. 3 (1980), 299–322.
——. "Urban Working-Class Life in Early Twentieth-Century Russia: Some Problems and Patterns." *Russian History*, 8 (1981), 360–78.
Bugaenko, P. A., et al. *Saratovskii universitet, 1909–1959*. Saratov, 1959.
Bul'in, N. P., et al. *Stranitsy zhizni (Iz istorii Serdobskoi organizatsii* KPSS*)*. Penza, 1961.
Burdzhalov, E. N. *Vtoraia russkaia revoliutsiia: Moskva, front, periferiia*. Moscow, 1971.
Chaadaeva, O. *Pomeshchiki i ikh organizatsii v 1917 g*. Moscow, 1928.
Chamberlin, W. H. *The Russian Revolution*. 2 vols. New York, 1935.
Chaniia, B. Kh. *Sovety v pervoi russkoi revoliutsii*. Moscow, 1972.
Chemu nauchilis' 1905 god rabochie i krest'iane? Saratov, 1925.
Chermenskii, E. D. *Fevral'skaia burzhuazno-demokraticheskaia revoliutsiia 1917 goda v Rossii*. Moscow, 1959.
——. "Vybory v IV gosudarstvennuiu dumu." *Voprosy istorii*, no. 4 (1947), pp. 21–40.
Dal'nii, S. "Kak derevnia prishla k Oktiabriu." *Kommunisticheskii put'*, no. 19 (1927), pp. 23–28.
Daniels, Robert V. *Red October: The Bolshevik Revolution of 1917*. New York, 1967.
D'dova, F. *Revoliutsionnye kruzhki v Saratove*. St. Petersburg, 1906.
Demochkin, N. N. "Partiia i Sovety v 1905 g." *Voprosy istorii* KPSS, no. 1 (1965), pp. 70–86; no. 2 (1965), pp. 89–92.
——. "Sovety 1905 g.—Organy vooruzhennogo vosstaniia i revoliutsionnoi vlasti." *Voprosy istorii*, no. 3 (1976), pp. 33–49.
Derenkovskii, G. M., et al. "1905 god v Saratove." *Istoricheskie zapiski*, 54 (1955), 74–104.
Diakevich, E. E. *Ocherk o deiatel'nosti Saratovskoi 'Birzhi truda' za god sushchestvovaniia (27 noiabria 1914 g. po 1 ianvaria 1916 g.)*. Saratov, 1916.
Druzhinin, N. M., and E. Mitskevich. "Sergei Ivanovich Mitskevich." *Istoriia* SSSR, no. 2 (1967), pp. 111–18.
Dubrovskii, S. M. *Stolypinskaia zemel'naia reforma: Iz istorii sel'skogo khoziaistva i krest'ianstva Rossii v nachale XX veka*. Moscow, 1963.
Ekonomicheskaia zhizn' Povolzh'ia: Sbornik statei. Pt. 1 (3). Saratov, 1919.
Elwood, Ralph Carter. "The Congress That Never Was: Lenin's Attempt to Call a 'Sixth' Party Congress in 1914." *Soviet Studies*, 31, no. 3 (1979), 343–63.
——. *Russian Social Democracy in the Underground: A Study of the* RSDRP *in the Ukraine, 1907–1914*. Publications on Social History Issued by the Internationaal Institut voor Sociale Geschiedenis, vol. 8. Assen, Netherlands, 1974.

Emmons, Terence. "Russia's Banquet Campaign." *California Slavic Studies*, 10 (1977), 45–86.

Erman, L. *Uchastie demokraticheskoi intelligentsii v stachechnom i profsoiuznom dvizhenii (1905–1907 gody)*. Moscow, 1955.

Ezergailis, Andrew. *The 1917 Revolution in Latvia*. Boulder, 1974.

Fedin, Konstantin. *Early Joys*. Trans. G. Kazanina. New York, 1960.

Ferro, Marc. "The Aspirations of Russian Society." In *Revolutionary Russia: A Symposium*, ed. Richard Pipes, pp. 183–209. New York, 1969.

——. *La Révolution de 1917*. Vol. 1, *La Chute du tsarisme et les origines d'Octobre*. Paris, 1967. Vol. 2, *Octobre: Naissance d'une société*. Paris, 1976.

Fleer, M. G. *Rabochee dvizhenie v gody voiny (Materialy po istorii rabochego dvizheniia v Rossii)*. Moscow, 1925.

——. "Vremennoe Pravitel'stvo v bor'be s agrarnoi revoliutsiei." *Krasnaia letopis'*, no. 2 (17) (1926), pp. 5–15.

Frantsev, V. "Agrarnye volneniia v 1905 godu po Saratovskoi gubernii." *Kommunisticheskii put'*, no. 37 (1925), pp. 37–40.

Frenkin, M. *Russkaia armiia i revoliutsiia, 1917–1918*. Munich, 1978.

——. *Zakhvat vlasti bol'shevikami v Rossii i rol' tylovykh garnizonov armii: Podgotovka i provedenie Oktiabr'skogo miatezha, 1917–1918 gg.* Jerusalem, 1982.

Frolova, N. C., ed. *Saratovskaia oblast'*. Saratov, 1947.

Gaponenko, L. S. "O chislennosti i kontsentratsii rabochego klassa Rossii nakanune Velikoi Oktiabr'skoi sotsialisticheskoi revoliutsii." *Istoricheskii arkhiv*, no. 1 (1960), pp. 76–116.

—— and V. M. Kabuzan. "Materialy sel'skokhoziaistvennykh perepisei 1916–1917 gg. kak istoricheskii istochnik." *Istoriia SSSR*, no. 6 (1961), pp. 97–115.

Genkina, E. "Pervye dni Oktiabr'skoi revoliutsii 1917 goda (Kak doshla vest' ob Oktiabr'skom perevorote na mestakh)." *Proletarskaia revoliutsiia*, no. 3 (1940), pp. 17–33.

——. "Pobeda Velikoi Oktiabr'skoi sotsialisticheskoi revoliutsii na mestakh." *Istoricheskii zhurnal*, no. 10 (110) (1942), pp. 49–50.

Geraklitov, A. A. *Melochi iz proshlogo Saratovskogo kraia po dokumentam Saratovskogo istoricheskogo arkhiva*. Saratov, 1911.

——. *Saratov: Kratkii istoricheskii ocherk*. Saratov, 1919.

Gerasimenko, G. A. "Bor'ba partii v Saratovskom Sovete Rabochikh i Soldatskikh Deputatov (mart-oktiabr' 1917 g.)." In *Trudy molodykh uchenykh: Vypusk istoriko-filologicheskii*, pp. 15–27. Saratov, 1964.

——. "Local Peasant Organizations in 1917 and the First Half of 1918," ed. Donald J. Raleigh. *Soviet Studies in History*, no. 3 (Winter 1977–78), pp. 1–129.

——. *Nizovye krest'ianskie organizatsii v 1917-pervoi polovine 1918 godov (Na materialakh Nizhnego Povolzh'ia)*. Saratov, 1974.

——. "Organizatsiia volostnykh zemel'nykh komitetov v Nizhnem Povolzh'e." *Povolzhskii krai*, no. 3 (1975), pp. 54–84.

——. "Partiinaia bor'ba na gubernskikh krest'ianskikh s"ezdakh Nizhnego Povolzh'ia, 1917 g." In *Materialy nauchnoi sessii Povolzhskogo Soveta po koordinatsii i planirovanii*, pp. 19–28. Saratov, 1964.

——. *Partiinaia bor'ba v sovetakh Nizhnego Povolzh'ia 1917 g.* Saratov, 1966.

——. *Pobeda Oktiabr'skoi revoliutsii v Saratovskoi gubernii*. Saratov, 1968.

——. *Sovety Nizhnego Povolzh'ia v Oktiabr'skoi revoliutsii*. Saratov, 1972.

——. "Ustanovlenie Sovetskoi vlasti v uezdakh Nizhnego Povolzh'ia." In *Iz istorii Saratovskogo Povolzh'ia*, ed. V. A. Osipov, pp. 71–102. Saratov, 1968.

——. "Vliianie posledstvii Stolypinskoi agrarnoi reformy na krest'ianskie organizatsii 1917 goda (Po materialam Saratovskoi gub.)." *Istoriia* SSSR, no. 1 (1981), pp. 37–54.

——. *Vozniknovenie sovetov rabochikh, soldatskikh i krest'ianskikh deputatov v Nizhnem Povolzh'e (1917-pervaia polovina 1918 gg.)*. Saratov, 1966.

——. "Vozniknovenie Sovetskoi vlasti v volostiakh Saratovskoi gubernii." *Povolzhskii krai*, no. 1 (1972), pp. 60–81.

——. "Vozniknovenie volostnykh obshchestvennykh ispolnitel'nykh komitetov v Nizhnem Povolzh'e (mart–mai 1917 goda)." *Povolzhskii krai*, no. 2 (1973), pp. 50–80.

—— and V. P. Sem'ianinov. *Sovetskaia vlast' v derevne na pervom etape Oktiabria (Na materialakh Povolzh'ia)*. Saratov, 1980.

—— and D. S. Tochenyi. *Sovety Povolzh'ia v 1917 godu: Bor'ba partii, bol'shevizatsiia sovetov, Oktiabr'skie dni*. Saratov, 1977.

Gerasimov, A. "God pervoi revoliutsii v Saratove." *Molodaia gvardiia*, no. 12 (1925), pp. 114–28.

Gershtein, E. E. "Oktiabr'skaia politicheskaia stachka 1905 goda v Saratove." *Uchenye zapiski Saratovskogo gosudarstvennogo universiteta*, 15 (1956), 305–41.

Gill, Graeme J. *Peasants and Government in the Russian Revolution*. New York, 1979.

Gokhlerner, V. M. "Iz istorii krest'ianskogo dvizheniia v Saratovskoi gubernii v gody pervoi russkoi revoliutsii (1905–1907 gg.)." *Uchenye zapiski Saratovskogo gosudarstvennogo universiteta*, 55 (1956), 219–45.

——. "Krest'ianskoe dvizhenie v Saratovskoi gubernii v gody pervoi russkoi revoliutsii." *Istoricheskie zapiski*, 52 (1955), 186–234.

—— and K. P. Kharlamova. "Iz istorii krest'ianskikh revoliutsionnykh komitetov v Saratovskoi gubernii v 1905 g." *Povolzhskii krai*, no. 5. (1977), pp. 89–119.

Golovkin, G. M. "Tsaritsynskaia gazeta 'Bor'ba' v period podgotovki i provedeniia Velikogo Oktiabria." In *Iz istorii partiinykh i komsomol'nikh organizatsii Povolzh'ia*, pp. 48–61. Volgograd, 1972.

"Golubeva, E. Mariia Petrovna." In *Slavnye bol'sheviki*, pp. 127–28. Moscow, 1958.

"Gorod Saratov: Sanitarno-topograficheskii ocherk." *Vestnik obshchestvennoi gigieny, sudebnoi i prakticheskoi meditsiny* (Saratov), no. 11–13 (1910), pp. 191–224.

Gubenko, P. T. "Agrarnaia programma bol'shevikov i revoliutsionnoe dvizhenie krest'ianstva ot fevralia k oktiabriu 1917 goda." *Trudy Saratovskogo instituta mekhanizatsii sel'skogo khoziaistva*, no. 23 (1960), pp. 42–49.

Haimson, Leopold H., ed. *The Mensheviks: From the Revolution of 1917 to the Second World War*. Trans. Gertrude Vakar. Hoover Institute Publications, vol. 117. Chicago, 1974.

——. "The Problem of Social Stability in Urban Russia, 1905–1914." *Slavic Review*, no. 4 (1964), pp. 619–42; no. 1 (1965), pp. 1–22.

Hamm, Michael F. "Kharkov's Progressive Duma, 1910–1914: A Study in Russian Municipal Reform." *Slavic Review*, 40, no. 1 (1981), 17–36.

Iakovlev, Ia. A. "'Mart–mai, 1917 goda' (Trekhmesiachnyi otchet 'otdela snoshenii s provintsiei' Gosudarstvennoi Dumy)." *Krasnyi arkhiv*, no. 2 (15) (1926), pp. 30–60.

Iatsunskii, V. K. "Izmeneniia v razmeshchenii naseleniia Evropeiskoi Rossii v 1724–1916 gg." *Istoriia* SSSR, no. 1 (1957), pp. 192–224.

Il'in, B. *Saratov: Istoricheskii ocherk*. Saratov, 1952.

Illeritskaia, E. V. *Agrarnyi vopros: Proval agrarnykh programm i politiki neproletarskikh partii v Rossii*. Moscow, 1981.

Ionenko, I. M. *Revoliutsionnaia bor'ba i natsional'noe osvoboditel'noe dvizhenie soldatskikh mass Povolzh'ia i Priural'ia nakanune Velikogo Oktiabria*. Kazan, 1966.

——. *Soldatskie massy v Oktiabr'skoi revoliutsii: Po materialam Povolzh'ia i Urala*. Kazan, 1982.

——. *Soldaty tylovykh garnizonov v bor'be za vlast' Sovetov (Po materialam Povolzh'ia i Urala)*. Kazan, 1976.

—— and R. S. Tseitlin. "Kazanskii voenno-okruzhnoi komitet (aprel'–oktiabr' 1917 goda)." In *Ocherki istorii narodov Povolzh'ia i Priural'ia*, no. 4, *Obshchestvenno-politicheskoe dvizhenie i klassovaia bor'ba na Srednei Volge (konets XIX–nachalo XX veka)*, pp. 89–110. Kazan, 1972.

Iudin, V. *Iakov Erman*. Volgograd, 1965.

Iurovskii, L. N. *Saratovskie votchiny*. Saratov, 1923.

Kabuzan, V. M. *Izmeneniia v razmeshchenii naseleniia Rossii v XVIII-pervoi polovine XIX v*. Moscow, 1971.

Kabytov, P. S. "O prichinakh krakha Stolypinskoi zemel'noi reformy v Povolzh'e (Po materialam Kazanskoi, Samarskoi, Saratovskoi, Simbirskoi, i Penzenskoi gubernii)." In *Sbornik aspirantskikh rabot*, no. 74, *Gumanitarnye nauki: Istoriia, pedagogika*, pp. 72–77. Kazan, 1973.

——. "Vliianie Stolypinskoi agrarnoi reformy na sel'skoe khoziaistvo Povolzh'ia (1907–1914 gg.)." *Ocherki istorii i kul'tury Povolzh'ia* (Kuibyshev), no. 1 (1976), pp. 52–56.

Katts, A. *Tysiacha deviat'sot piatyi god i professional'noe dvizhenie*. Moscow, 1926.

Kavunov, P. A. *Goroda Saratovskoi oblasti*. Saratov, 1963.

Keep, John. "October in the Provinces." In *Revolutionary Russia: A Symposium*, ed. Richard Pipes, pp. 180–216. Cambridge, Mass., 1968.

——. *The Russian Revolution: A Study in Mass Mobilization*. New York, 1976.

Khesin, S. S. *Stanovlenie proletarskoi diktatury v Rossii*. Moscow, 1975.

Khodakov, G. F. "Bor'ba Saratovskikh rabochikh pod rukovodstvom bol'shevikov v period revoliutsii 1905–1907 gg." *Uchenye zapiski Saratovskogo gosudarstvennogo universiteta*, 55 (1956), 85–123.

——. *Ocherki istorii Saratovskoi organizatsii* KPSS: *Chast' pervaia, 1898–1918*. Saratov, 1957. 2d ed. 1968.

——. "Rol' leninskoi 'Iskry' v sozdanii Saratovskoi organizatsii RSDRP." *Uchenye zapiski Saratovskogo gosudarstvennogo universiteta*, 58 (1956), 100–24.

Khodakov, V. G. "Rabochii kontrol' v Saratovskoi gubernii v period podgotovki Velikoi Oktiabr'skoi sotsialisticheskoi revoliutsii (mart–oktiabr' 1917 goda)." *Uchenye zapiski Saratovskogo gosudarstvennogo universiteta*, 47 (1956), 49–76.

Khodakova, S. B. "Vikhri vrazhdebnye." *Rabotnitsa*. no. 10 (1977), p. 8.

Khovanskii, N. F. *O proshlom goroda Saratova*. Saratov, 1891.

Kin, D. "Bor'ba protiv 'ob"edinitel'nogo udara' v 1917 g." *Proletarskaia revoliutsiia*, no. 6 (65) (1927), pp. 47–49, 68, 71.

Kirillov, B. S. *Bol'sheviki vo glave massovykh politicheskikh stachek v period pod"ema revoliutsii 1905–1907 gg*. Moscow, 1961.

Klein, N. L. "Ob osobennostiakh polozheniia i urovne ekspluatatsii promyshlennykh rabochikh Srednego Povolzh'ia v period kapitalizma." *Nash krai*, no. 1 (1974), pp. 19–27.

Kliachko, A. Kh. "Krizis pereproizvodstva 1900–1903 godov v Saratovskoi gubernii." *Trudy Saratovskogo ekonomicheskogo instituta*, 3 (1951), 113–34.

——. "Materialy o polozhenii promyshlennykh rabochikh Saratovskoi gubernii." *Trudy Saratovskogo ekonomicheskogo instituta*, 2 (1949), 61–74.

Klimov, P. I. *Revoliutsionnaia deiatel'nost' rabochikh v derevne v 1905–1907 gg*. Moscow, 1960.

Kochergin, P., comp. *Ves' gorod Saratov: Adres-kalendar'-ukazatel' na 1910 god*. Saratov, 1911.

Koenker, Diane. *Moscow Workers and the 1917 Revolution*. Princeton, 1981.

Kohn, Stanislav, and Baron Alexander F. Meyendorff. *The Cost of the War to Russia*. New Haven, 1932.

Kondrat'ev, V. V. *Bor'ba bol'shevikov v gody Stolypinskoi reaktsii za sokhranenie i ukreplenie nelegal'noi partii i ispol'zovanie legal'nykh vozmozhnostei*. Saratov, 1960.

Kon'kova, A. S. *Bor'ba kommunisticheskoi partii za soiuz rabochego klassa s bedneishim krest'ianstvom v 1917–1918 gg. (Po materialam Samarskoi, Saratovskoi i Simbirskoi gubernii)*. Moscow, 1974.

Konovalov, D. M. *Saratovskii agent "Iskry."* Saratov, 1969.

Konovalov, I. "V derevne (Iz Saratovskoi gubernii)." *Sovremennyi mir*, no. 2 (1909), pp. 14–33.

Korbut, M. "Strakhovaia kampaniia 1912–1914 gg." *Proletarskaia revoliutsiia*, no. 2 (73) (1928), pp. 107–8.

Kosenko, M. Ia. "Iz istorii bor'by krest'ian Saratovskoi gubernii letom i osen'iu 1917 g." *Uchenye zapiski Saratovskogo gosudarstvennogo universiteta*, 68 (1960), 55–69.

Kostrikin, V. I. *Zemel'nye komitety v 1917 godu*. Moscow, 1975.

Kovalevskii, A. G. *Ocherki po demografii Saratova (rozhdaemost' i smertnost' za 1914–1927 gg.)*. Saratov, 1928.

Kur'ianov, Iu. I. *Zhiznennyi uroven' rabochikh Rossii (konets XIX–nachalo XX v.)*. Moscow, 1979.

Kursanova, A. V. *Pervye sotsial-demokraticheskie organizatsii i iskrovtsy v Saratove*. Saratov, 1963.

Kutyrev, P. G., and A. G. Chulkov. "Sobytiia pervoi rossiiskoi revoliutsii v Vol'ske." *Voprosy istorii*, no. 6 (1981), pp. 184–87.

Kuz'mina, T. F. *Revoliutsionnoe dvizhenie soldatskikh mass Tsentra Rossii nakanune Oktiabria (Po materialam Moskovskogo voennogo okruga)*. Moscow, 1978.

Leikina, V. "Oktiabr' po Rossii." *Proletarskaia revoliutsiia*, no. 49 (1926), pp. 185–233; no. 58 (1926), pp. 234–55; no. 59 (1926), pp. 238–54.

Lepeshkin, A. I. *Mestnye organy vlasti sovetskogo gosudarstva (1917–1920 gg.)*. Moscow, 1957.

Levin, Sh. "Sotsialisticheskaia pechat' vo vremia imperialisticheskoi voiny." *Krasnyi arkhiv*, no. 2 (1922), pp. 202–25.

Liakhovetskii, I. "Banketnaia kampaniia v Saratove (1904–1905)." *Minuvshie gody*, no. 12 (1908), pp. 29–62.

Liebman, Marcel. *The Russian Revolution*. New York, 1970.

Liubomirova, L. N. "Vnenadel'naia arenda i ee vliianie na polozhenie krest'ian Saratovskoi gubernii (60 g. XIX–nach. XX v.)." *Povolzhskii krai*, no. 5 (1977), pp. 162–78.

Long, James W. "Agricultural Conditions in the German Colonies of Novouzensk District, Samara Province, 1861–1914." *Slavonic and East European Review*, 57, no. 4 (1979), 531–51.

Lubny-Gertsyk, L. I. *Dvizhenie naseleniia na territorii SSSR za vremia mirovoi voiny i revoliutsii*. Moscow, 1926.

Maizel', A. Ia. *Putevoditel' po g. Saratovu s 2-ia planami v kraskakh i svedeniiami o gubernii*. Saratov, 1917.

Maliavskii, A. D. "Bor'ba krest'ian za vnenadel'nye arendnye zemli v marte-oktiabre 1917 g." *Istoricheskie zapiski*, 102 (1978), 59–102.

——. *Krest'ianskoe dvizhenie v Rossii v 1917 g., mart–oktiabr'*. Moscow, 1981.

Malinin, G. A. *Saratov: Kratkii ocherk*. Saratov, 1974.

——. "Saratovskie zheleznodorozhniki v revoliutsii 1905–1907 gg." *Uchenye zapiski Saratovskogo gosudarstvennogo universiteta*, 55 (1956), 124–54.

——. "Saratovskii Sovet rabochikh deputatov v 1905 godu." *Uchenye zapiski Saratovskogo gosudarstvennogo universiteta*, 55 (1956), 155–72.

——. *Sviazhite nas s "Vavilonom"! (Iz istorii rasprostraneniia proizvedenii V. I. Lenina v Saratovskoi gubernii)*. Saratov, 1973.

Mal'kov, A. A. *Deiatel'nost' partii bol'shevikov sredi inostrannykh voennoplennykh v period imperialisticheskoi voiny i Brestskogo mira 1914–1918 gg. (Po materialam Srednego Povolzh'ia)*. Kazan, 1966.

Manturov, S. *Iz revoliutsionnogo proshlogo Kamyshina (1905–20)*. Volgograd, 1963.

Manusevich, A. Ia. *Pol'skie internatsionalisty v bor'be za pobedu Sovetskoi vlasti v Rossii, fevral'–oktiabr' 1917 g.* Moscow, 1965.

Martov, L., et al., eds. *Obshchestvennoe dvizhenie v Rossii v nachale XX-go veka*. 4 vols. St. Petersburg, 1909–14.

Martov, M. "Agrarnoe dvizhenie." *Krasnyi arkhiv*, no. 1 (14), (1926), pp. 182–226.

Maslov, P. *Kak krest'iane borolis' za zemliu v 1905–1906 godu, dvadtsat' let tomu nazad*. Moscow and Leningrad, 1925.

——. *Krest'ianskie dvizheniia v Rossii v epokhu pervoi revoliutsii (Agrarnyi vopros v Rossii)*. Vol. 2, bk. 2. Moscow, 1924.

Matasova, F. "Materialy dlia istorii russkogo rabochego dvizheniia za 1881–1895 gg." *Krasnaia letopis'*, no. 1 (1925), pp. 249–60.

Medvedev, Roy. *The October Revolution*. Trans. George Saunders. New York, 1979.

Medvedev, V. K., et al., eds. *Istoriia Saratovskogo kraia, 1917–1965: Khrestomatiia v pomoshch' uchiteliu istorii*. Saratov, 1967.

——. "Saratovskii Sovet ot fevralia k oktiabriu 1917 g." *Uchenye zapiski Saratovskoi oblastnoi partiinoi shkoly*, no. 1 (1948), pp. 47–87.

Miliutin, V. P. *O demokraticheskoi respublike*. Saratov, 1917.
——. *Zachem nam nuzhna demokraticheskaia respublika?* Saratov, 1917.
Miller, V. "Desiat' let professional'nogo stroitel'stva." *Kommunisticheskii put'*, no. 20 (1927), pp. 71–82.
Milonov, Iu. "Partiia i professional'nye soiuzy v 1905 godu." *Proletarskaia revoliutsiia*, no. 1 (48) (1925), pp. 94–118.
Milovzorov, A. F. *Sel'skokhoziaistvennye raiony Saratovskoi gubernii*. Saratov, 1924.
Minkin, G. Z. *Proletariat Nizhnei Volgi v revoliutsii 1905 g*. Saratov, 1932.
——. "Rabochee dvizhenie 1905 goda na Volge." *Kommunisticheskii put'*, nos. 21–22 (1930), pp. 66–79.
Mints, I. I., et al. *Oktiabr' v Povolzh'e*. Saratov, 1967.
Mixter, Timothy. "Of Grandfather-Beaters and Fat-Heeled Pacifists: Perceptions of Agricultural Labor and Hiring Market Disturbances in Saratov, 1872–1905." *Russian History*, 7 (1980), 139–68.
Mon'ko, A. *Letopis' geroicheskoi istorii*. Volgograd, 1967.
Morokhovets, E. A. *Krest'ianskoe dvizhenie i sotsial-demokratiia v epokhu pervoi russkoi revoliutsii*. Moscow, 1926.
——. "Krest'ianskoe dvizhenie 1905–1907 gg. i sotsial-demokratiia," *Proletarskaia revoliutsiia*, no. 2 (37) (1925), pp. 93–100; no. 4 (39) (1925), pp. 48, 56–64, 67, 80–83.
Morshanskaia, M. "Pervaia konferentsiia voennykh i boevykh organizatsii RSDRP v noiabre 1906 g." *Proletarskaia revoliutsiia*, no. 5 (28) (1924), pp. 86, 90, 96–97.
Mosse, W. E. "Revolution in Saratov (October–November 1917)." *Slavonic and East European Review*, 49, no. 117 (1971), 586–602.
——. "Stolypin's Villages." *Slavonic and East European Review*, 43, no. 101 (1965), 257–75.
Muliukov, M. A. "Nekotorye svedeniia o formirovanii politicheskikh vzgliadov levykh eserov." In *Itogovaia nauchnaia aspirantskaia konferentsiia za 1965 g.: Istoriia KPSS*, pp. 18–21. Kazan, 1967.
——. "O prichinakh raskola Kazanskogo komiteta partii sotsialistov-revoliutsionerov." In *Sbornik aspirantskikh rabot: Obshchestvennye nauki (Istoriia KPSS, filosofiia)*, pp. 56–66. Kazan, 1967.
Nafigov, R. I. "Iz istorii podpol'nykh sviazei partiinykh organizatsii Povolzh'ia." In *Istoriia partiinykh organizatsii Povolzh'ia: Mezhvuzovskii nauchnyi sbornik*, no. 8, pp. 3–13. Saratov, 1978.
Naiakshin, K. Ia., and G. N. Rutberg. *Bol'sheviki Povolzh'ia v pervoi russkoi revoliutsii, 1905–1907 gg*. Saratov, 1977.
Najdus, Walentyna. *Polacy w Rewolucji 1917 roku*. Warsaw, 1967.
Nevskii, V. I. "Ianvarskie dni 1905 g. v provintsii." *Krasnaia letopis'*, no. 4 (1922), pp. 120–32.
——. "Saratov." *Proletarskaia revoliutsiia*, no. 4 (1922), p. 358.
——. *Sovety i vooruzhennye vosstaniia v 1905 godu*. Moscow, 1932.
——. "Vooruzhennoe vosstanie v 1905 g." In *Istoriia proletariata SSSR*, nos. 3–4. Moscow, 1930.
Oppenheim, Samuel A. "The Making of a Right Communist—A. I. Rykov to 1917." *Slavic Review*, 36, no. 3 (1977), 420–40.
Osipov, V. A., ed. *Istoriia Saratovskogo kraia, 1590–1917: Khrestomatiia v*

pomoshch' uchiteliu istorii. 2 vols. Saratov, 1964, 1967.

——. *Saratovskaia organizatsiia RSDRP v 1905–1907 gg.* 2d ed. Saratov, 1947.

Osipova, T. V. *Klassovaia bor'ba v derevne v period podgotovki i provedeniia Velikoi Oktiabr'skoi sotsialisticheskoi revoliutsii*. Moscow, 1974.

Ovrutskaia, S. Sh. "Politicheskoe bankrotstvo eserov na vyborakh v Uchreditel'-noe sobranie (Po materialam Saratovskoi gubernii)." In *Nekotorye voprosy otechestvennoi i vseobshchei istorii*, pp. 42–59. Saratov, 1971.

——. "Proval politiki kontrrevoliutsionnoi voenshchiny v iiule–avguste 1917 g." *Istoricheskie zapiski*, 87 (1971), 351–82.

——. "Proval popytok eserov sderzhat' krest'ianskoe dvizhenie osen'iu 1917 goda (Po materialam Saratovskoi gubernii)." *Povolzhskii krai*, no. 3 (1975), pp. 85–102.

Owen, Launcelot A. *The Russian Peasant Movement, 1906–17*. New York, 1937.

Pankratova, A. M. *1905: Stachechnoe dvizhenie*. Moscow, 1925.

Pautov, D. I. *Bor'ba bol'shevistskoi partii za sochetanie demokraticheskikh i sotsialisticheskikh zadach rabochego klassa v gody mirovoi voiny*. Saratov, 1965.

Pereverzev, V. N. "Pervyi vserossiiskii zheleznodorozhnyi s"ezd 1905 g." *Byloe*, no. 4 (32) (1925), pp. 38–39.

Perrie, Maureen. *The Agrarian Policy of the Russian Socialist-Revolutionary Party from Its Origins through the Revolution of 1905–1907*. New York, 1977.

——. "The Russian Peasant Movement of 1905–1907: Its Social Composition and Revolutionary Significance." *Past and Present*, no. 57 (1972), pp. 123–55.

Pershin, P. N. *Agrarnaia revoliutsiia v Rossii*. 2 vols. Moscow, 1966.

——. *Uchastkovoe zemlepol'zovanie v Rossii: Khutora i otruba, ikh rasprostranenie za desiatiletie 1907–1916 gg. i sud'by vo vremia revoliutsii (1917–1920 gg.)*. Moscow, 1922.

Pisarev, V. I. "Mobilizatsiia revoliutsionnykh mass vokrug bol'shevistskoi munitsipal'noi platformy pri vyborakh gorodskikh dum v krupneishikh gorodakh Povolzh'ia 1917 g." In *Materialy nauchnoi sessii Povolzhskogo Soveta po koordinatsii i planirovaniiu rabot po gumanitarnym naukam*, no. 2, *Sektsiia istorii SSSR i vseobshchei istorii*, pp. 14–18. Saratov, 1964.

Pokrovskii, M. N. *1905: Istoriia revoliutsionnogo dvizheniia v otdel'nykh ocherkakh*. 2 vols. Moscow, 1925.

Poltavskii, S. "O 'Saratovskom Maiake.'" *Otkliki*, no. 12 (1913), pp. 13–14; no. 13 (1913), pp. 13–14; no. 15 (1913), pp. 11–12; no. 16 (1913), pp. 13–14.

Ponomarchuk, I. I. *Kuznetskii uezd posle Fevral'skoi revoliutsii (mart–iiun' 1917 g.)*. Kuznetsk, 1958.

Popova, E. D. *Leninskaia agrarnaia programma i bor'ba bol'shevikov za krest'ianstvo v 1917 godu*. Leningrad, 1980.

Pozdniakov, O. A. "Mestnaia pechat' bol'shevistskoi partii v gody novogo revoliutsionnogo pod"ema (1910–1914 gg.)." *Nauchnye zapiski Leningradskogo finansovo-ekonomicheskogo instituta, kafedra istorii KPSS*, no. 15 (1957), pp. 6, 15–17, 38, 46.

Pozoiskaia, V. N. "Bor'ba bol'shevikov pod rukovodstvom V. I. Lenina protiv otzovistov i ul'timatistov po voprosu dumskoi taktiki (1907–1910 gg.)." *Uchenye zapiski Saratovskogo gosudarstvennogo universiteta*, 59 (1958), 159–80.

——. "Saratovskaia partiinaia organizatsiia v gody tsarskoi reaktsii (1907–1910 gg.)." *Povolzhskii krai*, no. 4 (1975), pp. 39–62.

Presniakov, A. "1905 god." *Byloe*, no. 4 (32) (1925), p. 27.

"Professional'nye soiuzy Saratovskoi gubernii za 10 let." *Nizhnee Povolzh'e*, no. 10 (1927), pp. 151–76.

Rabinovich, S. E. "Bol'shevistskie voennye organizatsii v 1917 g." *Proletarskaia revoliutsiia*, no. 6–7 (77–78) (1928), pp. 179–98.

——. "Rabota bol'shevikov v armii v 1917 g." *Voina i revoliutsiia*, no. 6 (1927), pp. 96–108.

——. "Vserossiiskaia konferentsiia bol'shevistskikh voennykh organizatsii 1917 g." *Krasnaia letopis'*, no. 5 (38) (1930), pp. 105–32.

Rabinowitch, Alexander. *Prelude to Revolution: The Petrograd Bolsheviks and the July 1917 Uprising*. Bloomington, Ind., 1968.

——. *The Bolsheviks Come to Power: The Revolution of 1917 in Petrograd*. New York, 1976.

Radkey, Oliver H. *The Agrarian Foes of Bolshevism: Promise and Default of the Russian Socialist Revolutionaries, February to October 1917*. New York, 1958.

——. *The Election to the Russian Constituent Assembly*. Harvard Historical Monographs, vol. 21. Cambridge, Mass., 1950.

——. *The Sickle under the Hammer: The Russian Socialist Revolutionaries in the Early Months of Soviet Rule*. New York, 1963.

Raleigh, Donald J. "Revolutionary Politics in Provincial Russia: The Tsaritsyn 'Republic' in 1917." *Slavic Review*, 40, no. 2 (1981), 194–209.

Rashin, A. G. *Formirovanie rabochego klassa Rossii*. Moscow, 1958.

Rashitov, F. A. "Osnovnye etapy sovetskogo stroitel'stva v Saratovskoi gubernii v pervoi polovine 1918 goda." In *Materialy k nauchnoi konferentsii aspirantov i molodykh nauchnykh sotrudnikov*, pp. 1–48. Saratov, 1965.

Razgon, A. I. "O sostave sovetov Nizhnego Povolzh'ia v marte–aprele 1917 g." In *Sovety i soiuz rabochego klassa i krest'ianstva v Oktiabr'skoi revoliutsii*, pp. 83–122. Mocow, 1964.

——. "Sovety Srednego i Nizhnego Povolzh'ia v bor'be za demokraticheskie perevybory gorodskogo samoupravleniia (mart–avgust 1917 g.)." In *Oktiabr' i grazhdanskaia voina v SSSR*, pp. 109–24. Moscow, 1966.

Rimlinger, Gaston V. "The Management of Labor Protest in Tsarist Russia, 1870–1905." *International Review of Social History*, 5 (1961), 226–48.

Robbins, Richard G., Jr. *Famine in Russia, 1891–1892: The Imperial Government Responds to a Crisis*. New York, 1975.

Robinson, Geroid T. *Rural Russia under the Old Regime: A History of the Landlord-Peasant World and a Prologue to the Peasant Revolution of 1917*. New York and London, 1932.

Rodionov, V. A., et al., eds. *Saratovskaia oblastnaia organizatsiia KPSS v tsifrakh 1917–1975*. Saratov, 1977.

Romanov, F. A. *Rabochee i professional'noe dvizhenie v gody pervoi mirovoi voiny i vtoroi russkoi revoliutsii (1914–fevral' 1917): Istoricheskii ocherk*. Moscow, 1949.

Romanov, I., and N. Sokolov. *Ocherk istorii revoliutsii 1917 goda v Tsaritsyne (Stalingrade)*. Saratov, 1932.

Rosenberg, William G. "The Democratization of Russia's Railroads in 1917." *American Historical Review*, 86, no. 5 (1981), 983–1008.

——. *Liberals in the Russian Revolution: The Constitutional Democratic Party, 1917–1921*. Princeton, 1974.
——. "Workers and Workers' Control in the Russian Revolution." *History Workshop*, no. 5 (1978), pp. 89–97.
Rumianstev, E. D. "Fabrichno-zavodskaia militsiia i ee deiatel'nost' v Povolzh'e (mart–leto 1917 goda)." *Ocherki istorii narodov Povolzh'ia i Priural'ia*, no. 4, *Obshchestvenno-politicheskoe dvizhenie i klassovaia bor'ba na Srednei Volge (konets XIX–nachalo XX veka)*, pp. 78–88. Kazan, 1972.
——. "Istochniki izucheniia istorii rabochei militsii i krasnoi gvardii Povolzh'ia." In *Oktiabr' v Povolzh'e i Priural'e (Istochniki i voprosy istoriografii)*, pp. 31–47. Kazan, 1972.
——. "K istorii Krasnoi gvardii Povolzh'ia." In *Sbornik aspirantskikh rabot. Gumanitarnye nauki: Istoriia*, pp. 64–68. Kazan, 1971.
——. "K voprosu o voennom obuchenii Krasnoi gvardii v Povolzh'e (osen' 1917 g.)." In *Sbornik aspirantskikh rabot*, no. 74, *Gumanitarnye nauki: Istoriia, pedagogika*, pp. 77–84. Kazan, 1973.
——. "Rabochaia militsiia v Povolzh'e v 1917 g." In *Sbornik aspirantskikh rabot. Gumanitarnye nauki: Istoriia, zhurnalistika*, pp. 20–32. Kazan, 1971.
Saar, G. P. "Iz proshlogo Saratovskoi organizatsii (1904–1906)." *Vestnik Saratovskogo Gubkoma RKP*, no. 24 (1922), pp. 66–79; no. 25 (1922), pp. 122–27.
——. "Pervye popytki sotsial-demokraticheskoi raboty sredi Saratovskikh rabochikh." *Proletarskaia revoliutsiia*, no. 4 (75) (1928), pp. 128–53.
——. "Saratovskaia organizatsiia RSDRP do 1907 g." *Vestnik Saratovskogo Gubkoma RKP*, no. 3 (28) (1923), pp. 37–43.
——. "Saratovskaia organizatsiia RSDRP v nachale 900-kh gg." *Proletarskaia revoliutsiia*, no. 11–12 (82–83) (1928), pp. 112–32.
——. *Saratovskaia promyshlennost' v 90-kh godakh i v nachale 900-kh godov*. Saratov, 1928.
——. "Saratovskaia Sotsial-demokraticheskaia gruppa 1898–1899 gg." *Vestnik Saratovskogo Gubkoma RKP*, no. 5 (30) (1923), pp. 75–79.
——. "Vozniknovenie Saratovskoi organizatsii RSDRP." *Proletarskaia revoliutsiia*, no. 6–7 (77–78) (1928), pp. 265–92.
Sadriev, M. M., and N. A. Vakhrusheva. "Iz istorii bor'by bol'shevikov za soldatskie massy v Kazanskom voennom okruge v pervye mesiatsy posle Fevral'skoi revoliutsii." In *Sbornik aspirantskikh rabot. Gumanitarnye nauki: Istoriia, pedagogika*, pp. 110–18. Kazan, 1973.
Sagrad'ian, M. O. *Osushchestvlenie Leninskogo dekreta o zemle v Saratovskoi gubernii*. Saratov, 1966.
Saratov: Sputnik-ukazatel' 1911 god. Saratov, 1911.
Saratovskaia gubernskaia uchebnaia arkhivnaia komissiia. *K piatidesiatiletiiu zemskikh uchrezhdenii: K istorii organizatsii i pervykh shagov zemstva v Saratovskoi gubernii*. Saratov, 1911.
Saratovskaia oblast': Istoriko-kraevedcheskii ocherk. Saratov, 1947.
Saratovskaia oblast' za 50 let. Saratov, 1967.
Saratovskii krai: Istoricheskie ocherki, vospominaniia, materialy. Saratov, 1893.
Sbornik: Ves' Kuznetsk. Kuznetsk, 1927.
Semenov, K. T., and F. T. Misnik. "Aprel'skie tezisy V. I. Lenina—velikii obrazets tvorcheskogo marksizma." In *Kommunisticheskaia partiia—vdokhnovitel' i*

organizator pobedy Velikoi Oktiabr'skoi sotsialisticheskoi revoliutsii, pp. 46–47. Moscow, 1957.

Semenov, M. "1905 god v Saratovskoi gubernii." *Proletarskaia revoliutsiia*, no. 3 (50) (1926), pp. 197–218.

Serebriakova, Z. L. *Oblastnye ob"edineniia sovetov Rossii, mart 1917–dekabr' 1918*. Moscow, 1977.

Seregny, Scott J. "Politics and the Rural Intelligentsia in Russia: A Biographical Sketch of Stepan Anikin, 1869–1919." *Russian History*, 7 (1980), 169–200.

Sergeev, V. "Proidennyi put', 1904 god." *Vestnik Saratovskogo Gubkoma RKP*, no. 7 (32) (1922), pp. 95–96.

Sergievskii, N. L. "O kruzhke Tochinskogo. Prilozhenie: Doklad Departamenta politsii Ministra vnutrennykh del." *Krasnaia letopis'*, no. 7 (1923), pp. 342, 344–46, 348–49, 351, 359, 365, 372, 380–81.

Shanin, Teodor. *The Awkward Class: Political Sociology of Peasantry in a Developing Society, Russia, 1910–1925*. New York, 1972.

Sharov, N. I. "V. I. Lenin i Saratovskaia guberniia (Deiatel'nost' Saratovskogo Komiteta RSDRP)." In *Zhiznennost' leninskikh idei*. Saratov, 1970.

Shirokova, V. V. "Obshchestvennoe dvizhenie v Saratovskoi gubernii v period vtoroi revoliutsionnoi situatsii (1878–1882 gg.)." *Povolzhskii krai*, no. 4 (1975), pp. 89–105.

——. *Partiia "Narodnogo prava."* Saratov, 1972.

Sinitsyn, P. N. *Istoriia raboche-krest'ianskoi militsii po Saratovskoi gubernii*. Saratov, 1924.

Smirnov, A. G. *Biblioteki Saratova: Putevoditel'*. Saratov, 1963.

Smirnov, A. S. *Agitatsiia i propaganda bol'shevikov v derevne v period podgotovki Oktiabr'skoi revoliutsii*. Moscow, 1957.

——. "Bol'sheviki i krest'ianskie s"ezdy v iiule–oktiabre 1917 g." *Voprosy istorii KPSS*, no. 12 (1973), pp. 64–75.

——. "Bol'sheviki i revoliutsionnoe tvorchestvo na mestakh (iiul'–oktiabr' 1917 g.)." *Voprosy istorii KPSS*, no. 6 (1979), pp. 59–69.

Smith, S. A. "Craft Consciousness, Class Consciousness: Petrograd 1917." *History Workshop*, no. 11 (1981), pp. 33–58.

——. *Red Petrograd: Revolution in the Factories, 1917–1918*. Cambridge, Eng., 1983.

Snow, Russell. *The Bolsheviks in Siberia, 1917–1918*. Rutherford, O., 1977.

Sobolev, P. N. *Bedneishee krest'ianstvo—soiuznik proletariata v Oktiabr'skoi revoliutsii*. Moscow, 1958.

——. "Splochenie bedneishego krest'ianstva vokrug proletariata v 1917 g." *Istoricheskie zapiski*, 48 (1954), 42–80.

Sokolov, N. S. *Raskol v Saratovskom krae*. Vol. 1, *Popovshchina do piatidesiatykh godov nastoiashchego stoletiia*. Saratov, 1888.

Spiridovich, L. I. *Istoriia bol'shevizma v Rossii ot vozniknoveniia do zakhvata vlasti, 1883–1903–1917*. Paris, 1922.

Spravochnik-putevoditel' po gorodu Saratovu. Saratov, 1902.

Sputnik po gorodu Saratovu s illiustratsiiami i planom goroda. Saratov, 1898.

Starkmet, A. M. *Saratov: Putevoditel'*. Saratov, 1963.

Startsev, V. I. *Vnutrenniaia politika Vremennogo pravitel'stva pervogo sostava*. Leningrad, 1980.

Stishov, M. I., and D. S. Tochenyi. "Raspad esero-men'shevistskikh partiinykh organizatsii v Povolzh'e." *Voprosy istorii*, no. 8 (1973), pp. 15–28.
Suny, Ronald Grigor. *The Baku Commune, 1917–1918: Class and Nationality in the Russian Revolution.* Princeton, 1972.
——. "Labor and Liquidators: Revolutionaries and the 'Reaction' in Baku, May 1908–April 1912." *Slavic Review*, 34, no. 2 (1975), 319–40.
——. "Nationalism and Social Class in the Russian Revolution: The Case of Baku and Tiflis." In *Transcaucasia, Nationalism, and Social Change: Essays in the History of Armenia, Azerbaijan, and Georgia*, ed. Ronald G. Suny, pp. 239–58. Ann Arbor, 1983.
——. "Toward a Social History of the October Revolution." *American Historical Review*, 88, no. 1 (1983), 31–52.
Sushitskii, V. *V boiakh s samoderzhaviem: Saratovskie zheleznodorozhnye masterskie (rem. zavod RUZhD) v revoliutsii 1905 goda.* Saratov, 1933.
Suslov, Iu. P. *Leninskaia agrarnaia programma i bor'ba bol'shevikov Povolzh'ia za ee osushchestvlenie, mart 1917–mart 1918* gg. Saratov, 1972.
Sviatlovskii, V. "Professional'noe dvizhenie rabochikh v 1905 g." *Krasnaia letopis'*, no. 2–3 (1922), pp. 165–96.
Swain, G. R. "Bolsheviks and Metal Workers on the Eve of the First World War." *Journal of Contemporary History*, 16 (1981), 273–91.
Telitsa, G. M. "K voprosu o pobede proletarskoi revoliutsii v Nizhnem Povolzh'e." In *Iz istorii partiinykh organizatsii Nizhnego Povolzh'ia*, vol. 26, *Uchenye zapiski Volgogradskogo pedagogicheskogo instituta im. A. S. Serafimovicha*, pp. 173–98. Volgograd, 1969.
Terekhin, S. V. *Gody ognevye: Saratovskaia organizatsiia bol'shevikov v period Oktiabr'skoi revoliutsii.* Saratov, 1967.
Terekhov, I. S. "K voprosu o bor'be za vlast' Sovetov v Saratove." In *Iz istorii partiinykh organizatsii Povolzh'ia i Urala*, pp. 3–16. Saratov, 1968.
——. *V. I. Lenin i stroitel'stvo partii v period ot fevralia k oktiabriu, 1917* g. Saratov, 1969.
Tiutiukin, S. V. *Voina, mir, revoliutsiia: Ideinaia bor'ba v rabochem dvizhenii Rossii, 1914–1917* gg. Moscow, 1972.
Tochenyi, D. S. "Bankrotstvo politiki eserov: Povolzh'ia v agrarnom voprose, mart–oktiabr' 1917 g." *Istoriia* SSSR, no. 4 (1969), pp. 106–17.
——. "Iiul'skie sobytiia 1917 g. i nachalo krizisa melko-burzhuaznykh organizatsii (Na materialakh Povolzh'ia)." In *Iz istorii Srednego Povolzh'ia i Priural'ia*, vol. 115, *Nauchnye trudy Kuibyshevskogo gosudarstvennogo pedinstituta*, pp. 58–72. Kuibyshev, 1973.
——. "Raspad levoeserovskikh organizatsii v Povolzh'e." In *Nauchnye trudy Kuibyshevskogo gosudarstvennogo pedinstituta*, vol. 165, *Nash krai*, pp. 54–62. Kuibyshev, 1975.
Tokmakoff, George. "Stolypin's Agrarian Reform: An Appraisal." *Russian Review*, no. 2 (1971), pp. 124–39.
Tomarev, V. I. *Bol'sheviki Povolzh'ia vo glave bor'by proletariev protiv tsarizma.* Volgograd, 1977.
——. "Deiatel'nost' bol'shevikov Povolzh'ia nakanune pervoi russkoi revoliutsii i v period ee vysshego pod"ema." In *Iz istorii partiinykh i komsomol'skikh organizatsii Povolzh'ia*, pp. 5–47. Volgograd, 1972.

——. "Fevral' 1917 goda v Povolzh'e." *Povolzhskii krai*, no. 3 (1975), pp. 141–53.
——. "Pod"em rabochego dvizheniia v Povolzh'e v 1910–1914 gg." *Povolzhskii krai*, no. 1 (1972), pp. 82–97.
——. *Proletariat Tsaritsyna v bor'be za vlast' Sovetov*. Volgograd, 1957.
——. "Revoliutsionnaia rabota bol'shevikov Povolzh'ia sredi proletariev v period mirovoi imperialisticheskoi voiny." *Istoriia partiinykh organizatsii Povolzh'ia*, no. 4 (1975), pp. 3–19.
——. "Tsaritsynskaia gruppa RSDRP mezhdu dvumia revoliutsiiami (1907–1917 gg.)." *Istoriko-kraevedcheskie zapiski* (Volgograd), no. 5 (1977), pp. 4–53.
—— and N. O. Podlesnov. "Bor'ba bol'shevikov za ustanovlenie Sovetskoi vlasti v Tsaritsyne." *Istoriko-kraevedcheskie zapiski* (Volgograd), no. 1 (1973), pp. 54–74.
Topaz, S. E. *Nekotorye voprosy zakhvata vlasti Sovetami i podavleniia imi soprotivleniia ekspluatatorov v pervyi god Sovetskoi vlasti*. Ashkhabad, 1960.
——. "Pobeda Velikoi Oktiabr'skoi sotsialisticheskoi revoliutsii v Povolzh'e." *Uchenye zapiski Turkmenskogo universiteta*, no. 12 (1957), pp. 139–67.
Topilin, Petr, et al. *Saratovskaia oblast' za 40 let*. Saratov, 1957.
Treadgold, Donald W. *Lenin and His Rivals: The Struggle for Russia's Future, 1896–1906*. New York, 1955.
Trotsky, Leon. *The History of the Russian Revolution*. Trans. Max Eastman. 3 vols. Ann Arbor, 1957.
——. *1905*. New York, 1971.
Trukan, G. A. *Oktiabr' v Tsentral'noi Rossii*. Moscow, 1967.
Tseitlin, R. S. "Perekhod soldatskikh mass Kazanskogo voennogo okruga na storonu bol'shevikov (Po materialam vyborov v Sovety, gorodskie dumy i Uchreditel'noe sobranie)." In *Revoliutsionnoe dvizhenie v russkoi armii v 1917 godu: Sbornik statei*, ed. I. I. Mints et al., pp. 211–16. Moscow, 1981.
Tsypkin, G. A., and R. G. Tsypkina. *Krasnaia gvardiia—udarnaia sila proletariata v Oktiabr'skoi revoliutsii po materialam Tsentral'nogo promyshlennogo raiona, Urala i Povolzh'ia*. Moscow, 1977.
Tsypkina, R. G. "Set' voenno-revoliutsionnykh komitetov v Evropeiskoi chasti Rossii." *Voprosy istorii*, no. 2 (1975), pp. 18–30.
1905 god v Saratovskoi gubernii (Po materialam zhandarmskogo upravleniia): Sbornik statei. Saratov, 1925.
Urlanik, V. Ts. "Dinamika naseleniia Rossii nakanune oktiabria." *Uchenye zapiski Vsesoiuznogo zaochnogo ekonomicheskogo instituta*, no. 2 (1957), pp. 113–34.
Vakhrusheva, N. A. "Nastroeniia narodnykh mass i partiinaia pechat' Povolzh'ia v 1917 g." In *Sbornik aspirantskikh rabot. Gumanitarnye nauki: Istoriia, pedagogika*, pp. 3–10, Kazan, 1973.
Valeev, R. K. "Krizis mestnykh organov Vremennogo Pravitel'stva letom i osen'iu 1917 goda (Po materialam Povolzh'ia)." In *Oktiabr' v Povolzh'e i Priural'e (Istochniki i voprosy istoriografii)*, pp. 118–35. Kazan, 1972.
——. *Nazrevanie obshchenatsional'nogo krizisa i ego proiavlenie v Povolzh'e i na Urale v 1917 g*. Kazan, 1979.
Vas'kin, V. V. "Bor'ba bol'shevikov Nizhnego Povolzh'ia protiv formirovaniia kontrrevoliutsionnykh udarnykh chastei letom i osen'iu 1917 g." In *Nekotorye voprosy otechestvennoi i vseobshchei istorii*, pp. 29–41. Saratov, 1971.
——. "Iz istorii bor'by za bol'shevizatsiiu Saratovskogo garnizona v 1917 g." In

Materialy k nauchnoi konferentsii aspirantov i molodykh nauchnykh sotrudnikov, no. 1, pp. 96–120. Saratov, 1965.

——. "Kontrrevoliutsiia v bor'be za armiiu v 1917 g." In *Revoliutsionnoe dvizhenie v russkoi armii v 1917 godu: Sbornik statei*, eds. I. I. Mints et al., pp. 147–53. Moscow, 1981.

——. "Soldaty Nizhnego Povolzh'ia v Fevral'sko-martovskie dni 1917 goda." In *Iz istorii Saratovskogo Povolzh'ia*, pp. 92–110. Saratov, 1968.

—— and G. A. Gerasimenko. *Fevral'skaia revoliutsiia v Nizhnem Povolzh'e.* Saratov, 1976.

Venturi, Franco. *Roots of Revolution: A History of the Populist and Socialist Movements in Nineteenth-Century Russia.* Trans. Francis Haskell. New York, 1966.

Vodolagin, M. A. *Krasnyi Tsaritsyn.* Volgograd, 1967.

——. *Ocherk istorii Volgograda, 1589–1967.* Moscow, 1968.

Volobuev, P. V. *Proletariat i burzhuaziia Rossii v 1917 godu.* Moscow, 1964.

Von Laue, Theodore. *Sergei Witte and the Industrialization of Russia.* New York, 1963.

Wade, Rex A. *Red Guards and Workers' Militias in the Russian Revolution.* Stanford, 1983.

——. *The Russian Search for Peace, February–October 1917.* Stanford, 1969.

Wildman, Allan K. *The End of the Imperial Army: The Old Army and the Soldiers' Revolt (March–April 1917).* Princeton, 1980.

——. "Lenin's Battle with *Kustarnichestvo*: The *Iskra* Organization in Russia." *Slavic Review*, 23, no. 3 (1964), 479–503.

Willetts, Harry T. "The Agrarian Problem." In *Russia Enters the Twentieth Century, 1894–1917*, ed. George Katkov et al., pp. 111–38. London, 1971.

Wolf, Eric R. *Peasant Wars of the Twentieth Century.* New York, 1969.

Zakharov, F. F. *Samarskie bol'sheviki v Oktiabr'skoi revoliutsii.* Kuibyshev, 1957.

Zakharov, N. S. *Sovety Srednego Povolzh'ia v period bor'by za diktaturu proletariata.* Kazan, 1977.

Zamaraeva, T. B. "Nelegal'naia bol'shevistskaia pechat' v bor'be za prevrashchenie voiny imperialisticheskoi v voinu grazhdanskuiu (1914–1917 gg.)." In *V bor'be za pobedu Oktiabria: Sbornik statei*, pp. 18–47. Moscow, 1957.

Zelnik, Reginald E. "Russian Bebels: An Introduction to the Memoirs of Semen Kanatchikov and Matvei Fisher." *Russian Review*, no. 3 (1976), pp. 249–90; no. 4 (1976), pp. 417–47.

Zhukovskii, G., ed. *Kratkaia istoriia g. Saratova i Saratovskoi gubernii.* Saratov, 1881.

Znamenskii, O. N. *Iiul'skii krizis 1917 goda.* Moscow, 1964.

Dissertations

Fallows, Thomas Stuart. "Forging the Zemstvo Movement: Liberalism and Radicalism on the Volga, 1890–1905." Ph.D. dissertation, Harvard University, 1981.

Gol'dman, V. S. "Istoriia sozdaniia i uprocheniia Saratovskogo Soveta rabochikh, krest'ianskikh, krasnoarmeiskikh, kazach'ikh deputatov v 1917–1918 gg." Candidate dissertation, Leningrad Law Institute, 1954.

Khodakov, V. G. "Bor'ba rabochikh Saratovskoi gubernii pod rukovodstvom Kommunisticheskoi organizatsii za rabochii kontrol' nad proizvodstvom v 1917–18 gg." Candidate dissertation, Saratov Pedagogical Institute, 1953.

Kosenko, M. Ia. "Agrarnaia reforma Stolypina v Saratovskoi gubernii." Candidate dissertation, Moscow State Historical-Archival Institute, 1951.

Rumiantsev, E. D. "Rabochaia militsiia: Krasnaia gvardiia Povolzh'ia v bor'be za vlast' Sovetov." Candidate dissertation, Kazan State University, 1971.

Schaeffer, Mary Elizabeth. "The Political Policies of P. A. Stolypin." Ph.D. dissertation, Indiana University, 1964.

Skliar, M. I. "Gorod Saratov (ekonomiko-geograficheskaia kharakteristika)." Candidate dissertation, Moscow State University, 1958.

Index

Library of Congress Cataloging in Publication Data

RALEIGH, DONALD J.
Revolution on the Volga.

Bibliography; p.
Includes index.
1. Saratov (R.S.F.S.R.)—History—Revolution,
1917–1921. I. Title.
DK265.8.S37R34 1986 947.084′1 85-12792
ISBN 0-8014-1790-2 (alk. paper)